D0164077

THE HARMONIC DIMENSION

THE HARMONIC DIMENSION

by

GARY WHITE
Iowa State University

based on the works of:

BRUCE BENWARD
University of Wisconsin, Madison

Wm. C. Brown Publishers

Book Team

Editor *Meredith M. Morgan*
Developmental Editor *Dean Robbins*
Production Editor *Dave Welsh/Suzanne Guinn*
Designer *Elise A. Burckhardt*
Permissions Editor *Vicki Krug*
Visuals Processor *Amy Saffran*

Wm. C. Brown Publishers

President *G. Franklin Lewis*
Vice President, Publisher *George Wm. Bergquist*
Vice President, Publisher *Thomas E. Doran*
Vice President, Operations and Production *Beverly Kolz*
National Sales Manager *Virginia S. Moffat*
Senior Marketing Manager *Kathy Law Laube*
Marketing Manager *Kathleen Nietzke*
Executive Editor *Edgar J. Laube*
Managing Editor, Production *Colleen A. Yonda*
Production Editorial Manager *Julie A. Kennedy*
Production Editorial Manager *Ann Fuerste*
Publishing Services Manager *Karen J. Slaght*
Manager of Visuals and Design *Faye M. Schilling*

Consulting Editor
Frederick W. Westphal
California State University, Sacramento

Cover image: GRUS. Dan Christensen, 1968, acrylic on canvas, 123 × 99 inches. Hirshhorn Museum and Sculpture Garden, Smithsonian Institution, Gift of Joseph H. Hirshhorn, 1972.

Library of Congress Catalog Card Number: 90–55469

ISBN 0–697–03387–2

Printed in the United States of America by Wm. C. Brown Publishers, 2460 Kerper Boulevard, Dubuque, IA 52001

10 9 8 7 6 5 4 3 2 1

Contents

To the Instructor

The Harmonic Dimension is intended for use in colleges and universities with separate courses in harmony and analysis. It represents a compilation of the materials on harmony and voice-leading from the two volumes of Benward/White's *Music in Theory and Practice.* The materials contained in *The Harmonic Dimension* have thus met the test of time, having been perfected during the past decade in the various editions of the former book. Literally thousands of students and teachers have used these materials successfully and have made many suggestions for improvement. The text represents a complete package for the first years of study. The early chapters address the beginning student's need for a thorough grounding in the fundamentals before the study of harmony can begin. There are numerous assignments to aid the student in learning the course materials, with opportunities for creative work suggested in many of them. The text is written from a traditional point of view, placing emphasis on part writing, figured bass, melody harmonization, and analysis. The following features distinguish this book from many other harmony texts.

Historical Perspective

Nearly every chapter contains a short historical overview that deals with the topic under discussion as it applies to each historical period. This feature helps the beginning student to understand that music has changed over time, and that the principles he or she is learning have been applied in different ways at different times, and may not have been operating at all during other periods in the history of music. This will help the student avoid the common misconception that the rules of music theory are being propounded as an absolute prescription for the "correct" way of writing music.

Guided Review

Each chapter contains a suggested strategy for reviewing and learning the material. Students often find that the study skills they have developed for other courses don't work well in learning music theory. The guided review sections present a step-by-step process, involving reading, playing musical examples, and writing, which will establish good study habits and help insure success in learning the material.

Self-Testing

Each chapter concludes with a sample chapter test covering the essential concepts of the chapter. Answers for all chapter tests are contained in Appendix G. These tests allow the student to identify areas of strength and weakness before examinations, a further insurance of success.

Workbook-Anthology

The Harmonic Dimension is accompanied by a *Workbook-Anthology* containing a broad range of problems, exercises, and creative assignments. An additional feature of this learning resource is an anthology of music containing 51 complete pieces of music and excerpts from many more, making the purchase of a separate anthology unnecessary. The compositions are chosen to coordinate with the assignments, and are prepared for analysis, with extra space and blank staves provided for students' analytical notes.

Reviewers

Eddie C. Bass–University of North Carolina, Greensboro
Claire Boge–Miami University
Steven M. Bruns–University of Colorado
David Childs–Concordia College, Moorhead
Helen Hoekema Van Wych–Trinity Christian College

THE HARMONIC DIMENSION

PART
1

The Fundamentals of Music

Before you begin your study of the structure of music you must first understand the notation and basic elements of music: the *fundamentals of music.* As an experienced musician, you have probably learned many of these concepts in your previous studies. My purpose here is to present these basic musical facts in a systematic way to aid you in gaining fluency and filling any gaps in your knowledge. Even if you know the materials presented here, I urge you to take this opportunity to practice until you can recall the fundamentals without a moment of hesitation. Your success in understanding the structure of music will depend on this ability.

The goal of this book is to show you how music is put together. I will deal with a wide variety of music from very early to the most recent, from art music to folk and popular music. As a prelude to this adventure you must understand in broad terms the history of Western music and see the relationships among the various styles. For this reason I have included a brief overview of music history in Appendix B. I wish you success in your work and hope that you find here the beginning of a lifetime of exciting and serious study of the art of music.

Notation

Staff
Letter Names
Solfeggio Syllables
Clef
Treble Clef
Bass Clef
Grand Staff
Ledger Lines
C Clef
Alto Clef
Tenor Clef
Octave Identification
Accidentals
Intervals
Sharp
Flat
Natural
Double Sharp
Double Flat
Enharmonic Equivalents
Notation of Duration
Breve and Rest
Whole Note and Rest
Half Note and Rest
Quarter Note and Rest
Eighth Note and Rest
Sixteenth Note and Rest
Thirty-Second Note and Rest
Sixty-Fourth Note and Rest
Tie
Dot
Second Dot
Irregular Divisions and Subdivisions
Meter
Meter Signature
Simple Meter
Compound Meter
Asymmetrical Meters
Asymmetrical Divisions
Decimal Meter
Fractional Meter
Mixed Meter
Changing Meter
Polymeter
Dynamic Markings
History of Notation
Neumatic Notation
Mensural Notation
Present Notation
Manuscript Notation

Exposition

When we transcribe speech, we write symbols that will call to mind the spoken words, but the words we write do not show who should speak them or how fast or how loud they should be said. When we notate music, however, we use symbols that show three of the four properties of sound: pitch and duration are given accurately and relative intensity is indicated. Furthermore, pitch and duration are shown simultaneously. Music notation is therefore of necessity far more complicated than written words.

Notation of Pitch

The Staff

Figure 1.1

The staff consists of five lines.

Letter Names

The various pitches are referred to by the first seven letters of the alphabet (A B C D E F G), as shown on the piano keyboard below.

Figure 1.2

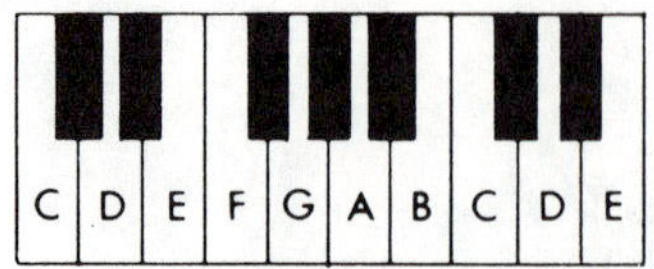
C D E F G A B C D E

Solfeggio Syllables

Certain systems of *solfeggio* (vocal exercises sung to a vowel, syllables, or words) use the syllables **do, re, mi, fa, sol, la, ti** to indicate the pitch.

The present solfeggio system derives from Guido d'Arezzo, an eleventh-century monk, who sought to teach sightsinging through the use of a well-known hymn to St. John, *Ut queant laxis.* The beginning notes of the first six phrases of Guido's melody form the first six notes of the scale: C, D, E, F, G, A. The syllables beginning these phrases are **ut, re, mi, fa, sol, la.**

Scale degree:	C	D	E	F	G	A
Syllable:	ut	re	mi	fa	sol	la

Figure 1.3

Hymn to St. John *(Ut queant laxis)*

Ut que-ant la - xis re-so-na-re fi-bris Mi - ra ge-sto - rum
fa-mu-li tu-o - rum, Sol - ve pol-lu-ti La-bi-i
re - a-tum, San - cte Jo - an-nes.

The significance of this system lay in the location of the half step that occurred between the syllables **mi** and **fa.** The *hexachord* (a scale of six notes) could begin on C, and on G or F as well. In the hexachord on F, a B-flat was added to insure the half-step interval (see figure 1.13) between **mi** and **fa.** The first syllable was eventually changed from **ut** to **do** and the modern system evolved.

Figure 1.4

Modern systems of solfeggio include several systems of "movable do" solfeggio, in which **do** is assigned to the keynote of the scale, in addition to the aforementioned "fixed do" system.

The Clefs

A *clef* is a symbol placed at the beginning of a line of music that establishes the letter names of the lines and spaces of the staff.

Treble Clef (G)

The *treble clef* or *G clef* is an ornate letter G. The curved line terminates at the second line of the staff, thus designating the letter name of a note on that line as G.

Figure 1.5

Staff with Treble or G Clef

Bass Clef (F)

The *bass clef* resembles a large comma followed by a colon. It is called the F clef because it was derived from the letter F. The dots of the colon are placed above and below the fourth line of the staff, designating that line as F.

Figure 1.6

Staff with Bass or F Clef

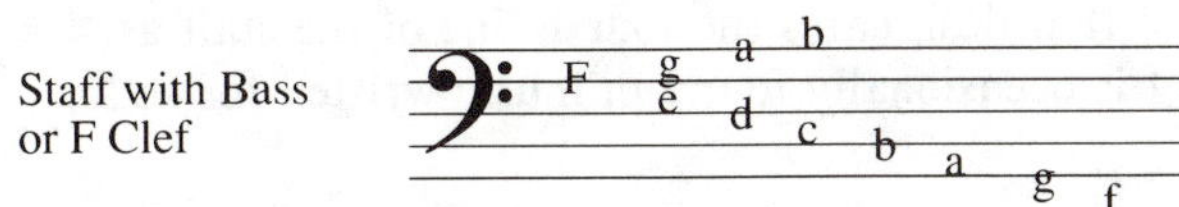

Grand Staff

Together, the treble and bass staves make up the *grand staff* associated with keyboard music. Figure 1.7 shows the point at which both clef signs converge. The two C's are the same pitch. The pitch is called *middle C.*

Figure 1.7

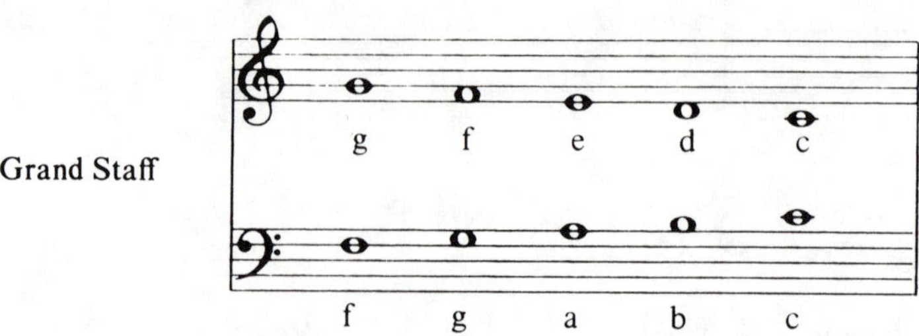

Ledger Lines

Pitches that go beyond the limits of the staff are written by adding *ledger lines* (sometimes spelled: *leger lines*) above or below the staff. Ledger lines, which parallel the staff, accommodate only one note.

Figure 1.8

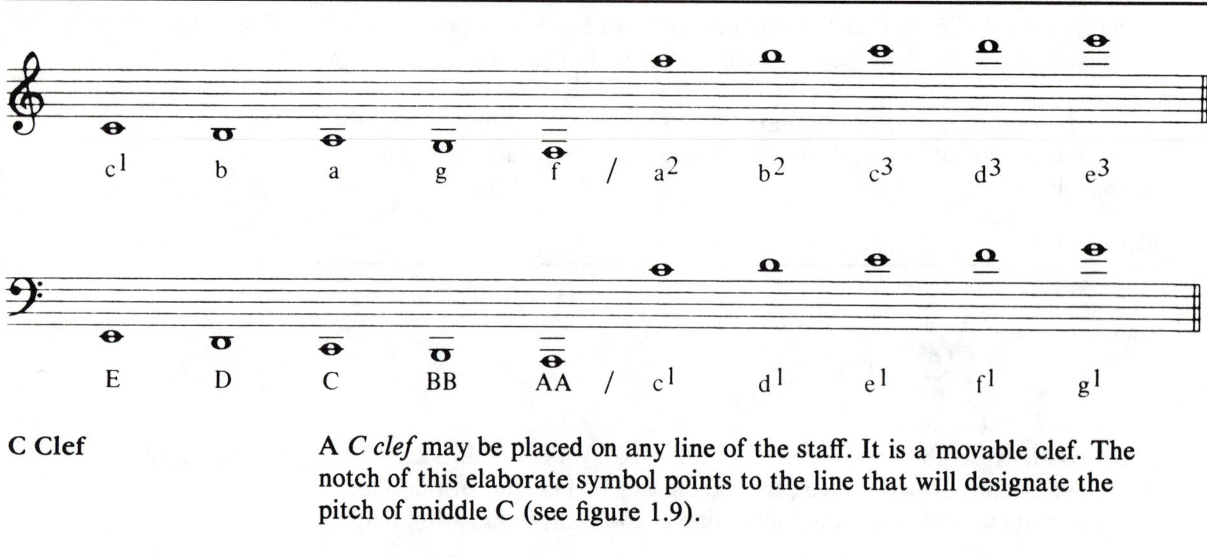

C Clef

A *C clef* may be placed on any line of the staff. It is a movable clef. The notch of this elaborate symbol points to the line that will designate the pitch of middle C (see figure 1.9).

Alto Clef

The *alto clef* is a C clef that designates the third line of the staff as middle C. It is the standard clef used in music for viola.

Tenor Clef

The *tenor clef* is a C clef that designates the fourth line of the staff as middle C. The tenor clef is occasionally found in music written for cello, bassoon, or trombone.

Soprano, Mezzo Soprano, and Baritone Clefs

The *soprano, mezzo soprano, and baritone clefs* are C clefs less often used than the alto and tenor clefs. In each case the line indicated by the notch of the clef is designated as middle *C*.

Figure 1.9

(Workbook-Anthology Assignments 1.1, p. 1, and 1.6, p. 4)

Octave Identification

Since the pitch spectrum is so wide, it is often necessary to identify a specific note by the octave in which it appears. Thus, middle C is distinguished from any other C in the pitch spectrum by the written designation c^1.

Figure 1.10

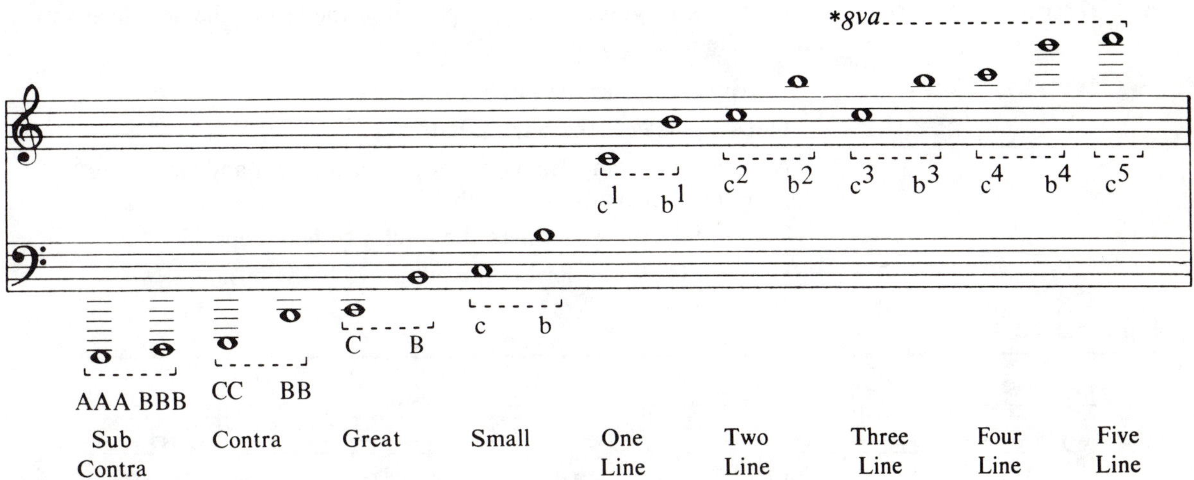

An alternate system of octave identification, which is recommended by the International Acoustical Society and used in Braille music notation, is gaining increased acceptance. In this system each octave is numbered beginning with 0 for the lowest three notes on the piano and extending to C8 for the highest note on the piano. Although the former system is used throughout this book, your instructor may prefer the latter.

Figure 1.11

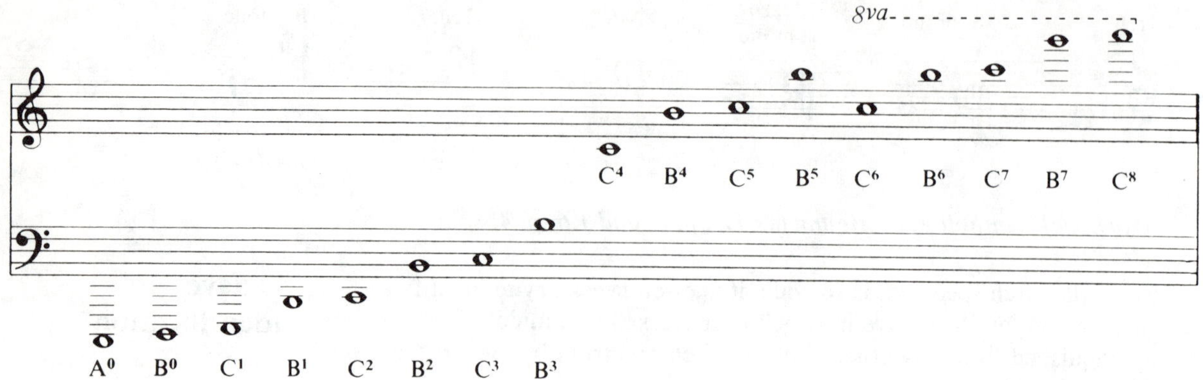

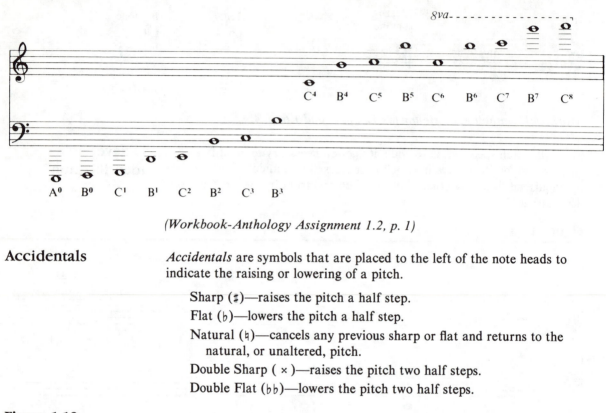

(Workbook-Anthology Assignment 1.2, p. 1)

Accidentals

Accidentals are symbols that are placed to the left of the note heads to indicate the raising or lowering of a pitch.

Sharp (♯)—raises the pitch a half step.

Flat (♭)—lowers the pitch a half step.

Natural (♮)—cancels any previous sharp or flat and returns to the natural, or unaltered, pitch.

Double Sharp (×)—raises the pitch two half steps.

Double Flat (♭♭)—lowers the pitch two half steps.

Figure 1.12

Intervals

An *interval* is the difference in pitch between two tones. In Western music the half step is the smallest interval used. It is the interval between any two adjacent tones on the piano keyboard.

Figure 1.13

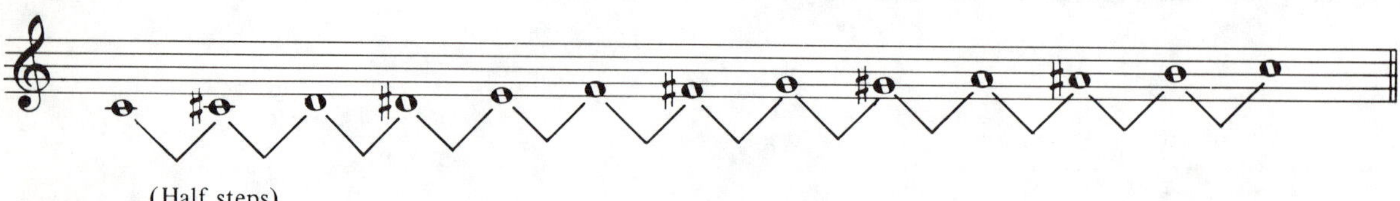

Enharmonic Equivalents

Enharmonic equivalents are tones that have the same pitch but different letter names.

Figure 1.14

In passages of music involving half-step motion, flatted tones are most often followed by a tone with a different letter name a half step lower.

Figure 1.15

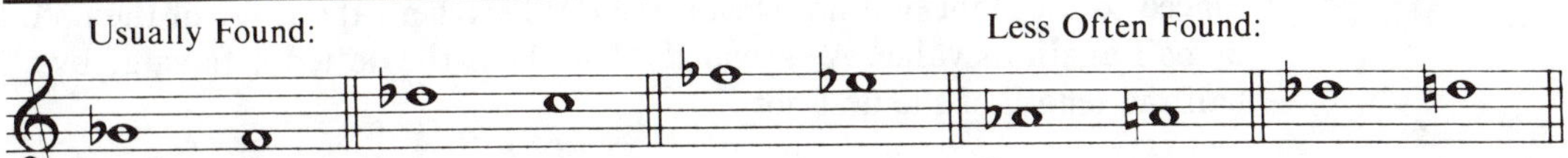

In passages of music involving half-step motion, sharped tones are most often followed by tones with a different letter name a half step higher.

Figure 1.16

(Workbook-Anthology Assignments 1.3, p. 2, and 1.7 and 1.8, p. 4)

Notation of Duration

Notation of duration is illustrated in the following chart:

Figure 1.17

Name	Note	Rest	Equivalents
Breve (double whole note)	or		Two Whole Notes
Whole Note		*	Two Half Notes
Half Note			Two Quarter Notes
Quarter Note			Two Eighth Notes
Eighth Note			Two Sixteenth Notes
Sixteenth Note			Two Thirty-second Notes
Thirty-second Note			Two Sixty-fourth Notes
Sixty-fourth Note			Two One Hundred Twenty-eighth Notes

*May be used to fill any whole measure of rest.

The Tie

The *tie* is a curved line that connects two adjacent notes of the same pitch into a single sound with a duration equal to the sum of both note values.

Figure 1.18

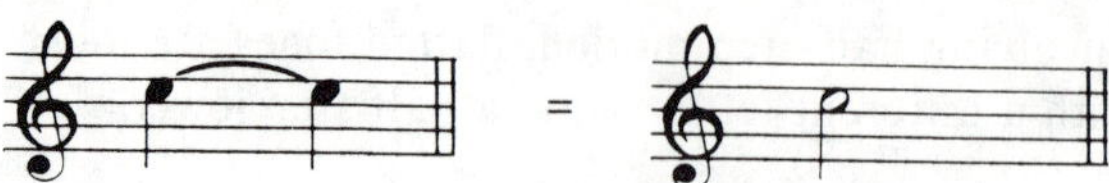

The Dot

Placed to the right of a note head, the *dot* lengthens the value of the note by half again its value. A *second dot* lengthens the dotted note value by half the length of the first dot:

Figure 1.19

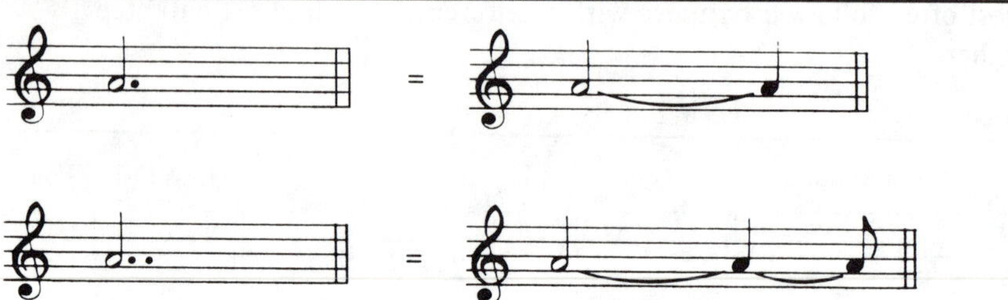

Dots may also be used with rests and affect them in the same way:

Figure 1.20

Irregular Division of Notes

A note value may be divided or subdivided into any number of equal parts, as shown in the following chart:

Figure 1.21

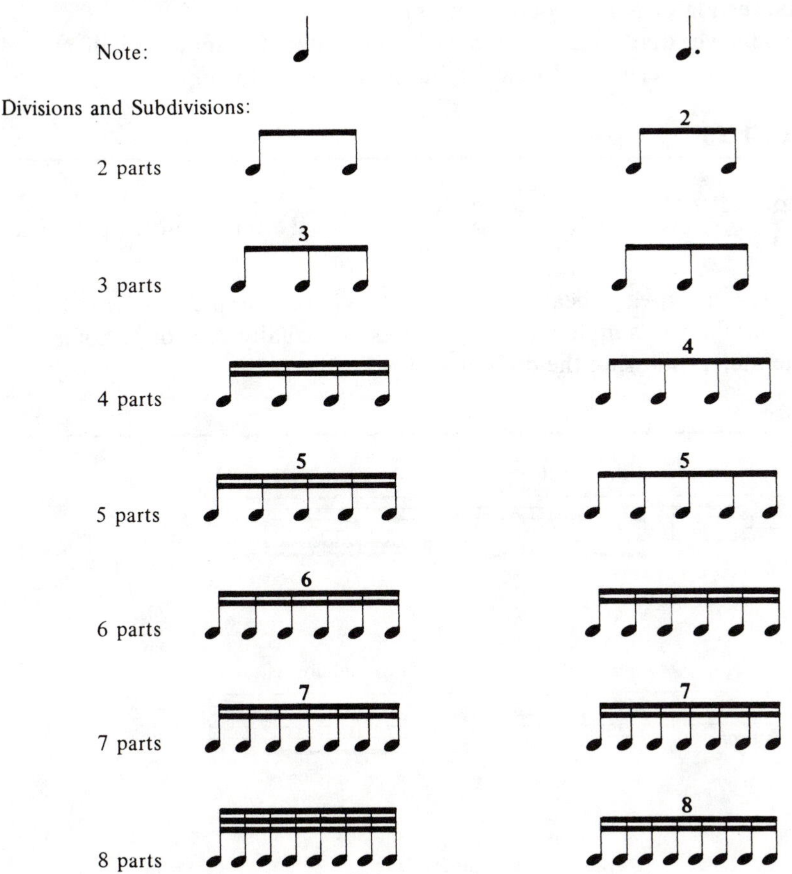

Those divisions and subdivisions that require added numbers are called *irregular divisions* and *subdivisions.*

Meter Signatures

Meter may be defined as a regular, recurring pattern of strong and weak beats of equal duration. This recurring pattern of durations is identified at the beginning of a composition by a *meter signature* (time signature) of two numbers.

Figure 1.22

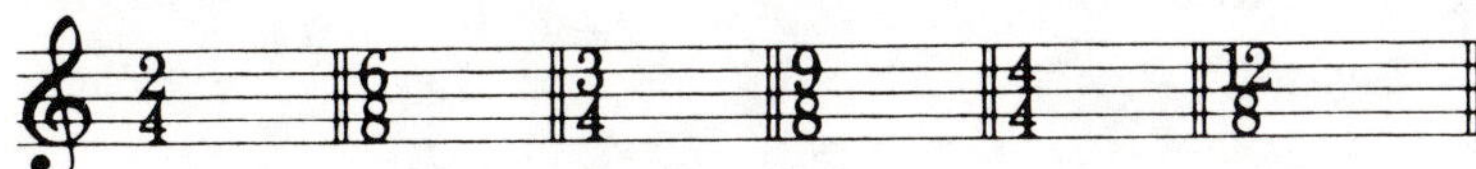

The upper digit indicates the number of basic note values per measure. It may or may not indicate the number of pulses per measure (as will be seen later in compound meters).

The lower digit indicates the basic note value: 2 signifies a half note, 4 refers to a quarter note, 8 to an eighth note, and so forth.

Figure 1.23

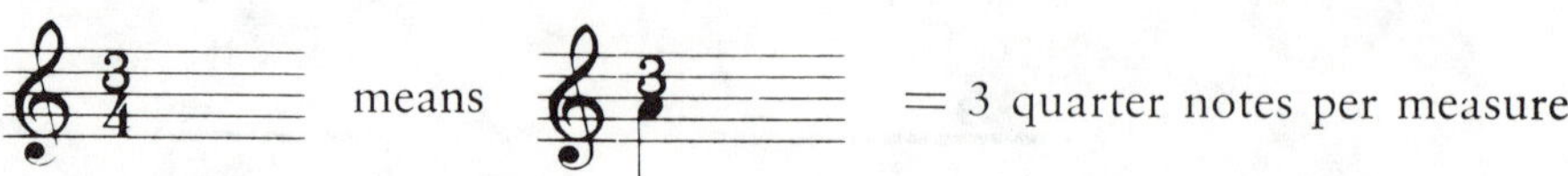

Simple Meter

In *simple meter,* each beat is divided in two parts (simple division). The upper numbers in simple meter signatures are usually 2, 3, or 4. Some simple meters showing the division of the beat are:

Figure 1.24

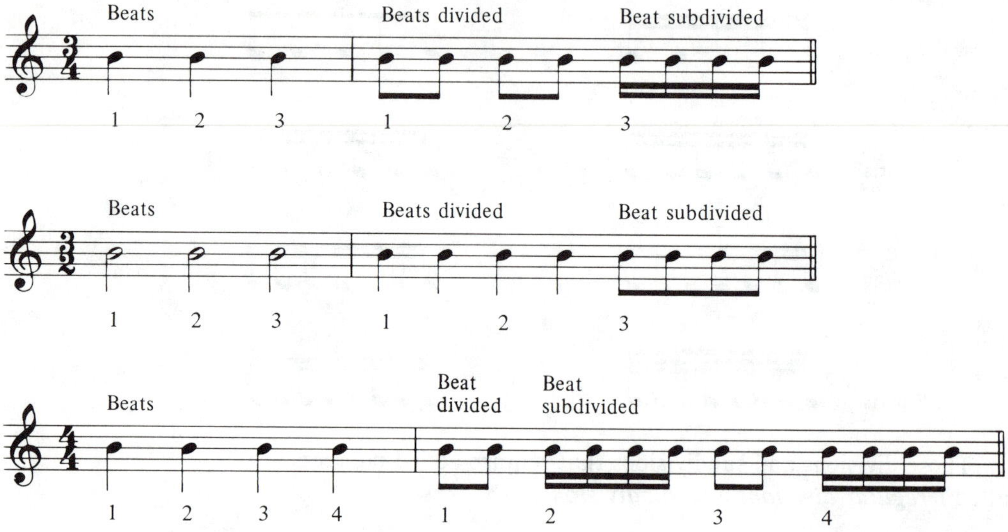

Beats — Beats divided — Beat subdivided

1 2 3 — 1 2 3

Beats — Beats divided — Beat subdivided

1 2 3 — 1 2 3

Beats — Beat divided — Beat subdivided

1 2 3 4 — 1 2 3 4

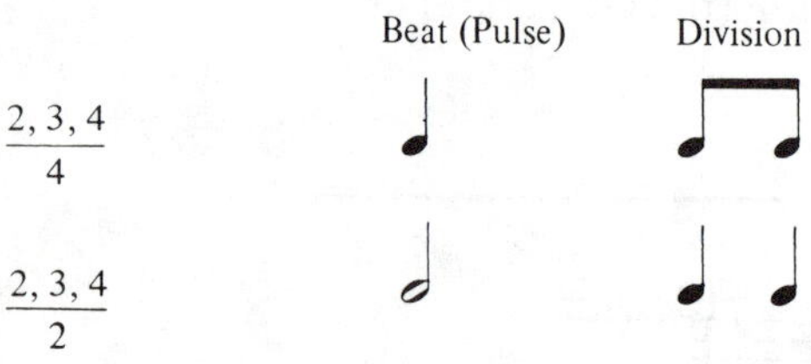

	Beat (Pulse)	Division
2, 3, 4 / 4		
2, 3, 4 / 2		

Compound Meter

In *compound meter,* each pulse is a dotted note, which is divided into groups of three parts (compound division). The most common compound meter signatures are 6/8, 9/8, and 12/8.

Figure 1.25

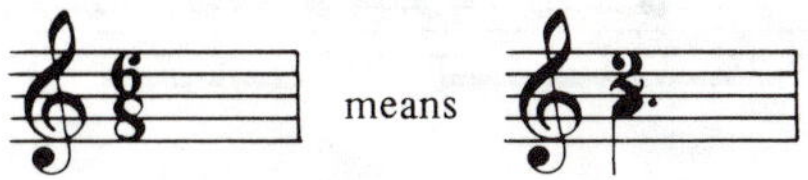

Compound meter signatures:

6	6	6	9	9	9	12	12	12
4	8	16	4	8	16	4	8	16

In 6/8 meter there are only two basic pulses, in 9/8 meter there are three, and in 12/8 meter there are four.

Figure 1.26

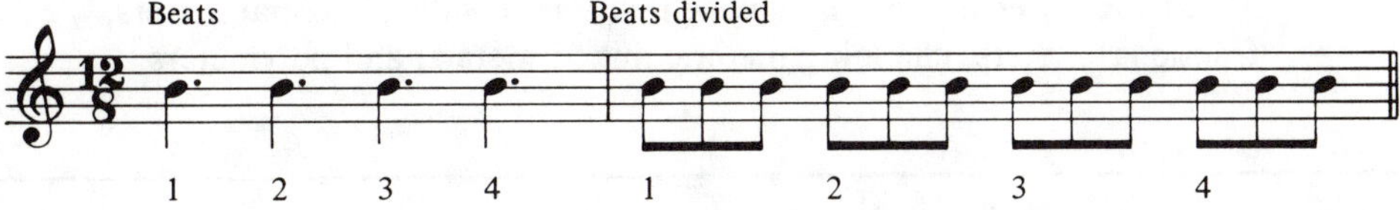

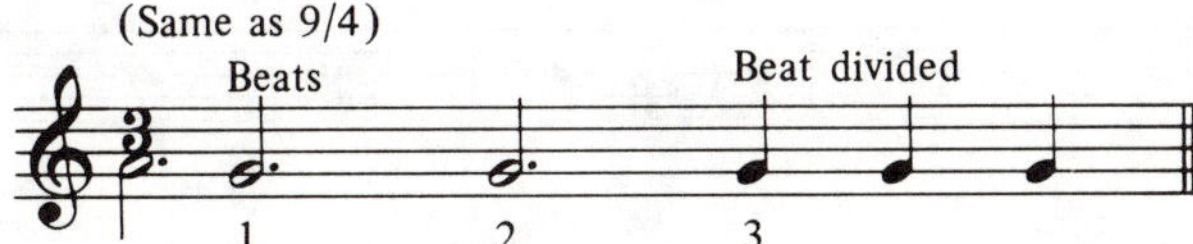

Note that the beat in compound meter will be some kind of dotted note value:

Figure 1.27

Meter Signature	Beat		Divisions
6, 9, 12 / 4	𝅗𝅥.	=	♩ ♩ ♩
6, 9, 12 / 8	♩.	=	♪ ♪ ♪ (beamed)
6, 9, 12 / 16	♪.	=	𝅘𝅥𝅯 𝅘𝅥𝅯 𝅘𝅥𝅯 (beamed)

Asymmetrical Meters

The term *asymmetrical* means not symmetrical and applies to those meter signatures that indicate the measure cannot be divided into equal groups of 2, 3, or 4.

Figure 1.28

Asymmetrical Divisions

Asymmetrical divisions are sometimes unconventional divisions of a measure (which might otherwise be fitted into a simple or compound meter) that are used consistently throughout a composition or an extended section.

Asymmetrical division of 9/8 $\frac{4+2+3}{8}$

Asymmetrical division of 8/8 or 4/4 $\frac{3+2+3}{8}$

New Trends

Innovations in music of the twentieth century include the use of meters in which the lower number is replaced by a note value, decimal meters, fractional meters, changing meters, mixed meters, and polymeters.

Figure 1.29

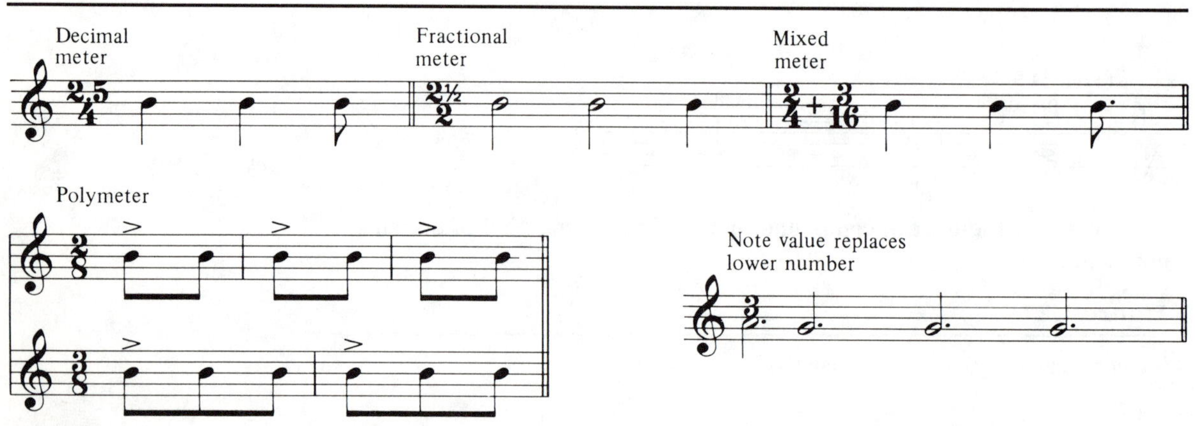

Changing meters

From Stravinsky: *Histoire Du Soldat*. Reproduced by permission © Copyright for all countries 1987. J & W Chester/Edition Wilhelm Hansen London Ltd.

Dynamic Marks

Dynamic marks indicate the general volume (amplitude) of sound. Although imprecise, such marks denote relative levels of intensity. The following words, abbreviations, and signs are common:

Symbol	Term	Definition
pp	Pianissimo	Very soft
p	Piano	Soft
mp	Mezzo piano	Moderately soft
mf	Mezzo forte	Moderately loud
f	Forte	Loud
ff	Fortissimo	Very loud
<	Cresc. or crescendo	Become louder
>	Decresc., decrescendo, or dim., diminuendo	Become softer
sfz sf	Sforzando, sforzato	Sudden accent on a single note or chord
sfp	Sforzando piano	Sudden accent followed immediately by soft
fp	Fortepiano	Loud followed immediately by soft

Some Directions for Notation in Manuscript

1. The stems of single notes within the staff should be about one octave in length.

Figure 1.30

One Octave

2. When a staff contains a single melodic line only, stems go down on those notes above the middle line and up when the notes are below the middle line. When the note is on the middle line, the stem is usually taken down except when the stems of adjacent notes are in the opposite direction.

Figure 1.31

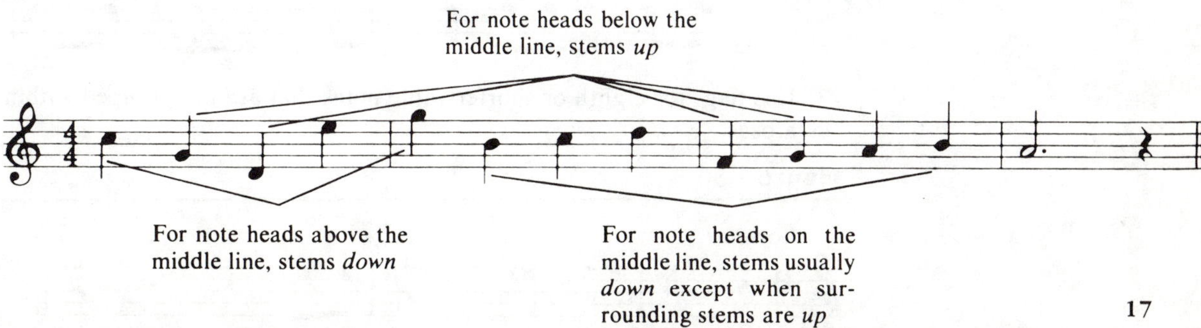
For note heads below the middle line, stems *up*
For note heads above the middle line, stems *down*
For note heads on the middle line, stems usually *down* except when surrounding stems are *up*

3. When stemmed notes are placed on ledger lines, the stems should extend to the middle line of the staff.

Figure 1.32

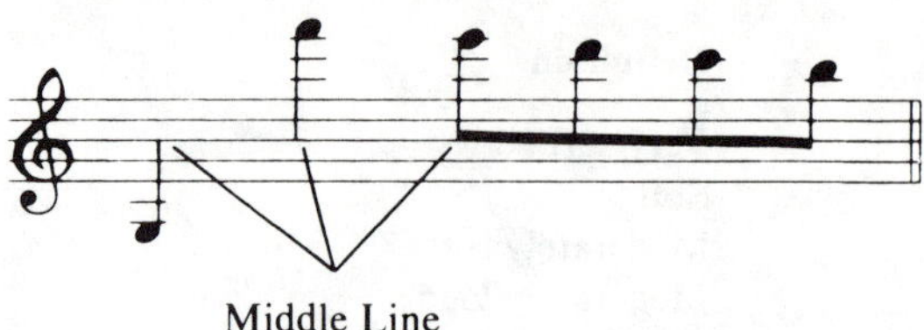

4. When connected by beams, stemmed notes should be modified so that the beams are slanted to cross no more than one line of the staff for each group of notes.

Figure 1.33

5. When two melodies occupy the same staff, the stems for one melody are up and for the other down. This makes it possible to distinguish each separate melody.

Figure 1.34

6. Beam groups of eighth notes (and smaller values) according to the beats in the measure.

Figure 1.35

7. Use flags for eighth or shorter value notes that are not grouped within a beat.

Figure 1.36

8. Avoid connecting more than six notes by beams unless all are a part of one beat.

9. Avoid mixing flagged and beamed notes except when notating vocal music. In vocal music, flagged notes have traditionally been used when the text-music relationship involves one note for each syllable. Modern practice has moved toward the use of "instrumental" notation for vocal music.

Figure 1.37

10. Irregular divisions of a beat or measure are indicated by showing the number of notes in the resulting group by means of an Arabic number. The note values of the irregular group are notated the same as the regular group, providing the number of notes in the irregular group is less than twice that of the regular (e.g., a triplet retains the same note values as a regular duplet).

Figure 1.38

Regular group is 8th notes. Irregular group is also 8th notes.

When the number of notes in the irregular group is more than twice the number of the regular, then the next smaller note value is used (e.g., a quintuplet would employ the next smaller note value).

Figure 1.39

Regular group is 8th notes. Irregular group is 16th notes. (Contains more than twice the notes of the regular group.)

11. In compound meter, try to show the basic pulse structure of the measure and the division into groups of three as clearly as possible.

Figure 1.40

12. The whole rest (▬) can be used to indicate a full measure rest in any meter.

13. Avoid half rests in 3/4 meter; use two quarter rests.

Figure 1.41

14. When notes of a chord are on an adjacent line and space, the higher of the two is always to the right regardless of the direction of the stem.

Figure 1.42

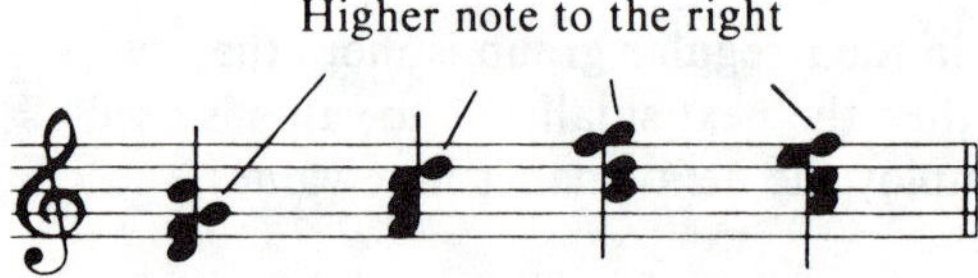

15. When a dotted note is on a line, the dot is usually placed slightly above the line. When two separate voices are placed on a single staff, the dots are below the line on the notes with stems down.

Figure 1.43

16. Dynamic markings should be added above, between, or below staves according to the nature of the music or score:

    Instrumental Music: The markings are usually placed beneath the staff to which they refer. Sometimes, because of inadequate space, it is necessary to place markings above the staff.

    Vocal Music: The markings are usually placed above the staff to which they refer. This is done to avoid confusion with the words of the text.

    Piano Scores: The markings are placed between the staves if the markings are to apply to both staves. If markings are needed for each staff individually, the markings should go just above or below the staff to which they refer.

    Generally avoid placing markings directly on the staff, although some, for example the crescendo ⟨ and diminuendo ⟩ , will protrude into the staff on occasion.

Figure 1.44

(Workbook-Anthology Assignments 1.4 and 1.5, pp. 2 and 3, and 1.9–1.16, pp. 5–8)

History

Neumatic Notation

From about A.D. 650 to A.D. 1200, music notation consisted of a set of symbols called *neumes* (pronounced "newms"). These symbols took their name from the Greek word meaning gesture. Written above the Latin texts associated with the liturgy of the Roman Catholic church, neumes could not convey pitch or duration, but rather served as a memory aid in recalling previously learned melodic lines. Figure 1.45 shows an example of neumatic notation from a twelfth-century gradual taken from a manuscript in the New York Public Library.

Figure 1.45

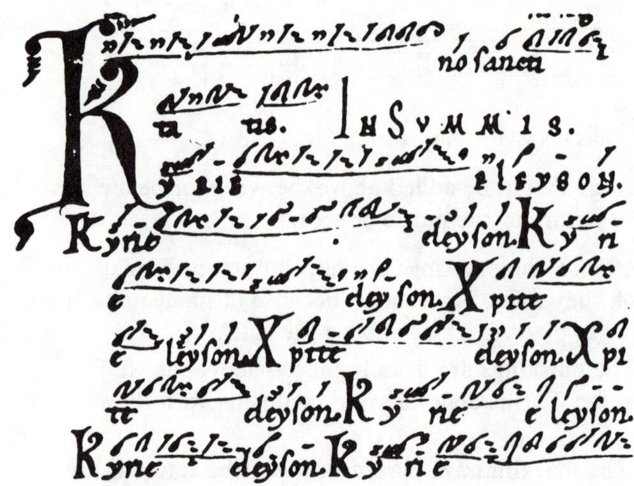

From Curt Sachs, *Our Musical Heritage: A Short History of Music,* 2d ed. Copyright © 1955 Prentice-Hall, Inc. Englewood Cliffs, NJ. Reprinted by permission of Gabrielle B. (Sachs) Forrest.

Horizontal lines were gradually added to indicate the locations of F and C. In the eleventh century, a four-line staff appeared that included the F line, the C line, and two additional lines. Later, neumes were square- or diamond-shaped. Combined with the staff, neumes now had the capability for indicating specific pitches. The four-line staff is still used to notate Gregorian chant.

Figure 1.46

Four-line staff and later types of neumes

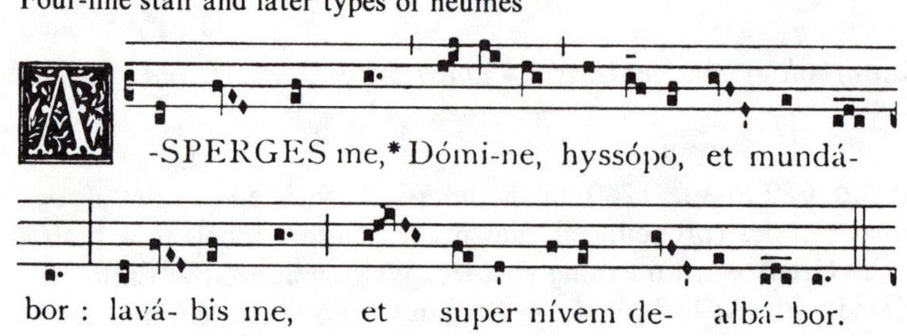
-SPERGES me,* Dómi-ne, hyssópo, et mundá-
bor : lavá- bis me, et super nívem de- albá- bor.

Transcribed into modern notation:

A - sper - ges me, Do - mi - ne, hysso - po et mun-da - bor;

Source: from *The Liber Usualis, No. 801,* ed. the Benedictines of Solesmes.

Mensural Notation

Mensural (measured) notation, a system that included durational values as well as pitch, developed during the thirteenth century as the single melody and free rhythm of Gregorian chant or plainsong gave way to measured music that included parts.

Figure 1.47

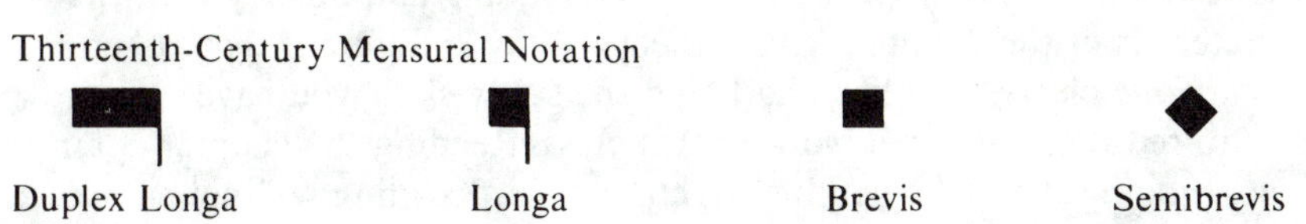

Present Notation

Our present system of notation evolved from thirteenth-century practices. The treatise on mensural notation, *De Musica Mensurabili* (*Ars Cantus Mensurabilis*), by Franco of Cologne (active 1250–80), contains fundamental rules of modern notation. The five-line staff appeared in the thirteenth century. Present-day conventional notation is more directly related to fifteenth- and sixteenth-century mensural notation. The later use of bar lines and square- or diamond-shaped notes brought notation very close to the form found today. Figure 1.48 shows the evolution of some of the more common notational signs.

Figure 1.48

HISTORICAL DEVELOPMENT OF NOTATION

Developed Approximately	Type	Examples of Notation
A.D. 650	Neumes	
A.D. 1250	Black Mensural	
A.D. 1450	White Mensural	
A.D. 1600	Modern	

In the sixteenth century, the short ledger lines were introduced, making it possible to extend the range of the staff. Round notes developed when it was realized that they were easier to write and print. Although a fairly basic system has prevailed during the past three hundred years and we often think of the present system as static, notation has always been undergoing transformation.

REVIEW

You will find sections labeled "Review" near the end of each chapter. The purpose of these sections is to provide a list of specific activities that you can do to improve your understanding and fluency with the materials of the chapter. Music theory study is different than other academic classes you have had, and the study skills you have acquired there may not work in this class. Reading the chapter again or studying the areas you highlighted on first reading will not suffice. These materials must be practiced on a regular basis until they become second nature to you. If you will take time to work on the following suggestions, you will find your knowledge and skills improving, and you will be well on your way to success in your study of music theory.

1. Look at the list of topics at the head of the chapter (p. 5). Try to recall as specifically as possible the content of each of the sections. If any topics seem unclear to you, those sections are targets for careful study.
2. Look at figure 1.4 and cover the letter names and solfeggio syllables below the staff. Look at a note in the bass staff and name it both with letter name and solfeggio syllable. Now choose one in the treble staff and do the same. Move around to random notes and see how fast you can name each one. Do the same exercise using figure 1.8.
3. Imagine the upper staff in figure 1.4 has an alto clef and the lower staff a tenor clef. Repeat exercise 2 above.
4. Sit at a piano keyboard. Play random white keys. For each key played, name the note, the solfeggio syllable and the specific octave identification (see figure 1.10 or 1.11).
5. Take a piece of music (any piece will do). Look at each note and name the half step above and below that note.
6. Look in the *Workbook/Anthology* at the anthology section. Examine the meter signature of each piece and identify it as simple meter or compound meter. Can you locate a division of the beat? A subdivision? Are there any irregular divisions?
7. Take a piece of music (any piece will do). Copy it on a blank piece of paper. In the days before copy machines, musicians regularly copied music, and it is said that many great composers learned their craft by copying other composers' music. You must learn to produce clear, legible manuscript, and copying music and comparing your work with the original is good practice.

Test Yourself 1

1. Write the letter name of each of the following notes and indicate the octave identification.

2. Find the pairs of enharmonic equivalents among the following ten notes:

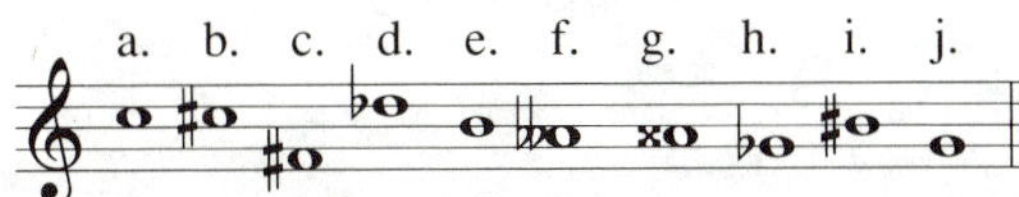

3. Find the errors in notation in each measure below:

4. Name the note one half-step above each of the following notes:

CHAPTER 2

Scales, Tonality, Key, and Modes

Scale
Pitch Class
Diatonic Scale
Major Scale
Transposition
Natural Minor Scale
Harmonic Minor Scale
Melodic Minor Scale
Relative Relationship
Circle of Fifths
Parallel Relationship
Tonality
Key
Pentatonic Scale
Nondiatonic Scale
Chromatic Scale
Whole-Tone Scale
Blues Scale
Nontraditional Scale
Authentic Mode
Plagal Mode
Pitch Inventory

Exposition

Scale

A *scale* is a series of ascending and descending pitches. Musicians use a scale as a convenient way of displaying the tones used in a melody or harmony. In figure 2.1, the melody consists of twenty-four notes, but only seven different *pitch classes.* (A *pitch class* contains all notes of the same name regardless of octave.) These pitch classes are arranged in ascending order to form a scale.

Figure 2.1

Haydn: Symphony in G (Surprise), Hob. I: 94 (3rd Movement)

Notes of the melody arranged as a scale:

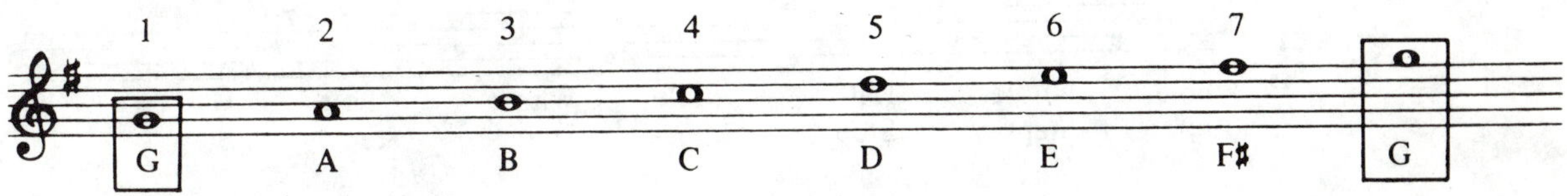

Although an infinite variety of pitch combinations is available, the following scales represent those in most common use during the past 200 years.

Diatonic Scales

Diatonic (literally "across the tones") defines a scale of mixed half and whole steps (and an occasional step-and-a-half) in which each individual tone plays a role. The first tone (the *tonic*) of a scale is a point of rest and is considered to be the most stable. Other tones lead toward or away from it, creating varying degrees of tension or relaxation.

Since the *tonic* (the first note) is the focal point of the scale, the most stable note, and the point of greatest relaxation, diatonic melodies are frequently shaped by composers to end on the tonic note. At times the word "diatonic" is used to indicate a tone that is part of a particular scale pattern—as distinguished from a *nondiatonic* tone that does not belong to the scale pattern.

Major Scale

The *major scale* is a scale of seven different pitches with whole steps separating adjacent tones except for half steps between the third and fourth degrees and between the seventh and eighth (or first) degrees. The eighth pitch has the same letter name as the first and thus is treated as a duplication.

Since all adjacent keys (black and white) on the piano are a half step apart, the following illustration shows that by beginning on C and playing in order only the white keys to the next C, a *C-major* scale results.

Figure 2.2

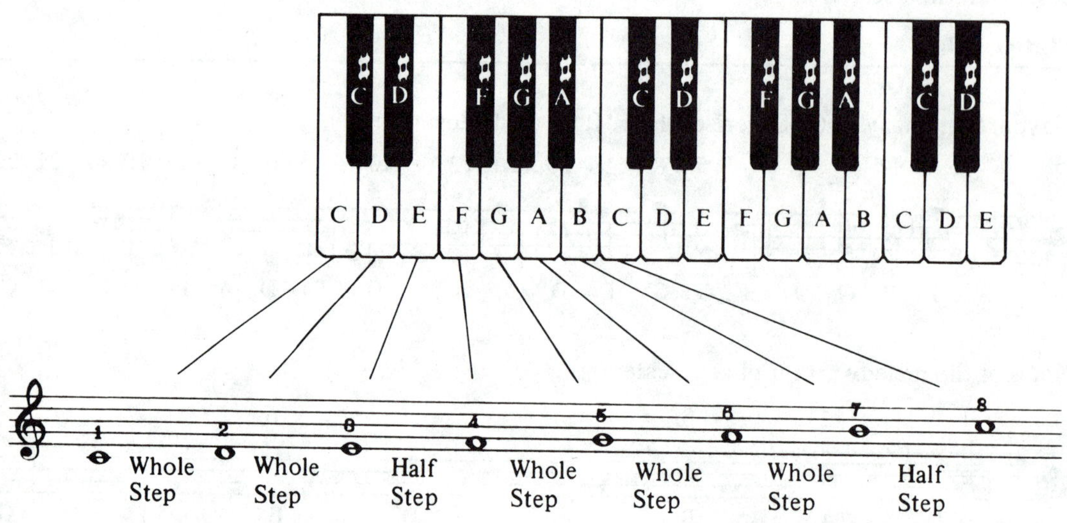

The melody in figure 2.3 utilizes the notes of the C-major scale:

Figure 2.3

Transposition

This same major-scale pattern of half and whole steps can be duplicated at any pitch. Such rewriting is called *transposition.* In figure 2.4 the major scale is transposed so that its first tone is G and it is called the *G-major scale:*

Figure 2.4

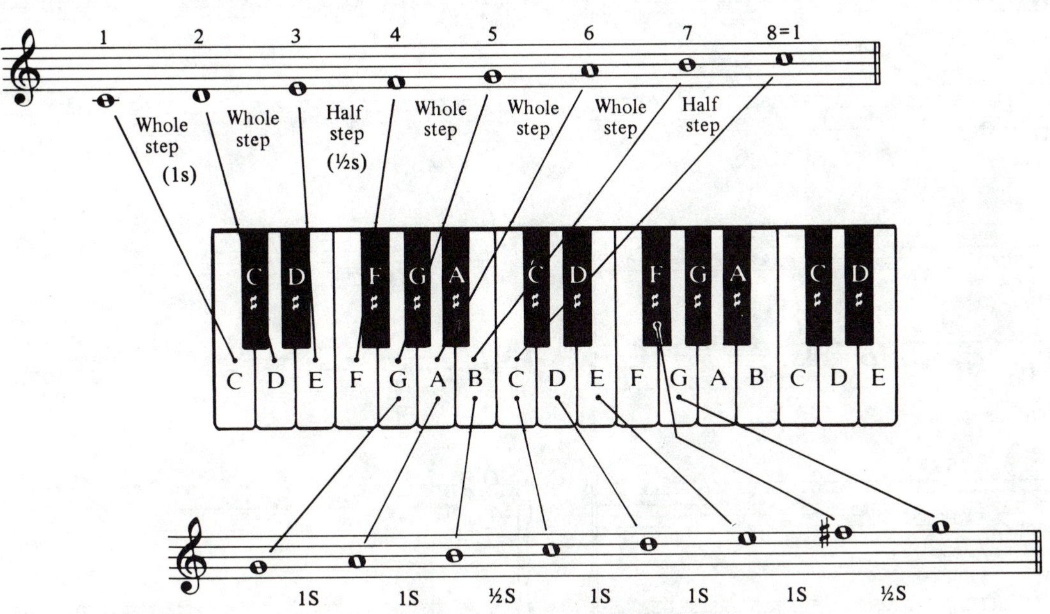

From figure 2.4, it can be seen that a sharp is necessary if the major-scale pattern of half and whole steps is to be carried out in the transposition. The following chart provides a convenient way to memorize the sharps or the flats needed when the scale begins on various pitches.

The arrangement of the necessary sharps or flats is called a *key signature* and appears at the beginning of each staff in a composition. Notice that each successive tonic, or beginning note, is five scale degrees (called a *perfect fifth*) above, or four scale degrees below (perfect fourth) the previous tonic. A new sharp is added to the key signature for each succeeding perfect fifth (P5), and in the flat signatures, a flat is dropped for each succeeding P5 (see figure 2.16).

Figure 2.5

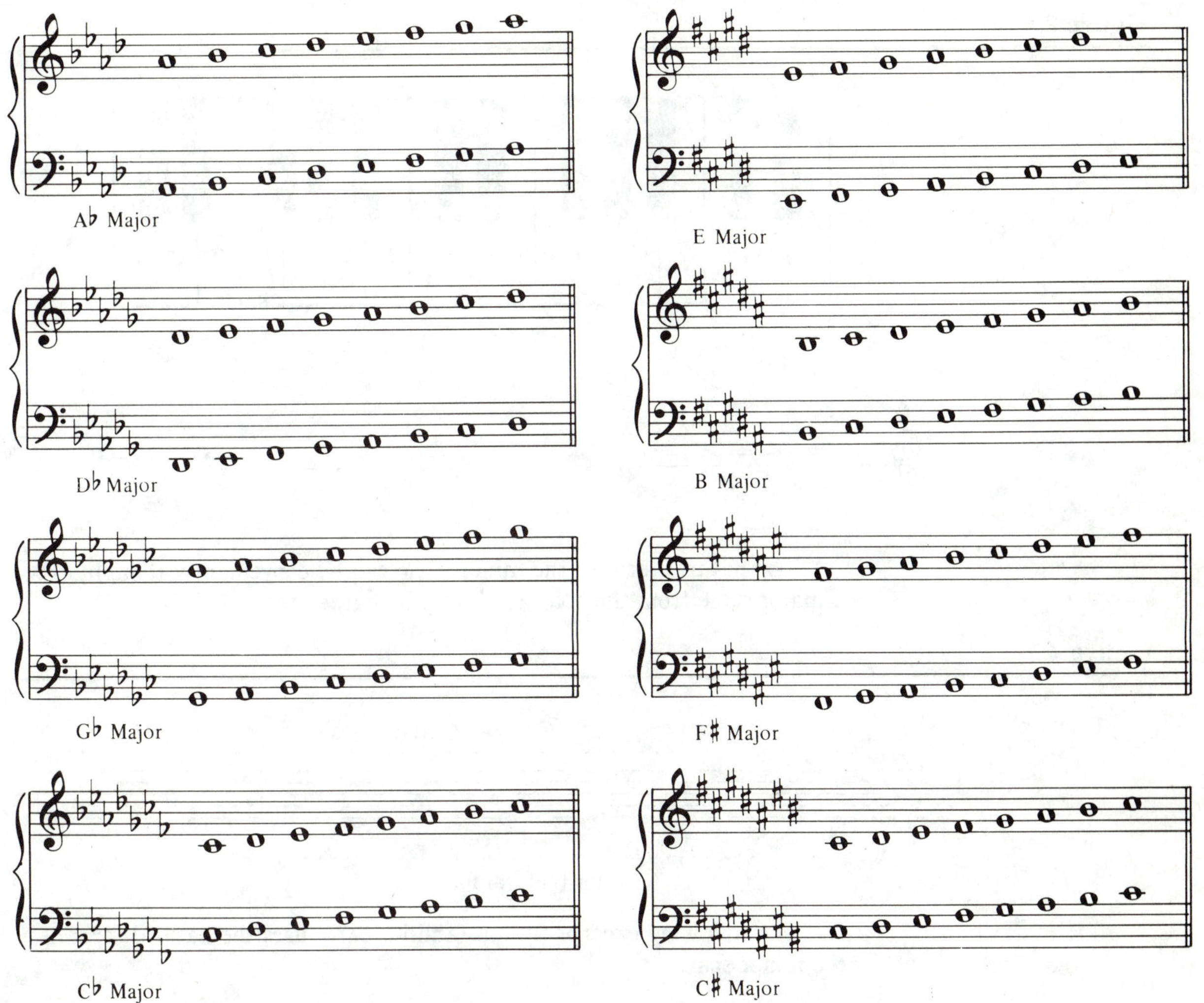

Minor Scale

Natural Form

The *natural form* of the *minor scale* contains seven different pitches with whole steps separating adjacent tones except for half steps between the second and third degrees and between the fifth and sixth degrees. One instance of this scale is formed by the white keys of the piano from A to A:

Figure 2.6

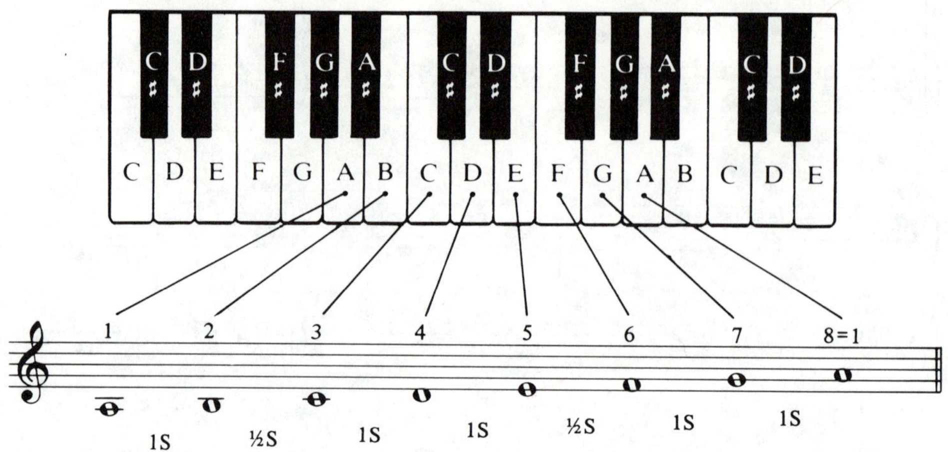

The natural form of the minor scale can be conveniently thought of as a major scale from the sixth to the sixth degree.

Figure 2.7

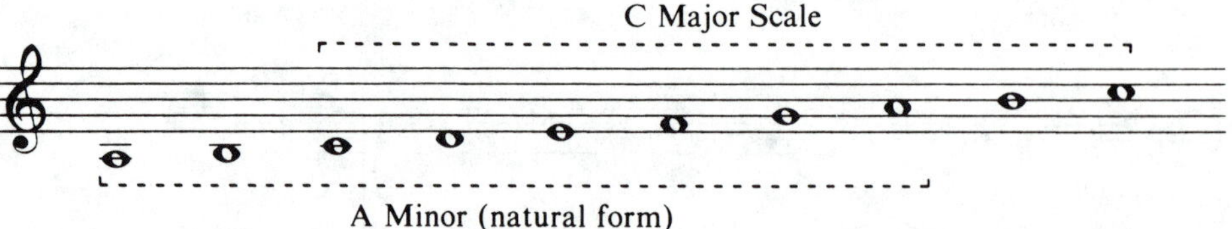

The following excerpt from a familiar carol uses the natural form of the minor scale:

Figure 2.8

The *harmonic* form of the minor scale is the natural minor scale with a raised seventh degree. The added impetus of a raised seventh degree gives more melodic thrust toward the tonic and provides for a major dominant triad (see chapter 4). Raising the seventh degree creates a step-and-a-half between the sixth and seventh degrees and a half-step between the seventh and eighth degrees. Accidentals used to raise the seventh degree do not appear in the key signature. The pattern of half steps (2–3, 5–6, 7–8) is shown in figure 2.9.

Harmonic Form

Figure 2.9

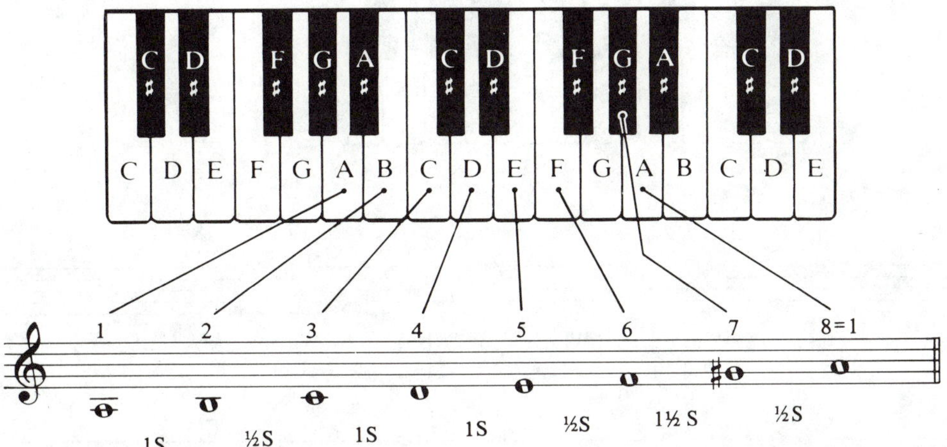

This Mozart excerpt utilizes the harmonic form of the minor scale. Notice the presence of G-sharps in every measure except 5 and 6.

Figure 2.10

Mozart: Piano Sonata in A minor, K. 310 (3rd Movement)

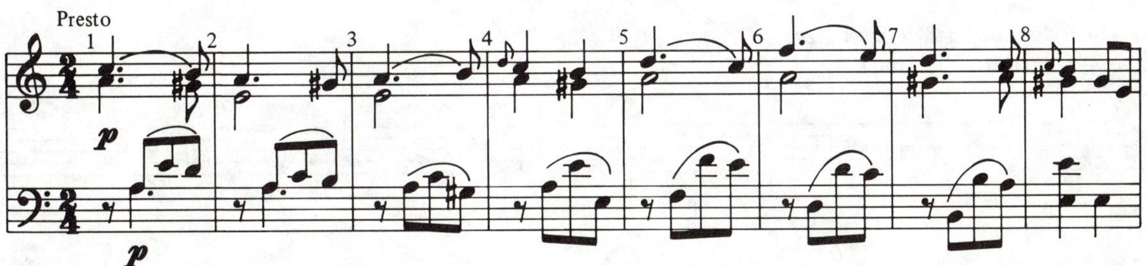

The *melodic* form of the minor scale is different in its ascending from its descending form. The ascending form includes raised sixth and seventh scale degrees, producing half steps between the second and third and between the seventh and eighth degrees. The descending form is exactly the same as the natural minor.

Melodic Form

The melodic form of the minor scale developed because composers liked the urgency of the raised seventh, but found the step-and-a-half interval between the sixth and seventh degrees of the harmonic minor scale too rough, especially for smooth vocal writing. In descending melodic passages, no need existed for the raised seventh, so composers most often used the natural minor with the lowered seventh and sixth degrees.

Figure 2.11

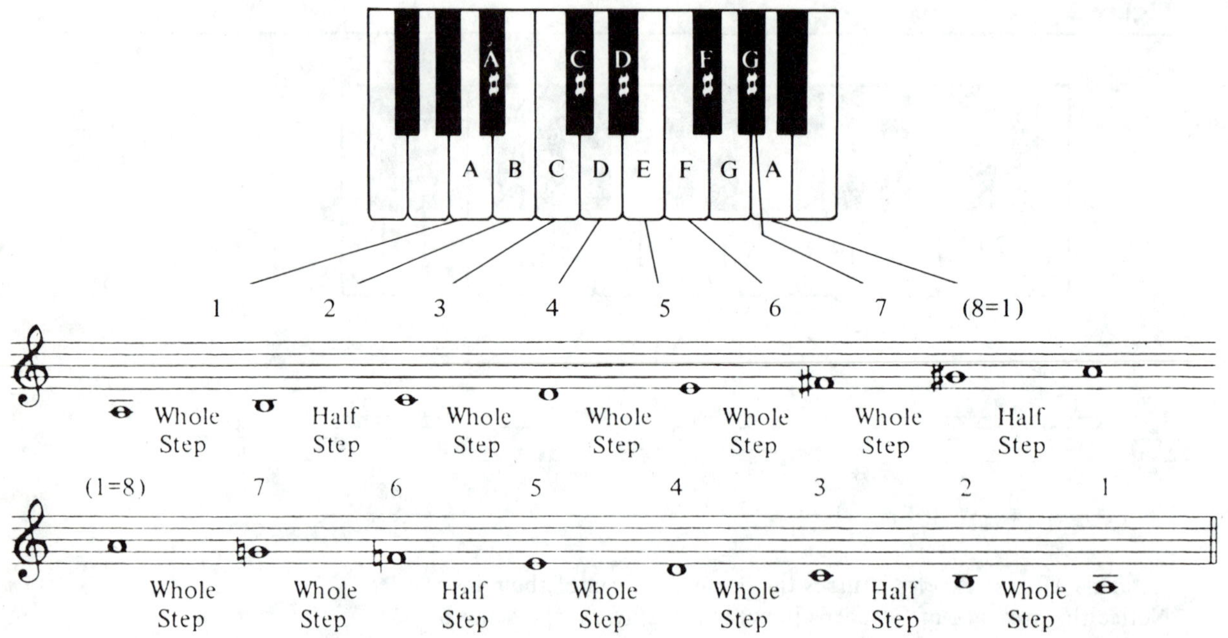

The following excerpt includes the ascending and descending forms of the melodic minor scale:

Figure 2.12

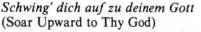

Schwing' dich auf zu deinem Gott
(Soar Upward to Thy God)

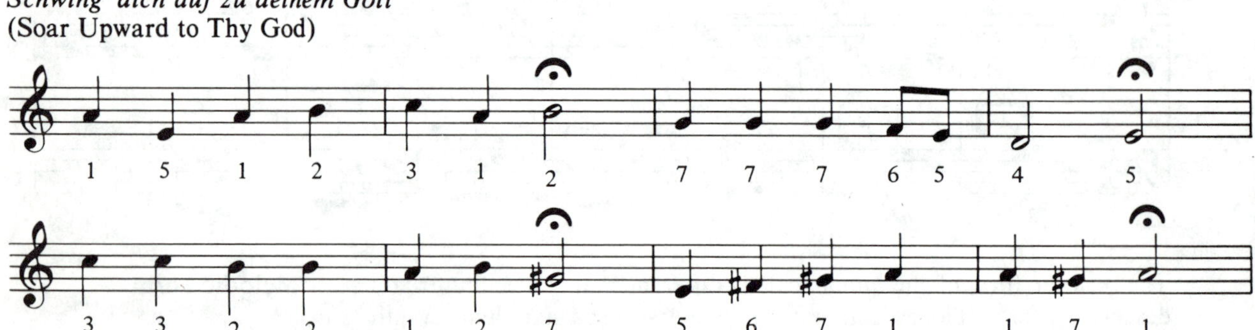

An examination of music literature, especially vocal and choral, reveals that composers considered the natural, harmonic, and melodic minor as arrangements of the same scale with each form to be used according to need. This excerpt, by Bach, utilizes the various forms of the A-minor scale in a single phrase of music:

Figure 2.13

Bach: *Herr Jesus Christ, du höchstes Gut* (transposed)
(Lord Jesus Christ, Thou Highest Good) BWV 113

(Workbook-Anthology Assignments 2.1–2.3, pp. 9 and 10, and 2.8 and 2.10, pp. 14 and 15)

Scale Relationships

It is important on occasion to associate and compare the patterns of the major and minor scales. Two relationships will be described: the relative and the parallel.

Relative Relationship

A major and a minor scale that have the same key signature are said to be in a *relative relationship*. To find the *relative minor* of any major scale, proceed to the sixth degree of that scale. This tone is the tonic of the relative minor.

Figure 2.14

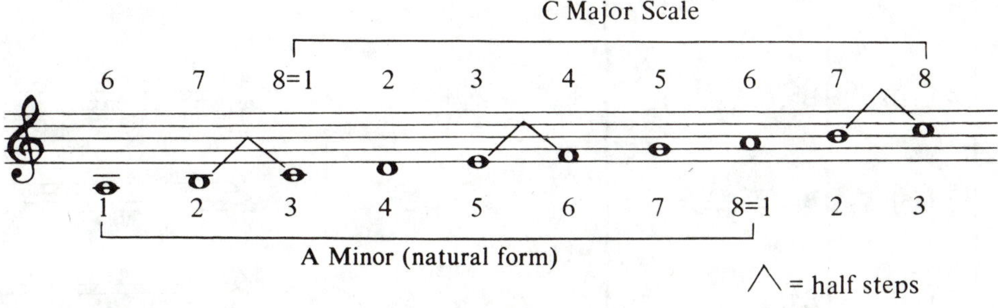

To find the *relative major* of a minor key, proceed to the third degree of the minor scale. This tone is the tonic of the relative major key.

Figure 2.15

MAJOR-RELATIVE MINOR RELATIONSHIPS

Major Scale	Relative Minor Scale	Number of Sharps or Flats	Letter Names	Key Signatures and Key Notes (Major and Minor)
C	a	None		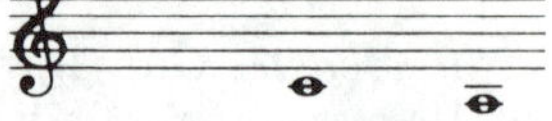
G	e	1 Sharp	F♯	
D	b	2 Sharps	F♯, C♯	
A	f♯	3 Sharps	F♯, C♯, G♯	
E	c♯	4 Sharps	F♯, C♯, G♯, D♯	
B = C♭	g♯ = a♭	5 Sharps 7 Flats	F♯, C♯, G♯, D♯, A♯, B♭, E♭,A♭, D♭, G♭, C♭, F♭	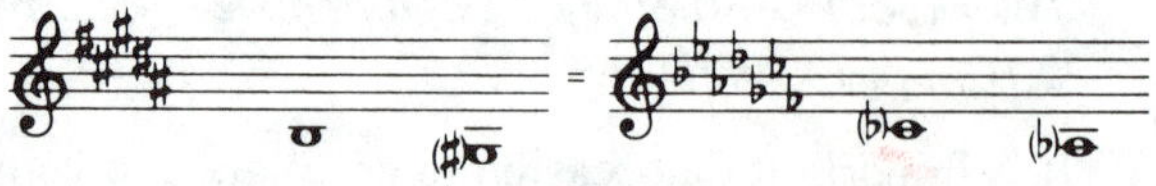 =
F♯ = G♭	d♯ = e♭	6 Sharps 6 Flats	F♯, C♯, G♯, D♯, A♯, E♯, B♭, E♭, A♭, D♭, G♭, C♭	 =
C♯ = D♭	a♯ = b♭	7 Sharps 5 Flats	F♯, C♯, G♯, D♯, A♯, E♯, B♯, B♭, E♭, A♭, D♭, G♭	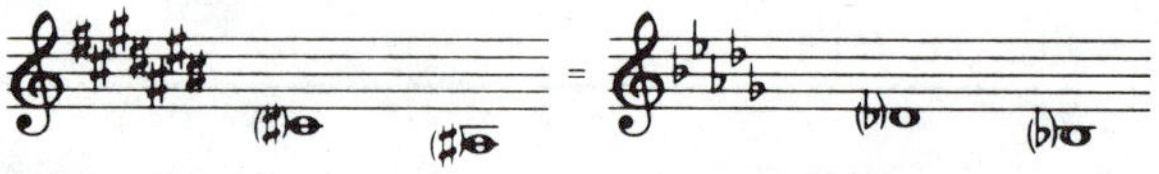 =
A♭	f	4 Flats	B♭, E♭, A♭, D♭	
E♭	c	3 Flats	B♭, E♭, A♭	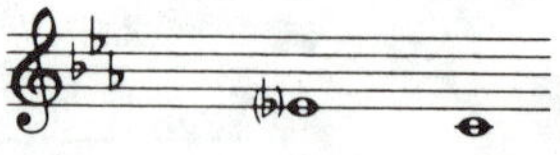
B♭	g	2 Flats	B♭, E♭	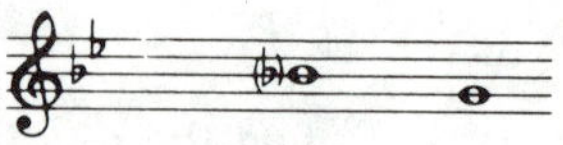
F	d	1 Flat	B♭	

Figure 2.16

Another way to visualize the relationship between the major scales and their relative minors is on the circle of fifths:

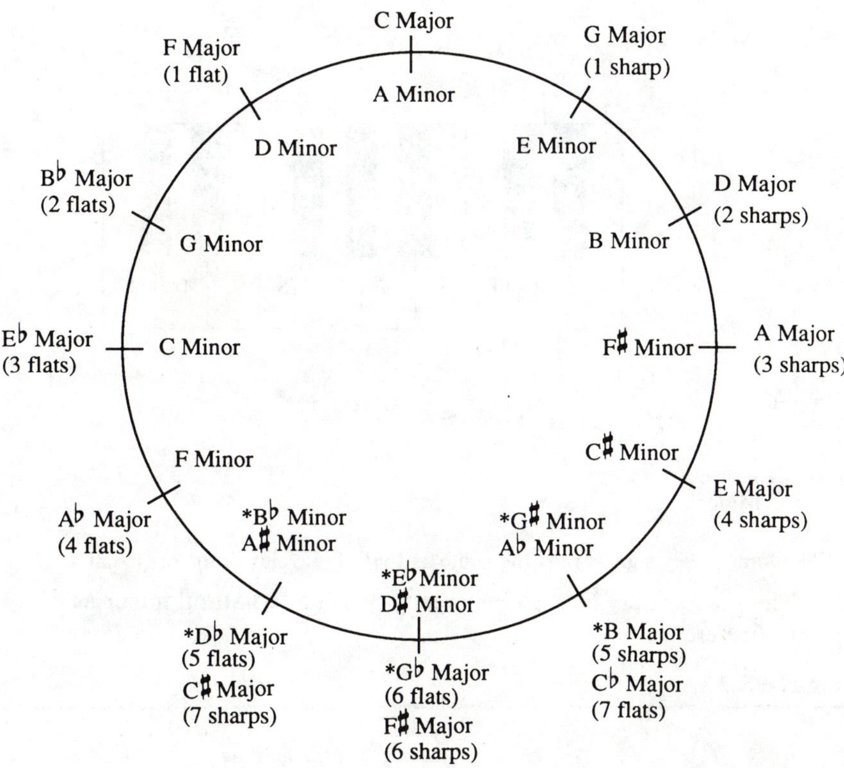

Parallel Relationship

A major and a minor scale that have the same tonic note are said to be in *parallel* relationship. In the following example using C as the tonic, the major scale is written without accidentals. Using C as the tonic of the natural form of a minor scale requires accidentals to produce the required sequence of whole and half steps. The accidentals required for this change become the key signature for C minor.

Figure 2.17

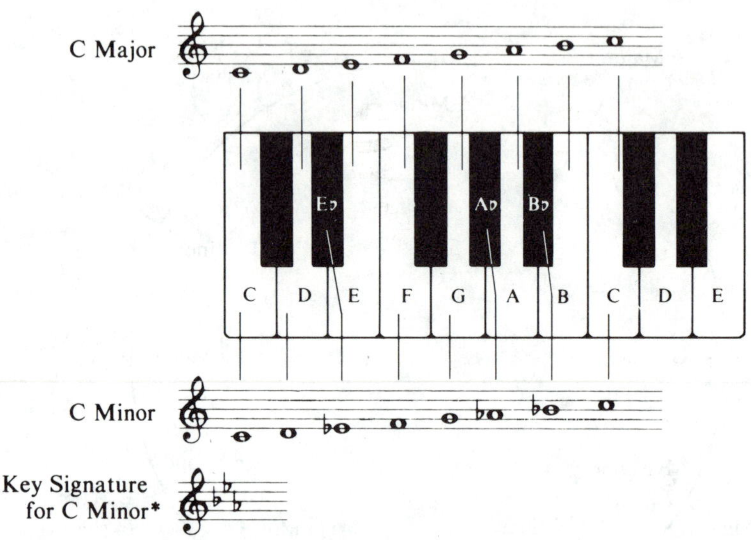

*The C minor key signature is the same as that of its relative major, E-flat.

The process may be seen in reverse by using A-natural minor as a point of reference:

Figure 2.18

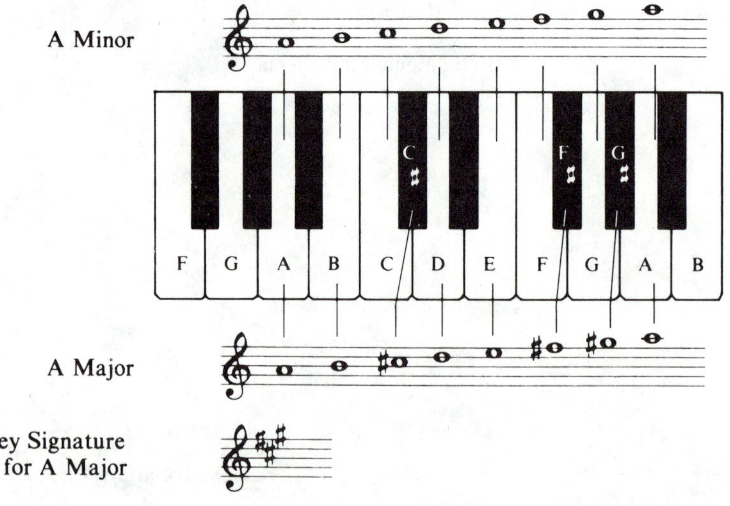

Figure 2.19 shows the D-major scale and the scale degrees affected in the parallel natural, harmonic, and melodic minor scales:

Figure 2.19

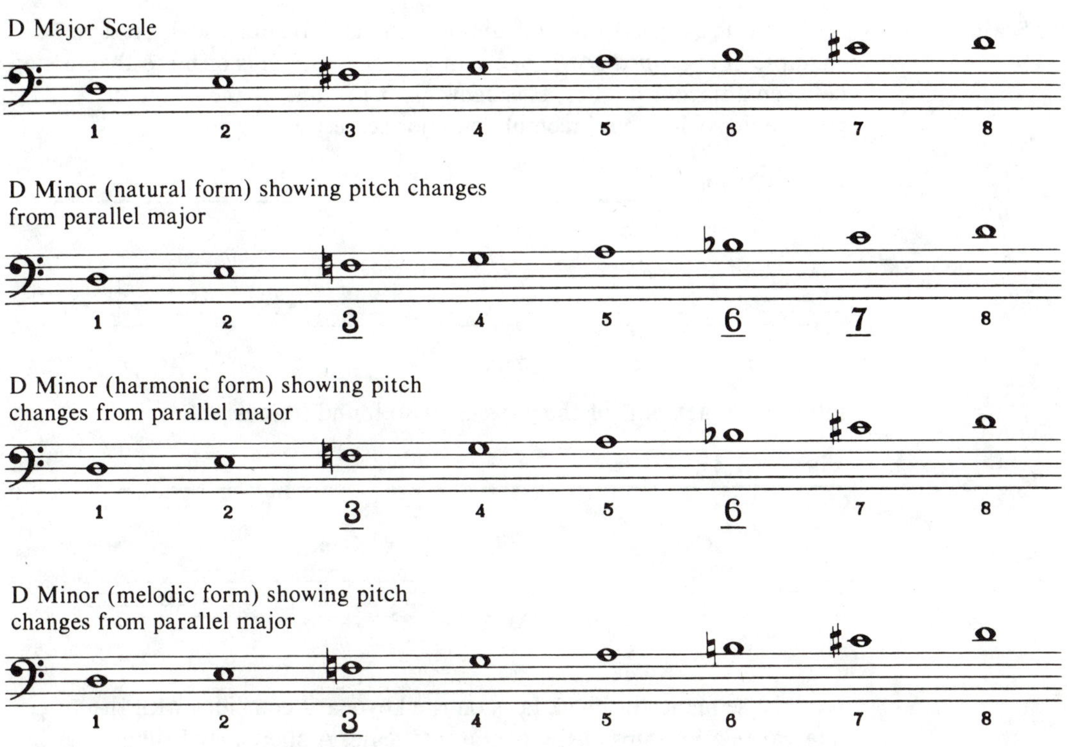

(Workbook-Anthology Assignments 2.4, p. 10, 2.11, p. 15, and 2.12, p. 16)

Tonality

Tonality refers to a system of tones (example: the tones of a major or minor scale) functioning in such a way that one tone becomes the central point to which the remaining tones are related in varying degrees of importance. In tonality, the tonic (tonal center) is the tone of complete relaxation, the target toward which (to reduce tension) or from which (to create tension) other tones lead. Although most musicians consider the meaning of the term tonality obvious, the exact definition is difficult because the term describes a subjective perception that differs from person to person.

Key

Key refers to the tonal system based on the major and minor scales. This system is by far the most common tonal system, but tonality can be present in music not based on the major and minor scales (see chapter 22).

Other Scales

While the major scale and the three forms of the minor scale represent by far the largest percentage of Western music written from the seventeenth century to the end of the nineteenth century, a number of other scale formations are found now and then. Some of these are listed as follows.

Pentatonic Scale

As its name suggests, the *pentatonic scale* is a five-tone scale. It is an example of a *gapped scale,* one that contains intervals of more than a step between adjacent pitches. It is convenient to think of the common pentatonic scale as an incomplete major scale.

Figure 2.20

Other arrangements of the gaps are also found in music:

Figure 2.21

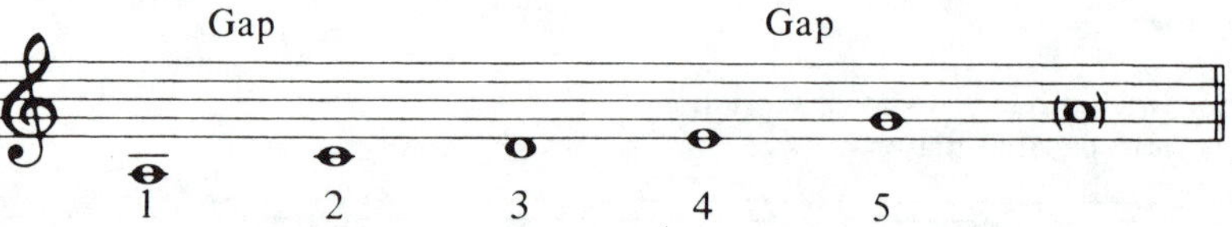

The sequence of black keys on the keyboard coincides with the interval relationships of the pentatonic scale. A singularly brilliant exploitation of the pentatonic scale occurs in the right-hand melodic line of Chopin's Étude in G-flat Major, op. 10, no. 5, the popular "Black Key" Étude.

Ravel utilized pentatonic material to evoke Oriental images in a movement from *Ma Mere l'Oye:*

Figure 2.22

Ravel: *Ma Mere l'Oye* (Mother Goose)

Examples of the use of pentatonic scales are often found in folk tunes:

Figure 2.23

Swiss Folk Tune

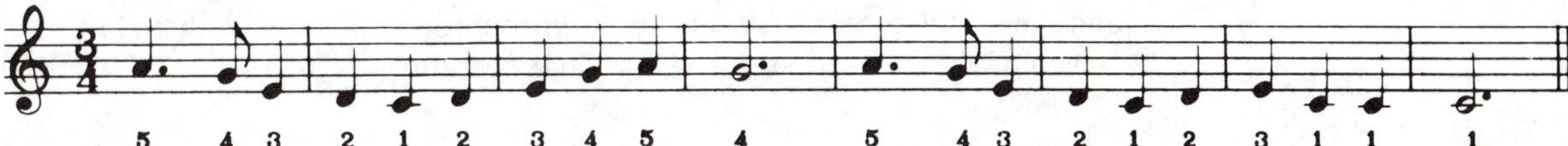

The first two phrases of the following familiar tune are based on a pentatonic scale:

Figure 2.24

Foster: Oh, Susanna

While all the aforementioned examples illustrate gapped scales typical of Western music, nongapped pentatonic scales (all adjacent intervals of the same size) occur in the music of other cultures. One such culture is Java, where a pentatonic scale consisting of five nearly equal intervals (whole plus a quarter step) forms the basis for a large body of music literature.

Nondiatonic Scales

A scale that does not observe the interval sequence of the diatonic or pentatonic scales is called a *nondiatonic scale.* Many nondiatonic scales have no identifiable tonal center (tonic).

Chromatic Scale

A *chromatic scale* is a nondiatonic scale consisting entirely of half-step intervals. Since each tone of the scale is equidistant from the next, it has no tonic.

Figure 2.25

Chromatic Scale

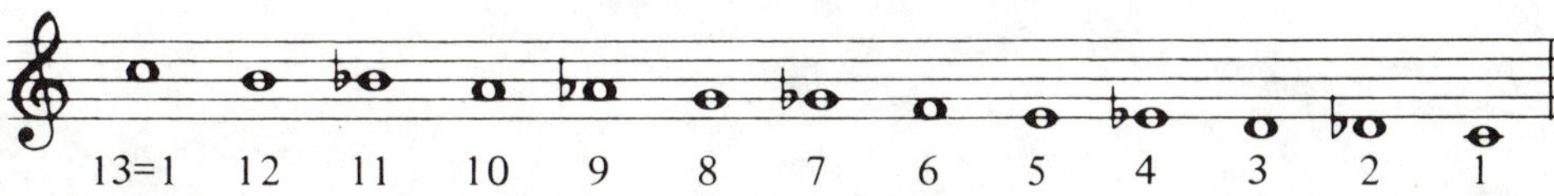

Sometimes, however, a melody based on a regular diatonic scale (major or minor) is laced with many accidentals, and although all twelve tones of the chromatic scale may appear, the tonal characteristics of the diatonic scale are maintained. The following excerpt from Purcell's Dido and Aeneas demonstrates this use of chromatic half steps by including eleven of the twelve tones in its gradual descent:

Figure 2.26

Purcell: "Thy Hand, Belinda" from Dido and Aeneas, Z. 626

*Note the chromatic descent.

A *whole-tone scale* is a six-tone scale made up entirely of whole steps between adjacent scale degrees.

Whole-Tone Scale

Figure 2.27

Examples of whole-tone material are found in music from the late Romantic and Impressionistic periods:

Figure 2.28

Source: Debussy: *Voiles* (Sails), copyright © 1910, Durand et Cie. Elkan-Vogel, Inc. sole representative, United States.

(Workbook-Anthology Assignment 2.5, p. 10)

The *blues scale* is a chromatic variant of the major scale with flat third and flat seventh scale degrees. These notes alternating with the normal third and seventh scale degrees are used to create the blues inflection. Actually these "blue notes" represent the influence of African scales on this music. (See Gunther Schuller's *Early Jazz,* pp. 46–52 for a complete discussion of the blue notes.)

Blues Scale

Figure 2.29

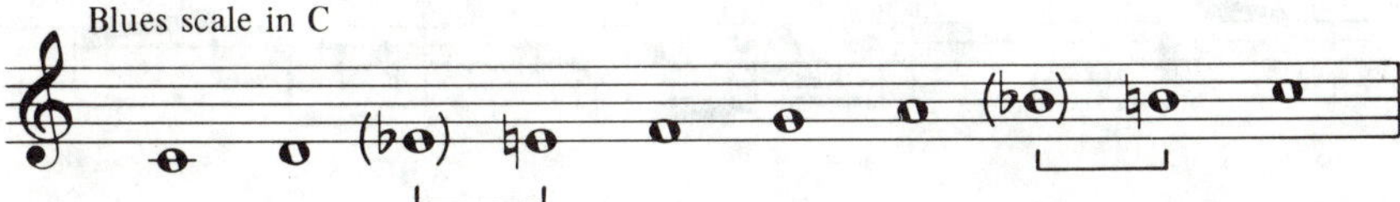

Nontraditional Scales

A number of *nontraditional scales* occur occasionally in the music of the late-nineteenth and twentieth centuries. Most of these scales are made of a symmetrical pattern of intervals.

Figure 2.30

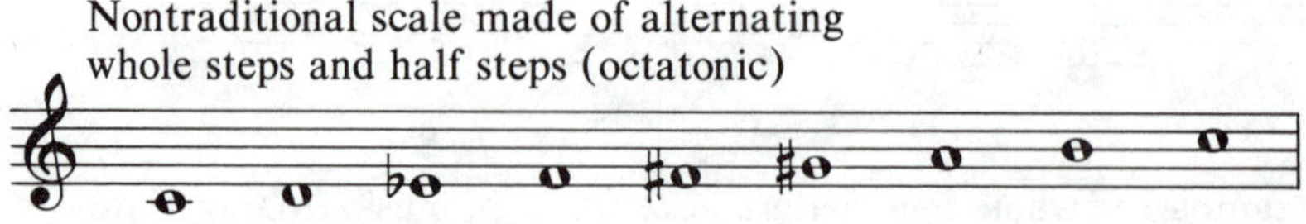

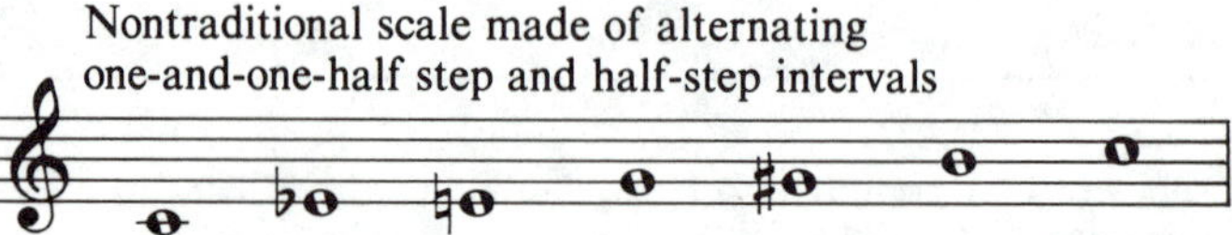

Pitch Inventory

As a first step in understanding the structure of a piece of music, it is important to determine its scalar basis. This can be done by forming a pitch inventory. A *pitch inventory* is a scalewise list of the tones used in a composition or section thereof. For purposes of organization, the pitch inventories in this text always begin with the pitch A.

Many students will have no need to prepare a pitch inventory. But for those students who have yet to develop a "hearing eye" that would allow instantaneous recognition of keys and tonal centers, a pitch inventory may be a necessity. A pitch inventory permits quick assessment of the selected pitches without prejudice as to key or tonality. From there a fairly accurate determination of key may be determined by observing the location of half and whole steps, accidentals such as raised 7ths, etc., and particular notes of the melody that are emphasized.

With practice the need for a pitch inventory will diminish and the calculations will become automatic. Figure 2.31 shows a melody, its pitch inventory, and finally, its scale.

Figure 2.31

(Workbook-Anthology Assignments 2.7, p. 12, 2.14 and 2.15, pp. 17–20)

History

The scales used in music developed and changed over the various historical periods. For a more complete explanation of the historical periods listed below see Appendix B.

Middle Ages and Renaissance Period (800–1600)

From roughly 800 to 1500, the church modes formed the basis for nearly all Western music. Notice in the following illustration that modal scales are divided by range, and that the beginning tone is called the final rather than the tonic, as in the other diatonic scales.

Figure 2.32

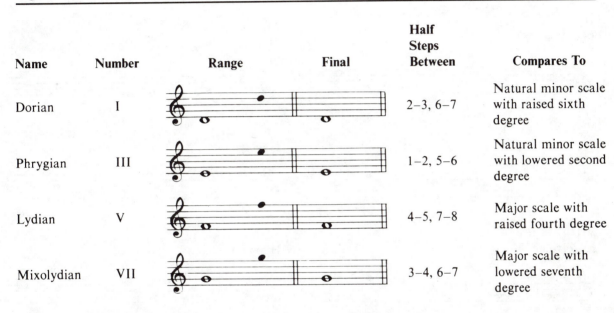

Name	Number	Range	Final	Half Steps Between	Compares To
Dorian	I			2–3, 6–7	Natural minor scale with raised sixth degree
Phrygian	III			1–2, 5–6	Natural minor scale with lowered second degree
Lydian	V			4–5, 7–8	Major scale with raised fourth degree
Mixolydian	VII			3–4, 6–7	Major scale with lowered seventh degree

Modes I, III, V, and VII are called *authentic* because the final is at the bottom of the range. Modes II, IV, VI, and VIII are called *plagal* (the plagal modes are given the prefix *hypo-*) and contain the same pattern of half and whole steps as the authentic forms, except that their range surrounds the Final (o = Final):

Figure 2.33

Early in the Renaissance (1450–1600) period, four other modes were acknowledged. The *Aeolian* is the same as the natural minor scale, and the *Ionian* is the same as the major scale.

Figure 2.34

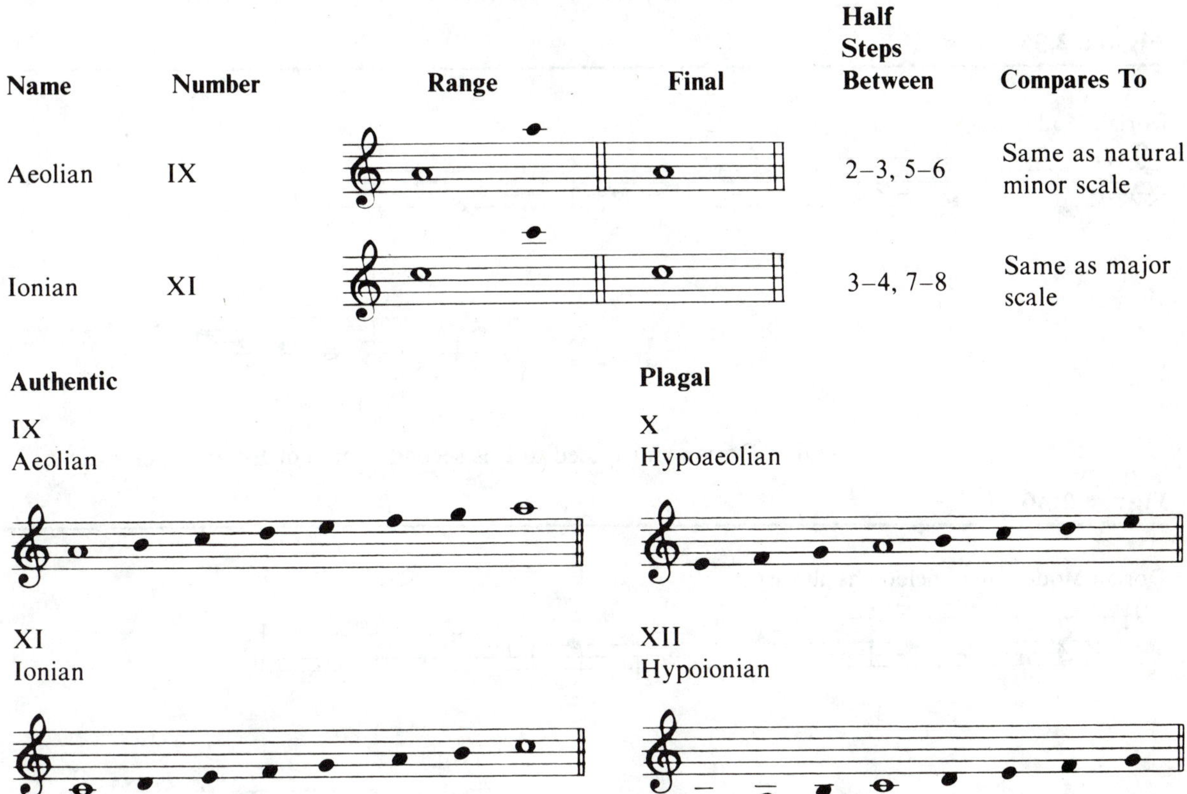

Name
Number
Range
Final
Half Steps Between
Compares To
Aeolian
IX
2–3, 5–6
Same as natural minor scale
Ionian
XI
3–4, 7–8
Same as major scale
Authentic
IX
Aeolian
Plagal
X
Hypoaeolian
XI
Ionian
XII
Hypoionian

As with the major and minor scales, the modes may begin on any tone as long as the arrangements of half and whole steps remain the same.

Since the final of each transposed mode lies in the same relationship to the tonic of the major scale with the same key signature, the identity of a transposed mode can be quickly determined—

1. The final of the *Dorian* mode is always the *second* degree of a major scale.
2. The final of the *Phrygian* mode is always the *third* degree of a major scale.
3. The final of the *Lydian* mode is always the *fourth* degree of a major scale.
4. The final of the *Mixolydian* mode is always the *fifth* degree of a major scale.
5. The final of the *Aeolian* mode is always the *sixth* degree of a major scale.
6. The final of the *Ionian* mode is always the *first* degree of a major scale.

To illustrate:

Final of nontransposed Dorian is second degree of C-major scale

Figure 2.35

Final of Dorian transposed to F is second degree of E-flat major scale

Figure 2.36

(Workbook-Anthology Assignments 2.6, p. 11, and 2.13, p. 16)

Baroque Period (1600–1750)

The system of major and minor scales developed during the early part of the Baroque period. This coincided with the emergence of key consciousness. By the end of the Baroque period the church modes had generally ceased to have any influence in music.

Classical Period (1750–1825)

The major and minor keys were the basis of music in the Classical period. Chromaticism was decorative for the most part and shifts from one key to another (see Modulation) were used to create formal divisions (see chapters 14 and 15).

Romantic Period (1825–1900)

During the Romantic period chromaticism increased to the point that the major-minor key system began to be threatened. By the end of the period, keys often shifted so rapidly in the course of a composition that tonality itself began to break down.

Post-Romantic and Impressionistic Period (1875–1920)

With the breakdown of the major-minor key system Impressionist composers began to experiment with other scales. They were particularly fond of pentatonic, modal, and whole-tone scales.

Contemporary Period (1920–present)

Twentieth-century composers have continued to expand the scalar basis of their music. The chromatic scale has predominated in much of the music of our period, but a number of composers have experimented with nontraditional scales (Bartók, Scriabin) and microtonal (Ives, Partch) scales (scales with intervals smaller than a half step).

Jazz and Popular Music (1900–present)

Twentieth-century popular music has remained as the last bastion of the major-minor key system. Until the 1960s, the great majority of popular songs were written in major keys. This preference for the major keys persists today, but songs in minor keys have become somewhat more common. The blues scale is often found in jazz and popular music with blues influence.

REVIEW

1. Starting with "C," write the key signature for the major scale on each half step on the piano keyboard. Check your work by referring to figure 2.5. Now do the same for minor scales. Check your work using figure 2.15.
2. At the piano keyboard, play the major, and the three forms of the minor scales beginning on each pitch. Name the notes using letter names as you play the scale.
3. Name the major and the minor scale for each of the key signatures from 7 sharps through 7 flats.
4. Look at the anthology. For each composition look at the key signature and name the major and the minor scale for that key signature. (Can you tell if the piece is in a major or a minor key?)
5. Work with a friend in spelling the major and the three forms of the minor scales. Take turns asking for a scale and check each other's work. See who can spell the most scales without making an error.
6. Look at the list of topics at the beginning of the chapter and review any areas for which you can't remember specific details.
7. Take familiar melodies or your sight-singing book. Do a pitch inventory of several melodies. Can you identify the scale basis from your inventory and by examining the melody?
8. If you have computer software available for the major and minor scales, use it to review.

Test Yourself 2

1. Identify each of the following scales (Major, Natural Minor, Harmonic Minor, Melodic Minor):

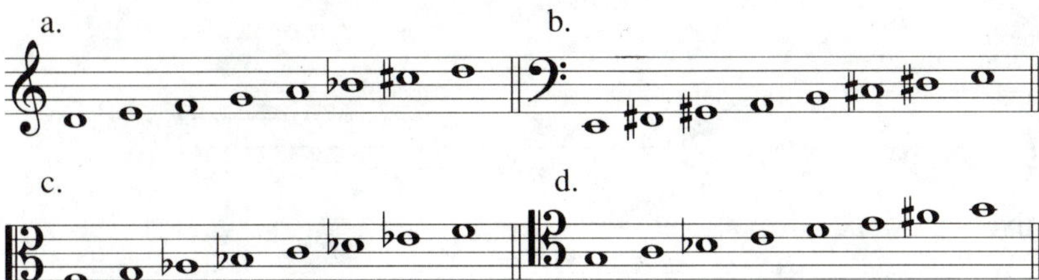

2. Name the major and the minor scale for each of the following key signatures:

3. Each of the following groups of notes is part of two major scales. Name the two scales.

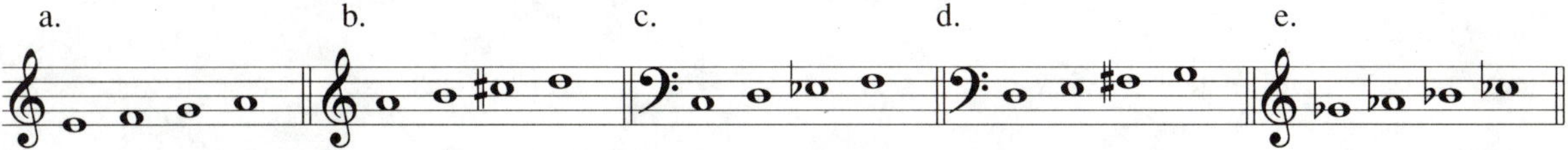

4. Add the sharps or flats (on the staff, to individual notes) to form the scale requested.

a. D major

b. A♭ major

c. B ascending melodic minor

d. C♯ harmonic minor

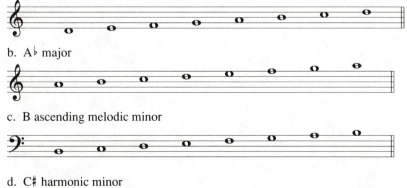

5. Add the correct accidentals to form the mode requested.

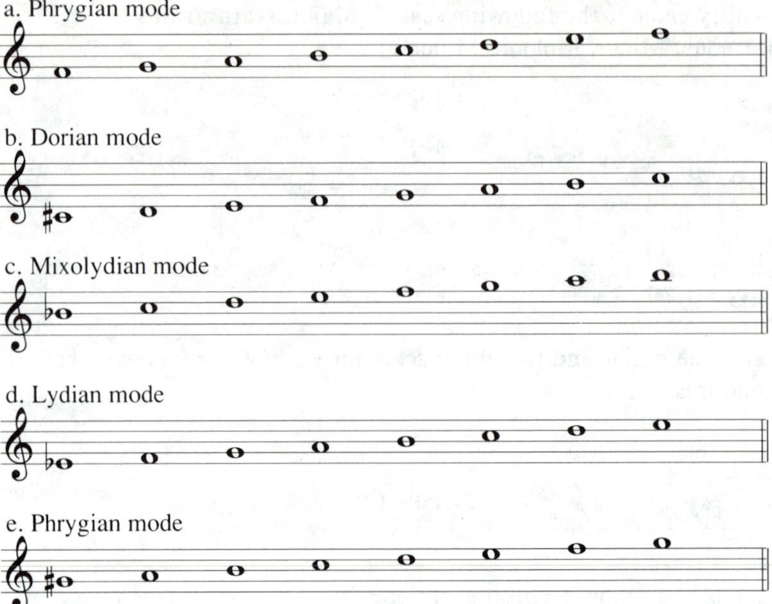

Intervals

Major, Minor, and Perfect Intervals
Consonance and Dissonance
Augmented and Diminished Intervals
Enharmonic Intervals
Inversion of Intervals
Compound Intervals
Invertible Counterpoint
Pythagorean Tuning
Mean-Tone Tuning
Equal Temperament

Exposition

An *interval* is the difference in pitch between two tones.

Major, Minor, and Perfect Intervals

Major, minor, and perfect intervals are illustrated in figure 3.1.

Figure 3.1

Name	Illustration	Number of Half Steps	Convenient Example
Perfect Unison (Also Prime)		0	
Minor 2nd (m2)		1	7-8 of Major Scale
Major 2nd (M2)		2	1-2 of Major Scale

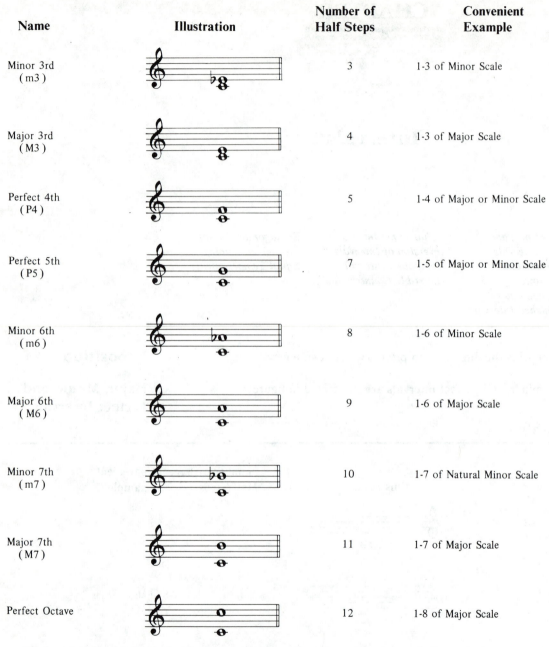

Name	Illustration	Number of Half Steps	Convenient Example
Minor 3rd (m3)	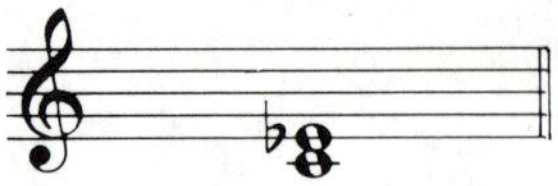	3	1-3 of Minor Scale
Major 3rd (M3)		4	1-3 of Major Scale
Perfect 4th (P4)		5	1-4 of Major or Minor Scale
Perfect 5th (P5)		7	1-5 of Major or Minor Scale
Minor 6th (m6)	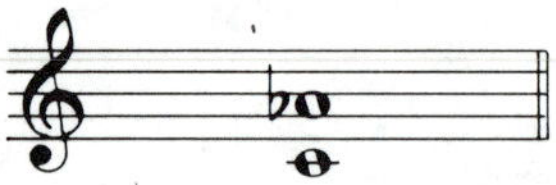	8	1-6 of Minor Scale
Major 6th (M6)	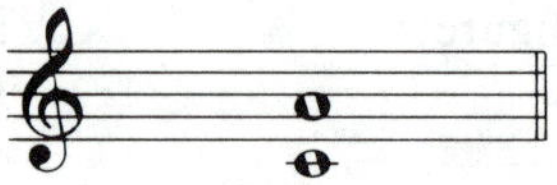	9	1-6 of Major Scale
Minor 7th (m7)	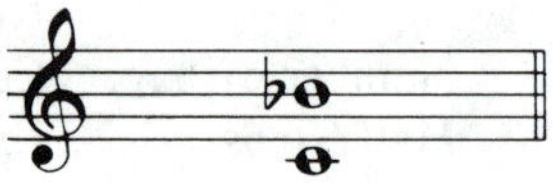	10	1-7 of Natural Minor Scale
Major 7th (M7)	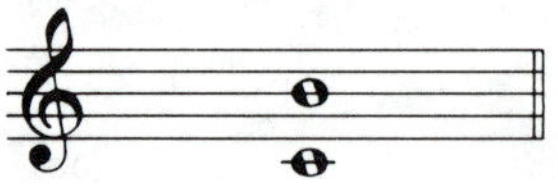	11	1-7 of Major Scale
Perfect Octave	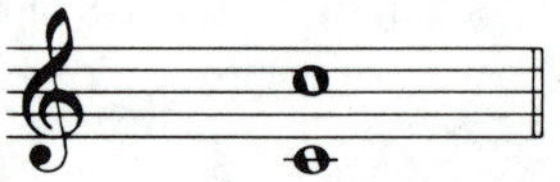	12	1-8 of Major Scale

Only seconds, thirds, sixths, and sevenths are referred to as major and minor. Only fourths, fifths, octaves, and unisons are referred to as perfect.

Consonance and Dissonance

The terms *consonance* and *dissonance* are defined in a variety of ways, depending on the context of the terms. In an acoustical context the consonances are those intervals that are found in the Harmonic Series (see pages 62 and 438). Throughout this book the term consonance will be used in a musical sense, and will be defined as intervals that are treated as stable and not requiring resolution. The consonant intervals under this definition are: P1, m3, M3, P5, m6, M6, P8. All other intervals are considered dissonant.

Augmented and Diminished Intervals

An *augmented interval* is a half step larger than either a major or perfect interval, but it retains the same letter names. A *diminished interval* is a half step smaller than either a minor or perfect interval, but it retains the same letter names.

The order in which a perfect interval is augmented or diminished is:

1. Perfect—interval as is
2. Diminished—a half step smaller than the perfect interval
3. Augmented—a half step larger than the perfect interval

Figure 3.2

The following chart illustrates augmented and diminished perfect intervals.

Figure 3.3

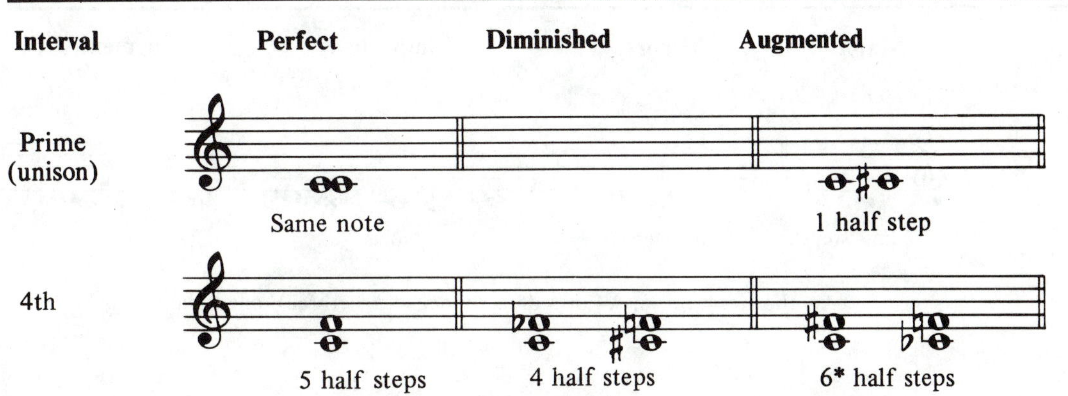

*Another term for an A4 or a d5 is *tritone* = tri (three) tone (whole steps)

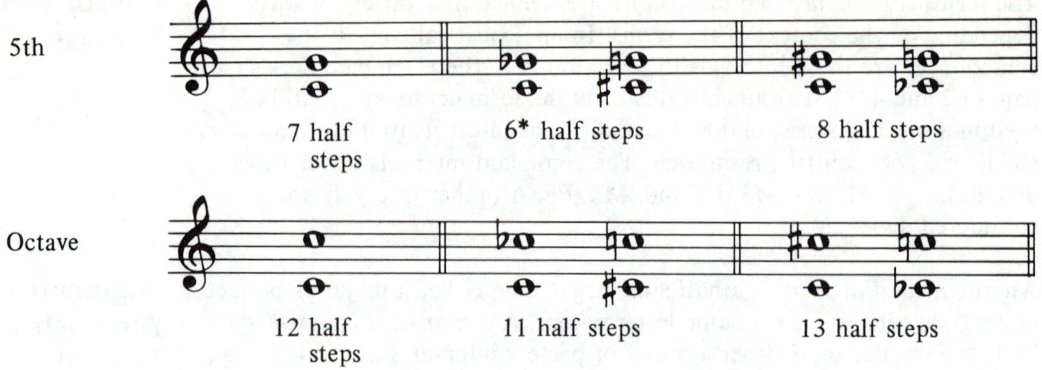

The order in which a major or minor interval is augmented or diminished appears here:

1. Major—interval as is
2. Minor—a half step smaller than a major interval
3. Diminished—a half step smaller than a minor interval
4. Augmented—a half step larger than a major interval

Figure 3.4

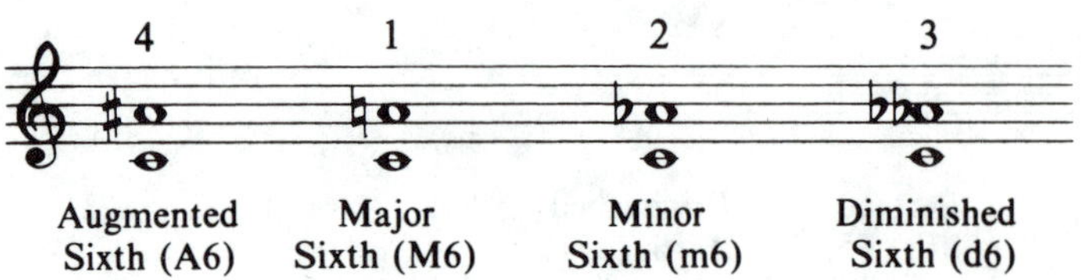

Figure 3.5 illustrates augmented and diminished major or minor intervals.

Figure 3.5

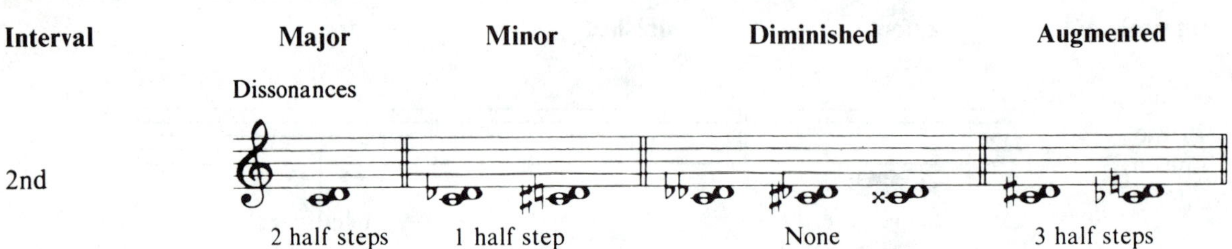

*Another term for an A4 or a d5 is *tritone* = tri (three) tone (whole steps)

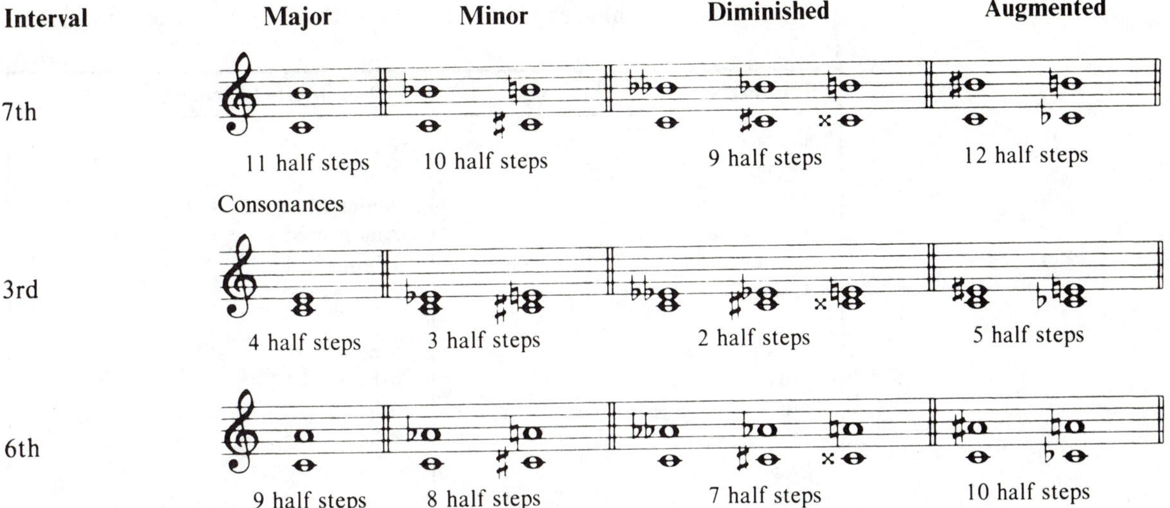

Enharmonic Intervals

Enharmonic intervals are intervals with the same quality (sound), but which are spelled differently. Such intervals result, of course, from enharmonic tones (see Enharmonic Equivalents, pages 10 and 11). All of the following intervals have the same sound but are spelled differently:

Figure 3.6

Care must be taken in spelling intervals. If a specific interval is requested, the enharmonic-equivalent spelling is not correct.

Thus, if a major third below G is called for, a diminished fourth is not correct even though the sound is the same:

Figure 3.7

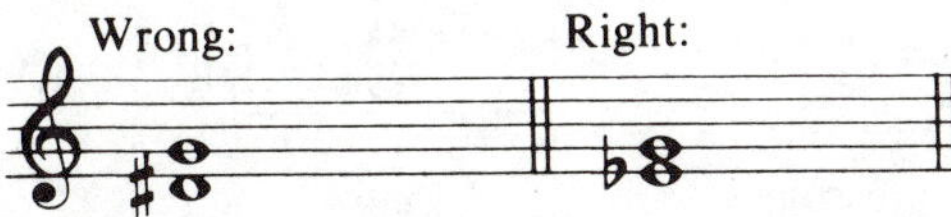

Inversion of Intervals

The inversion of an interval means that the lower tone of an interval becomes the higher tone, or the higher tone becomes the lower tone. The interval is literally turned upside down:

Figure 3.8

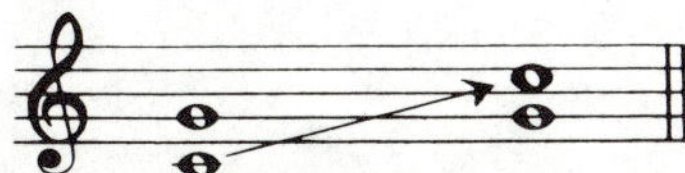

The following table shows various intervals and their inversions:

Interval Name	When Inverted Becomes
Perfect	Perfect
Major	Minor
Minor	Major
Diminished	Augmented
Augmented	Diminished
Unisons	Octaves
2nds	7ths
3rds	6ths
4ths	5ths
5ths	4ths
6ths	3rds
7ths	2nds
Octaves	Unisons

Figure 3.9 shows some typical intervals and their inversions:

Figure 3.9

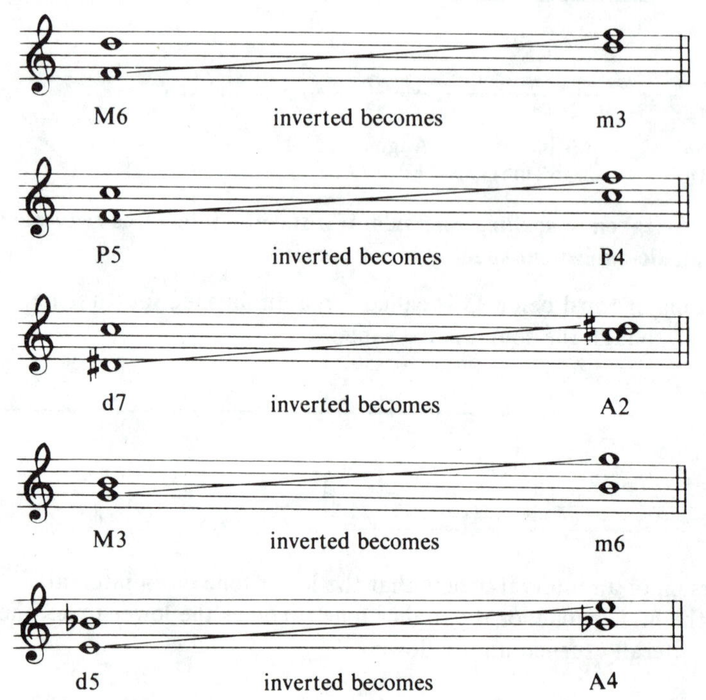

Compound Intervals

Intervals greater than an octave are called *compound intervals*. These intervals are named in a similar manner to the intervals within an octave *(simple intervals)*.

Figure 3.10

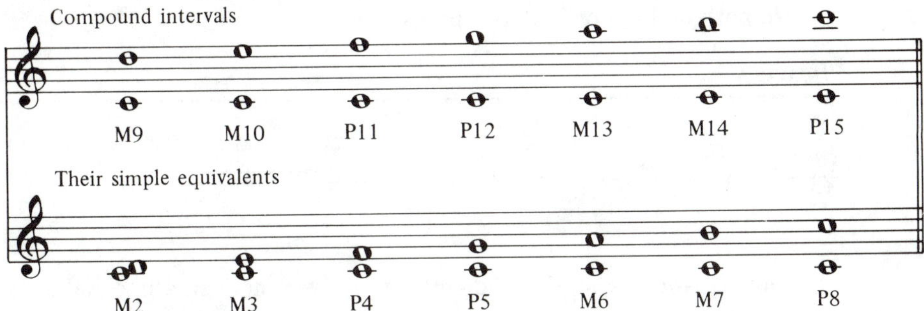

The compound intervals are often labeled as their simple equivalents—as if an octave were removed from the interval. The compound names are used only if it is important to stress the exact interval size.

Invertible Counterpoint

The following is an excerpt of a two-voice composition from music literature. In the second version, the same excerpt is inverted. This inversion of parts is referred to as *invertible counterpoint*.

Figure 3.11

Bach: The Art of Fugue, *Contrapunctus VIII,* BWV 1080

The same excerpt inverted

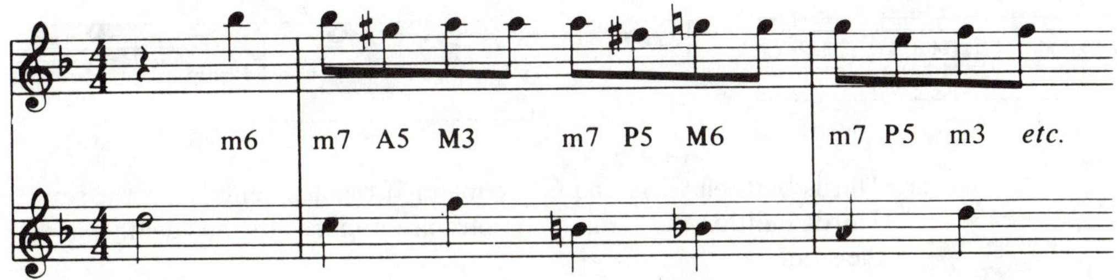

Summary

It is vital that you become fluent in the identification and spelling of intervals. Much of your future work in music theory will depend on this ability. The following observations may be of assistance to you in developing speed and accuracy with intervals.

1. Notice that in writing thirds, fifths, and sevenths that either the notes are both on lines or both on spaces.

Figure 3.12

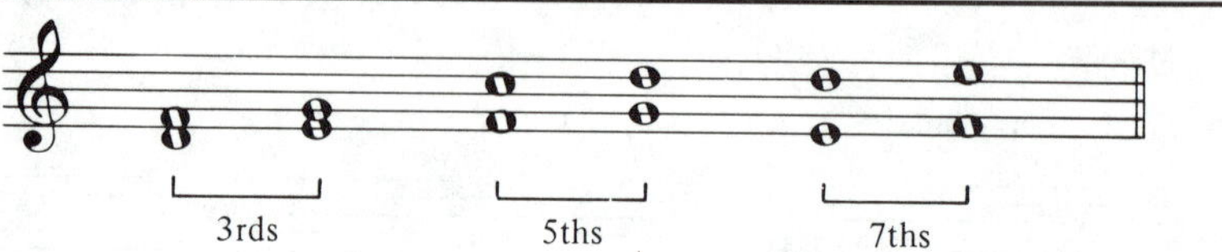

2. Seconds, fourths, sixths, and octaves involve a note on a line and a note on a space.

Figure 3.13

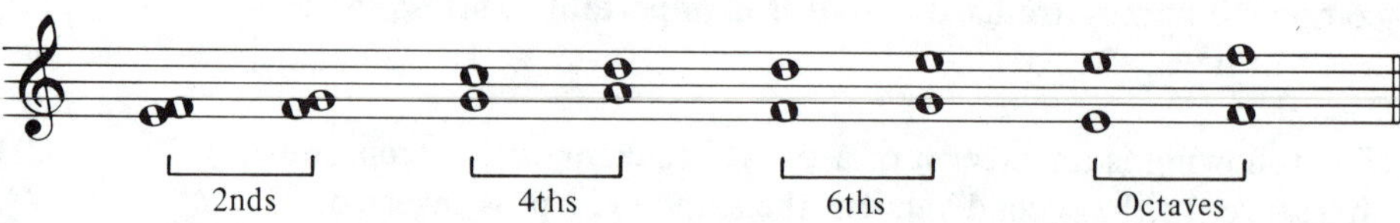

3. Fourths, fifths, and octaves are perfect if the accidentals are the same, except for the fourth and fifth involving B and F.

Figure 3.14

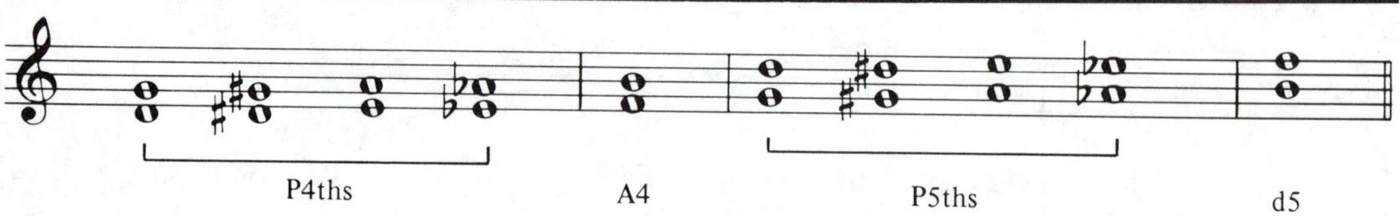

4. Seconds are major and sevenths are minor if the accidentals are the same, except for those involving E–F and B–C.

Figure 3.15

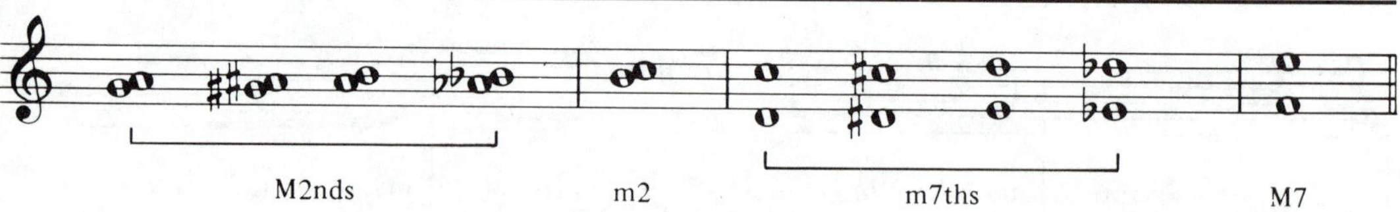

5. Thirds built on C, F, and G are major if the accidentals are the same. Thirds built on the remaining notes are minor if the accidentals are the same.

Figure 3.16

6. Sixths whose upper tones are C, F, or G are minor if the accidentals are the same. Sixths whose upper tones are any of the remaining notes are major if the accidentals are the same.

Figure 3.17

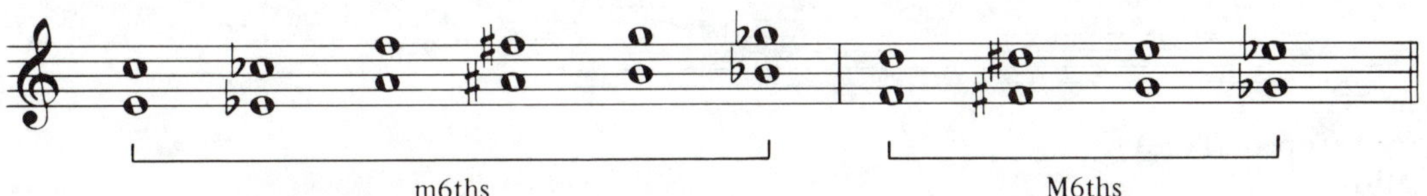

7. Other interval qualities may be quickly determined by reducing the interval to the "same accidental" form and then noting the effect on interval size when the accidentals are replaced.

Figure 3.18

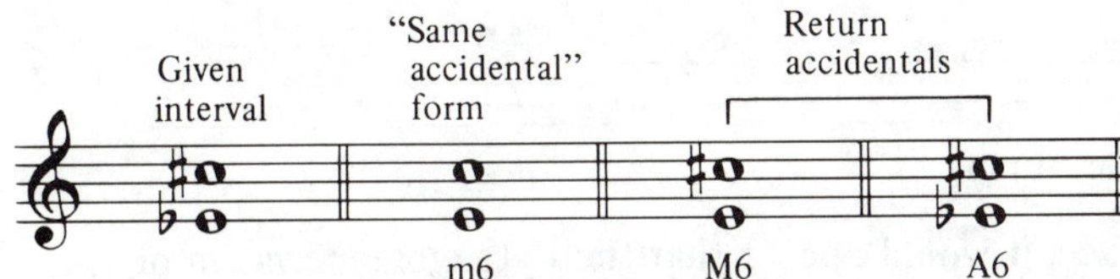

With sufficient practice the size of intervals will be easily determined, and little conscious thought will be necessary. In the assignments work first for accuracy and then try to develop speed in writing and identifying intervals.

(Workbook-Anthology, Assignments 3.1–3.14, pp. 21–27)

History

Tuning Systems

In modern times the *equal temperament* system of tuning has been accepted as the standard for nearly all music written in the Western world (see page 63). Most musicians trained in the twentieth century find it difficult to conceive that other systems of tuning were ever in use. Nevertheless, the history of music reveals a variety of methods that preceded equal temperament. The two most important of these were Pythagorean tuning and mean-tone tuning.

Pythagorean Tuning

Attributed to the philosopher Pythagoras in the sixth century B.C., *Pythagorean tuning* prescribes the tuning of scale pitches that conform to the *pure fifth*. The harmonic series, illustrated on page 438, shows the pure fifth between the second and third partial (c to g). Thus, if the G were vibrating at 300 cycles per second, the C below it would be vibrating at 200 cycles per second—a ratio of 3:2. Figure 3.19 demonstrates how a C scale could be derived by applying a series of 3:2 ratios:

Figure 3.19

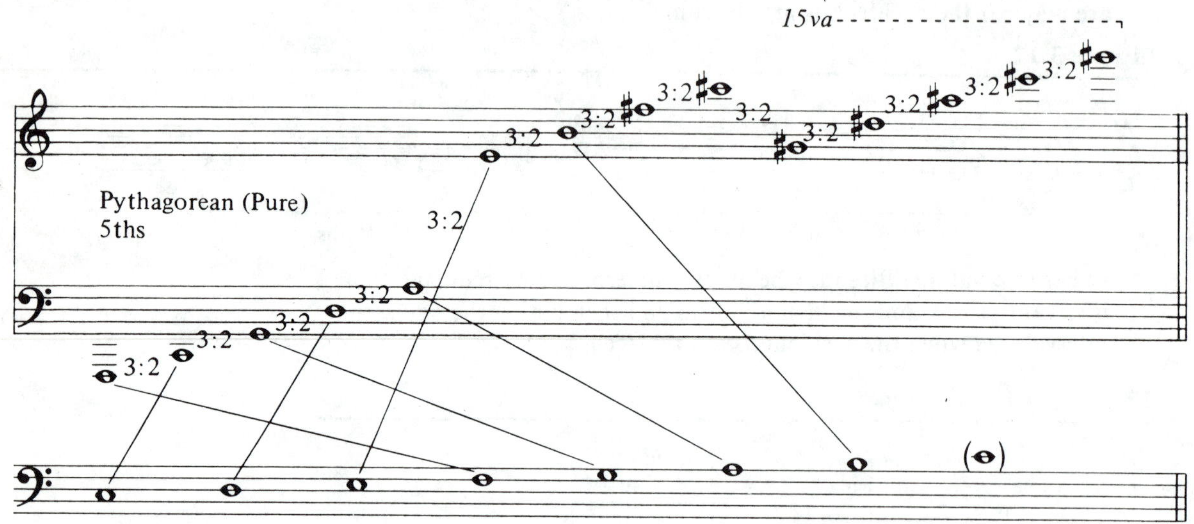

C major scale derived from Pythagorean tuning

On the surface, it would appear that the Pythagorean system of tuning is ideal because it provides the pure fifth (3:2). However, if the octaves at a ratio of 2:1 were extended from the same pitch up to the same octave as that of the 3:2 fifth, the B-sharp derived by the fifths is higher than the C derived by the 2:1 octaves.

By starting both series at the pitch of 33 vibrations per second for CC, the final pitch of c^5 derived by octaves is 4,224 cycles per second (Hz.), while that of the same note derived by fifths is 4,282 cycles per second, a substantial difference in pitch.

Figure 3.20

Mean-Tone Tuning

In addition to the Pythagorean method, musicians employed a variety of tuning systems. By the early sixteenth century, *mean-tone tuning* gained considerable acceptance. This system made the pure fifth slightly smaller, but retained the *pure third* of the fourth to fifth partial of the harmonic series. (See page 438.)

Musicians continued to experiment with tuning. During the seventeenth and eighteenth centuries a variety of temperaments were in use, some of which allowed the performance of music in all keys. This led gradually to the adoption of equal temperament.

Equal Temperament

Equal temperament divides the octave into twelve equal half steps, thus compromising both the pure fifths and thirds, but preserving the 2:1 octave. The fretted string instruments were responsible for the early interest in equal temperament since the frets passed under all the strings and this required that all the half steps be as equal as possible. During the later nineteenth and twentieth centuries equal temperament became the standard system of tuning, and most modern instruments approximate this system as nearly as possible. There are, however, a number of deviations from equal temperament that deserve mention. In blues music the so-called "blue notes" are tones that are intentionally tuned below the equal-tempered pitches, and this blues intonation has had a major effect on intonation in popular music and jazz. A number of twentieth-century composers have experimented with tuning systems as the basis for new musical styles, and the interest in historically accurate performance has led to the construction of instruments employing various historical tunings.

REVIEW

1. Look at the list of concepts at the beginning of the chapter. Define each term in your own words and check your definition with the book.
2. Take one note and name each of the following intervals above that note (m2, M2, A2, m3, M3, P4, A4, d5, P5, A5, m6, M6, A6, m7, M7). Now name the same list of intervals below that note. Now select a new note.
3. Sit at a piano keyboard. Play two tones at random. Name the interval. Spell one of the tones enharmonically and name the interval. Move the lower tone up an octave. Now name the interval.
4. Select a major scale. Identify all pairs of scale degrees that are a M2 apart, spelling each. Repeat this process for each interval type (refer to item 2 above). This exercise also should be practiced using a minor scale.
5. In a major scale, name the interval between each scale degree and the remaining scale degrees. In the same way name the intervals in the three forms of the minor scale.
6. Look at a piece of music. Name the interval between each note in the melody.
7. Work with a friend on spelling intervals.
8. Use computer software if it is available.

Test Yourself 3

1. Name the seven consonant intervals.
2. Identify each of the following intervals:

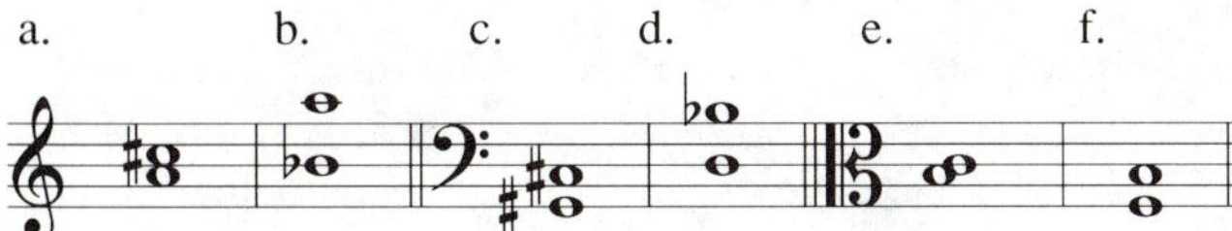

3. Name the inversion of each of the intervals in question 2.
4. Identify the intervals between the two voices below.

5. Name the note that is the requested interval *above* each of the following notes:

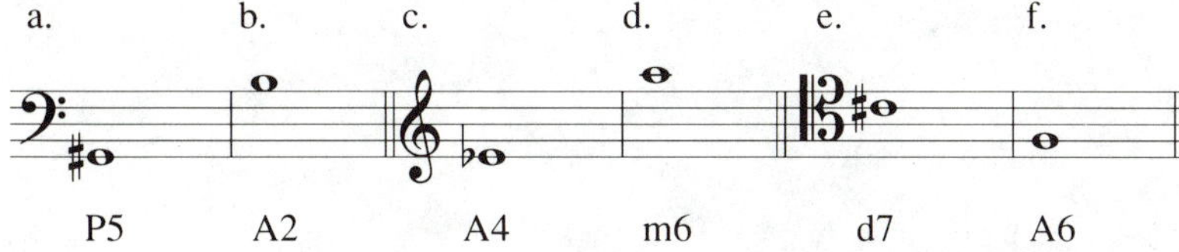

6. Name the note that is the requested interval *below* each of the notes in question 5.

CHAPTER 4

Chords

Harmony
Chord
Triad
Triad Roots
Major Triad
Minor Triad
Diminished Triad
Augmented Triad
Scale Degree Names
Primary Triads
7th Chords
Dominant 7th Chord
Triad Stability
Triad Inversion
Triad Position
Root Position
First Inversion
Second Inversion
Triad Analysis Symbols
7th Chord Analysis Symbols
Figured Bass
Figured Bass Symbols
Popular Music Symbols
Added 6th Chord

Exposition

Harmony

Harmony is the study of tones sounding together. Whereas melody implies the linear (horizontal) aspect of music, harmony refers to the vertical dimension of music.

Chord

A *chord* is a harmonic unit with at least three different pitch classes sounding simultaneously. The term *chord* applies to all sonorities with three or more different pitch classes.

Figure 4.1

Triad

Strictly speaking, a *triad* is any three-tone chord. However, since Western music of the seventeenth through nineteenth centuries is *tertian* (chords containing a superposition of harmonic thirds), the term has come to mean a three-note chord built in superposed thirds.

Triad Roots

The term *root* refers to the note upon which a triad is built. A "C major triad" refers to a major triad whose root is "C." The root is the pitch from which a triad is generated, and the other notes are referred to as the *third* and *fifth*.

Four types of triads are in common use:

Major Triad

A *major triad* consists of a major third and a perfect fifth.

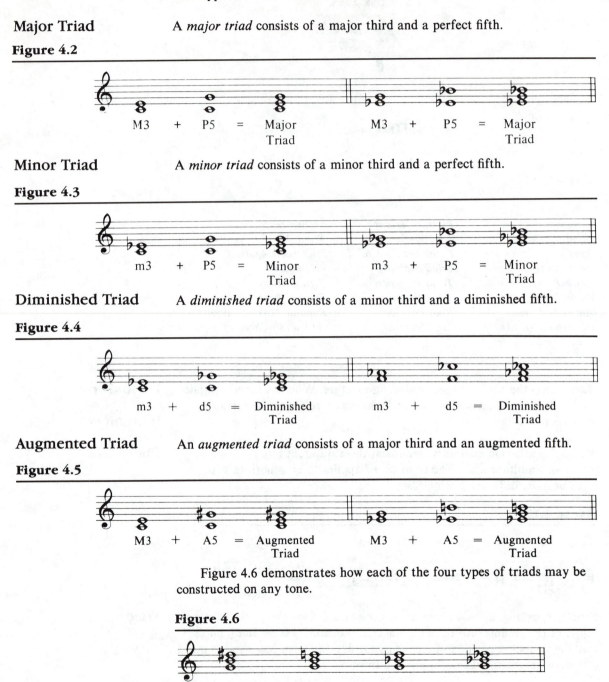

Figure 4.2

Minor Triad

A *minor triad* consists of a minor third and a perfect fifth.

Figure 4.3

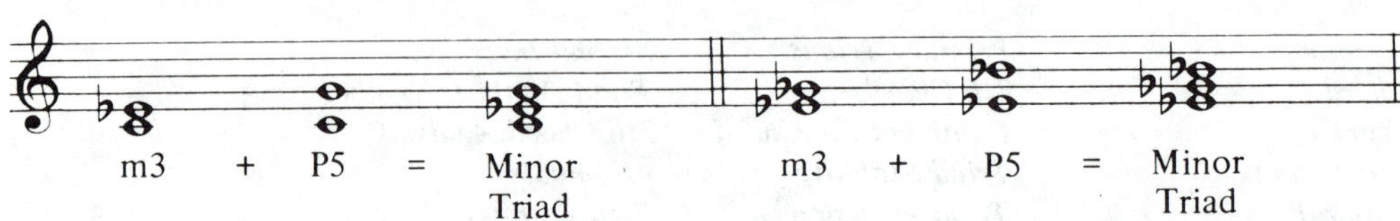

Diminished Triad

A *diminished triad* consists of a minor third and a diminished fifth.

Figure 4.4

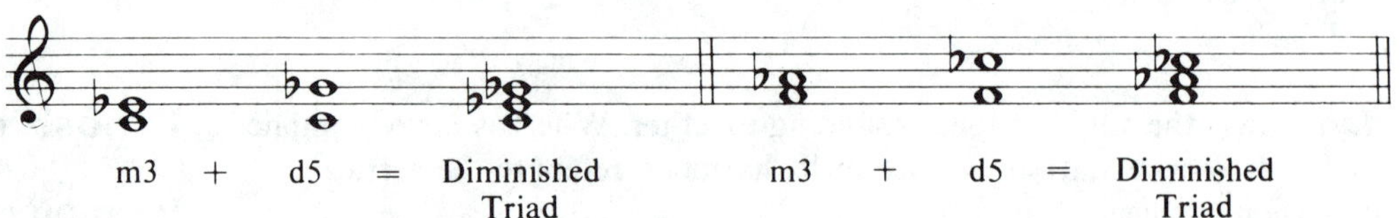

Augmented Triad

An *augmented triad* consists of a major third and an augmented fifth.

Figure 4.5

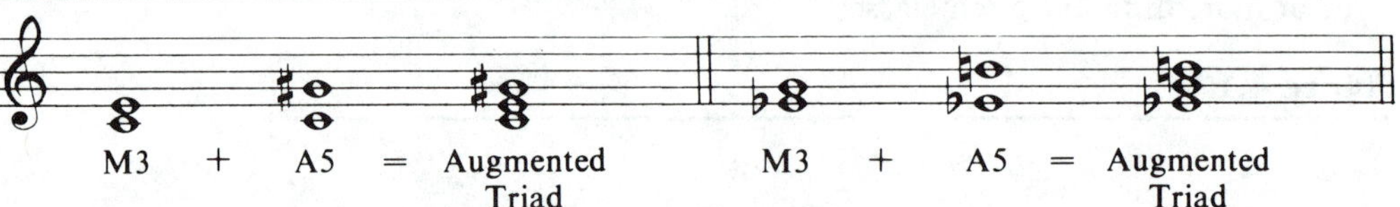

Figure 4.6 demonstrates how each of the four types of triads may be constructed on any tone.

Figure 4.6

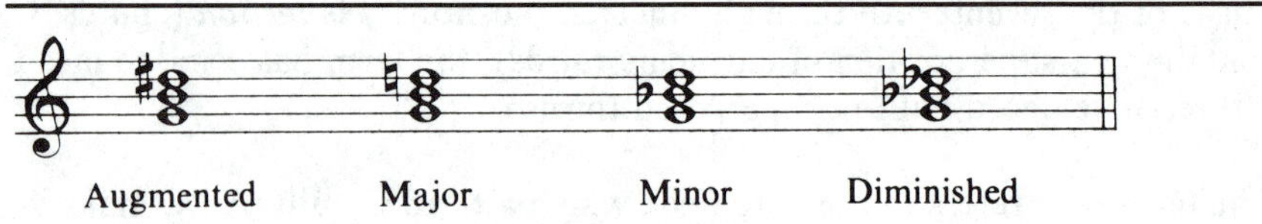

(Workbook-Anthology Assignments 4.1, p. 29, and 4.11, p. 35)

Scale Degree Names

Each degree of the seven-tone diatonic scale has a name that relates to its function. Thus, the major scale and all three forms of the minor scale share these terms.

Scale Degree	Name	Meaning
1st	Tonic	Tonal center—the final resolution tone
2nd	Supertonic	One step above the tonic
3rd	Mediant	Midway between tonic and dominant
4th	Subdominant	The lower dominant—the fifth tone down from the tonic (also the fourth tone up from the tonic)
5th	Dominant	So called because its function is next in importance to the tonic
6th	Submediant	The lower mediant. Halfway between tonic and lower dominant (subdominant). The third tone down from the tonic (also the sixth tone up from the tonic)
7th	Leading tone	Leads melodically to the tonic
7th	Subtonic	Used only to designate the seventh degree of the natural minor scale (a whole step below the tonic)

Figure 4.7

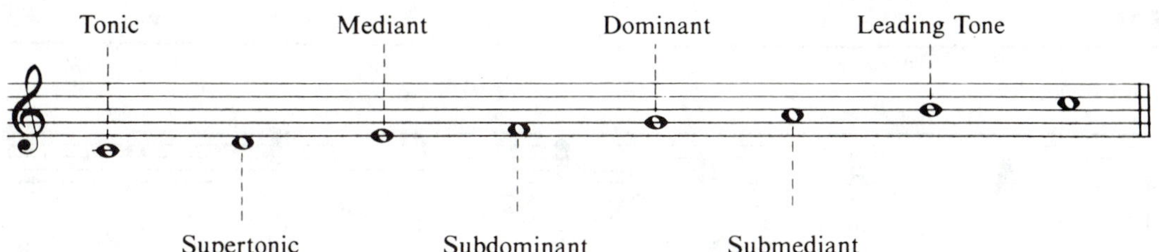

Primary Triads

The triads built on the tonic, subdominant, and dominant are often referred to as the *primary triads* due to their strong relationship to each other. The tonic is seen as standing in the center of the tonal system with the dominant a perfect fifth above and the subdominant a perfect fifth below.

Figure 4.8

7th Chords

A *7th chord* is formed by adding another third above the fifth of a triad.

Figure 4.9

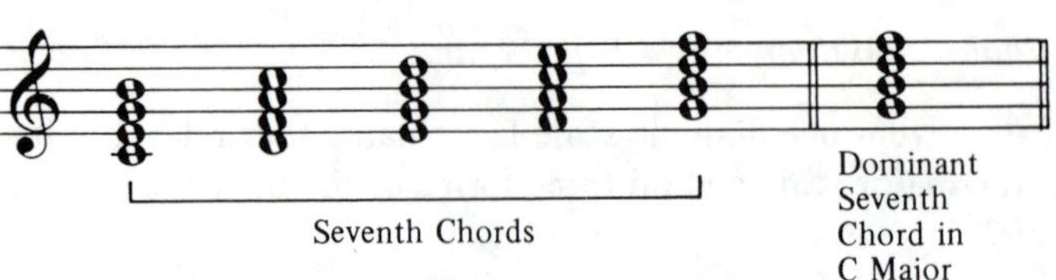

Triads and 7th chords by no means exhaust the possible tertian sonorities. One can continue adding thirds to tertian chords, resulting in 9th chords, 11th chords, and 13th chords (these chords will be discussed in detail in chapter 19). The 7th chord built on the dominant is the most common 7th chord in tonal music (see figure 4.9).

(Workbook-Anthology Assignments 4.2, p. 29, and 4.12 and 4.13, p. 35)

Triads on Scale Tones

A triad may be constructed on any pitch. Memorize the type of triads that appear on each tone of the major scale and the three forms of the minor scale.

In analysis, roman numerals are used to distinguish triads based on scale degrees; arabic numerals are used for scale degrees themselves.

Uppercase roman numerals	I IV V = *Major* triads
Lowercase roman numerals	ii iii vi = *Minor* triads
Lowercase roman numerals with °	vii° = *Diminished* triads
Uppercase roman numerals with +	III+ = *Augmented* triads

Figure 4.10

In the major scale:

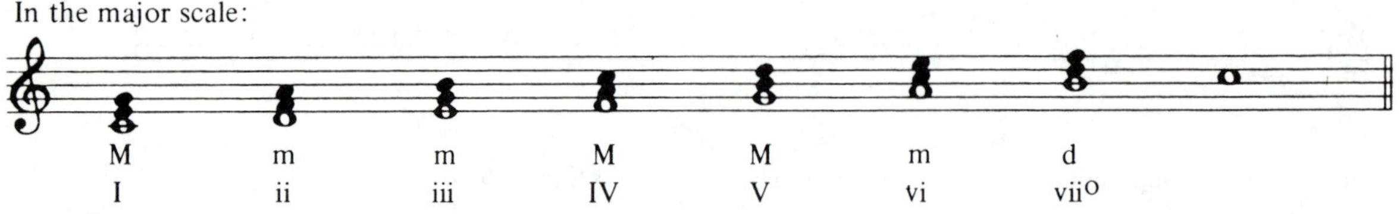

In the natural minor scale:

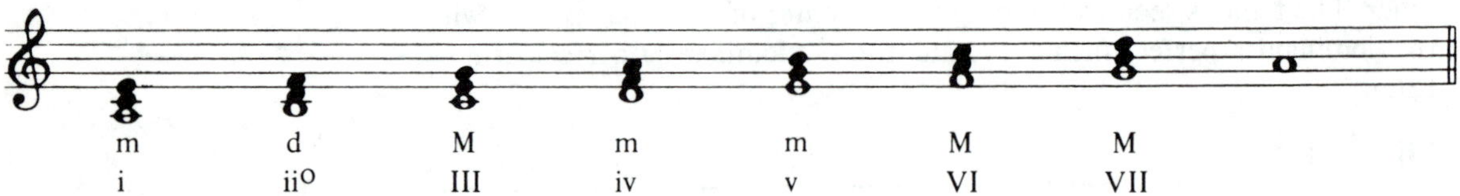

In the harmonic minor scale:

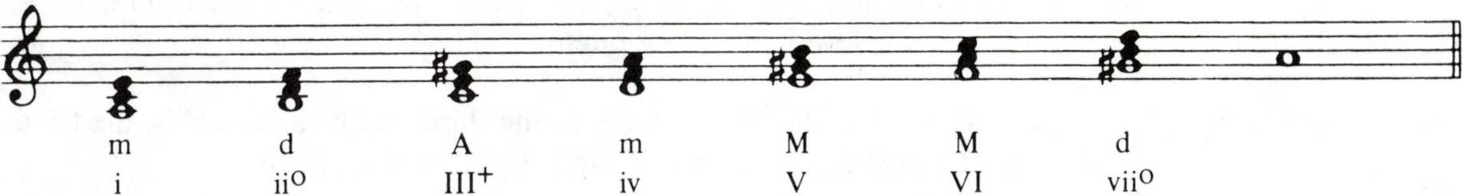

In the melodic minor scale:

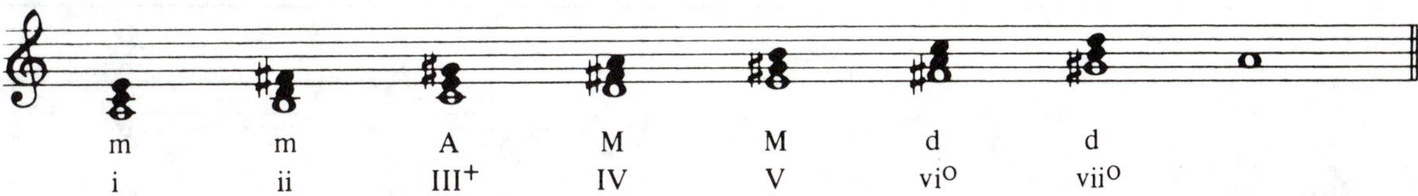

The following chart is a summary of triad types in the diatonic scales:

Scale	Major Triads on	Minor Triads on	Diminished Triads on	Augmented Triads on
Major	I, IV, V	ii, iii, vi	vii°	None
Natural Minor	III, VI, VII	*i, iv, v	ii°	None
Harmonic Minor	V, VI	*i, iv	ii°, vii°	III+
Melodic Minor	IV, V	*i, ii	vi°, vii°	III+

(Workbook-Anthology Assignments 4.3, p. 29, 4.4 and 4.5, p. 30, and 4.14, p. 36)

Triad Stability

A triad that is a combination of the strongest intervals is the most stable. The perfect fifth is by far the strongest interval and this accounts for the superior stability of the Major and Minor triads.

Strongest and most stable	Major triad
Strong and quite stable	Minor triad
Weak and unstable	Diminished triad
Weak and unstable	Augmented triad

Triad Inversion

An *inversion* of a triad occurs when the root (the lowest pitch forming the triad) is placed higher than another factor. In other words, the root is not the lowest-sounding pitch.

Figure 4.11

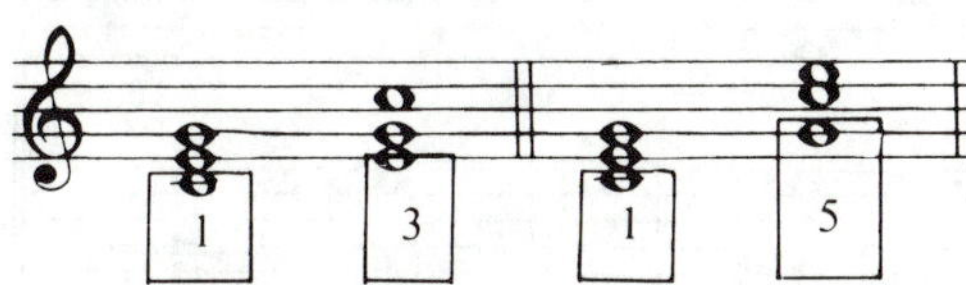

*Occasionally, a composition written in a minor key will end with a major triad. This is known as a *picardy third.*

Triad Position

Triad position identifies the note of the chord that appears as the lowest-sounding pitch of the harmony. Any of the three notes of the triad may appear as the lowest-sounding pitch.

Root Position

No matter what the arrangement of the third and fifth factors is, the triad is in *root position* if the root is the lowest-sounding pitch.

All are in *root position:*

Figure 4.12

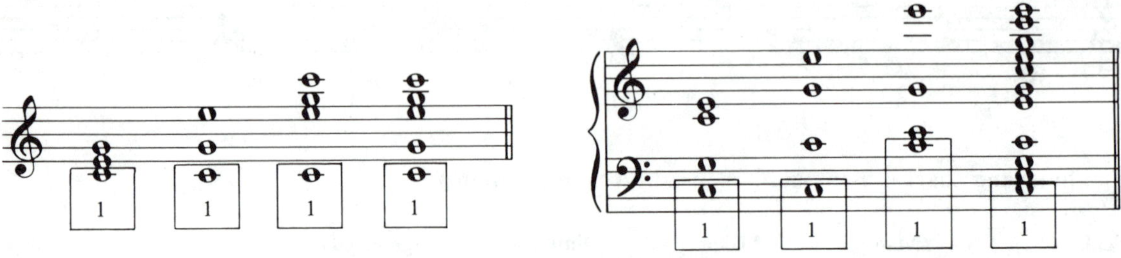

First Inversion

No matter what the arrangement of the root and fifth factors, the triad is in *first inversion* if the third factor of the triad is the lowest-sounding pitch.

Figure 4.13

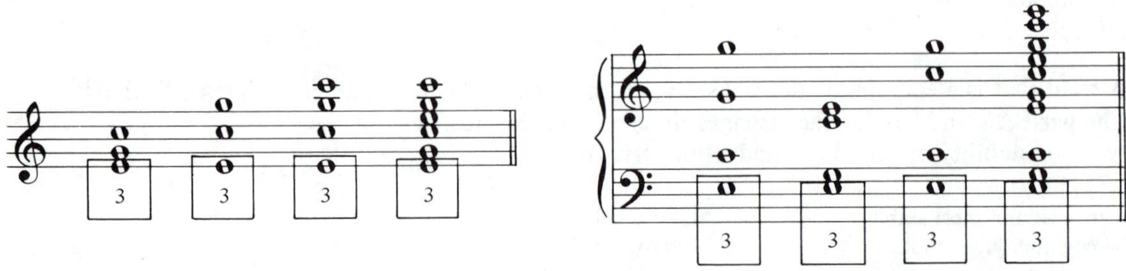

Second Inversion

No matter what the arrangement of the root and third factor, the triad is in *second inversion,* if the fifth factor is the lowest-sounding pitch.

Figure 4.14

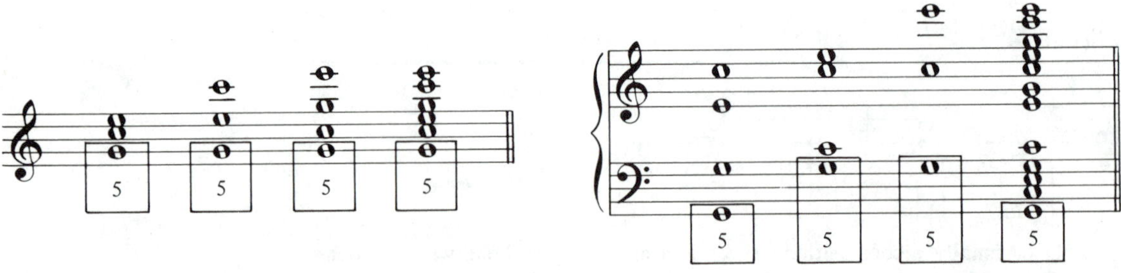

Triad Analysis Symbols

Root position triads are indicated with roman numerals without additional symbols.

First-inversion triads are indicated with a small superscript ^{6} to the right of the roman numeral.

Second-inversion triads are indicated with a superscript $^6_4$ to the right of the roman numeral.

When triads are reduced to three notes spaced as closely together as possible, this position is referred to as *simple position.* Simple position chords are written on the staff below musical examples throughout this book as an aid to analysis. These chords are normally written with the bass note at the bottom to show the inversion.

Figure 4.15

Chords reduced to simple position:

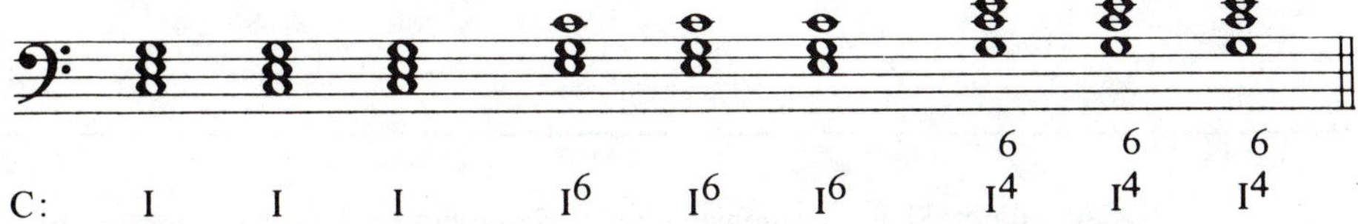

7th Chord Analysis Symbols

Root position 7th chords are indicated by adding a small superscript ^{7} to the right of the roman numeral.

Figure 4.16

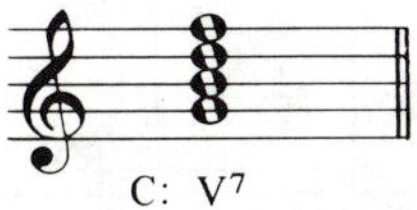

Other symbols associated with 7th chords and their inversions will be presented in chapter 9.

(Workbook-Anthology Assignments 4.6, pp. 30 and 31, and 4.15, p. 36)

Figured Bass

Figured bass consists of a bass part (single line) with figures (mostly numbers) below to indicate the type of harmony. It is an intervallic shorthand method of showing the harmony (along with nonharmonic tones—see chapter 6).

Figured Bass Symbols

The numbers ^{6} and $^6_4$ refer to intervals above the base note, but they imply others such as 3, 8, or an additional 6 or 4 to fill out the four voices. (Note the following example.) Also, figured bass numbers do not denote specific arrangements. That is, they do not indicate what note should be placed in a particular voice (soprano, alto, or tenor). Composers of the Baroque period could have indicated all intended notes above the bass note—including octaves, thirds, and doublings where they occur—but this would have proven burdensome. In actual practice they chose only those figures that would specifically define a position (root, first inversion, or second inversion)—a quick and efficient system. Thus, a ^{6} clearly distinguishes first inversion from root position (no numbers) and second inversion $^6_4$.

Some standard figured bass symbols along with their realizations are:

Symbol	Meaning
None	A triad in root position (short for $\begin{smallmatrix}8\\5\\3\end{smallmatrix}$, $\begin{smallmatrix}5\\5\\3\end{smallmatrix}$, or $\begin{smallmatrix}5\\3\\3\end{smallmatrix}$).
6	A triad in first inversion (short for $\begin{smallmatrix}8\\6\\3\end{smallmatrix}$ or $\begin{smallmatrix}6\\6\\3\end{smallmatrix}$).
$\begin{smallmatrix}6\\4\end{smallmatrix}$	A triad in second inversion (short for $\begin{smallmatrix}8\\6\\4\end{smallmatrix}$, $\begin{smallmatrix}6\\6\\4\end{smallmatrix}$, or $\begin{smallmatrix}6\\4\\4\end{smallmatrix}$).

Figure 4.17

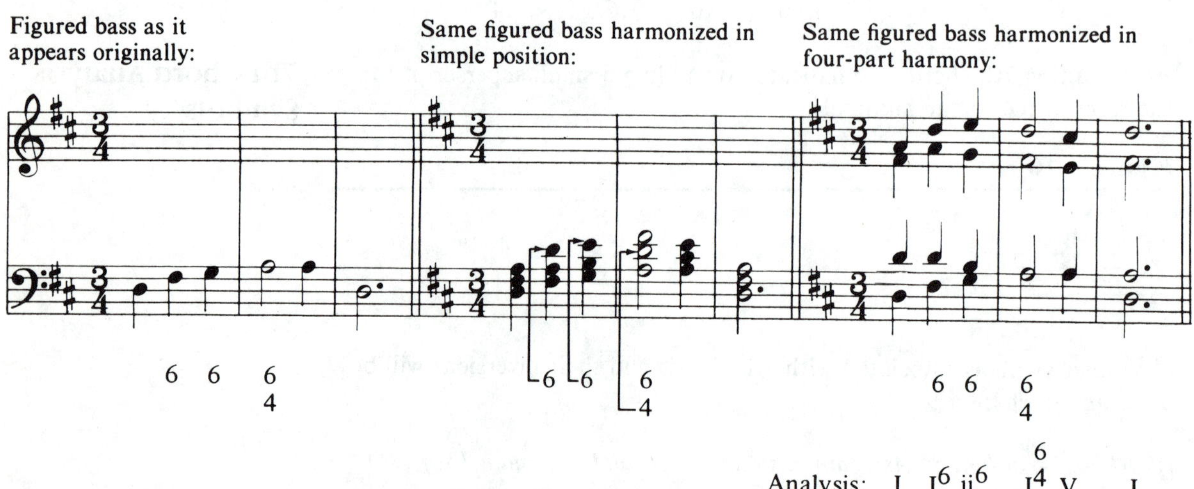

Figures indicating all intervals above the bass note:

The same as reduced to actual figured bass by composers of the Baroque period:

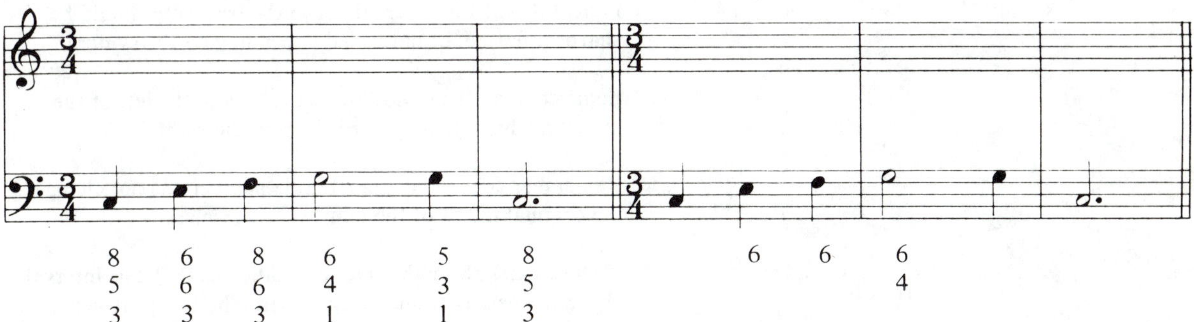

The same figured bass as it might be realized:

The same figured bass realized correctly also but with different arrangment of chord factors above the bass notes:

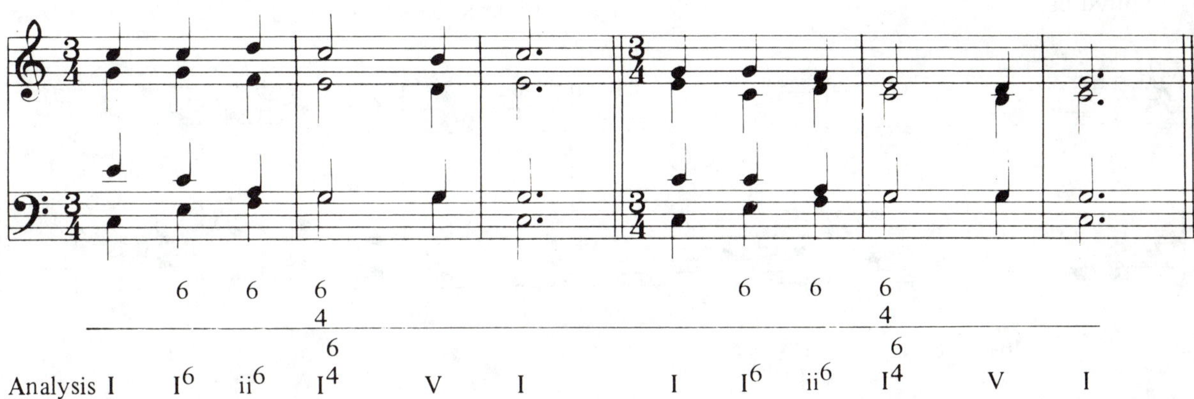

Sometimes it is necessary to indicate sharps, flats, or naturals above the bass note. These are shown in the following manner:

Symbol	**Meaning**
♯, ♭, or ♮	**A sharp, flat, or natural alone beneath a bass note indicates a triad in root position with the third interval above the bass note sharped, flatted, or naturaled.**
6, 6, or 6 ♯ ♭ ♮	**A sharp, flat, or natural below a 6 indicates a first-inversion triad with the third interval above the bass note sharped, flatted, or naturaled.**

♯6 ♭6, ♮6, ♯6
4 ♭4

Any sharp, flat, or natural sign on either side of a number indicates that this interval above the bass note should be sharped, flatted, or naturaled depending on the symbol.

Some composers placed the accidentals to the left of the number, while others placed them to the right.

Remember that accidentals beside numbers do not change the original intent of the numbers themselves.

6̸, 5̸, 4+

A slash mark through a number indicates that this interval above the bass note should be raised a half step. It means the same as a sharp sign beside the number and was employed by some composers instead of the sharp sign. The plus sign (4+) has the same meaning.

Figure 4.18

Figured bass: Figured bass as realized:

To summarize, any figured bass that contains a 6 but *not* a 4 means first inversion:

8 6 6
All mean first inversion: 6 6 6 3 6 6 etc.
3 3 3 3 6

Any figured bass that contains a 6 *and* a 4 means second inversion:

8 6 6
All mean second inversion: 6 6 6 4 etc.
4 4 4 4

All of these arrangements are correct:

Figure 4.19

Intervals, such as ^{6} and $^{6}_{4}$ may be positioned in any octave above the bass note. A good example of a composition that includes figured bass is found on pages 42 and 43.

(Workbook-Anthology Assignments 4.7 and 4.8, pp. 31 and 34, and 4.16–4.18, pp. 37 and 38)

Popular Music Symbols

As figured bass was the shorthand of the eighteenth century, *popular music symbols* are the shorthand of the twentieth century—a system for notating chords when the performer is expected to improvise the specific details. Instead of writing out the exact notes on score paper, popular music composers and arrangers indicate the chords they wish used for accompaniment with chord symbols written above the melody line of the composition. Such a score, with the melody and the popular music symbols, is called a *lead sheet* or *fake sheet*.

Figure 4.20

Popular music symbols, like the figured bass symbols, give the performer information about the chords required, but popular music symbols usually give no information about the bass line. The performer is expected to improvise that part.

The chord indications are quite simple to master and may be read and interpreted by guitar players and keyboard players alike. The addition of rhythmic patterns and arrangements of the chord factors is left entirely to the performer, and most of these musicians are well trained in the art of improvisation. Although chord indications are given in root position, most performers will *voice* the chords, that is, arrange them for the best voice leading, which may mean placing some chords in inversion. In some recent popular music the bass position is indicated by a slash followed by the base note: C/G means a C-major chord with G in the bass.

The following examples illustrate popular music chord symbols for triads and the dominant 7th chord. Chord symbols for additional chord types can be found in Appendix D.

Major Triad

A major triad is shown by a capital letter designating the root.

Figure 4.21

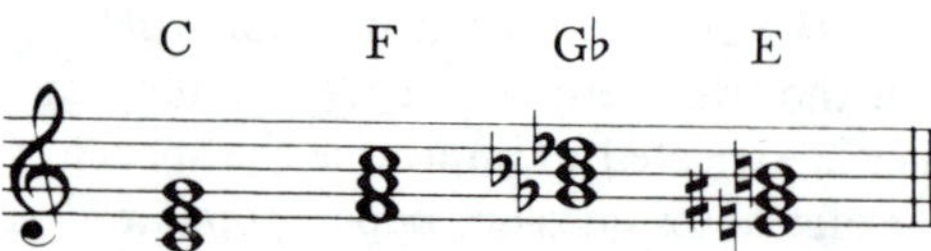

Minor Triad

A minor triad is shown by a capital letter with a lowercase m added (Dm). Sometimes the minor triad is indicated simply by a lowercase letter (d).

Figure 4.22

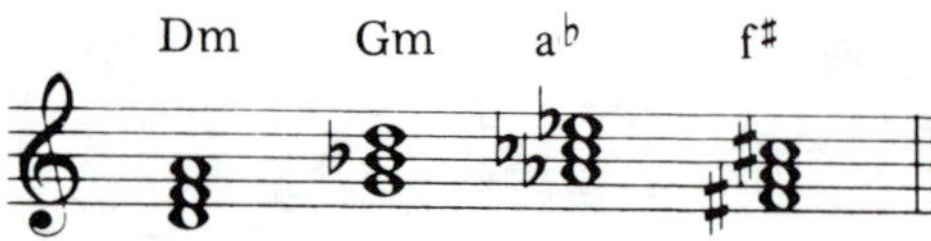

Diminished Triad

A diminished triad is shown by a capital letter with "dim" added (Bdim), or by a letter with ° added (B°).

Figure 4.23

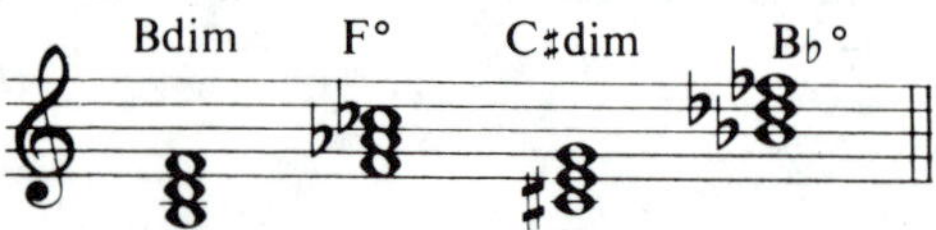

An augmented triad is shown by a capital letter with either "aug" (Caug) or + added (C+).

Augmented Triad

Figure 4.24

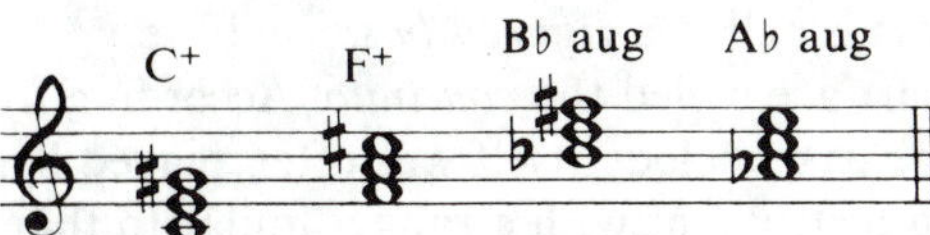

A triad with an added tone a major 6th above the triad root (common in popular music) is indicated by adding 6 after the letter designating the triad (C6).

Added 6th Chord

Figure 4.25

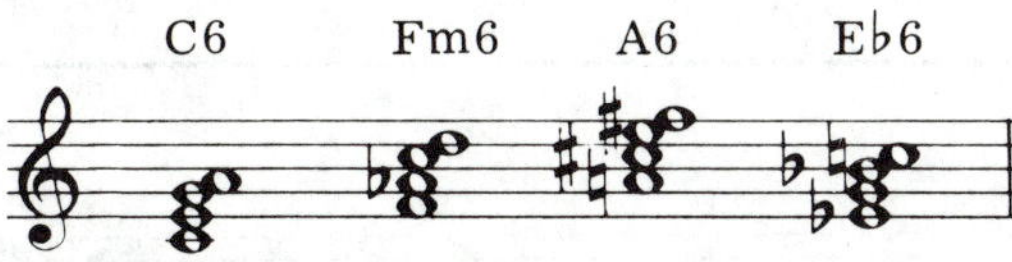

The major-minor 7th chord (dominant 7th) is indicated by adding 7 after the letter designation of the triad (C7).

Major-Minor 7th Chord

Figure 4.26

(Workbook-Anthology, Assignments 4.9 and 4.10, p. 34)

Summary

Three methods for labeling chords have been presented in this chapter: roman numerals, figured bass, and popular music symbols. Each system has advantages and disadvantages. The roman-numeral system's advantage is that it shows both the quality of the chord and its relationship to a diatonic scale. This relationship is vital to your understanding of harmony, and for this reason the roman-numeral system will be the primary system for labeling chords in the book. The figured bass system is useful in learning voice leading, and will be used for many assignments. The popular music symbols are universally used in jazz and popular music, and an understanding of these symbols is vital when this music is studied. Your instructor may choose to emphasize one or another of these labeling systems, depending on the musical context.

History

Emerging during the thirteenth century from a style known as organum, harmony developed gradually and grew to full stature by the late 1600s. In the Renaissance period (1450–1600) harmony was the result of the combination of melodic lines, and the study of harmony was a study of the consonant and dissonant relationships between melodic lines.

During the Baroque period (1600–1750) the concept of accompanying a melody with chords was developed. The keyboard performer was expected to improvise the accompaniment from a given bass line and a set of symbols to indicate in a general way the chords to be used. The bass line with its accompanying symbols is called a *figured bass,* and the instruments that play from this part are called the *continuo.* According to Baroque performance practice, the bass melody itself was often played by both a viola da gamba (a stringed instrument with a range similar to that of the cello) and a keyboard instrument (usually a harpsichord or organ), while at the same time the keyboard player realized (filled in) the harmony according to the meaning of the figures. Practical editions of the present day are generally printed with the figured bass already realized.

Figure 4.27 is from a Baroque composition as it appeared originally:

Figure 4.27

Cesti: *Bella Clori* (Beautiful Chloris) Opera

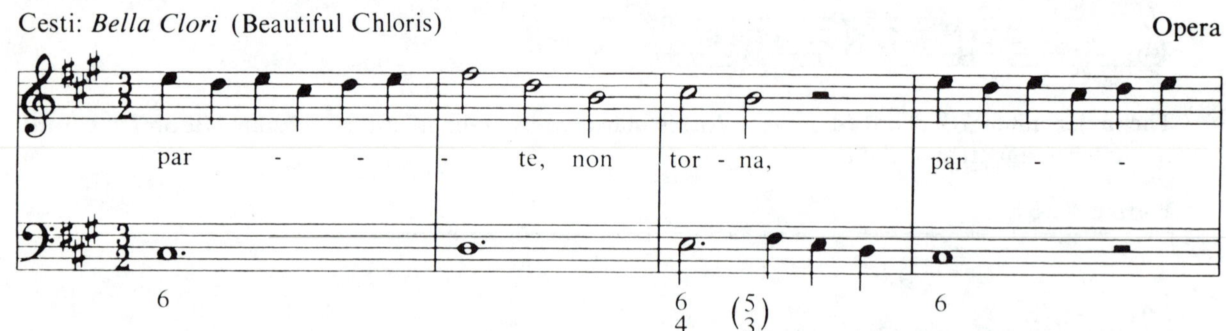

Figure 4.28 is the same excerpt as it appears in a modern edition:

Figure 4.28

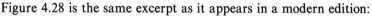

Cesti: *Bella Clori* (Beautiful Chloris) Opera

The figured bass system saved time, and was employed throughout the Baroque period for keyboard accompaniments and keyboard parts for solo songs, solo instrumental compositions, and small and large ensembles. It also exemplifies the Baroque tendency to emphasize the outer voices (S/B) as opposed to the renaissance tradition of equal voices (SATB).

In 1722 Jean-Philippe Rameau wrote a treatise, *Traitê de l'Harmonie* (Treatise on Harmony), which described a theory of harmony. In chapter 8 of his Treatise on Harmony, Book One (1722), Rameau discusses the inversion of chords, a concept that profoundly influenced later theoretical writing. Many of the principles presented in this book are a direct outgrowth of Rameau's ideas.

REVIEW

1. Take a single note. Spell a major, a minor, an augmented, and a diminished triad with that note as the root. Now make that note the third of each of the four triad qualities. Now make it the fifth of each triad quality. Choose another note.
2. Review the concepts listed at the beginning of the chapter.
3. Take a single note. Make it the tonic, the supertonic, the mediant, the subdominant, the dominant, the submediant, the leading tone of a major scale. Now make it the subtonic of a minor scale. Choose another note.
4. Look at figure 2.5 (that's right, 2.5!) For each of the major scales spell the tonic, dominant, and subdominant triad.
5. Choose a note and write the major scale and then a triad on each scale degree. Identify the quality of each triad and write the appropriate roman numeral below the chord. Repeat this exercise using the natural minor scale, the harmonic minor scale, and the melodic minor scale. Repeat this exercise using a different note.
6. Take a familiar hymn or look at the Hallelujah chorus from Handel's Messiah in the anthology. Examine the notes in the four parts on a given beat and identify a chord, if possible (there may be tones that are not a part of the chords in this music, so don't be surprised if you can't always identify a chord). Identify the inversion for each chord you find.
7. Use computer software if it is available.

Test Yourself 4

1. Indicate the quality (major, minor, augmented, diminished) of each of the following triads:

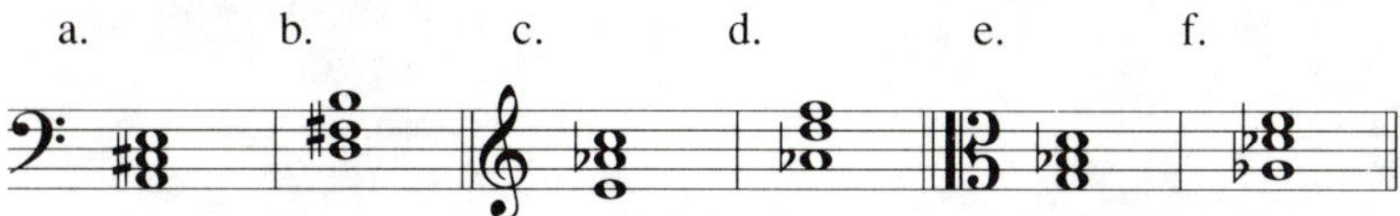

2. Give the popular music chord symbol for each of the triads above.
3. For each of the following chords name the scale degree on which it is built, and give the correct roman numeral. Indicate the inversions in the standard way.

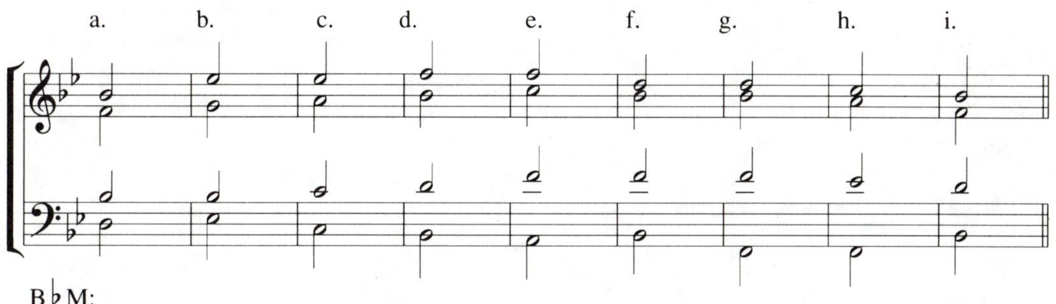

4. Indicate the proper roman numeral for the given chord if it occurred in each of the following keys:

a. A-flat major. b. G minor. c. B-flat major. d. C minor.
e. E-flat major. f. F minor.

5. Indicate the proper roman numeral for the given chord if it occurred in each of the following keys:

a. D major. b. F-sharp minor. c. A major. d. E minor
e. G major. f. B minor.

CHAPTER 5

Cadences, Phrases, and Periods

Cadence
Perfect Authentic Cadence
Imperfect Authentic Cadence
Half Cadence
Plagal Cadence
Deceptive Cadence
Phrase
Phrase Member
Period
Parallel Period
Contrasting Period
Three-Phrase Period
Double Period
Repeated Phrases
Dissimilar Phrases

Exposition

Cadence

A *cadence* is a musical punctuation. A *harmonic cadence,* which will be discussed in this chapter, usually consists of just two chords and signals the end of a composition or section thereof. Cadences differ considerably in musical strength. Some signify the end of a complete musical thought and may be compared to the period (.) in our written language. Others bring an incomplete idea to a close but suggest something else to come. These may be compared to the comma (,) in written language. Most cadences end on either the **V** or **I** chord.

Perfect Authentic Cadence

The *perfect authentic cadence* consists of two chords, both in root position, **V** to **I** in major keys and **V** to **i** in minor keys. In this cadence the *tonic must also be the highest-sounding pitch in the tonic triad.* From the standpoint of finality, it is the strongest cadence of all, and is found frequently at the end of entire compositions, sections, or wherever a forceful termination of a musical thought is needed.

Imperfect Authentic Cadence

The term *imperfect* signifies an authentic cadence that is slightly weaker than *perfect*.

A perfect cadence may be made into an *imperfect authentic cadence* if any of the following conditions exist:

1. The highest-sounding tone in the tonic triad is exchanged for either the third or fifth factor.

2. The **vii°** triad is substituted for the **V,** making the cadence **vii**$^{\circ 6}$ to **I** or **i.**
3. One or both of the chords (**V** or **I**) is inverted. Examples are: **V**^{6} or **I** or **V** to **i**^{6}.

Figure 5.1 illustrates both perfect and imperfect authentic cadences.

Figure 5.1

Half Cadence

If the last chord of a cadence is **V,** it is a *half cadence.* This permits a large number of possibilities, but composers actually employ only a few. **I** to **V, IV** to **V,** or **ii** to **V** account for about 90 percent of all half cadences.

Figure 5.2

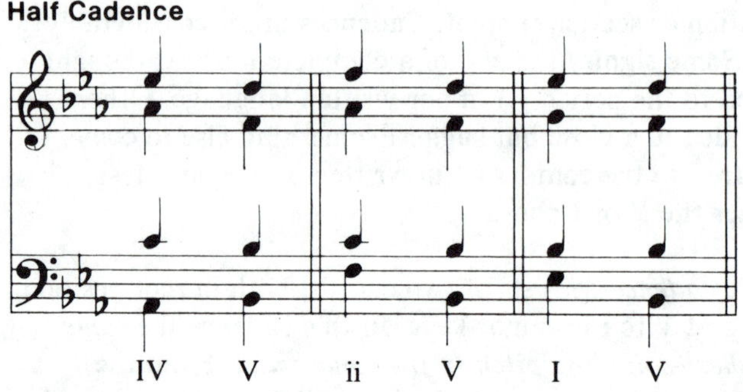

Plagal Cadence

The *plagal cadence* is nearly always one progression: **IV** to **I** in major, or its equivalent **iv** to **i** in minor keys. Infrequently, a cadence, **ii**^{6} to **I,** is interpreted as plagal.

Figure 5.3

Deceptive Cadence

If the first chord is **V** and second is *not* **I,** the cadence is *deceptive.* While there are a large number of possibilities, composers most often select **vi** (**VI** in minor).

Figure 5.4 illustrates the deceptive cadence:

Figure 5.4

(Workbook-Anthology Assignments 5.1, p. 39, and 5.5, p. 44)

Phrase

A *phrase* is a substantial musical thought usually ending with both a harmonic and melodic cadence. The length of a phrase and the presence of a cadence usually distinguishes it from a motive. Phrases are frequently four measures long, but may be longer or shorter so long as a complete (though sometimes dependent) thought is present.

Figure 5.5

Haydn: Symphony in B-flat Major, Hob I:102 (4th Movement)

Phrase

Phrase Member

Phrases frequently contain slight melodic interruptions and thus divide into two *phrase members.* Phrase members are sufficiently separated, usually by a longer note value or rest, to distinguish them as individual units. Sometimes the second phrase member is either a repeat or sequence (repetition at a higher or lower pitch) of the first, while it is just as often contrasting.

Figure 5.6

Haydn: Symphony in C (Toy) (Attributed to Haydn)

Leopold Mozart: Keyboard Trio in G Major, Hob. XV:25 (Finale)

Mozart: Piano Sonata in D Major, K. 284 (1st Movement)

Under certain conditions phrase members may be nearly indistinguishable from phrases themselves. This excerpt from a Mozart sonata might be interpreted as two phrases or two phrase members. However, the lack of cadence at the end of measure 2 tends to favor a single phrase analysis.

Figure 5.7

Mozart: Piano Sonata in C Major, K. 309 (2nd Movement)

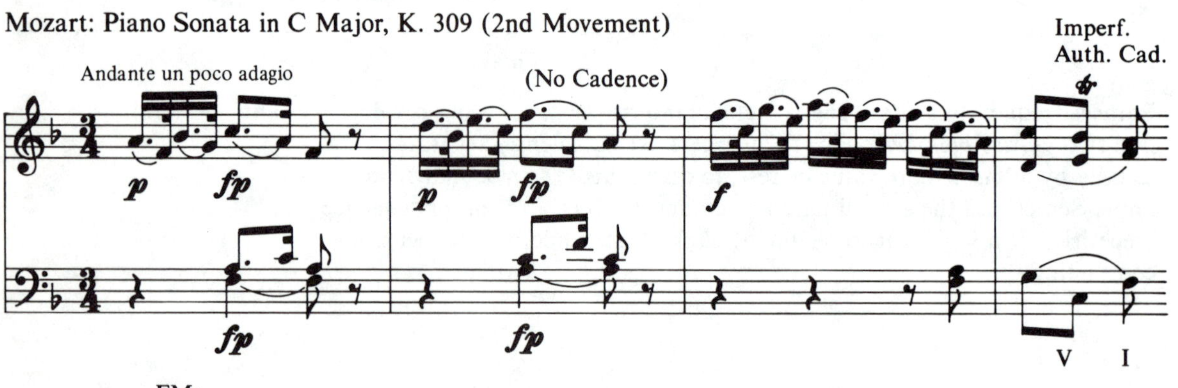

FM:

Two (or sometimes more) adjacent phrases may combine to form a *period*. Characteristics found in all periods (assuming two phrases for the moment) follow:

Period

1. *Closure (finality) must be achieved at the end of the second phrase*—usually with a perfect authentic cadence.
2. *The first phrase must end with a weaker cadence than that of the second.* A half cadence is common at the end of the first phrase:
   Strongest Possible Cadence—Perfect Authentic
   Less Strong—Imperfect Authentic
   Weaker—Half
3. *The two phrases must bear some musical relationship to one another.* Often, they will create a kind of question-answer effect called *antecedent-consequent*. The first phrase acts as the *antecedent* (question) and the second phrase as the *consequent* (answer).

Parallel Period

A *parallel period* results when the melodic content of two adjacent phrases is similar. Conditions needed to create a parallel period are:

1. Harmonically the first phrase ends with a half cadence (infrequently an imperfect authentic cadence). The second phrase ends with a perfect authentic cadence (infrequently with an imperfect cadence—if a half cadence ends the first phrase).
2. Melodically the two phrases contain similar material near the beginning—sometimes only a few notes or as much as the entire phrase except for the cadence (melodic and harmonic).

In these examples the similar (or same) material is two measures long:

Figure 5.8

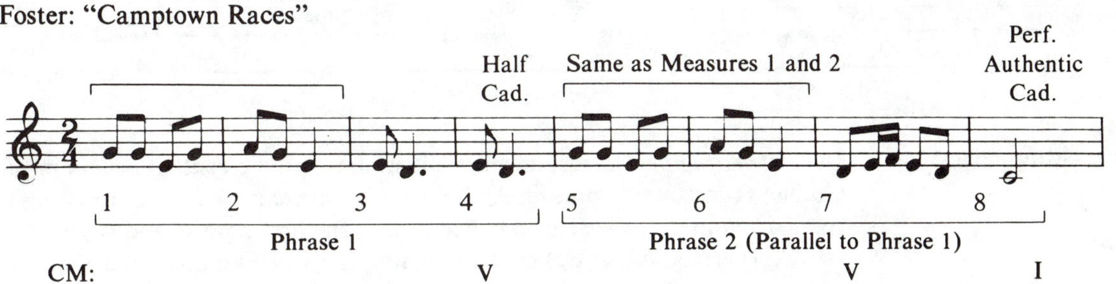

"Cockles and Mussels"

Irish Folk Song

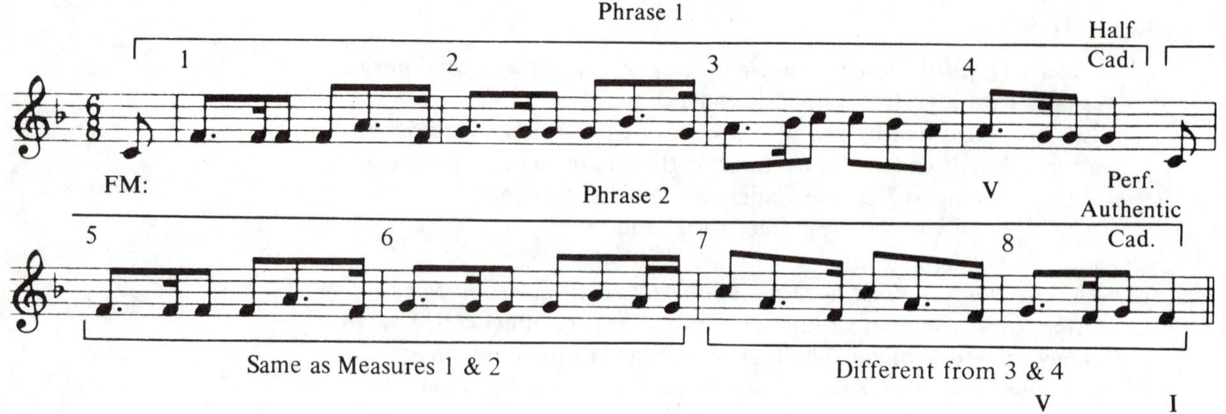

In this example only the three final notes of the second phrase are different from the first:

Figure 5.9

Schubert: Impromptu op. 90, no. 1, D. 899

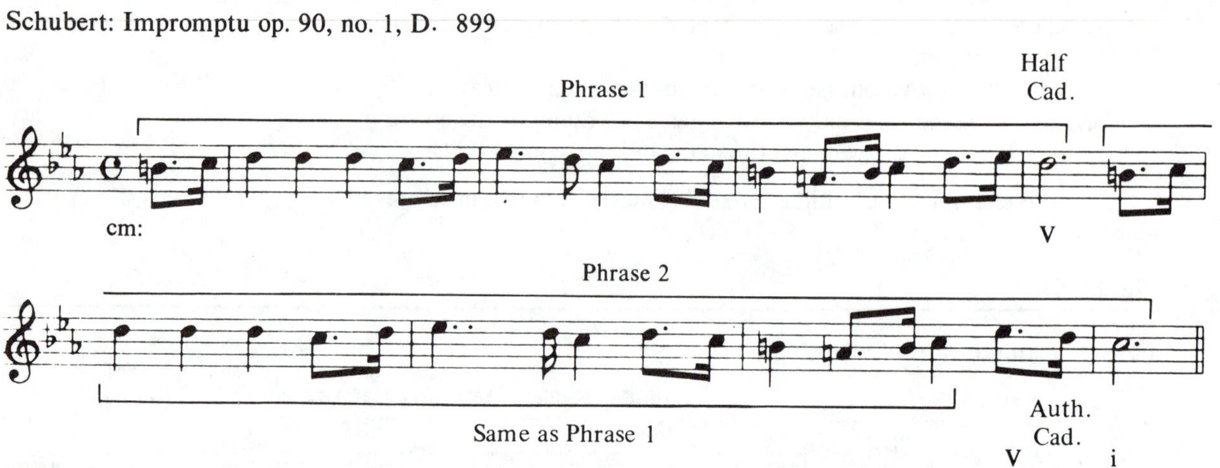

Contrasting Period

A *contrasting period* results when dissimilar melodic content occurs in the second (consequent) phrase. As for all two-phrase periods, a contrasting period requires (1) a weak cadence ending the first phrase, and (2) a strong (perfect authentic) cadence ending the second phrase. But the differing melodic content of the two phrases clearly distinguishes a *contrasting* period from a *parallel* period. Usually the melodic contours (outline of the notes) of the two phrases are different.

Figure 5.10

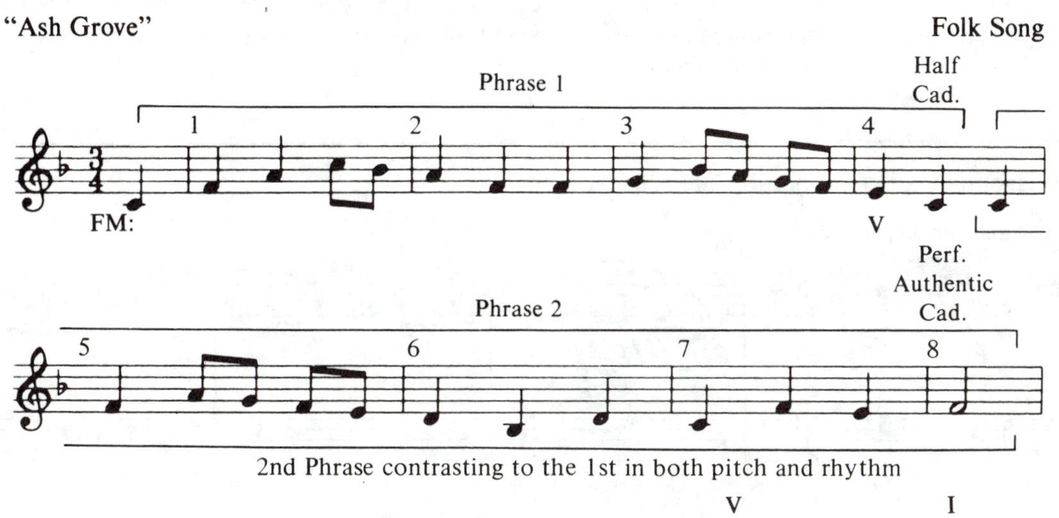

While most periods are composed of just two phrases, those of three (and even more) do occur. The three phrases may consist of A A B (antecedent, antecedent, consequent) or A B B (antecedent, consequent, consequent). The third phrase must end with a stronger cadence than either of the other two.

Three-Phrase Period

Figure 5.11

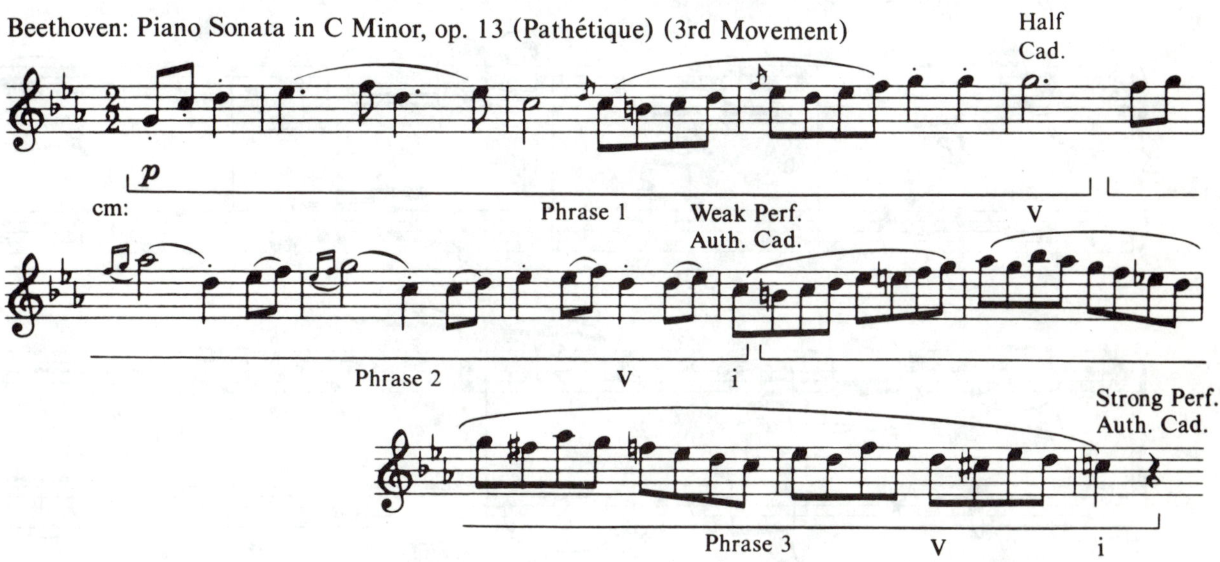

Double Period (Four-Phrase Period)

The variety of phrase relationships in *double periods* are too numerous to classify here. However, the same principle governing two-phrase periods applies here as well—the fourth phrase must bring the period to closure and should be at least as strong as any of the other three.

Figure 5.12

Mozart: Piano Sonata in C Major, K. 309 (2nd Movement)

Analysis:

Measures	Phrases	Cadence
1–4	a	Imperfect Authentic
5–8	b	Half
9–12	a′	Imperfect Authentic
13–16	b′ or c	Perfect Authentic

Repeated Phrases

Repeated phrases, whether identical or modified, are not typically regarded as period structures because the second phrase is not dependent on the first. Thus the antecedent-consequent concept cannot be applied here. This excerpt, from the light opera "The Fortune Teller" by Victor Herbert, illustrates a modified repeated second phrase and a perfect authentic cadence as the completion of both phrases.

Figure 5.13

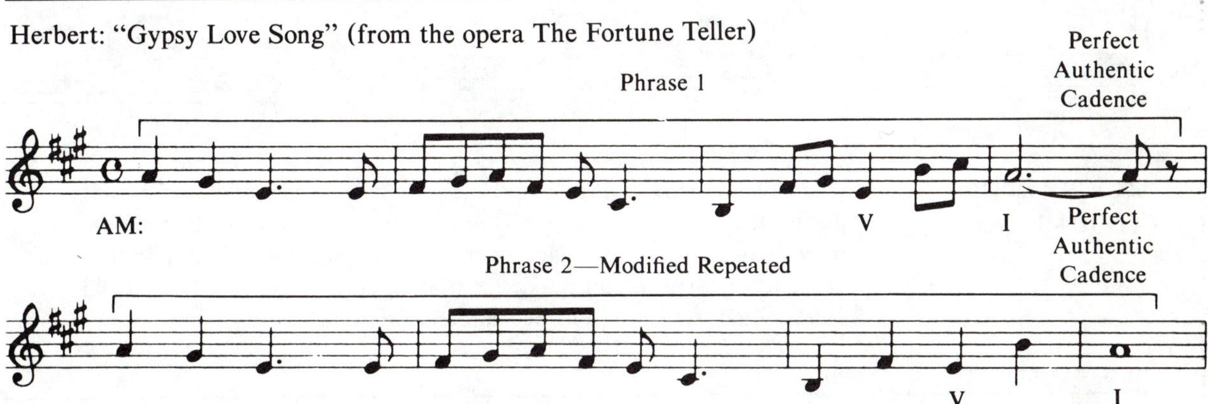

Dissimilar Phrases

A series of phrases, some of which may be unrelated or lacking closure, do not arrange themselves conveniently into periods. Terms for such groupings range from phrase groups, or phrase chains, to dissimilar phrases, or dissolved periods. For purposes of analysis here, these nonperiod combinations may be called *dissimilar phrases.*

(Workbook-Anthology Assignments 5.2, p. 40, and 5.3, pp. 41 and 42)

History

Renaissance Period (1450–1600)

The idea of the four-bar phrase, so common in the mid-to-late seventeenth century, was developed gradually during the late Renaissance period. Although examples of fairly strict phrasing can be found, the following excerpt of music, for the virginal (a type of harpsichord) by Thomas Morley (1557–1603?) is perhaps representative of the period. Perfect authentic cadences occur in measures 2, 6, and 8, and the phrases are not intended to be balanced. The composition is a mixture of both modal and tonal influence.

Figure 5.14

Morley: "Nancie" (from the Fitzwilliam Virginal Book)

Baroque Period (1600–1750)

The development of phrase and period construction advanced rapidly during the years 1600 to 1675, and by the latter half of the Baroque period, all devices mentioned in this chapter were in place. The following excerpt of instrumental music from an opera by Henry Purcell (1653–1695) illustrates clear-cut period construction.

Figure 5.15

Purcell: Chaconne (from the opera King Arthur, Act V)

Classical Period (1750–1825)

This period, represented by the works of Haydn, Mozart, and Beethoven, is perhaps the culmination of formal phrase and period construction. This chapter contains six excerpts from compositions by these three composers.

Romantic Period (1825–1900)

While the highly formal style of the Classical period began to fade in the years from 1800 to about 1830, the freer style of the Romantic period maintained the basic elements of phrase and period construction.

Post-Romantic and Impressionistic Period (1875–1920)

As functional harmony and major/minor tonality gradually diminished in importance, so did the earlier ideas concerning phrase relationships. Nevertheless, in a new setting bedecked with a freer use of tonality and only the bare existence of functional harmony, phrase and period construction can still be detected in the works of composers of this period.

Contemporary Period (1910–Present)

In such a wide range of new musical styles as are present in this period, the musical phrase, although stylistically much changed from that of its progenitors of the Baroque period, is still a dominant influence in music.

Jazz and Popular Music (1900–Present)

Phrase and period construction have always been a staple procedure in American popular music.

Note the strict 8-bar units in the following popular song of the 1960s.

Figure 5.16

"Try to Remember"—Tom Jones & Harvey Schmidt. Copyright © 1960 by Tom Jones and Harvey Schmidt. Chappell & Co., Inc., owner of publication and allied rights.

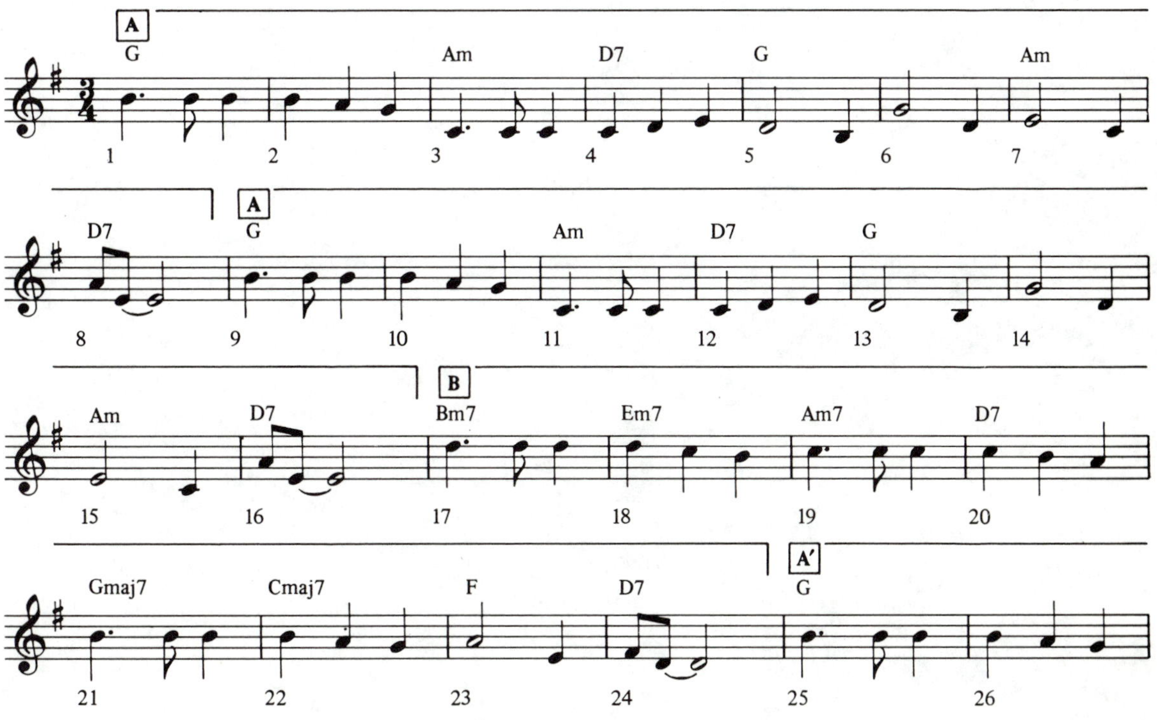

Jazz, up to about 1945, also maintained a balanced phrase structure, but with the rise of Charlie Parker and other noted improvisers of that period, irregular and unbalanced phrases become more fashionable as a means of expression.

REVIEW

1. Play all the examples of cadences (figures 5.1–5.4) on the piano and identify the features of each cadence as described in the accompanying text. **Even if your piano skills are minimal you will find this to be a helpful exercise.**
2. Choose a few pieces from a collection of traditional and patriotic songs, a hymnal, or some similar music with clear phrases and a text.
   a. Find the key of each piece.
   b. Identify phrases by the given punctuation marks in the text.
   c. For each phrase identify the cadence type (authentic, plagal, etc.). Some phrases may be in keys other than the key of the piece as a whole and you may not be able to identify the cadence type in every case.
   d. Examine the length of the phrases. Are all phrases the same length?
   e. Are the phrases grouped together into periods? How do you know? Are the periods parallel, contrasting, three-phrase periods, or double periods? How can you tell?
   f. Does the melody contain repeated melodic motives?
3. Look over the assignments you have completed for this chapter, paying particular attention to any difficulties you encountered. Think through the process for completing each exercise.
4. Since you are likely to find problems similar to the assignments on an examination, work through some of the assignments that you were not required to complete during your study of the chapter. This will give practice in working with the concepts of the chapter.

Test Yourself 5

Name the cadence type in the following short excerpts (each ending with a cadence). The cadence types are:

Imperfect Authentic	Plagal
Perfect Authentic	Deceptive
Half	

*Occasionally a 5th is missing. In this instance analyze as if the 5th ("B") were present.

10.
fm:
11.
cm:
12.
AM:
13.
em:
14.
FM:
15.
GM:
16.
B♭M:
17.
fm:
18.
AM:
19.
em:
20.
gm:
21.
bm:

25. The following melody by Schubert contains four phrases. Identify the beat where each of the phrases ends and describe the melody in terms of its period structure (parallel period, contrasting period, three-phrase period, double period, dissimilar phrases).

Schubert: Piano Sonata in A Major, D. 959

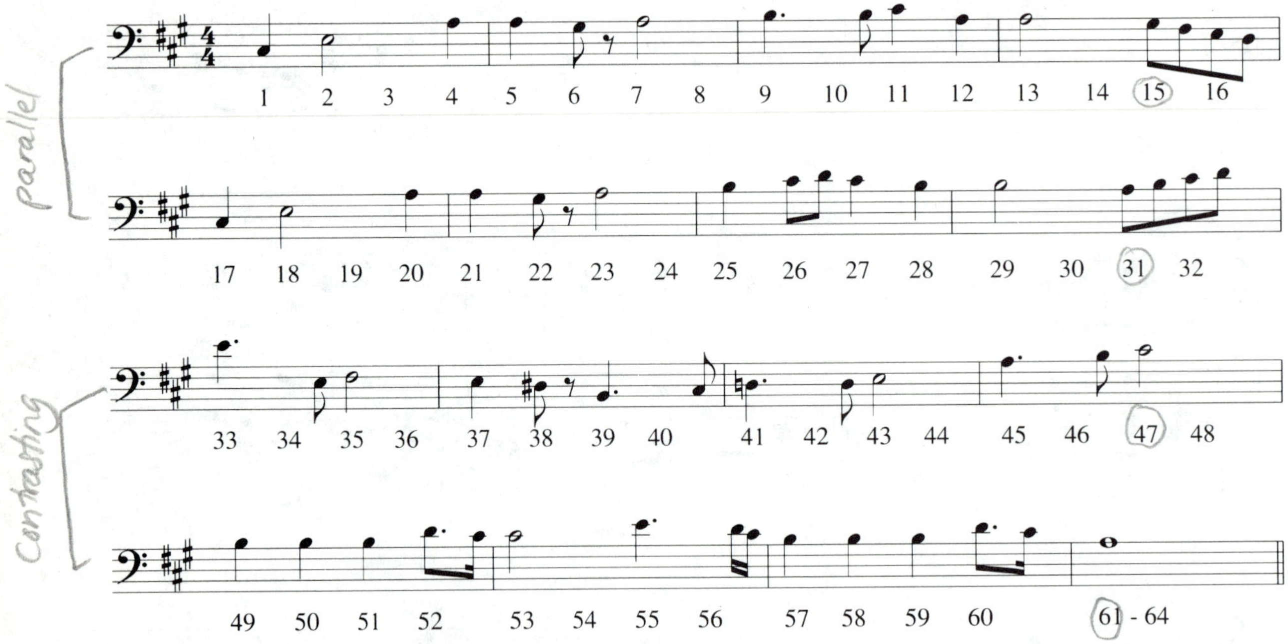

1 2 3 4 5 6 7 8 9 10 11 12 13 14 15 16

17 18 19 20 21 22 23 24 25 26 27 28 29 30 31 32

33 34 35 36 37 38 39 40 41 42 43 44 45 46 47 48

49 50 51 52 53 54 55 56 57 58 59 60 61 - 64

PART 2

Harmony and Voice Leading

The study of harmony includes:

1. Harmonic vocabulary—the types of vertical structures found in music.
2. Harmonic progression—the patterns of chord change.
3. Harmonic rhythm—the rate of harmonic change, the number of changes per unit of music, the patterns of harmonic duration.
4. Tonal implications of the harmony. The key or keys established by the harmony.
5. Harmonic elaboration—the ways in which harmony is sustained. A chord is generally considered to be a simultaneous combination of tones, and yet, composers have developed different techniques for continuing the effect of a single chord over a span of time, including: repeated note patterns, arpeggiation, sustained chords, use of pedal tones, and embellishing tones.

The study of voice leading includes:

1. Methods of creating smooth melodic connections between chords.
2. A study of the relationship among the various lines in the musical texture.
3. The use of dissonance to increase the interest and variety in the music.

Music is a multidimensional art, where harmony and voice leading represent two complimentary dimensions—the vertical and the horizontal. Considerable skill is required to balance the need for strong harmony and good melodic lines, and the following chapters will help you develop your ability to work in both dimensions simultaneously.

The harmonic theory in this book is based on the theories of Jean-Philippe Rameau (1683–1764), whose *Traité de l'harmonie* (1722) first elucidated the relationship between the bass and the harmony and established the principle of inversion of chords. The musical style presented is that of the so-called "common practice" period—a period that extends from the late Baroque period (the early eighteenth century) to the Romantic period (the late nineteenth century). In the common practice period, music exhibited strong tonal centers based on the major and minor scales, and a balance between the horizontal and vertical dimensions.

CHAPTER 6

Nonharmonic Tones and Harmonic Rhythm

Passing Tone
Neighboring Tone
Escape Tone
Appoggiatura
Suspension
Retardation
Anticipation
Pedal Tone
Changing Tone
Harmonic Rhythm

Exposition

Nonharmonic Tones

Harmonic tones should be well known by now. They are the triad tones: root, third, or fifth. *Nonharmonic tones* are pitches that sound along with a chord but are not triad pitches.

Before studying the variety of nonharmonic tone types, some information regarding all nonharmonic tones is in order.

1. Most nonharmonic tones are dissonant and create intervals of a 2nd, 4th, or 7th. Diminished or augmented intervals are also considered dissonant.
2. The dissonance created by nonharmonic tones is calculated against the lowest-sounding tone of a chord—no matter how many other voices are present. An exception occurs when the nonharmonic tone occurs in the lowest-sounding voice itself (usually bass).
3. Think of nonharmonic tones as a pattern of three pitches:

	1		2		3
Pattern:	**Preceding Tone**	—	**Nonharmonic Tone**	—	**Following Tone**
	(Consonance)		**(Dissonance)**		**(Consonance)**

The pedal tone, changing tones, and consecutive passing tones are exceptions to the pattern.

4. A very important distinction among the various nonharmonic tones is their rhythmic placement—whether the dissonance occurs on the beat (accented) or off the beat (unaccented). Dissonances placed on the

beat are much stronger and often create a powerful emotional impact, while those placed off the beat generally pass almost unnoticed, and serve to smooth or embellish melodic lines. Some nonharmonic tones occur both in accented and unaccented contexts, while others appear only as accented or as unaccented dissonances.

5. Nonharmonic tones are named for the type of approach and departure they receive.

Passing Tone

A nonharmonic tone leading by step from one chord tone to another different pitch is called a *passing tone.* As shown in figure 6.1, passing tones may occur as unaccented (a) or accented (b), two at a time (c), and in any voice (d). Sometimes, when filling in the interval of a 4th, two consecutive passing tones are used (e).

Figure 6.1

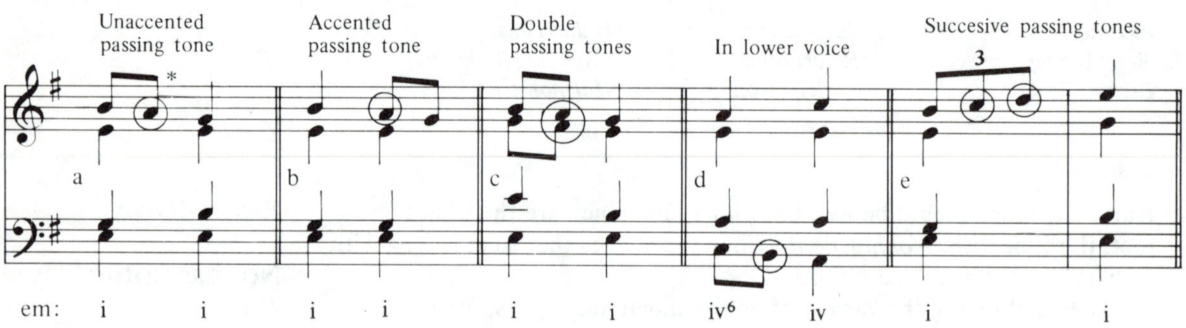

*Circles indicate nonharmonic tones.

Neighboring Tone

A nonharmonic tone that leads by step from one chord tone and returns to another of the same pitch is called a *neighboring tone.* Neighboring tones may occur as accented or unaccented.

Figure 6.2

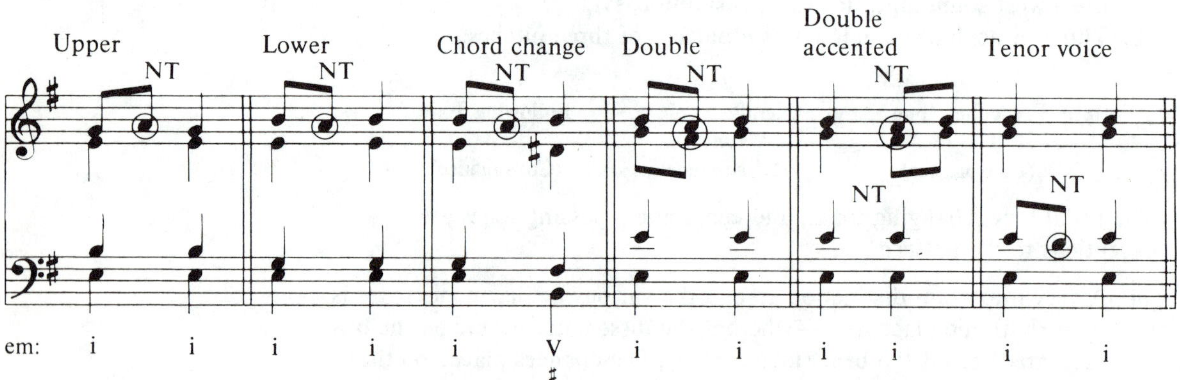

An *escape tone* is a nonharmonic tone that leads by step from a chord tone and skips in the opposite direction to another chord tone. The escape tone found in most music covered by this book leads *up* by step from the chord tone and skips a *3rd down.*

Escape Tone

Figure 6.3

*Indicates the nonharmonic tone.

The *appoggiatura* is a nonharmonic tone that is approached by skip and resolved by step in the opposite direction. It generally occurs on an accented beat.

Appoggiatura

Figure 6.4

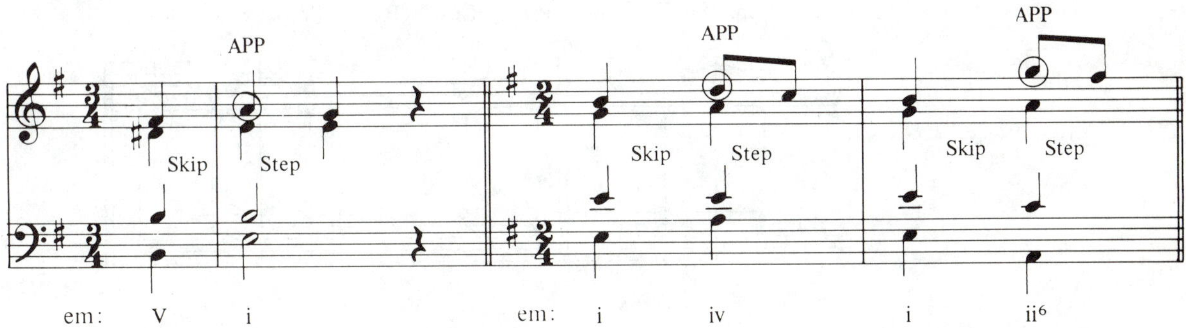

A *suspension* is a nonharmonic tone that includes a prepared dissonance and a resolution down one scale step.

Suspension

1. To form a suspension, three melodic notes in succession are required.
2. The melodic pattern of the suspension figure is always as follows:

Figure 6.5

3. The middle (repeated) note of the suspension figure is the suspended tone. Suspensions contain three phases:

Figure 6.6

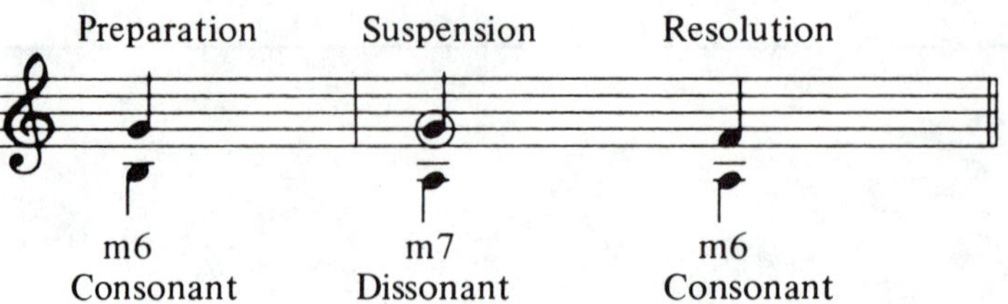

4. The suspended tone (the middle tone of the figure) is always in a stressed position. Suspensions are of the following types, designated by the interval forming the suspended tone and resolution with the lowest sounding voice (usually the bass voice):

Type	Suspended Tone	Resolution
9–8	9th	8th
7–6	7th	6th
4–3	4th	3rd

Figure 6.7

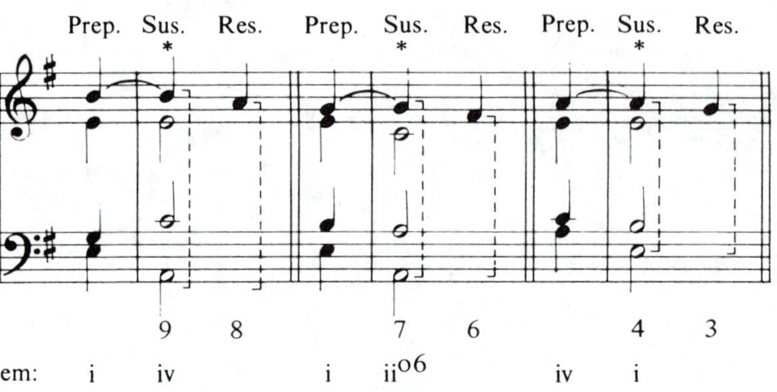

5. There is one other type of suspension—the 2–3. Whereas the suspension figure (note, same note, one step lower) is in one of the upper voices in all of the previously described suspension types, in the 2–3 suspension the suspended tone is in the lower voice.

Type	Suspended Tone	Resolution
2–3	2nd	3rd

*In determining the interval of suspension, the octave is usually removed. Thus 4–3 instead of 11–10. The exception is 9–8.

Figure 6.8

2–3 suspension showing suspension figure in lower voice.

6. The other voice (not containing the suspension figure) may move in almost any way so long as it provides the necessary preparation, suspension, and resolution phases for the suspension figure.

Figure 6.9

7. Remember that suspensions occur between only two voices—even in four-voice writing. The other voices do not take part and for the present moment may be ignored. Figure 6.10 shows suspensions (between only two voices) found in a four-voice setting.

Figure 6.10

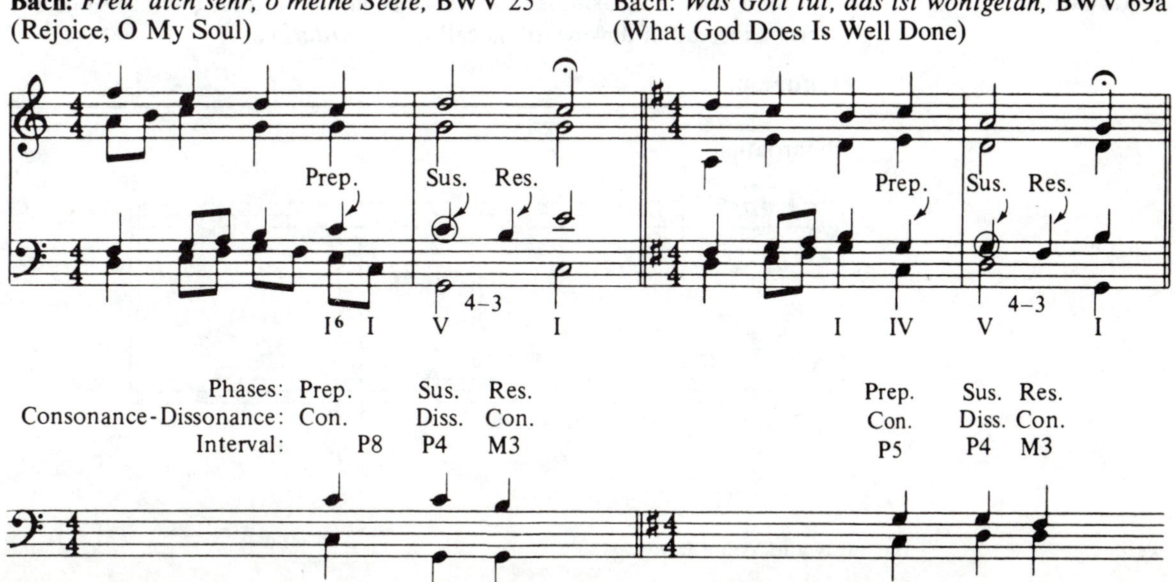

8. Suspensions may occur in pairs simultaneously, have decorated resolutions, and occur in chains.

Figure 6.11

In pairs

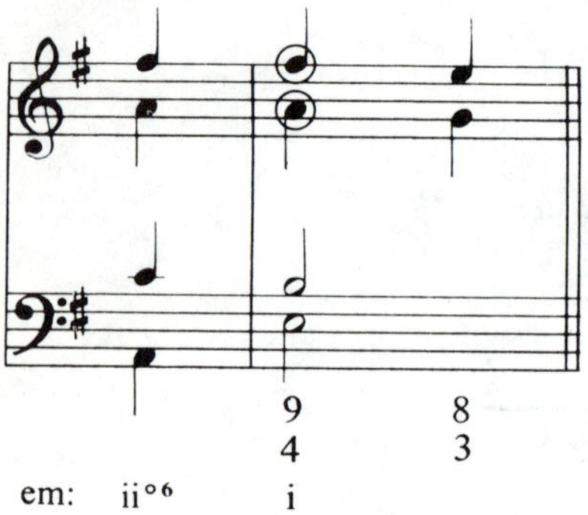

9 8
4 3

em: ii°6 i

Decorated resolutions

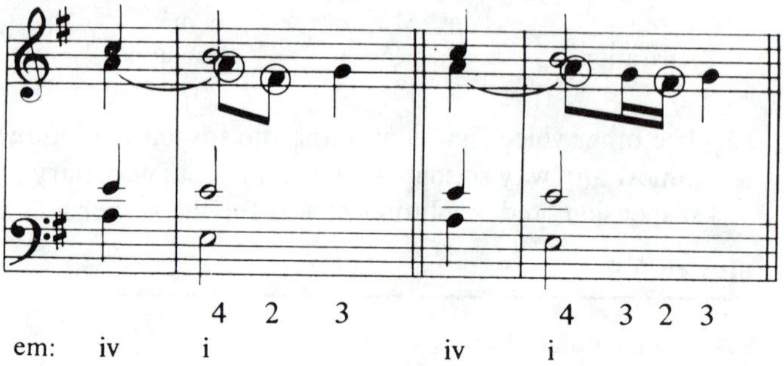

4 2 3 4 3 2 3

em: iv i iv i

In chains

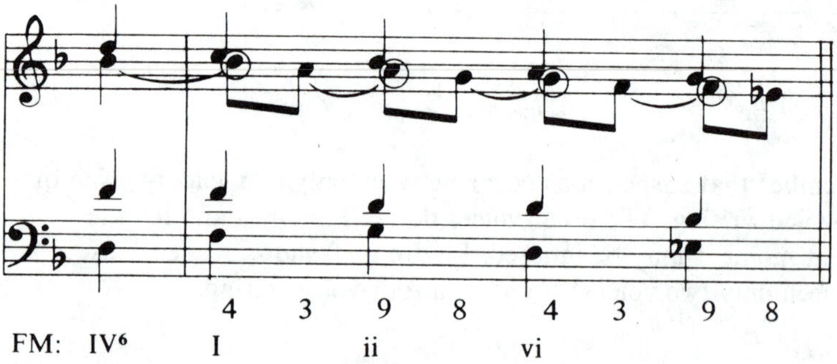

4 3 9 8 4 3 9 8

FM: IV6 I ii vi

Retardation

A nonharmonic tone, similar to a suspension, except that the resolution is *upward* instead of downward, is called a *retardation.*

Figure 6.12

Anticipation

An *anticipation* is a nonharmonic tone that anticipates a tone of the chord that follows. The anticipation departs by step from a chord tone and progresses by repetition to a chord tone. Occasionally it is approached by skip.

Figure 6.13

Anticipation

Pedal Tone

A *pedal tone* (also called a pedal point) is a held or repeated note, usually in the lowest voice, that alternates between consonance and dissonance with the chord structures above it. When a pedal tone occurs above other voices it is called an *inverted pedal tone.*

Figure 6.14

Changing Tone

Changing tones consist of two consecutive nonharmonic tones. The first leads by step from a chord tone, skips to another nonharmonic tone, and then leads by step to a chord tone (often the same chord tone). More recent terms often used instead of changing tones are *double neighboring tones* or *neighbor group.* In many ways the two changing tones resemble neighboring tones with a missing (or perhaps implied) middle tone.

Figure 6.15

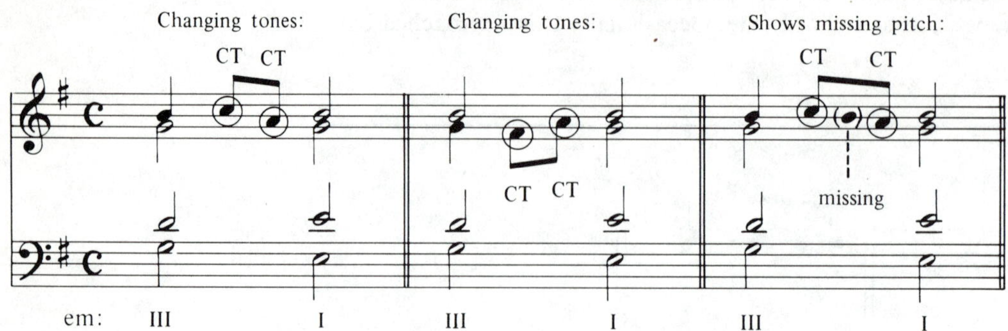

Summary

The following chart is a summary of nonharmonic tones studied in this chapter:

PT—Passing Tone
APP—Appoggiatura
ANT—Anticipation
NT—Neighboring Tone
SUS—Suspension
PD—Pedal Tone
ET—Escape Tone
RE—Retardation
CT—Changing Tones

Type	Approach	Departure	Voice	Accented or Unaccented
PT	Step	Step	Any	May be either
NT	Step	Step	Any	May be either
ET	Step	Skip	Soprano	Unaccented
APP	Skip	Step	Usually Soprano	Accented
SUS	Same pitch	Step down	Any	Accented
RE	Same pitch	Step up	Usually Soprano	Accented
ANT	Prefer step	Same tone	Usually Soprano	Unaccented
PD	NA		Usually Bass	Both
CT	NA		Any	Usually neither note accented

(Workbook-Anthology Assignments 6.1–6.3, pp. 45–49, and 6.5–6.8, pp. 51–56)

Harmonic Rhythm

Harmonic rhythm is the frequency of harmonic change in a composition. In some compositions each successive melody tone is harmonized with a different chord. Thus, the harmonic rhythm is that of one chord per melody tone.

Figure 6.16

Bach: *Wer nur den lieben Gott lässt walten,* BWV 434
(If We Will But Let God Guide Us)

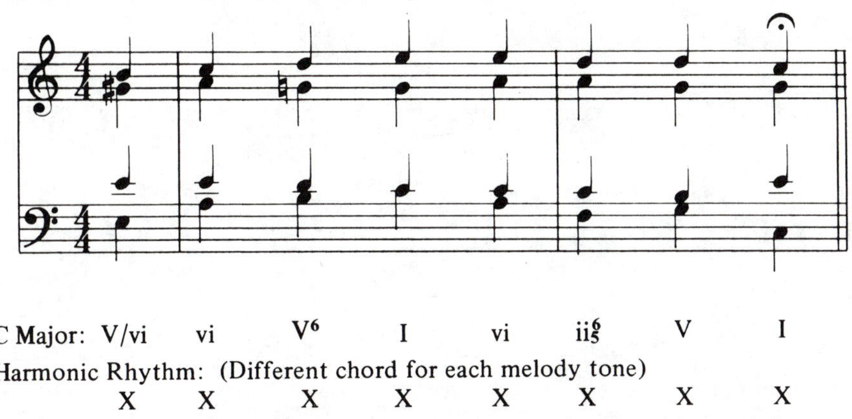

Other compositions may exhibit a very slow harmonic rhythm even though the tempo is fast and the rate of change in melody tones is very rapid.

Figure 6.17

La Cucaracha
(The Cockroach)

Folk Song

On occasion a single melody tone may be harmonized with several different chords.

Figure 6.18

Schumann: *Papillons,* op. 2, no. 12

Fast harmonic rhythm—harmony changes on each successive melody tone (14 chords in all; 13 changes):

Figure 6.19

Medium harmonic rhythm—same melody with only half as many harmony changes (8 chords in all; 7 changes):

Figure 6.20

Slow harmonic rhythm—same melody harmonized with only one chord per measure (4 chords in all; 3 changes):

Figure 6.21

(Workbook-Anthology Assignments 6.4, pp. 49–50, and 6.9, p. 56)

REVIEW

1. Play the examples of nonharmonic tones (figures 6.1–6.15) on the piano and pay particular attention to the three-tone pattern: **preceding tone, nonharmonic tone,** and **following tone.**
2. Study the summary of nonharmonic tones on page 112 and memorize the approach and departure characteristics of each. Also memorize the list of abbreviations at the top of the chart. You will need these abbreviations to label nonharmonic tones in assignments and examinations.
3. Review the fundamentals (chapters 1–5). You must review these basic facts on a regular basis and practice to achieve fluency. This repeated review will pay big dividends in future chapters.

Test Yourself 6

Questions 1–3 refer to these examples:

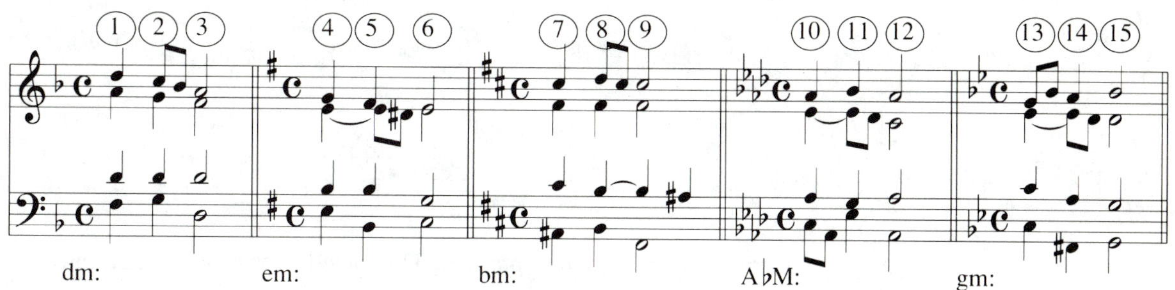

1. Cadences:
   a. The cadence at chord **3** is a(n) ________________ cadence.
   b. The cadence at chord **6** is a(n) ________________ cadence.
   c. The cadence at chord **9** is a(n) ________________ cadence.
   d. The cadence at chord **12** is a(n) ________________ cadence.
   e. The cadence at chord **15** is a(n) ________________ cadence.
2. Nonharmonic tones:
   a. The nonharmonic tone at chord **2** is a(n) ________________ .
   b. The nonharmonic tone at chord **5** is a(n) ________________ .
   c. The nonharmonic tone at chord **8** is a(n) ________________ .
   d. The nonharmonic tone at chord **9** is a(n) ________________ .
   e. The nonharmonic tone at chord **11** is a(n) ________________ .
   f. The nonharmonic tone at chord **13** is a(n) ________________ .
   g. The nonharmonic tone at chord **14** is a(n) ________________ .
3. Describe the harmonic rhythm in the examples above.

Questions 4–7 refer to the Lullaby by Brahms:

Brahms: Lullaby, op. 49, no. 4

4. Divide this melody into phrases. The melody consists of _____ phrases.
5. Examine the phrases for period construction. This melody contains ___ period(s).
6. Describe the period(s) by type (parallel period, contrasting period, three-phase period, double period).
7. Describe the harmonic rhythm in Brahms' Lullaby.

CHAPTER 7

Voice Leading in Four-Part Chorale Writing

Voice Leading
Chorale
Stylistic Practices
Doubling
Parallel P5ths
Parallel P8ths
Stylistic Departures
Unstylistic Departures—Inviolate and Occasionally Broken
Overlap
Order of Voices
Crossed Voices
Spacing of Voices
Cadenza
Common Tone

Exposition

Voice leading is the term used to describe the linear aspect of music. A chord is made up of tones that sound together, but the nature of the various voices (melodic lines) that come together to produce the chord are also of considerable musical importance. Think of *chords* as telephone poles and the wires they support as the individual voices. *Voice leading* is the art of creating smooth melodic connections between chords.

The best way to understand eighteenth-century voice-leading practices is to examine compositions by composers of the period. The following phrases from chorale harmonizations by J. S. Bach have furnished models of good voice leading to generations of students. The following excerpts from these chorales will be examined in detail to illustrate typical voice-leading practice.

Five chorale phrases:

Figure 7.1

1. Bach: *Lobt Gott, ihr Christen, allzugleich,* BWV 151
   (Praise God, Ye Christians, All Together)

2. Bach: *Ermuntre dich, mein schwacher Geist,* BWV 43
   (Rouse Thyself, My Weak Spirit)

3. Bach: *Wer weiss, wie nahe mir mein Ende,* BWV 166
(Who Knows How Near My End May Be)

4. Bach: *Der Tag, der ist so freudenreich,* BWV 294
(This Day is So Joyful)

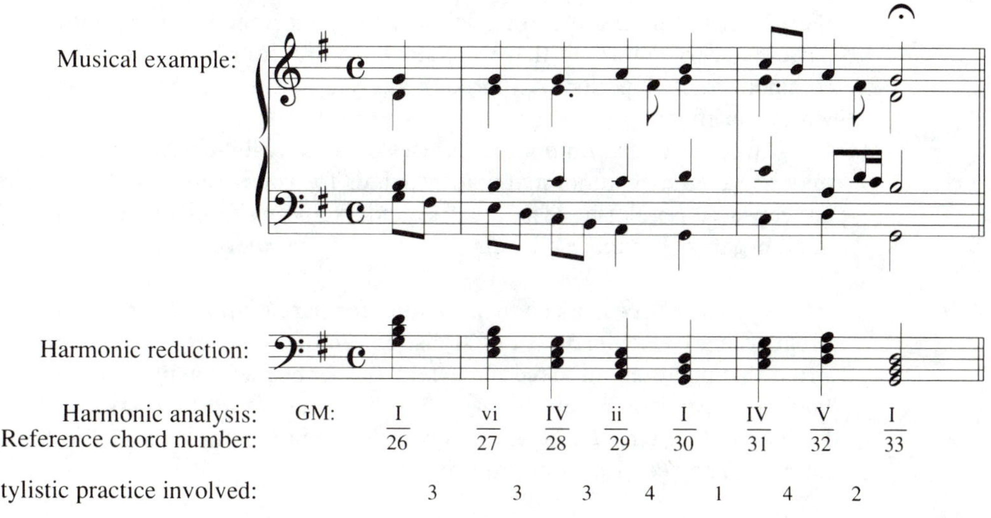

5. Bach: *Nun danket alle Gott,* BWV 386
(Now Let Us All Thank God)

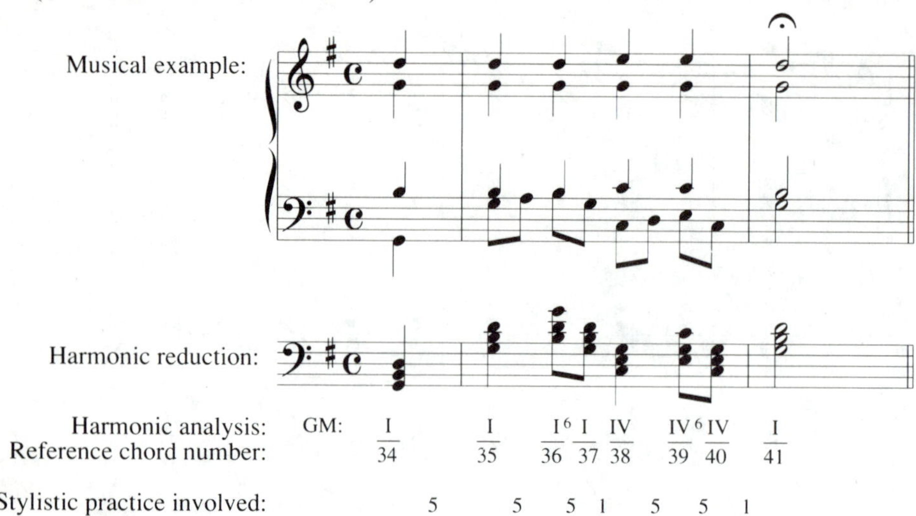

Analysis of the Chorale Phrases

Although the forty-one chords comprising these five phrases do not by any means constitute a sample large enough for a thorough and valid study, they do, nevertheless, illustrate some of the important and recurring patterns in voice leading that were standard procedures during the common-practice period. A thorough analysis of the five phrases is well worth the effort.

Rather than examining the phrases on a chord-by-chord basis, time may be saved by examining adjacent triads for voice-leading patterns that are repeated regularly. Also, a better understanding results if this is done in an organized manner—by classification of root movement.

Stylistic Practices

A *stylistic practice* is a common method for part-writing a particular progression. (A complete list of stylistic practices is found in Appendix A. From this point on, all listed material from Appendix A will appear in boldface.) Stylistic practices 1 and 2 refer to chords whose roots are a P5th or P4th apart. There are no fewer than nine examples in the five phrases. They connect root position chords:

3–4	12–13	30–31
6–7	15–16	37–38
11–12	20–21	40–41

The following two are additional examples of stylistic practice no. 2. They occur between chord numbers:

8–9
32–33

Root Position

When the two roots lie a perfect 5th or 4th apart (one common tone):

1. **Keep the common tone (tone shared by both triads) and move the remaining two upper voices stepwise to the chord tones of the next triad. If handled correctly, the roots of the chords will be doubled.**
2. **Do not keep the common tone, especially when the soprano voice descends scale steps 2 to 1. Move all three upper voices in similar motion to the nearest chord tone. If handled correctly, the roots will be doubled.**

Figure 7.2

Keep Common Tone
Move other upper voices by step to nearest chord tone

Do Not Keep Common Tone
Move all 3 upper voices in similar motion to nearest chord tone

For chord roots that lie a third apart there are three examples. These connect chords at numbers:

26–27 27–28 28–29

All adhere to the following stylistic practice:
When roots lie a third (major or minor) apart (two common tones):

3. **Keep both common tones and move remaining upper voice stepwise. If handled properly the roots of the two chords will be doubled.**

Figure 7.3

For adjacent chord roots that lie at the interval of a second (major or minor), five examples, all following stylistic practice no. 4, can be cited. These occur in figure 7.1 between chords:

7–8 13–14 21–22 29–30 31–32

When roots lie a second apart (no common tones):

4. **Move the three upper voices in contrary motion to the bass, making sure that each voice moves to the nearest chord tone of the next chord. If handled correctly, the roots of the two chords will be doubled. An exception is the progression V to vi or VI. In this case, double the third factor of the vi or VI triad. Only two upper voices will move in opposite direction to the bass.**

Figure 7.4

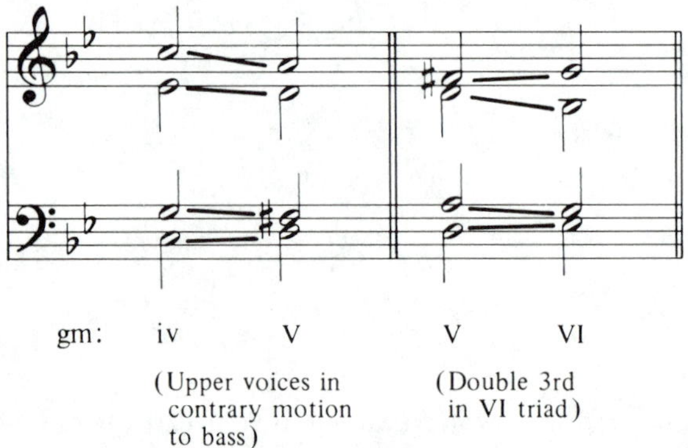

Often in the five chorale phrases two adjacent chords are the same (example: I followed by another I). The second chord is simply a continuation of the first and is not called a chord progression. Much flexibility is available and only two general warnings are necessary. In the five chorale phrases there are ten examples of repeated triads, and they connect chords:

2–3	17–18	35–36	39–40
4–5	24–25	36–37	
5–6	34–35	38–39	

When chords are repeated:

5. **Maintain proper doubling, range of voices (see Appendix e), and keep the usual order of voices (Soprano, Alto, Tenor, and Bass). But, otherwise, freedom to exchange chord factors among voices is quite acceptable. Sometimes a change of position takes place (example: I to I^6). (See pages 126–132.)**

Nearly all progressions in the five phrases (pages 120–122) are now accounted for. Those with other numbers will be discussed later in this chapter, but those marked "Exc.," meaning exception, require explanation.

Exceptions to Stylistic Practices

Sometimes stylistic practices are not followed. Chorale phrase no. 2 *Ermuntre dich* contains two such departures (numbers 10–11 and 14–15). Occasionally, voice-leading conditions make it impossible to apply stylistic practices, and at other times composers simply seek a better melodic line in inner voices. So, while stylistic practices are the norm, they must not be considered as unbreakable laws. Later in this chapter you will be introduced to *stylistic departures,* which provide guidelines to help you when the voice-leading practices listed in this chapter cannot or should not be followed.

First-Inversion Triads

First-inversion triads are used for a number of purposes, including smoother bass lines, and to provide melodic motion in repeated chords.

First-Inversion Triads for Smooth Bass Melodies

Triads in root position establish stability in the chorale and are considered anchor positions, but if all chorales or hymns were comprised only of root positions, bass lines would be disjointed and capable of bringing about stepwise movement only with adjacent chords that are a step apart (**IV** to **V, V** to **vi,** etc.). So, one of the reasons first inversions are employed is to provide smooth bass lines with a musical balance of steps and skips. A good example of this is in chorale phrase 3, chords 18 through 20 (reprinted here for convenience). Chord 19 is a $\mathbf{V^6}$ triad in first inversion, and it is substituted here for the V in root position because it adds stepwise movement to the bass line (**G F♯ G**).

Figure 7.5

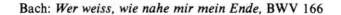

Bach: *Wer weiss, wie nahe mir mein Ende,* BWV 166

First-Inversion Triads to Provide Melodic Motion

Not only do first-inversion triads diminish the angularity of a bass line, but they may also add another ingredient not available to root positions. Chorale phrase no. 5, (chords 35–37) illustrates this point. The first-inversion triad at 36 provides an opportunity to incorporate melodic motion (**G B G**) in the bass melody and avoid repeating the **G.** Reprinted here for convenience:

Figure 7.6

Bach: *Nun danket alle Gott,* BWV 386

There are a number of other fundamental reasons for the use of first-inversion triads, but these will be discussed as they are found in music literature.

Voice Leading in First-Inversion Triads

The five chorale phrases, harmonized by Bach (figure 7.1), contain six first-inversion triads. First-inversion triads occur in the following places:

1–2	5–6	22–23	36–37
2–3	18–19	23–24	38–39
4–5	19–20	35–36	39–40

Careful examination of all of these examples indicates that each first-inversion triad must be treated in relation to surrounding chords, and therefore does not form preferred patterns of voice leading, as in the case of root-position triads.

One general stylistic practice statement suffices for voice leading in first-inversion major and minor triads as they occur in chorales or hymns:

Recommended voice leading for first-inversion triads:

6. Double any triad factor that facilitates smooth voice leading. Favored notes are the soprano (found often) and bass (slightly less common). Never double the leading tone (7th scale degree). Observe general recommendations regarding voice ranges, order of voices, and spacing. (See appendixes C and E for specific information.)

The vii°^{6} Triad

Since the five chorale phrases used to discover and demonstrate voice-leading principles contain no vii°^{6} triads, voice leading as applied to this triad will be shown with special illustrations.

The leading tone triad is nearly always found in first inversion and progresses most often to the tonic. It is to be thought of as a dominant function because the two (**V** and **vii°^{6}**) have two pitches in common (in CM: G **B D** and **B D** F).

Voice leading for the vii°^{6}:

7. Double the third (bass note) or fifth factor. The bass note is preferred. Move all voices with as much stepwise movement as possible. Avoid melodic skips of a tritone.

Figure 7.7

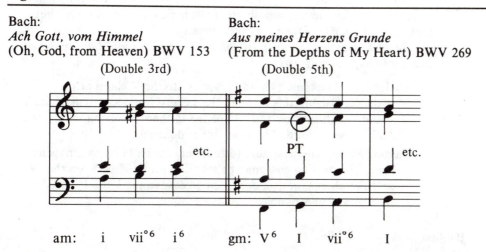

Bach:
Ach Gott, vom Himmel
(Oh, God, from Heaven) BWV 153

Bach:
Aus meines Herzens Grunde
(From the Depths of My Heart) BWV 269

(Double 3rd) (Double 5th)

etc. PT etc.

am: i vii°^{6} i^6 gm: V^6 I vii°^{6} I

One final detail remains. Chord no. 23 of the five chorale phrases (page 121) is a **ii°⁶** triad that has not yet been discussed. The **vii°⁶** and **ii°⁶** are both diminished triads but do not function in a similar manner. **vii°⁶** is related to the dominant and usually progresses to the tonic. But, **ii°⁶** has predominant (precedes the dominant) function.

Voice leading for the ii°⁶ triad in minor keys:

8. **Double the bass note (third factor) or the root, which will be in an upper voice. When approaching or leaving the ii°⁶, make voice leading stepwise whenever possible and avoid melodic tritones.**

Chord 23 (page 121), reprinted here, represents typical use—the bass note (third of the triad) is doubled.

Figure 7.8

Bach: *Wer weiss, wie nahe mir mein Ende* (Who Knows How Near My End May Be), BWV 166

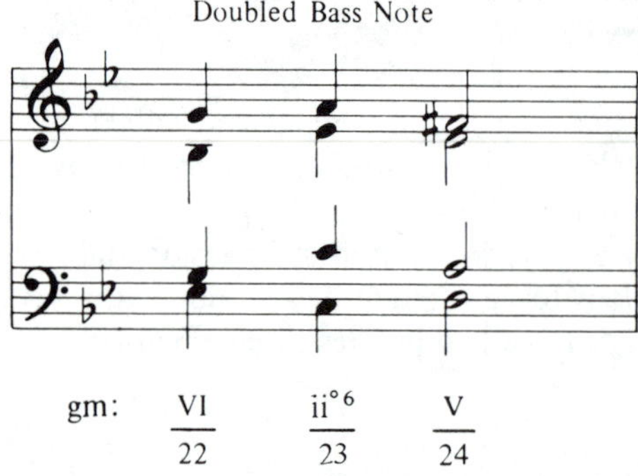

$^6_4$ Chords

The second inversion of any triad should be used with extreme caution because of its unstable nature. The chord contains the interval of a fourth (considered a dissonance to be resolved) above the bass and cannot be used in the functional way that typifies both root position and first-inversion triads. The second-inversion position of the tonic chord is common, but that of other triads is found only occasionally.

Second-inversion triads (particularly the tonic) should be employed in one of the following ways only:

Cadential—The tonic $^6_4$ chord "resolves" to the V chord at the cadence. Used in this manner, the $^6_4$ chord is a decoration of the V chord—with the "6" and "4" of the I^6_4 chord resolving to "5" and "3" of the V chord. The bass note is doubled.

Passing Bass—The bass note (5th factor) of the $^6_4$ acts as a passing tone. The passing bass may be found as a tonic $^6_4$ between the IV and IV^6 chords, or as a dominant $^6_4$ between the I and I^6 chords. The bass note is doubled.

Arpeggiated Bass—The bass note (5th factor) participates in an arpeggiation of the same chord. This usage of $^6_4$ chords occurs occasionally with triads other than the tonic. The bass note is doubled.

Pedal Bass—Also known as *static bass* or *neighboring tone* chords, the bass note (5th factor) is preceded and followed by the same tone and is interspersed between two root positions of the same triad. This type also occurs occasionally with the IV$^6_4$ as well as the tonic. The bass note is doubled.

Figure 7.9

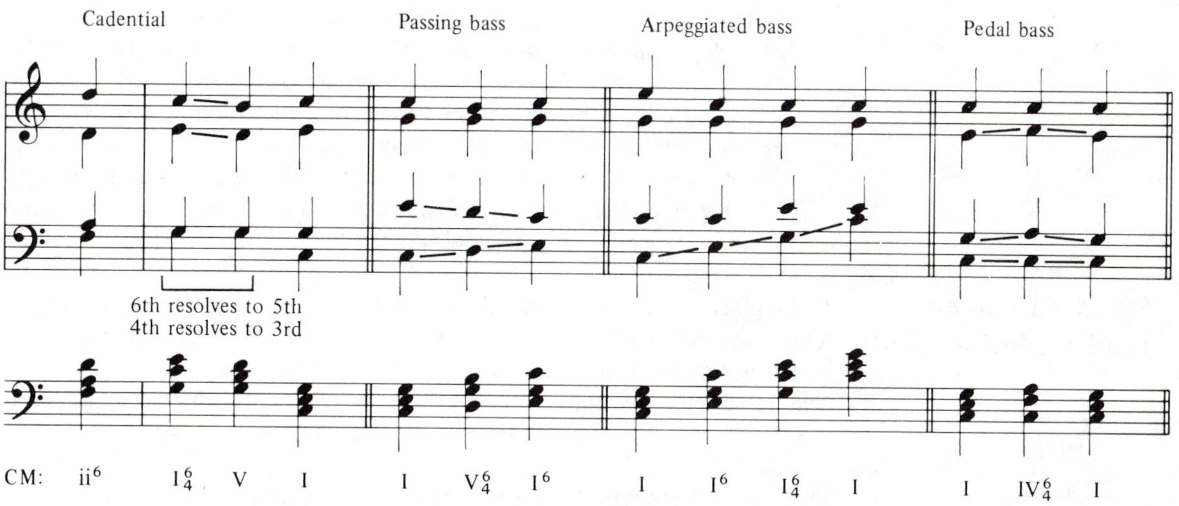

General Rule: The bass of a $^6_4$ chord must be prepared either by step or repetition and must resolve by step or repetition. The exception is the arpeggiated bass.

$^6_4$ Chords in a Cadenza

A *cadenza* is an improvised section of a composition, especially of the Classical period, where performers traditionally display their technical brilliance. Typically found in the concerto, the cadenza is usually inserted between the I$^6_4$ and the V chord at the final cadence of one or more movements, usually the first.

Summary of $^6_4$ Chords: (Stylistic Practice)

9. a. Except under unusual circumstances double the bass note (5th of the chord).

b. Approach and depart from $^6_4$ chords with as few skips as possible.

c. Only in the arpeggiated $^6_4$ chord is the bass note approached or left by skip.

d. Use only the four types of $^6_4$ chords described in this chapter: cadential, passing bass, arpeggiated bass, and pedal bass.

The nine *stylistic practices* discussed so far represent conventional practices in the voice leading of diatonic triads and may be applied to the large majority of cases. However, you may recall that in the five phrases from which the principles were formulated, there were two significant examples (between chords 10–11 and 14–15) where other voice-leading solutions were necessary.

Departures from conventional voice leading occur for a number of reasons, but two of the important ones are:

1. *To accommodate given notes.* A "given" note is one that is predetermined, for example, the notes of a chorale melody or a folk tune that cannot be changed. Voice leading must accommodate such notes and sometimes requires nonstandard practices.
2. *To make inner voices more interesting.* If inner voices are continually sacrificed to make the outer voices (soprano and bass) more interesting, they themselves tend to become dull. Sometimes, especially in chorales, it is extremely difficult to write four interesting voices. However, you should try to make each line as attractive as possible, and this may require an occasional departure from one of the standard voice-leading principles listed here.

Standard Voice-Leading Guidelines

As long as you follow *stylistic practices* 1–9, you need not worry about the following guidelines. But, as you already observed in the chorale phrases by Bach, exceptions do, indeed, occur, and when a phrase cannot be completed with conventional part writing, you will need further guidelines to prevent you from making unstylistic or unmusical mistakes.

Unstylistic Departures

Inviolate

There are no exceptions to these practices under any conditions:

1. **Avoid parallel perfect octaves (P8s), perfect fifths (P5s), or perfect unisons. Successive perfect intervals containing the same pitches are not considered parallel.**
2. **Never double the leading tone (7th) of the scale.**
3. **Do not write pitches out of the range of that particular voice. Keep all four voices within their ranges at all times (see appendix E for voice ranges).**
4. **Avoid the melodic augmented second (A2) and fourth (A4) in all voices.**

Occasionally Broken

These practices should be carefully observed unless particular situations permit no other alternative.

5. **Avoid crossing voices. Keep voices in proper order (from highest to lowest); soprano, alto, tenor, bass. On rare occasions crossing of voices is justified if it improves voice leading.**
6. **Spacing between adjacent voices should not exceed an octave in the three upper voices. The spacing between bass and tenor voices can be of any reasonable interval (never greater than two octaves).**

7. **Do not overlap two adjacent voices more than a whole step. An overlap occurs between two chords when one voice moves above or below the previous pitch of an adjacent voice. (See figure 7.10.) Overlaps of a half- or whole-step may be employed if they improve voice leading.**
8. **Do not leap in the same direction to perfect intervals in the two outer voices (soprano and bass). Such motion, especially in outer voices is thought by some theorists to create the effect of parallel perfect intervals.**
9. **Unequal fifths, P5ths to d5ths or vice-versa, are found in chorale harmonizations, and may be used sparingly. The progression vii°6 to I, under certain circumstances, requires the use of unequal fifths.**
10. **Melodic augmented 2nds and 4ths are almost never found in chorale literature of the eighteenth century.**
    a. **The melodic descending d5th appears sometimes in bass voices, but rarely in the soprano.**
    b. **The d4th is a diatonic interval in the harmonic minor scale (from the third down to seventh scale degrees), and may be written in isolated situations.**
11. **The leading tone should progress upward to tonic when in an outer voice (soprano or bass).**

Figure 7.10 shows examples of the preceding unstylistic departures—inviolate and occasionally broken.

(Workbook-Anthology Assignments 7.1–7.11, pp. 57–72)

Figure 7.10

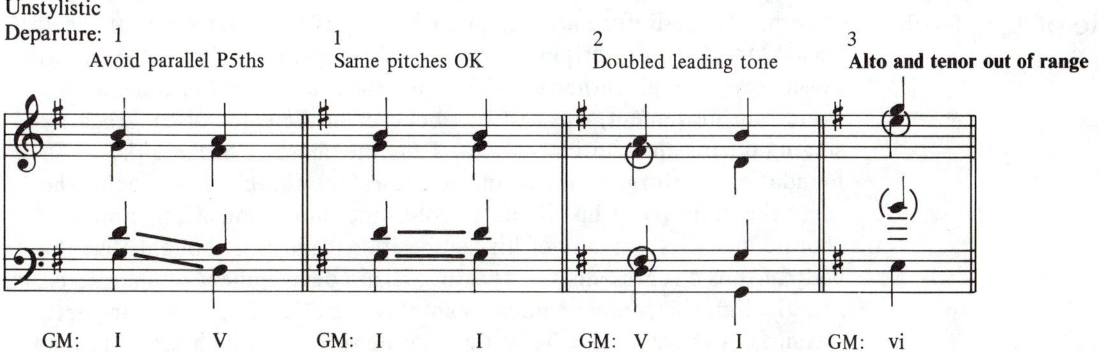

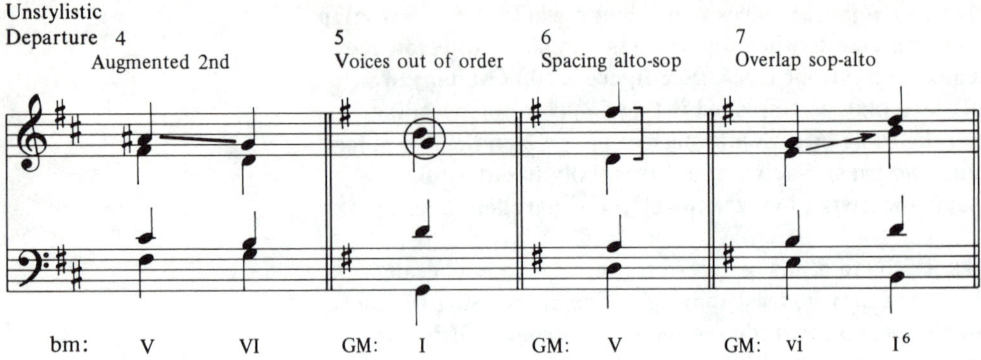

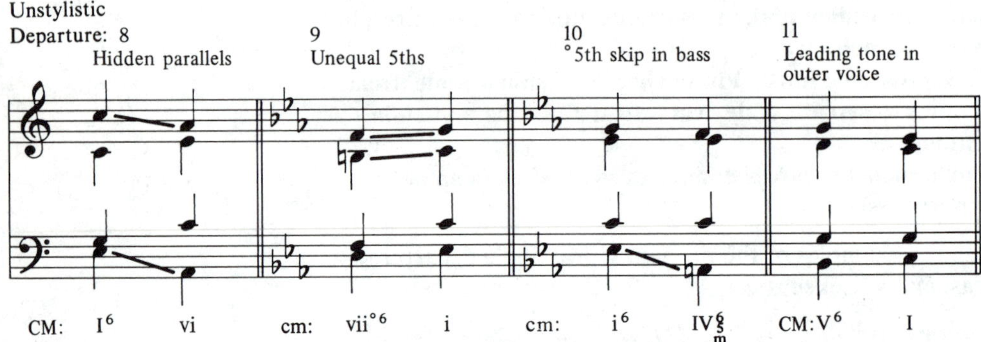

History

The Chorales in the Music of J. S. Bach (1685–1750)

The *chorale* was the congregational hymn in the German Protestant church at the time of Bach. The chorale melodies of the eighteenth century derived from a variety of sources: (1) Latin hymns of the Catholic church, (2) pre-Reformation popular hymns, (3) popular songs of the period, and (4) some original hymn tunes composed by Protestant church musicians. Martin Luther (1483–1546), the founder of the German Protestant movement, was a strong believer in the value of congregational singing during the church services. Thus the chorales became the foundation of liturgical music in the Protestant church. J. S. Bach, who spent the majority of his life as a Protestant church musician, employed chorale melodies in many of his compositions, and it is thought that this body of music represents the apex of artistic development of chorale-based liturgical music. Many of Bach's cantatas are climaxed by a four-part setting of a chorale tune. Thus the chorale settings, which are examined throughout this book, form an important part of the artistic output of Bach and are worthy models for study. They illustrate voice-leading principles that remain valid throughout the "common practice" period, and represent these principals in a relatively simple context, in short compositions that may be sung in class.

REVIEW

The techniques of voice leading allow you to connect chords smoothly, creating parts that are easily singable. These techniques will not, in themselves, allow you to produce interesting music, but they are important standard procedures that you will use many times in future chapters, so it is important that they be thoroughly mastered.

1. Review stylistic practices 1–9 on pages 123–129. These procedures are the heart of the chapter. For each stylistic practice play the musical illustration several times and observe the movement of each voice from chord to chord (figures 7.2–7.9). Restate each stylistic practice in your own words.
2. Play through the examples of unstylistic departures (figure 7.10). These examples show situations you should avoid in connecting chords. In each case identify the problem and relate it to the list of unstylistic departures. Remember that these problems will never occur as long as you follow the stylistic practices, but must be carefully checked in those cases where the stylistic practices cannot be followed.
3. Turn to figure 7.1, select a chorale phrase and cover the lower staff and the list of "stylistic practices involved" with a piece of music paper. Do a harmonic reduction of each chord in the chorale phrase and check your work by comparing it with the analysis staff you covered. Now complete a roman-numeral analysis and check your work with the analysis provided. For each pair of chords identify the stylistic practice involved and check your work with the "stylistic practices involved" line. This process of reconstructing the analysis of a chorale phrase is an invaluable review technique that will cement the ideas of the chapter in your mind. The five chorale phrases provide ample practice to insure thorough learning.
4. Complete assignments that you were not asked to do during your study of the chapter. For those that list the stylistic practice involved, restate that practice before completing each chord. For those that do not list the stylistic practice involved, give the stylistic practice you used to complete the chord.

Test Yourself 7

Each of the examples below demonstrates one of the nine Stylistic practices. Identify the stylistic practice involved.

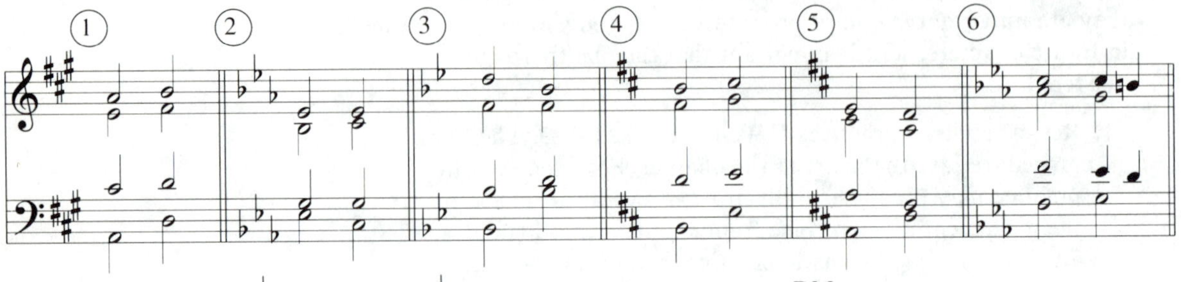

(1) AM: (2) E♭M: (3) B♭M: (4) bm: (5) DM: (6) cm:

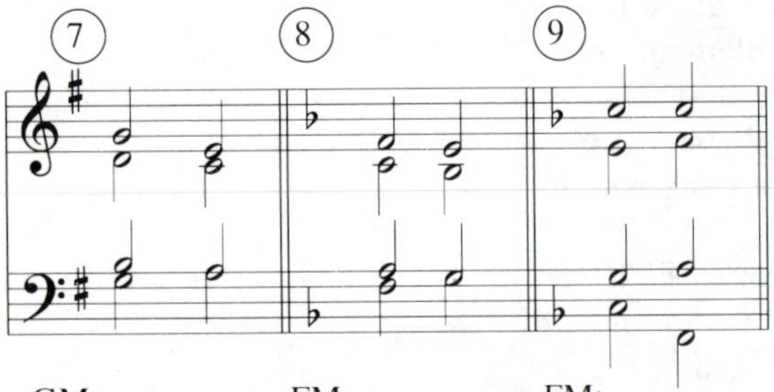

(7) GM: (8) FM: (9) FM:

1. _____
2. _____
3. _____
4. _____
5. _____
6. _____
7. _____
8. _____
9. _____

Each of the examples below demonstrates one of the Unstylistic departures (inviolate). Identify at least one error in each case.

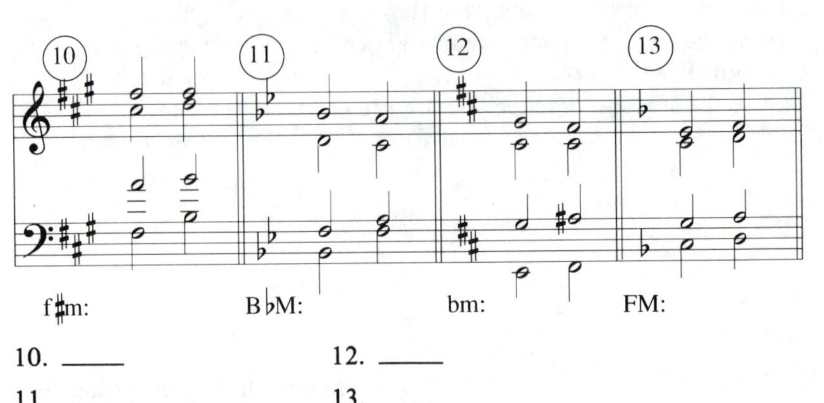

10. _____
11. _____
12. _____
13. _____

CHAPTER 8

Harmonic Progression

Root Relationships
Chord Progressions
Circle of 5ths
Descending 5ths
Ascending 4ths
Ascending 2nds
Descending 3rds
Ascending 3rds
Target Chord

Exposition

Harmonic Progression

In the previous chapters, attention has been focused on the vertical aspects as well as the voice leading of harmony. Now the study will concentrate on harmonic progressions—the way in which chords are selected to succeed each other in a section of music.

The Relationship of Chords

From the Baroque through the Classical and Romantic periods, composers employed the relationship of chords as a principal organizing force. The movement from one chord to another provides an additional impetus to music and contributes a stimulus not found in melody or rhythm alone. Throughout the entire gamut of music involving conventional harmony, the shape of a composition is to a large extent determined, or at least influenced, by the design and fashioning of the chord progressions. As an example, play the two sets of progressions in figure 8.1 and determine which is the most effective. Both have the same soprano melody:

Figure 8.1

Which set are you most accustomed to hearing? The opening triad of the first example seems to lead strongly to the final triad, almost as if it were a predetermined target—which it actually is. The second example seems confusing, lacks direction, and appears to wander about aimlessly.

Root Relationships

Two forces govern the relationship of chords in succession. Together they help form the organization of phrases, periods, sections, and other musical units. These two forces are:

1. The Relationship of Chord Roots to the Prevailing Tonality.

The diatonic pitches of a scale (major or minor) all relate to the tonic—in one way or another. The triads constructed upon those pitches also relate to the tonic triad, which, as you already know, is the strongest of all. The dominant (V) triad relates strongly to the tonic and most frequently resolves to the tonic. How many **V** to **I** progressions have you heard in your lifetime? Ask the same question concerning the **vii°** followed by **iii.** Far fewer certainly. In both progressions (**V** to **I** and **vii°** to **iii**) the interval between the chord roots is the same—a descending P5th. Yet the relationship between the dominant and tonic makes that particular descending P5 a much stronger connection.

2. The Intervals Formed by the Roots of Adjacent Chords

Along with the relationship of chord roots to tonic is the affinity of one chord root for the next. Take the same example, **V** to **I,** a descending P5 relationship. This is a very common occurrence in music. On the other hand, how often does **V** progress to **ii,** for instance? Note in the previous illustration, second set, that one of the progressions was indeed a **V** to **ii,** and we found it confusing: it did not seem to provide direction. So, just from a cursory investigation, it is quite obvious that the relationship of adjacent chord roots does indeed make a difference.

Chord Progressions

So, the two factors, relationship of chord roots to (1) tonic, and (2) to one another, are essential. In planning the movement of chord progressions, the entire musical unit—a phrase, a period, etc.—must be taken into consideration. Each single progression must be analyzed for its relation to the entire phrase or other unit.

Perhaps the most meaningful way to do this is to sort progressions into interval types—that is, according to the interval produced by the roots of adjacent chords. The categories are:

Category	Ascending	Descending	Examples
1	*P4	P5	vi–ii, ii–V, V–I
2	P5	P4	I–V, V–ii, ii–vi
3	M2 or m2	m7 or M7	IV–V, I–ii, V–vi
4	m6 or M6	M3 or m3	I–vi, vi–IV, iv–ii
5	M3 or m3	m6 or M6	I–iii, ii–IV, IV–vi
6	m7 or M7	M2 or m2	ii–I, vi–V, V–IV

The Circle Progression—
iii–vi vi–ii
ii–V V–I

Undoubtedly the most common and the strongest of all harmonic progressions is the circle progression—adjacent roots in ascending 4th or descending 5th relationship. This progression has the capability, more than any other, to determine a tonality, to give direction and thrust, and to provide order in a section or phrase of music. Throughout the remainder of this text, emphasis will be placed on this very important harmonic progression, and a slur will be used to indicate all circle progressions.

The circle progression, like no other, provides direction and drive toward a goal—toward the completion of momentum, from tension to relaxation.

Some characteristics of the *circle progression* follow.

*Underlined progressions or chords occur most often.

1. Very often circle progressions are found in succession—for example, **ii** to **V** or **I,** or even **vi** to **ii** to **V** to **I.** The following example by Beethoven illustrates a complete circle—from tonic, through all seven diatonic chords and a return to the original tonic:

Figure 8.2

*Augmented 4th or diminished 5th.

Note that ascending P4s may be used in place of descending P5s and descending P4s may be used in place of ascending P5s.

2. Circle progressions may be descending (P5th below—**C** down to **F,** down to **B♭**, down to **E♭**, etc.) or ascending (P4th above—**C** up to **F** up to **B♭**, up to **E♭**, etc.). The pitches will be the same in either direction. See figure 8.3:
   a. An extended circle progression (**iii–vi–ii–V–I**) occurs in chords 4 through 8. These are marked with a line connecting the roots of the chords.
   b. The circled notes indicate that they are nonharmonic tones.
   c. The first three chords are **I–IV–V,** helping to set the tonality.
   d. The circle progression begins immediately after the first three chords and continues to its final destination—the tonic triad.
3. Circle progressions usually occur in greater profusion near a cadence. Very often phrases of music end with **ii** to **V** to **I.**
4. The final chord of a circle series (like **ii–V–I**) releases the tension built up during the circle and, because of this property, is called a *target* or *goal.*
5. Not all series of circle progressions come to a halt on the tonic chord. Frequently, composers will end a phrase with the progression **ii** to **V,** thus creating increased tension, since the circle does not complete its movement toward the tonic. The half cadence, when it consists of **ii** to **V,** is an example of such an occurrence. Concerning figure 8.4 (Praise God, Ye Christians, All Together):
   a. The phrase ends with the **ii–V** progression, creating a half-cadence. Because the circle progression (**ii–V**) does not (in this phrase) proceed to its final destination (the tonic triad, **I**), tension is not released and depends on the next phrase for final resolution. In fact, full release is withheld (prolonged) for two more phrases (not printed here).
   b. Note also that a **vi–ii–V** circle progression does exist from chords 5 to 8, but a **I** triad is placed between the **vi** and the **ii** triads. This is an example of a continuing cycle progression that has been temporarily interrupted. The interruption is shown by a dotted line.

Figure 8.3

Bach: *Straf' mich nicht in deinem Zorn* (Punish Me Not in Thy Wrath), BWV 115

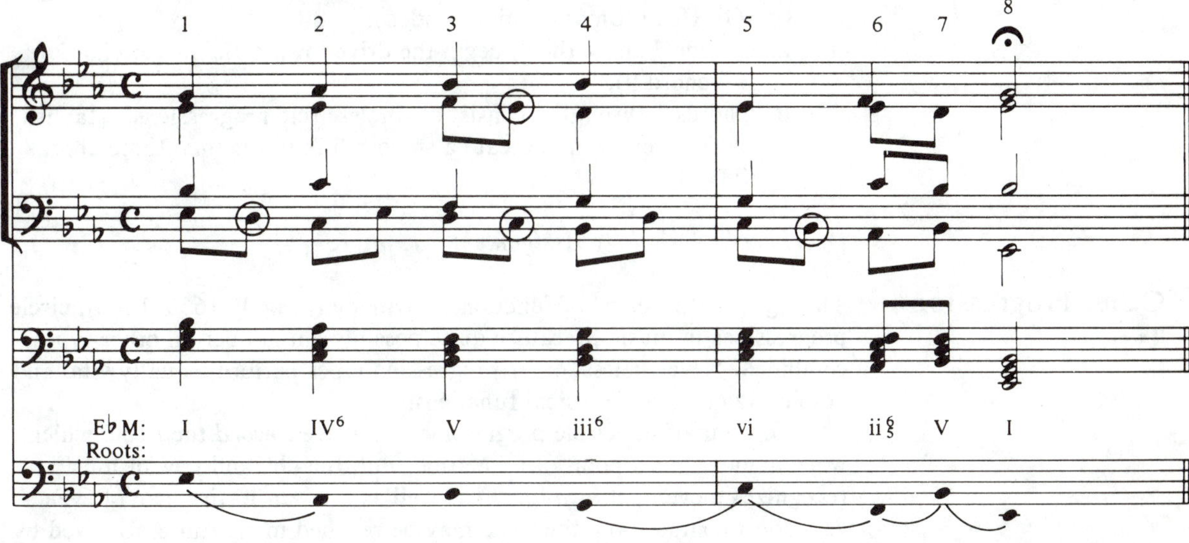

Figure 8.4

Bach: *Lobt Gott, ihr Christen, allzugleich* (Praise God, Ye Christians, All Together), BWV 151

6. Many phrases open with a mixture of circle and noncircle types, and, as the cadence approaches, a strong succession of circle progressions leads convincingly to the final cadence, as illustrated by Bach in figure 8.5 (Oh Head, Bloody and Wounded):
   a. Chords 7 and 8 (**ii–V**) begin the drive toward the target chord (**I**—chord 9).
   b. Chords 1 through 6 consist of single-circle progressions, establish the key center, and create a smooth link to the final three chords (**ii–V–I**).

(Workbook-Anthology Assignment 8.1, pp. 73–74)

Other Progression Types

Throughout the period of functional harmony (roughly 1650–1880), circle progressions in music literature quite possibly outnumber all other types combined. Nevertheless, other progression types perform equally vital and absolutely necessary musical functions.

We think of the circle progression as a drive *toward* the tonic, which, when achieved, is a point of relaxation. But, the ebb and flow of music recognizes movement *away from* as well as *toward*. In the span of even a very short composition, the tonic may be reached many times, followed by a motion away and another approach toward the goal (tonic).

Ascending 5ths and Descending 4ths

Most Common: **I–V and IV–I**
Others: **V–ii, vi–iii, iii–I, ii–vi**

This so-called backward motion, especially the **I–V,** (moving away from tonic) is used by composers as an alternative to the circle progression—relief from the constant motion toward tonic is essential.

Ascending 2nds

Most Common: **IV–V, V–vi, I–ii**
Others: **ii–iii, iii–iv**

This progression is employed often to prepare a switch from the circle, **I–IV,** to another circle, **V–I.** The resulting progression is **I–IV–V–I,** and is often considered as a substitute for **I–ii–V–I.**

Concerning figure 8.6:

a. Chord 1 to 2 (**I–V**) illustrates a typical example of an *ascending 5th* progression—departure from tonic.
b. Chord 3 to 4 (**I–ii**) shows how an *ascending 2nd* prepares a switch from one circle (chords 2 to 3) to another (chords 4 through 6).
c. Circle progressions, dominating the phrase, are marked with slurs.

Figure 8.5

Bach: *O Haupt voll Blut und Wunden* (Oh Head, Bloody and Wounded), BWV 271

Figure 8.6

Tchaikovsky: Symphony no. 5 in E minor, op. 64 (2nd Movement)

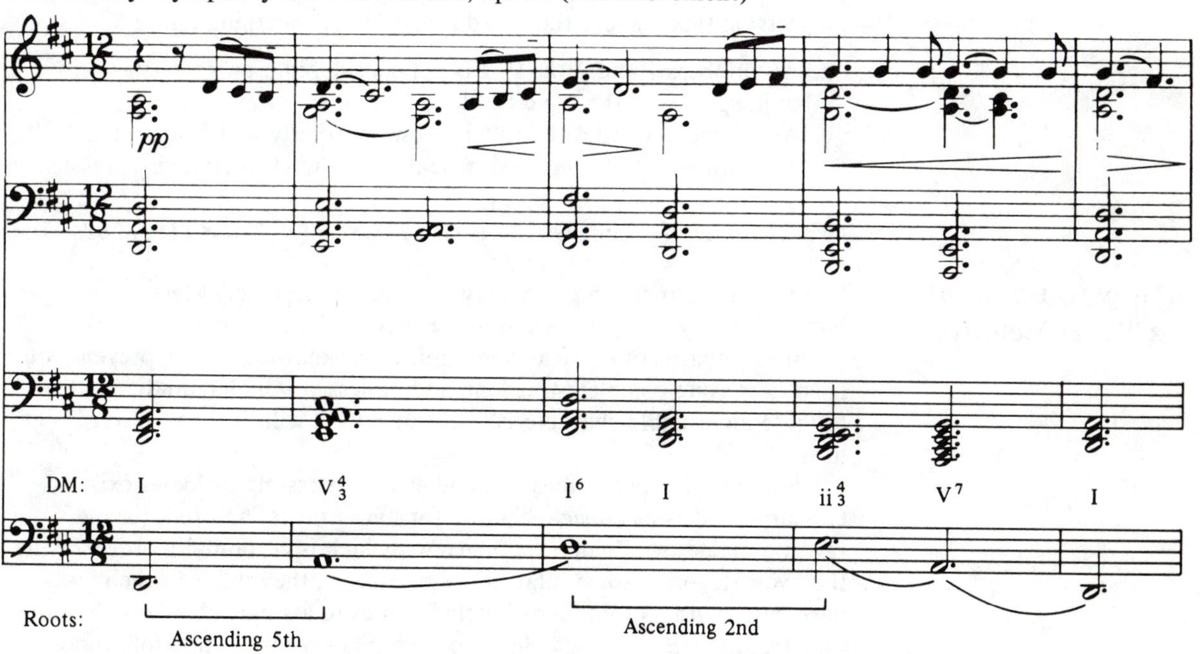

Descending 3rds

Most Common: **I–vi, vi–IV, IV–ii**
Others: **iii–I, V–iii**

I–vi, vi–IV, and **IV–ii,** are progressions that find applications (1) immediately after the tonic (**I–vi**), (2) as a means to get from a completed circle to the beginning of the next (**IV–ii**), or (3) occasionally in series (**I–vi–IV–ii**)—see figure 8.7.

The vii° Triad

Since the **vii°** triad contains two pitches (root and 3rd) in common with the V triad (3rd and 5th), **vii°** is closely related to dominant function and should be so considered. Thus, the progression **vii°⁶–I,** although weaker, functions for all practical purposes as a **V–I.** It is appropriate to include the usual slur associated with circle progressions, but a dotted slur (‿‿‿) indicates its weaker nature.

The Tonic $^6_4$

The second-inversion tonic triad, especially in the cadence formula **I^6_4–V–I,** reflects little of the stable quality normally associated with the tonic function, and should for all practical purposes be ignored as a chord progression. In analysis, the chord may be shown as a decoration of the **V** chord that follows it.

Repeated Chords

In instances where the same triad is repeated or recurs in a different position, no progression takes place. For purposes of analysis, indicate both triads and position (root–1st–2nd–inversions). However, in assessing the progression type, ignore the chord repetition. Concerning figure 8.8:

a. At numbers 1 and 2 the **I^6–I** is not considered a progression—only a prolongation of the tonic triad.
b. At numbers 3 and 4 the **$vii^{\circ 6}$** is shown correctly with a dotted slur.
c. At number 6 a **I^6_4** is ignored, revealing the **ii^6–V–I** circle progression.

(Workbook-Anthology Assignments 8.2–8.3, p. 74, and 8.11, pp. 83–85)

How to Harmonize a Tonal Melody

Ultimately, harmonizing a melody is a matter of personal taste. Nevertheless, while you have some leeway in the selection of chords, certain standards of musical communication, known as *style,* prevent you from exercising complete freedom; and, unless you understand and adhere to these identifiable characteristics, your efforts will likely be inconsistent in style.

Some of the most endearing and easily accessible melodies exist in two large bodies of music—chorale (or hymn tunes) and folk (or old favorite melodies). Some experience with each is certainly in order. While the two categories are similar in some respects, they differ in their harmonic rhythms (number of melody notes to a single chord). A hymn tune traditionally uses one chord to each melody note, while folk tunes

Figure 8.7

Bach: *Der Tag, der ist so freudenreich* (This Day Is So Joyful), BWV 294

Figure 8.8

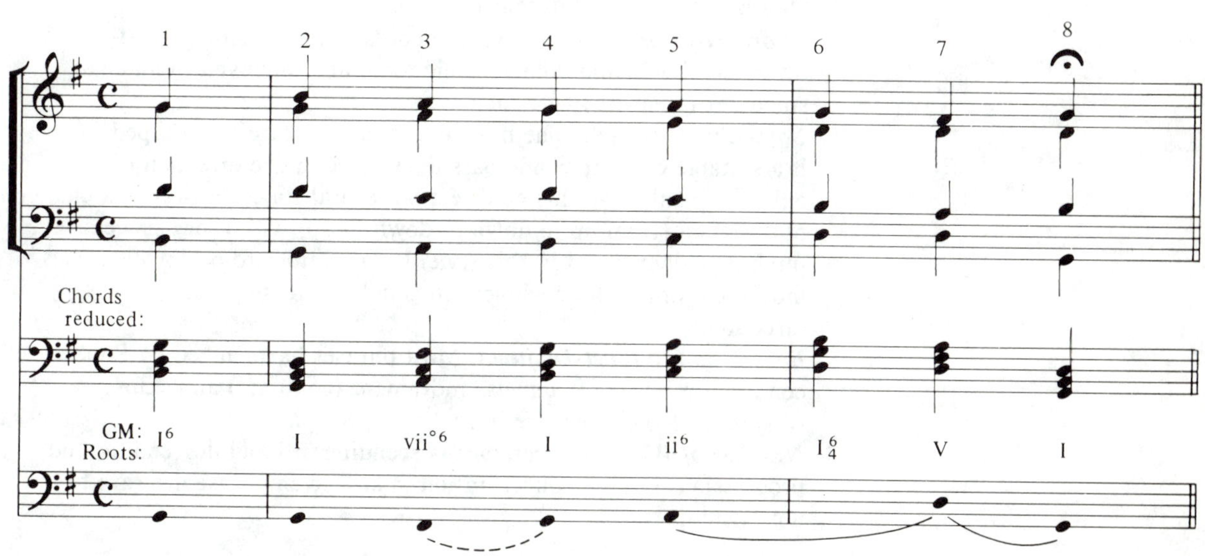

often use one chord for each measure. So, let us first harmonize a chorale phrase, then we can transfer some of that information to a well-known folk melody.

Harmonizing a Chorale Phrase

Earlier in this chapter several examples of chorale phrases were included. The chorales, harmonized by Bach, represent a large body of respected literature. Furthermore, in the learning stage of development, it is quite appropriate to imitate the harmonic construction of these magnificent works. After your skills have matured, individual choice and creative selectivity may be tested. However, for the duration of this chapter, try to make your chorale harmonization as much like those of Bach as possible. From observing these chorale phrases, a number of logical patterns develop, and these should be taken into account as the task of harmonization takes place.

1. *Cadence.* Half (**I–V, IV–V,** or **ii–V**) or authentic (**V–I**) cadences are employed to harmonize the final two notes of the melody.
2. *Circle Progressions.* Circle progressions should appear prominently and should highlight each phrase. These progressions are more often longer and more abundant near the cadence than at the beginning of the phrase.
3. *Harmonic Rhythm.* Harmonize each melody note with one chord even though it is not unusual for a chord to be repeated. Adjacent repeated chords are often in different positions.
4. *Chord Positions.* Seldom are all chords in root position. First-inversion chords and nonharmonic tones are employed to make a smoother (stepwise) bass melody.
5. *Bass-Line Direction.* The bass line should be carefully shaped to give it a suitable contour. Some bass lines move in one direction (down only or up only), or change direction several times. However, a change of direction (from up to down or down to up) with every successive pitch is seldom found in this style. Isolated upward or downward movement of a half or whole step is not considered a change of direction.
6. *Bass-Line Conjunct-Disjunct.* Most phrases harmonized by Bach contain a mixture of stepwise movement (conjunct) and skips (disjunct). Exceptions are infrequent.
7. *Number of Weak Progressions.* Ascending 3rd and descending 2nd progressions in high concentration in any given phrase are rare to nonexistent.

Three harmonizations (of the same melody) are printed here for comparison. Play each one so you will be familiar with its sound, then criticize each. Only one of the three is by Bach.

Figure 8.9

The following are a set of conclusions about the three preceding examples. You must learn to criticize your own work in this way to develop skill in the harmonization of melodies. Remember also that music analysis, like the music itself, is open to differing viewpoints. Do you see any below that you question?

1. *Cadence.*
   No. 1—No recognized cadence.
   No. 2—Authentic cadence.
   No. 3—Authentic cadence.
   Conclusion: Numbers 2 and 3 have acceptable cadences.

2. *Circle Progressions.* (indicated with slurs)
   No. 1—No circle progressions.
   No. 2—Three circle progressions.
   No. 3—Three circle progressions.
   Conclusion: Numbers 2 and 3 contain circle progressions. With no circle progressions, Number 1 is atypical.
3. *Harmonic Rhythm.*
   No. 1—Each melody note harmonized separately. One repeated harmony.
   No. 2—Each melody note harmonized separately. One repeated harmony.
   No. 3—Each melody note harmonized separately. One repeated harmony.
   Conclusion: All three are suitable from this standpoint.
4. *Chord Positions.*
   No. 1—All chords are in root position, except 1.
   No. 2—Contains three chords in first inversion.
   No. 3—All chords are in root position.
   Conclusion: Numbers 1 and 3 fail to take advantage of the variety afforded by a mixture of positions.
5. *Bass-Line Direction.*
   No. 1—A well-defined, two-directional (down-up) shape.
   No. 2—Three-directional (up-down-up) shape.
   No. 3—Four-directional (up-down-up-down) shape.
   Conclusion: Numbers 1 and 2 have an acceptable shape. Number 3 is marginally acceptable.
6. *Bass-Line Conjunct-Disjunct.*
   No. 1—Entirely stepwise (conjunct).
   No. 2—A mixture of steps (conjunct) and skips (disjunct).
   No. 3—Entirely made up of skips (disjunct).
   Conclusion: Number 2 is the more natural—mixture of steps (conjunct) and skips (disjunct).
7. *Number of Weak Progressions.*
   No. 1—Contains three descending 2nd and one ascending third progressions.
   No. 2—No weak progressions.
   No. 3—No weak progressions. (Same progressions as Number 2.)
   Conclusion: Only Number 1 contains a high concentration of weak progressions (four out of a total of seven).

To summarize:

1. All three versions appear acceptable from the standpoint of harmonic rhythm and bass-line direction.
2. However, in example 1, the cadence is nonexistent, circle progressions are entirely absent, and a high concentration of weak progressions is present. Example 1 is not an acceptable harmonization.

3. Criticizing example 3, the bass line is too disjunct—there is not a single stepwise movement in the bass. Also, all chords are in root position. Thus, example 3 is inferior to example 2, which passes all seven critical analyses. Example 2 is the first phrase of Bach's harmonization of *Was Gott tut, das ist wohlgetan* (What God Does Is Well Done), BWV 69.

Harmonization of Folk and Familiar Melodies

The suggestions (page 144) for harmonizing a chorale melody also apply here. The most important difference is the harmonic rhythm. While in in most chorale or hymn tunes each note of the melody is harmonized separately (partly because of the slow stately tempo and partly due to traditions of previous style periods), folk or familiar melodies imply a slower harmonic rhythm—often one or two chords per measure.

The following suggestions for harmonizing a well-known melody are in addition to those given for chorale melodies and are related primarily to harmonic rhythm. Remember also that these are only general guidelines and are not to be interpreted as immutable. Special musical situations may render any one of them invalid. With your intuition alone, and no suggestions, you might be able to construct excellent harmonizations on your own. But, even if that is so, it is important to know the factors that influence a good harmonization.

Determining the Harmonic Rhythm

A. *Metric Implications.* Metric accents play an important part in the style of folk or old favorite melodies. Change harmony from weak to strong beats:

Meter (Change harmony between)	**Weak Beat** (and)	**Strong Beat**
2/4	2	1 (next meas.)
4/4	4	1 (next meas.)
4/4	2	3
3/4	3	1 (next meas.)
6/8	6	1 (next meas.)
6/8	3	4

B. *Skips.* Of course, harmonic changes may be made anywhere that is appropriate, but two melody notes forming a skip are usually expected to be part of the prevailing harmony, and thus consonant.

1. *Skips without Change of Harmony.* When you find skips in a melody, look carefully to determine whether the two notes forming the skip could both be part of a single important triad (**I, IV, ii,** or **V**). If so, then that harmony is implied by the melody and should be selected.

2. *Skips with Change of Harmony.* If the two notes forming a skip do not fit into a single important harmony, a change of harmony is implied—all other forces being equal.

C. *Steps with Change of Harmony.* Changes in harmony may take place almost at will during stepwise passages providing the metric placement (weak to strong beats) is observed.

D. *Nonharmonic Tones.* Changes in harmony almost never occur at the point where nonharmonic tones are present in the melody.

To test the above general guidelines, figure 8.10 is shown below with four different harmonizations. Play each version, and determine which you think is the most acceptable.

Figure 8.10

Assessment of the Four Versions

Version 1: Fails to fulfill letter A (above); change harmony from weak to strong beats. In numbers 1 through 3 (above the melody), the change of harmony from beat 2 (weak) to beat 3 (weak) is unnecessary and creates a mild harmonic syncopation that is not in keeping with the straightforward nature of the melody. Also, the two final chords (**ii–I**^{6}) do not create any of the established cadences (authentic, half, plagal, or deceptive) that are a part of the style.

Version 2: At numbers 1–3 the three changes of harmony within one measure (at the prescribed tempo) might be acceptable for a chorale melody, but they create a busy harmonic effect—not characteristic for harmonizations of folk melodies. Also, the attempt to harmonize the sixteenth note between numbers 7 and 8 is an infraction of letter D above, and causes the note at number 8 to be harmonized with a chord that does not contain the melody note D.

Version 3: This version is simple, direct, and in keeping with typical harmonizations of such melodies. It does not violate any of the suggestions given above. It makes no attempt to interject the personality of the arranger, and serves simply to highlight the qualities of the melody itself.

Version 4: Perhaps the least effective harmonization of the four, version 4 attempts to harmonize the 16th notes consistently, creating a harmonic rhythm faster than is called for—eleven harmonic changes in a melody of only fourteen notes! The cadence (9–10) attempts to alter the tonal center (C) and creates a movement to A minor, which is not inherent in the melody itself. If this version were part of a composition in which novel variations were the norm, it might be acceptable, but as a natural and uncomplicated harmonization, it falls far short.

(Workbook-Anthology Assignments 8.4–8.10, pp. 75–82, and 8.12–8.15, pp. 86–89)

History

Renaissance Period (1450–1600)

The Baroque, Classical, and Romantic periods are generally assumed to be the exclusive domain of harmonic progression, that is, vertical sonorities (chords) functioning as identifiable harmonies. Nevertheless, a Renaissance composer, Adrian Willaert (1490–1562), in a stylistic environment known primarily for pure modal polyphony, produced some early examples of what we now know as circle progressions. Although these compositions were probably of an experimental nature, the seeds of the ensuing Baroque period were indeed sown.

Baroque Period (1600–1750)

The Baroque period brought forth the tonal system, and with it came functional harmony. The early seventeenth century witnessed a gradual shift from modality (use of modes) to tonality (key systems). Equal temperament, born in the Renaissance period, and applied first to fretted instruments, began to gain a measure of acceptance in the Baroque period. Chord progressions, and especially circle progressions, are clearly in evidence in the works of early representative composers such as Samuel Scheidt (1587–1654) and Claudio Monteverdi (1567–1643). The middle and latter part of the Baroque period brought functional harmony to a high level of sophistication.

Classical Period (1750–1825)

Continuing the practices of the Baroque period, harmonic progression is an essential parameter of music written during this period.

Romantic Period (1825–1900)

While the style of the Romantic period is characterized by increased chromaticism and a freer attitude toward musical structure, harmonic progressions continue as an important element of the period. The last quarter of the century (about 1875–1900) marks the gradual decline of functional harmonic progression.

Post-Romantic and Impressionistic Period (1875–1920)

Here composers, such as Ravel (1875–1937), Richard Strauss (1864–1949), and Mahler (1860–1911) continued to rely heavily on traditional harmonic progression; but others, such as Debussy (1862–1918), Satie (1866–1925), and Scriabin (1872–1915) looked for alternatives—and found them.

Contemporary Period (1920–Present)

Some traces of functional harmony can be recognized here and there in twentieth century music, but for the most part, such examples are not intrinsic to the period.

Jazz and Popular Music (1900–Present)

Most jazz and popular music is structured around standard harmonic progressions (which jazz musicians refer to as "changes"). The most common of these progressions is the twelve-bar blues progression. The table in figure 8.11 shows common variants of this progression. Notice that the chords are all notated as major triads with a minor 7th (see chapter 9), which is typical of the blues style.

Figure 8.11

Standard Twelve-Bar Blues Progressions:

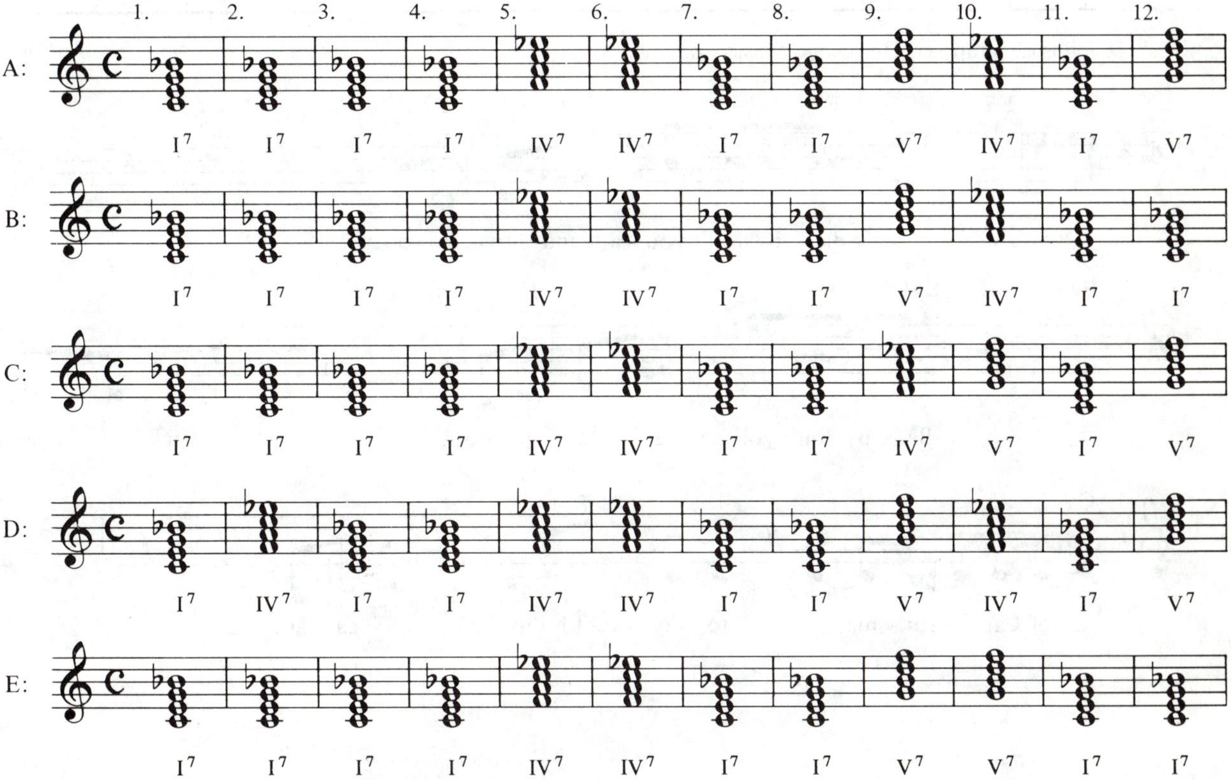

	1.	2.	3.	4.	5.	6.	7.	8.	9.	10.	11.	12.
A:	I^7	I^7	I^7	I^7	IV^7	IV^7	I^7	I^7	V^7	IV^7	I^7	V^7
B:	I^7	I^7	I^7	I^7	IV^7	IV^7	I^7	I^7	V^7	IV^7	I^7	I^7
C:	I^7	I^7	I^7	I^7	IV^7	IV^7	I^7	I^7	IV^7	V^7	I^7	V^7
D:	I^7	IV^7	I^7	I^7	IV^7	IV^7	I^7	I^7	V^7	IV^7	I^7	V^7
E:	I^7	I^7	I^7	I^7	IV^7	IV^7	I^7	I^7	V^7	V^7	I^7	I^7

"Sweet Home Chicago," recorded by Robert Johnson in 1936, is a blues song using the first chord progression (A):

Figure 8.12

Robert Johnson, composer, Horoscope Music Co.

REVIEW

The technique of melody harmonization is at the heart of this chapter, and the central importance of the circle of 5th progression (circle progression) in achieving a satisfactory harmonization cannot be overemphasized.

1. Choose a few pieces from a collection of traditional and patriotic songs, a hymnal, or some similar music. Name the root of each chord. (You may not be able to do a roman-numeral analysis of the entire piece because the chord vocabulary may not have been covered yet.) Mark each example of a circle progression you discover. Try to find examples of several circle progressions in succession. How often do these progressions reach the tonic chord as a target?
2. Examine the five chorale phrases in chapter 7 (figure 7.1) and mark each example of a circle progression you discover. Note every case of ascending 2nd and descending 3rd progressions. How many examples of progressions other than circle progressions, ascending 2nd, and descending 3rd progressions are used in these phrases?
3. Review the sections on the vii° and the second-inversion tonic triad on pages 127–129. Remember that the leading-tone triad is closely related to the dominant and counts as a weaker circle progression when it progresses to the tonic chord. The tonic triad in second inversion is usually a decoration of the dominant chord that follows immediately.
4. Practice harmonizing chorale melodies, using examples from the assignments or familiar hymn tunes. Try to use as many circle progressions as possible in your harmonizations. Remember that each phrase must end with one of the standard cadences.
5. This would be a good opportunity to review the materials of chapters 5, 6, and 7, which you will need to have clearly in mind as you work on your chorale harmonizations. Music theory is a cumulative subject, and you must constantly review previous materials to keep them fresh in your mind.

Test Yourself 8

Below are several phrases from a chorale setting by Otto Nicolai (1810–1849) with each pair of chords identified by a number.

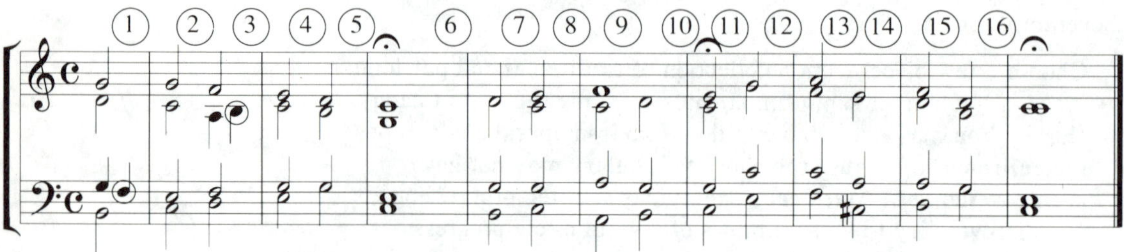

1. List all the progressions according to type as follows:
   a. Circle progressions
   b. Descending third progressions
   c. Ascending second progressions
   d. Other progressions
2. What conclusion could you reach by studying the tabulation of progression types in question 1?
3. On the following page is a chorale melody with possible chords for a harmonization (only one choice is given for the first note of the melody and the final note of each phrase). Mark all possible circle progressions with a line between the roman numerals. Mark all weaker circle progressions with a dotted line. Choose a single chord for each quarter note that takes advantage of the maximum number of circle progressions. If no circle progression is possible, try to choose an ascending 2nd or descending 3rd progression. You should have at least twelve circle progressions in your harmonization.
4. Compare your chord choices with the setting of this chorale by Bach. (Bach's setting uses 7th chords and some chromatic harmony that you have not studied as yet.) How often does your chord choice agree with that of Bach?

O Ewigkeit, du Donnerwort (Oh Eternity, Thou Word of Thunder), BWV 20

CHAPTER 9

The Dominant 7th Chord

Figured Bass Symbols
V⁷ in Major Keys
V⁷ in Minor Keys
Inversions
Voice Leading
Resolutions

Exposition

Dominant 7th Chord

The *dominant 7th chord* is a diatonic 7th chord built on the fifth scale degree of the major, harmonic minor, and melodic minor scales. The major triad (root, 3rd, 5th) and minor 7th (from root to 7th) create a distinctive sound elsewhere found diatonically only as $\mathbf{IV^7}$ in the melodic minor and $\mathbf{VII^7}$ in the natural minor. Since the $\mathbf{IV^7}$ is relatively rare, and the $\mathbf{VII^7}$ sounds like a dominant 7th when it progresses to **III** (natural minor), the major triad and minor 7th interval from root to 7th are universally linked to the dominant function.

The $\mathbf{V^7}$ is found almost as frequently as the dominant triad. The following illustration from a Beethoven concerto is typical of the widespread use of the $\mathbf{V^7}$.

Figure 9.1

Beethoven: Piano Concerto no. 2 in B-flat, op. 19 (3rd Movement)

Inversions of the V^7

The various positions of the $\mathbf{V}^7$ are illustrated in figure 9.2. The numbers you see designate the various positions of the chord and indicate intervals *above the bass note.* Interpret the first example in the chart as:

7 = Interval of a diatonic 7th above bass
5 = Interval of a diatonic 5th above bass
3 = Interval of a diatonic 3rd above bass

Viewing the chart you will see that the 7 (7th above G) is F, the 5 (5th above G) is D, and the 3 (3rd above G) is B.

Baroque-period composers often deleted some of the full set of three numbers to make manuscript copying less tedious when writing continuo parts. In figure 9.2 the column on the right shows the symbols as simplified for conventional use. This conventional system is used throughout the text.

Resolution of V^7

Circle Progression

The $\mathbf{V}^7$ in a circle progression moves to **I.** This is by far the most common resolution for $\mathbf{V}^7$ chords and is perhaps the most frequently used progression in all music containing functional harmony. The following is important information regarding the $\mathbf{V}^7$ in a circle progression.

1. *The 7th of the V^7 resolves down one scale step* to the third factor of the tonic triad. The 7th may be in any voice (soprano, alto, tenor, bass).
2. *When the 7th is the bass note* ($\mathbf{V}^4_2$), it must resolve to third factor of **I,** and *the tonic triad must automatically be in first inversion* ($\mathbf{I}^6$).
3. In figure 9.3, you will observe that if you will *first* part-write the seventh factor, the three remaining voices move to notes of the **I** triad, as described in stylistic practices 1 and 2, on page 123. In the first-, second-, and third-inversion examples *the common tone (G) is retained* in the same voice (like stylistic practice 1). In the root example, *all three upper voices move in similar motion* to the nearest chord tones (stylistic practice 2).
4. In all four examples, *all four factors of the V^7 are present.* In unusual instances an *incomplete V^7* may be necessary. In such cases *omit the 5th factor.*

Figure 9.2

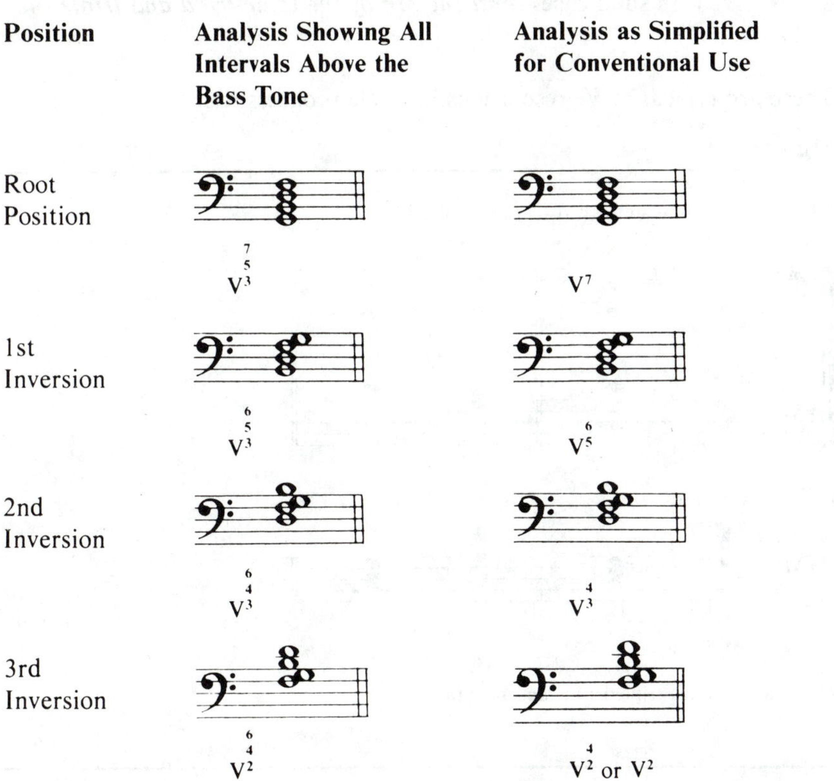

Position
Analysis Showing All Intervals Above the Bass Tone
Analysis as Simplified for Conventional Use
Root Position
$V^{7}_{5}{}_{3}$
V^{7}
1st Inversion
$V^{6}_{5}{}_{3}$
V^{6}_{5}
2nd Inversion
$V^{6}_{4}{}_{3}$
V^{4}_{3}
3rd Inversion
$V^{6}_{4}{}_{2}$
V^{4}_{2} or V^{2}

Figure 9.3

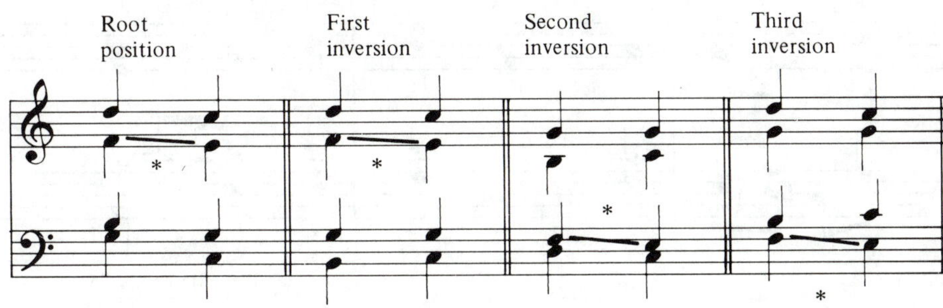

Chords reduced to simple position:

5. In figure 9.4, the 7th of the chord and the leading tone are both resolved. In such cases *omit the 5th of the tonic triad and triple the root.*

These are typical of **V**^{7} resolutions in circle progressions.

Figure 9.4

*Tonic triad has tripled root and no 5th

Figure 9.5

Bach: *Es ist Genúg* (It Is Enough), BWV 60

Joplin: "Maple Leaf Rag"
7th resolves down
Chords reduced to simple position:
Root descends P5
A♭M: V6/5 I V7 I
Schubert: Erlkönig, D. 328
(Erl King)
Est ist der Vat - er mit sein - em Kind;
7th resolves
7th resolves
Root descends P5
cm: V7 i B♭M: I6/4 V7 I

Noncircle Progressions with Resolution

Sometimes a V^7 is diverted temporarily from its normal resolution to **I.** A typical example is $\mathbf{V^7}$ to **vi** or **VI** (see figure 9.6). The triad roots are the interval of a second apart, and, except for the 7th factor, the remaining three voices follow stylistic practice No. 4 on page 124. The **vi** chords contain a doubled 3rd factor.

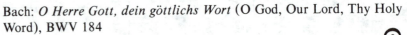

Figure 9.6

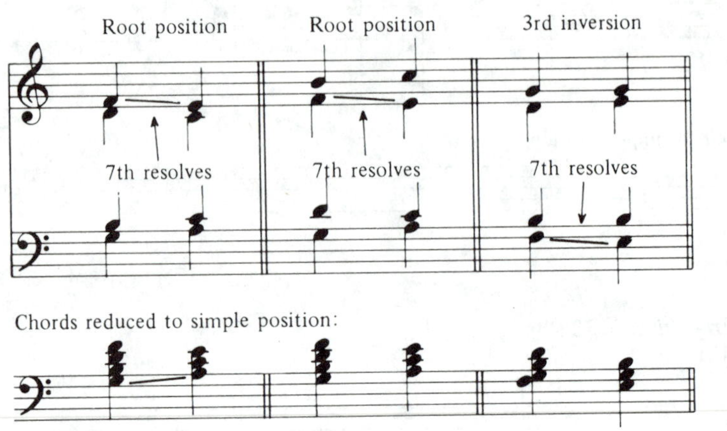

Bach: *O Herre Gott, dein göttlichs Wort* (O God, Our Lord, Thy Holy Word), BWV 184

Nonresolution of 7th Factor

In rare instances the 7th of the V^7 chord cannot be resolved. No single voice-leading recommendation can be given because so few examples exist and no single voice-leading pattern emerges. Treat each occurrence as a special case, and follow those unstylistic departures (pages 130–132) that apply.

Figure 9.7

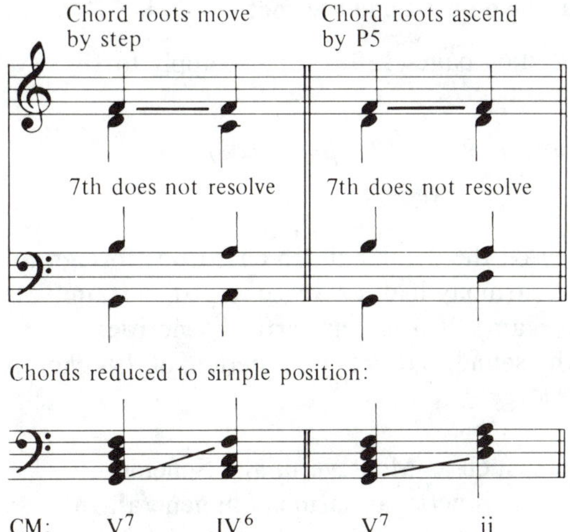

The following illustration by Mozart shows the **iv**^{6} triad as an embellishment of the $\mathbf{V^7}$.

Figure 9.8

Stylistic Practices for Voice Leading in V^7 Chords

We now add the following *stylistic practices* to the list that begins on page 123 (also see Appendix C):

10. **Resolve the 7th of the** V^7 **chord down one scale degree in the same voice.** In the few instances where the resolution tone is not present, either keep the 7th as a common tone or move it by the smallest melodic interval possible.
11. **All four factors of the** V^7 **are usually present, but for smoothness of voice leading, the fifth may be omitted and the root doubled.**

Unstylistic departures, listed on pages 130–132, also apply to $\mathbf{V^7}$ chords and inversions.

(Workbook-Anthology Assignments 9.1–9.12, pp. 91–108)

History

Renaissance Period (1450–1600)

In music of the Renaissance period the dominant 7th chord was foreign to the style. Yet, while functional harmony had not yet emerged, certain nonharmonic tones gradually became "frozen" as vertical sonorities (combinations of tones), and the sound, but not the function, of 7th chords came into existence.

Baroque Period (1600–1750)

Early Baroque period composers, such as Monteverdi and Scheidt, introduced the V^7 chord, as well as functional harmony in general. In early seventeenth-century music, examples of dominant 7th chords are scarce and are treated very conservatively. In figure 9.9, for example, the seventh is prepared and resolved as a suspension, clearly indicating its dissonant status.

As the Baroque period progressed V^7 chords became more plentiful and an integral part of the style.

Classical Period (1750–1825)

The Classical period saw a continued use of the dominant 7th chord without a marked difference in treatment.

Romantic Period (1825–1900)

In the Romantic period, consistent use of dominant 7th chords was perpetuated, but freer voice-leading became more prevalent. In figure 9.10, note the descending nature of the bass and the absence of resolution. No roman-numeral analysis is provided because dominant function (resolution to tonic) has been temporarily suspended. The 7th factor does not resolve in any of the three major-minor 7th chords, showing that the chord had achieved near-consonant status.

Figure 9.9

Monteverdi: *Lasciatemi Morire* (Oh, Let Me Die) from *Lamento d'Arianna*

Figure 9.10

Chopin: Mazurka in F minor, op. 68, no. 4

Post-Romantic and Impressionistic Period (1875–1920)

As the Romantic movement in Europe waned, so did the functional use of the dominant 7th chord (as well as functional harmony in general). Chords weighted more heavily with dissonance (9ths, 11ths, and 13ths) became common, and as divergent musical styles multiplied during this period, the major-minor 7th chord declined in use as dominant function.

Contemporary Period (1920–Present)

For most music written for performance in concert halls or opera houses, the V^7 chord ceased to exist except for those styles that make conscious use of functional harmony.

Jazz and Popular Music (1900–Present)

Throughout both Europe and America, music in the popular vein continued to use functional harmony. Folk and popular songs, as well as the earlier forms of jazz and blues, were laced with dominant 7th chords. Even into the 1960s the popular culture—folk and popular songs, mainstream jazz, and blues—had changed little in regard to the dominant 7th. Indeed, at the present moment, V^7 is alive and well in the hands of rock and rock-derivative styles, as shown by the first phrase of the Beatles' "Hey Jude" (figure 9.11).

Figure 9.11

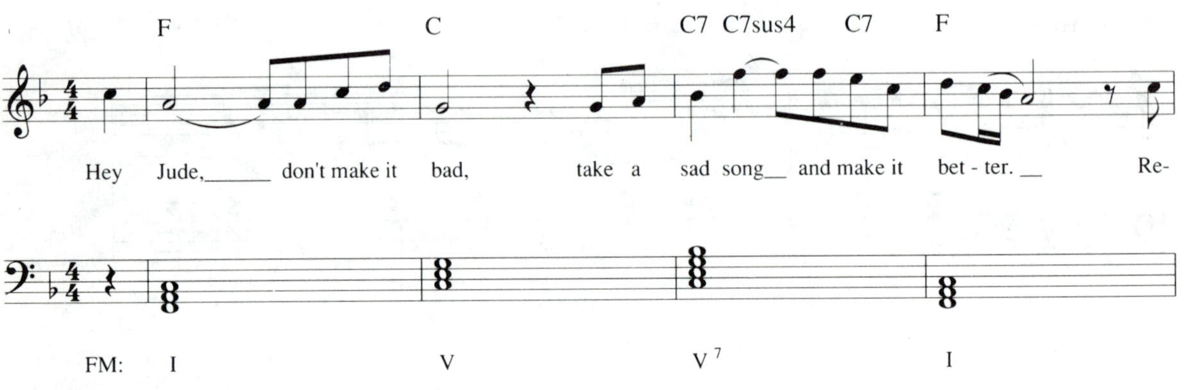

REVIEW

1. Look at the circle of 5ths on page 37. Spell the dominant 7th chord in each major and minor key. *Remember to use the harmonic form of the minor scales.* Write the dominant 7th in four parts and resolve it to the tonic chord, making sure that the 7th resolves downward by step. Use the first example in figure 9.4 as a model for your progression. Play the progressions on the piano.
2. Repeat the procedure above, resolving the dominant 7th chord to VI or vi. Use the second example in figure 9.6 as a model for this progression. Play this progression at the piano.
3. Review Appendix C, **Summary of Part-Writing Practices,** taking particular note of numbers 10 and 11, which refer specifically to the dominant 7th chord. This appendix will prove useful in reviewing each of the following chapters, since it contains a summary of part-writing principles for each chord.
4. Remember that the list of terms at the beginning of each chapter forms a convenient list of important concepts you need to understand. See if you remember the important information about each of the listed terms. Pay particular attention to the specific figured bass symbols for the inversions of the 7th chords.
5. Work out assignments that were not completed during your study of the chapter for practice in dealing with the dominant 7th chord.
6. Dominant 7th chords are by far the most common 7th chords in tonal music. Find examples of dominant 7ths in music that you are familiar with and see if the part-writing principles contained in this chapter are observed. Does the 7th of the chord move downward by step? If not, can you see how its resolution is accounted for in the music?

Test Yourself 9

Question 1 refers to this musical example:

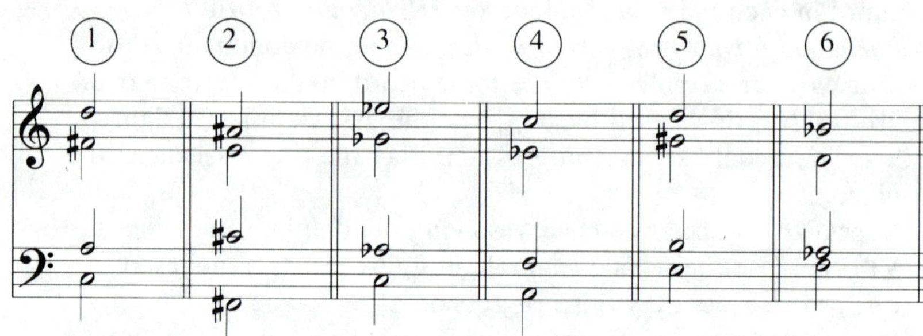

1. Each of the chords is a dominant 7th chord. Determine the chord and its inversion and answer the following questions.
   a. Chord number **1** is the dominant 7th chord in _____ major. The 7th is in the _____ voice and will resolve to _____ (note name) in the tonic triad.
   b. Chord number **2** is the dominant 7th chord in _____ minor. The 7th is in the _____ voice and will resolve to _____ (note name) in the tonic triad.
   c. Chord number **3** is the dominant 7th chord in _____ major. The 7th is in the _____ voice and will resolve to _____ (note name) in the tonic triad.
   d. Chord number **4** is the dominant 7th chord in _____ minor. The 7th is in the _____ voice and will resolve to _____ (note name) in the tonic triad.
   e. Chord number **5** is the dominant 7th chord in _____ minor. The 7th is in the _____ voice and will resolve to _____ (note name) in the tonic triad.
   f. Chord number **6** is the dominant 7th chord in _____ major. The 7th is in the _____ voice and will resolve to _____ (note name) in the tonic triad.

Questions 2–5 refer to the musical examples below:

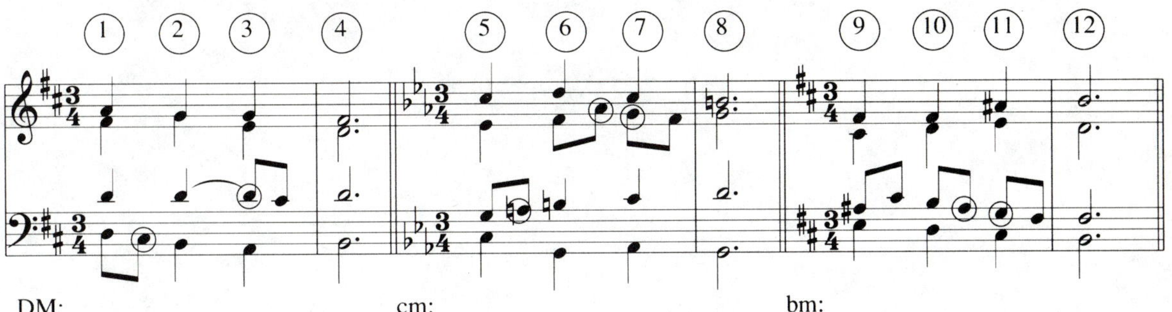

2. Dominant 7th chords appear at chord numbers _____ , _____ , _____ , and _____ .
3. At chord number _____ the 7th of the dominant does not resolve in the normal manner.
4. Nonharmonic tone review:
   a. The nonharmonic tone at chord number **1** is a(n) ____________ .
   b. The nonharmonic tone at chord number **3** is a(n) ____________ .
   c. The nonharmonic tone at chord number **5** is a(n) ____________ .
   d. The nonharmonic tone at chord number **6** is a(n) ____________ .
   e. The nonharmonic tone at chord number **7** is a(n) ____________ .
   f. The nonharmonic tone at chord number **10** is a(n) ____________ .
   g. The nonharmonic tone at chord number **11** is a(n) ____________ .
5. Cadence review:
   a. The cadence at chord number **4** is a(n) ________________ cadence.
   b. The cadence at chord number **8** is a(n) ________________ cadence.
   c. The cadence at chord number **12** is a(n) ________________ cadence.

CHAPTER 10

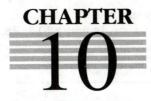

The Leading-Tone 7th Chords

Diminished-Minor 7th Chord
Half-Diminished 7th Chord
Diminished-Diminished 7th Chord
Full-Diminished 7th Chord
Resolution of 7th Factor
Resolution of Tritone

Exposition

Leading-Tone 7th Chord

The **vii** indicates a chord on the 7th scale step, the ø shows that the quality of the chord is *diminished-minor* (also known as *half-diminished),* and the 7 means that it is a 7th chord. The ° in the **vii°7** designates a *diminished-diminished* (usually referred to as diminished or *fully diminished*) 7th chord. The **viiø7** occurs diatonically in major keys and **vii°7** diatonically in minor keys.

Both the **viiø7** and **vii°7** are associated very closely with dominant sound since both contain three notes of the **V7**:

Figure 10.1

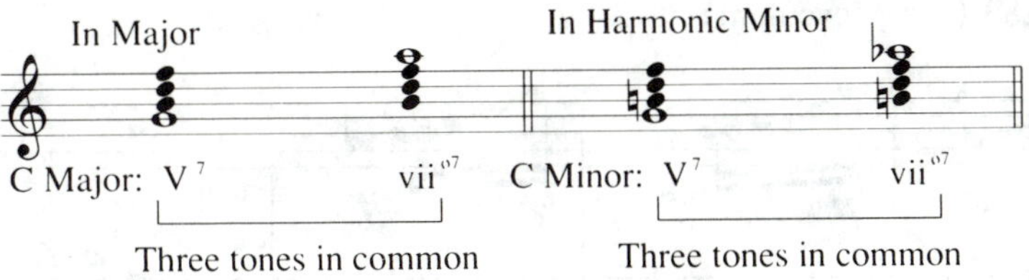

Composers frequently substituted leading-tone triads and 7th chords for the dominant to lend variety. In figure 10.2, Beethoven alternates the **V**^{7}, **vii**$^{\circ 6}$, and **vii**$^{\circ 7}$ freely to represent dominant harmony.

Figure 10.2

Beethoven: Piano Sonata in C Minor, op. 10, no. 1 (1st movement)

Since **V**^{7}, **vii**$^{\circ 7}$, and **vii**$^{ø 7}$ all represent dominant harmony, composers occasionally intermixed them, allowing especially the **vii**$^{\circ 7}$ to dissolve (not resolve) into the **V**^{7} chord. Examples of this treatment occur more often in instrumental than in vocal or choral writing. In figure 10.3, the 7th (B♭) of the **vii**$^{\circ 7}$ moves down to the root (A) of the **V**$^6_5$.

Figure 10.3

Mozart: Piano Sonata in G Major, KV 283 (3rd Movement)

Like the dominant 7th, with which they share three notes, **vii**^{ø7} and **vii**^{o7} usually resolve to the tonic (**I** or **i**):

Progressions from vii^{ø7} **and vii**^{o7}

Figure 10.4

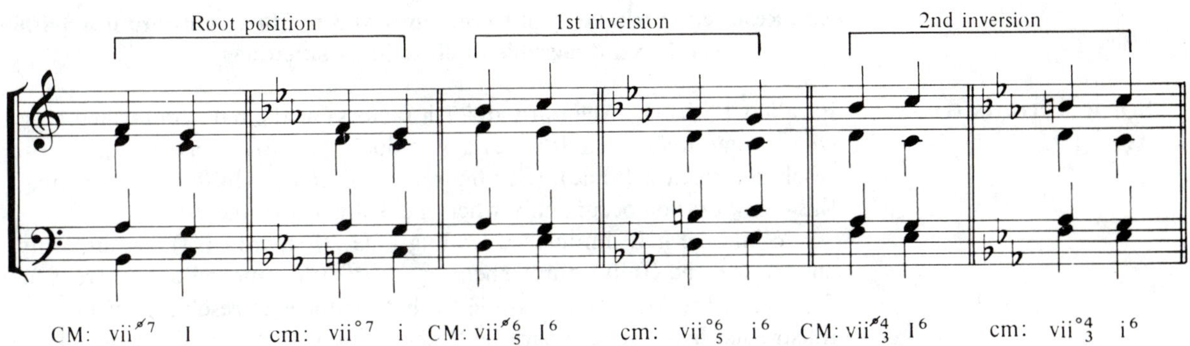

Diminished 5ths resolve inward (by half step), while augmented 4ths resolve outward (by half steps). Both the half-diminished (**vii**^{ø7}) and diminished (**vii**^{o7}) permit this resolution when progressing to the tonic. In this excerpt by Mozart, the diminished 5th (A♯ to E) as well as the 7th factor (G) of the 7th chords resolve inward by step.

Resolution of Tritone and Seventh Factor

Figure 10.5

Mozart: *Don Giovanni,* K. 527 (Act I, Scene XIV)

Partwriting the vii$^{\varnothing 7}$ and vii$^{\circ 7}$

These procedures continue the list on pages 123–129 and 164. (See also Appendix C.)

12. Resolve the 7th factor of the *vii*$^{\varnothing 7}$ or *vii*$^{\circ 7}$ (and inversions) down one diatonic scale degree.

13. Resolve the tritone (root to 5th) inward if a °5th an outward if a +4th. However, it is not possible to do so in all situations.

Some Pitfalls to Avoid

Parallels P5ths (between 3rd and 7th factors) of the half-diminished type (**vii**$^{\varnothing 7}$) sometimes make it necessary to double the 3rd factor of the resolution triad, **I** (tonic). (See figure 10.6 E and F.) In four-part writing this configuration occurs only when the 3rd is below the 7th.

While the half-diminished leading-tone 7th chord (**vii**$^{\circ 7}$) contains only one tritone, the (fully) diminished type (**vii**$^{\circ 7}$) is comprised of two (root to 5th and 3rd to 7th). It is possible for both tritones to resolve properly. (See illustration B.) Also, the parallel P5ths, so difficult to handle in the **vii**$^{\varnothing 7}$, become d5ths in **vii**$^{\circ 7}$, and are sometimes written by composers in preference to a tonic triad with a doubled 3rd. (See illustration D.) Items A, B, D, and F may be found in music literature.

Figure 10.6

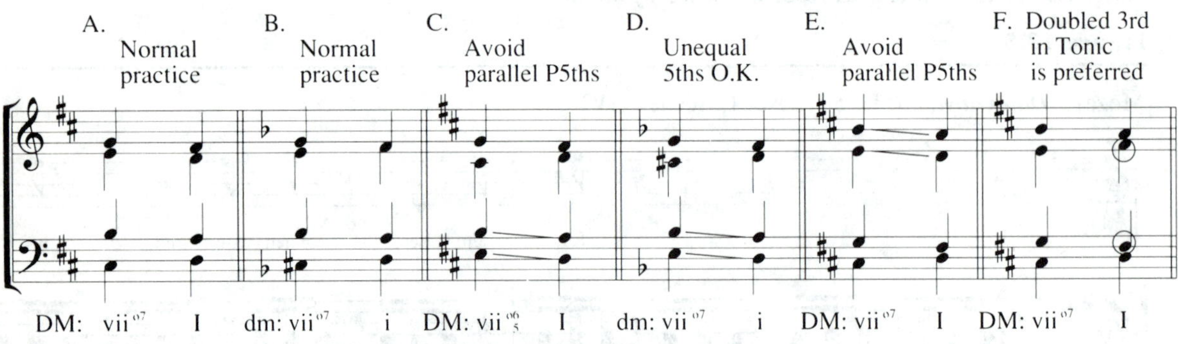

(Workbook-Anthology Assignments 10.1–10.14, pp. 109–119)

History

Renaissance Period (1450–1600)

Both the **vii**$^{\varnothing 7}$ and **vii**$^{\circ 7}$ were so rare as to be virtually nonexistent in the Renaissance period.

Baroque Period (1600–1750)

With the development of equal-tempered tuning and the ascendancy of the major and minor key systems, leading-tone 7th chords took their place as a basic part of the harmonic vocabulary of the Baroque period. Figure 10.7 shows typical use of the **vii**$^{\circ 7}$ during the middle and late Baroque period.

Figure 10.7

Bach: *Wir Christenleut'* (We Christian People) BWV 40

Chords reduced to simple position:

Classical Period (1750–1825)

The Classical period continued the use of leading-tone 7th chords with little change in stylistic application. Figure 10.8 is representative of the general treatment given these chords.

Figure 10.8

Mozart: Piano Sonata in D Major, K. 284 (3rd movement)

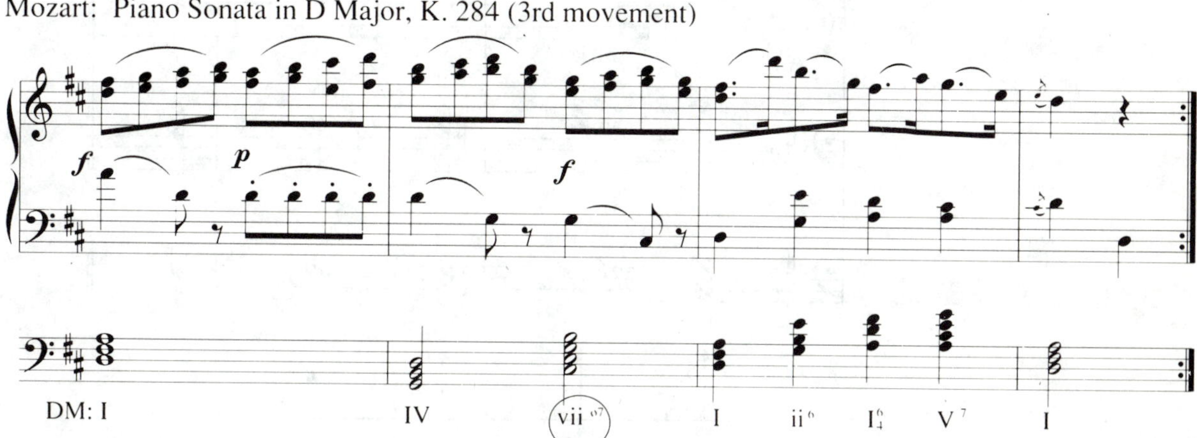

Romantic Period (1825–1900)

This period saw a more relaxed and somewhat freer use of leading-tone 7th chord. Figure 10.9 illustrates six consecutive diminished 7th chords. In each succeeding chord all voices descend a half step, preventing the diminished 7th interval (sometimes augmented 2nd) from resolving. No analysis is given for the first five measures since functional harmony is temporarily suspended.

Figure 10.9

Wagner: Overture to the Opera *Rienzi*

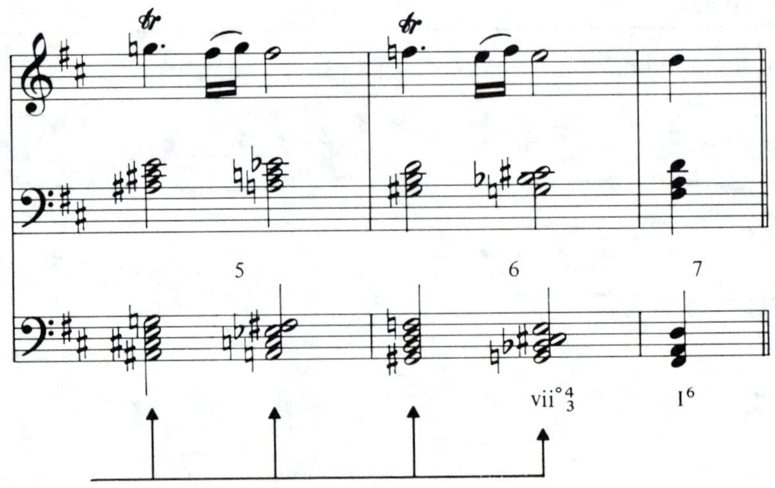

With the gradual breakup of functional harmony, leading-tone 7th chords fell into disuse. Nevertheless, nonfunctional diminished and half-diminished 7th chords were still very much a part of the harmonic vocabulary of this period. The following excerpt by Debussy illustrates the use of the half-diminished 7th chord, substituting for dominant harmony, as part of the final cadence in an extended work.

Post-Romantic and Impressionistic Period (1875–1920)

Figure 10.10

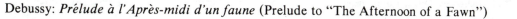

Debussy: *Prélude à l'Après-midi d'un faune* (Prelude to "The Afternoon of a Fawn")

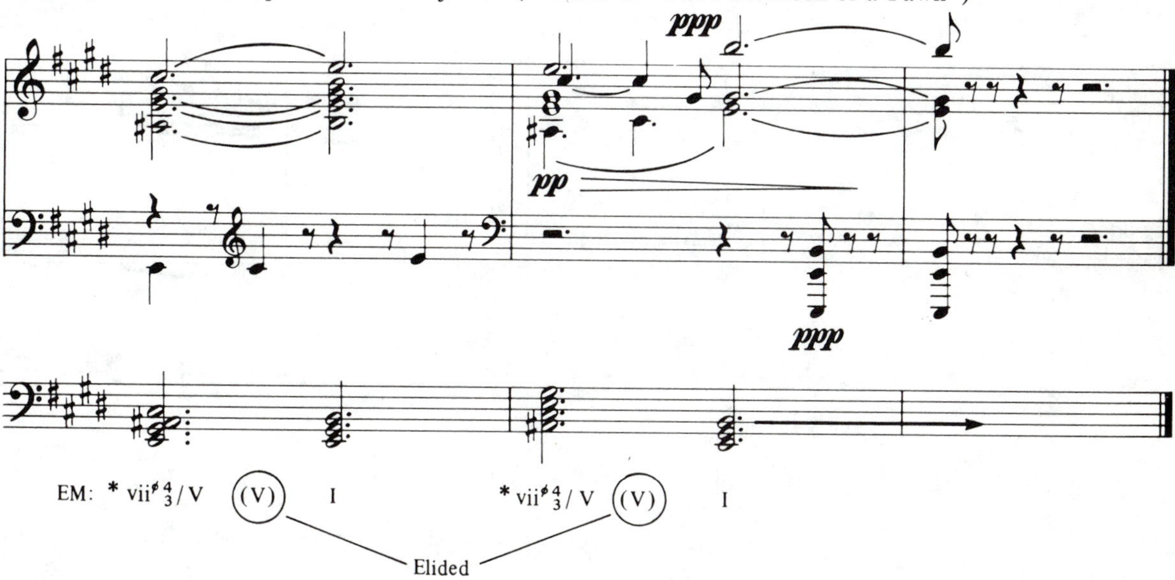

*See chapter 13.

For most music written for performance in concert halls or opera houses, leading-tone 7th chords ceased to exist except for those styles that make a conscious use of functional harmony.

Contemporary Period (1920–Present)

Jazz and Popular Music (1900–Present)

Popular songwriters and jazz artists considered leading-tone 7th chords an integral part of their style, although the half-diminished (**vii**$^{\varnothing 7}$) was by far the more favored. Even ragtime, one of the early forms of music that contributed to the jazz style, found use for these 7th chords:

Figure 10.11

Johnson: "A Black Smoke Rag"

REVIEW

1. Practice spelling leading-tone 7th chords in all major and minor keys. Remember that the leading-tone 7th in major is half-diminished while that in minor is fully diminished. How is the half-diminished 7th chord indicated in roman numerals? The fully diminished 7th chord?
2. Play the examples in figure 10.6 (page 174) at the piano, observing the resolution of the 7th and the treatment of the tritones. Review the text associated with these examples.
3. Write the leading-tone 7th chord in a major or a minor key in four parts. Now resolve the chord to the tonic chord, observing Stylistic practices 12 and 13. (Remember, **Summary of Part-Writing Practices** in Appendix C). The half-diminished 7th chord contains one perfect 5th (between the 3rd and 7th of the chord.) Did you avoid parallel perfect 5ths in resolving this chord?
4. Look again at figure 10.6. Play examples A and B at the piano. Now transpose these two examples to the keys of E-flat major and E-flat minor. Next move them to E major and E minor. Continue transposing these examples until you have played them in all keys.
5. Review the figured bass symbols for the inversions of 7th chords found on page 159 (chapter 9). Now complete several of the figured basses that were not assigned, paying particular attention to the resolution of the 7th and the tritones of the leading-tone 7th chords.

Test Yourself 10

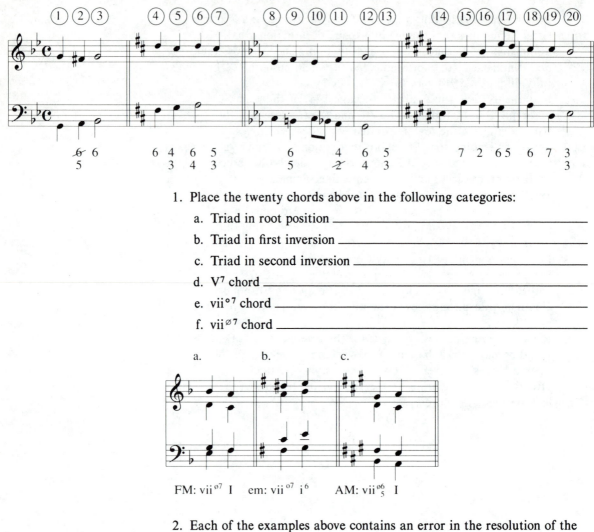

1. Place the twenty chords above in the following categories:
   a. Triad in root position __________
   b. Triad in first inversion __________
   c. Triad in second inversion __________
   d. V^7 chord __________
   e. $vii^{\circ 7}$ chord __________
   f. $vii^{\o 7}$ chord __________

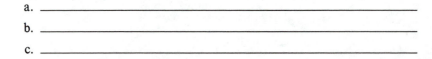

FM: $vii^{\o 7}$ I em: $vii^{\circ 7}$ i^6 AM: $vii^{\o 6}_{5}$ I

2. Each of the examples above contains an error in the resolution of the leading-tone 7th chord. Describe the error in each case.
   a. __________
   b. __________
   c. __________

CHAPTER 11

Nondominant 7th Chords

Exposition

Nondominant 7th chords are those diatonic 7th chords that do not possess dominant function:

Type	**Chords whose roots are:**
Dominant Function—	**V** or **vii°**
Nondominant Function—	**I i ii iii IV iv vi VI**

Analysis Symbols

The quality of a 7th chord is indicated in analysis by:

1. Type of triad: **I** (major) **ii** (minor) **vii°** (diminished) **III+** (Augmented)
2. Type of 7th:
   a. When the triad and 7th have the same quality, add ^{7} only:

      I^7 (major-major) **ii**^{7} (minor-minor)
      iii^7 (minor-minor) **IV**^{7} (major-major)
      vii$^{\circ 7}$ (diminished-diminished)

   b. When the triad is diminished and 7th is minor, add the half-diminished symbol ($^{\varnothing}$):

      ii$^{\varnothing 7}$ (diminished-minor)
      vii$^{\varnothing 7}$ (diminished-minor)

c. When the quality of the triad is *different* from that of the 7th, write the quality of the 7th, (interval from root to 7th) below the ^{7}:

i^7_M (minor-major)

d. Since the dominant 7th is so frequently used and so easily recognized, the small m beneath the ^{7} is omitted:

(V^7) instead of (V^7_m).

Nondominant 7th Chords in Major and Minor Keys

Illustrated here are the symbols for all diatonic 7th chords in the major and three forms of the minor scale:

Figure 11.1

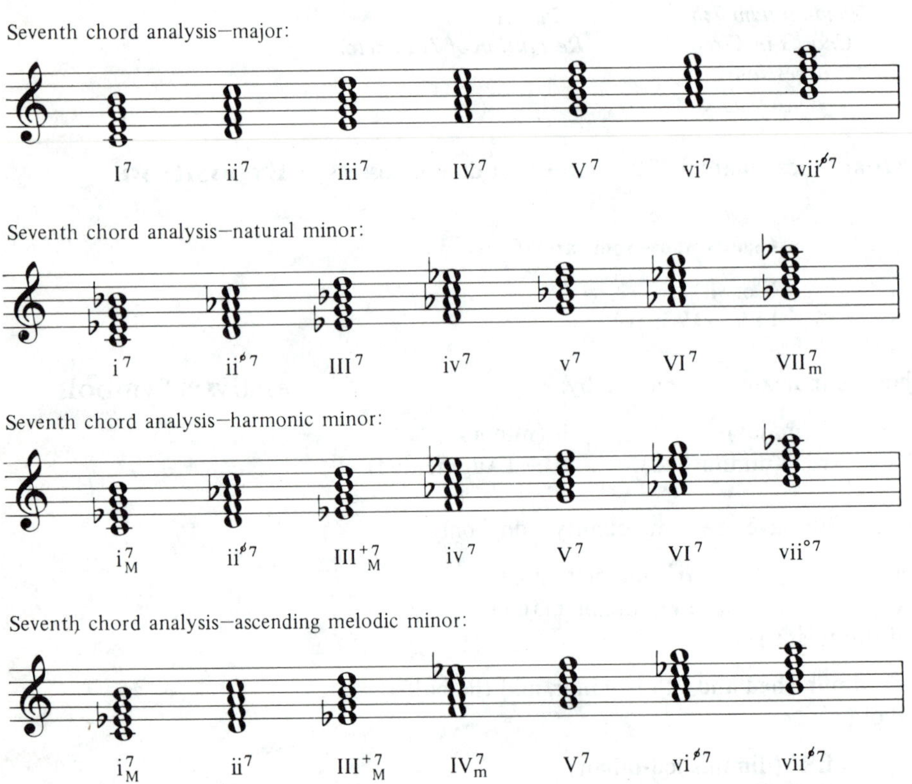

Nondominant 7th Chords in Circle Progressions

As with the dominant 7th (see chapter 9), nondominant 7th chords usually progress according to the circle pattern (descending 5th root movement). Circle Pattern: **iii vi ii V I (IV)**

Nondominant 7th Chord	Resolves to:
ii^7 and **ii°7** **vi**^{7} and **VI**^{7} **iii**^{7} and **III+**^{7}	**V** **ii** or **ii°** **vi** or **VI**

Noncircle Treatment of Nondominant 7th Chords

Nondominant 7th chords depart from circle progressions occasionally for one reason or another:

1. The **IV**^{7} (in major) and **iv**^{7} (in minor), like their triad counterparts, progress most often to **V.**
2. In circle progressions all nondominant 7th chords eventually resolve to **V.** However, sometimes the circle is interrupted, allowing **vi**^{7}, for instance, to resolve to **IV** (and then **V**) instead of **ii** (and then **V**). Some common circle interruptions are:

Chord	Resolves to	Instead of	Illustrated in Figure 11.2
IV^7	**V**	**vii°**	a
vi^7	**IV** (then **V**)	**ii** (then **V**)	
vi^7	**V**	**ii (then V)**	b
iii^7	**IV** (then **V**)	**vi** (then to **ii V**)	
I^7	**ii**	**IV**	c

Figure 11.2

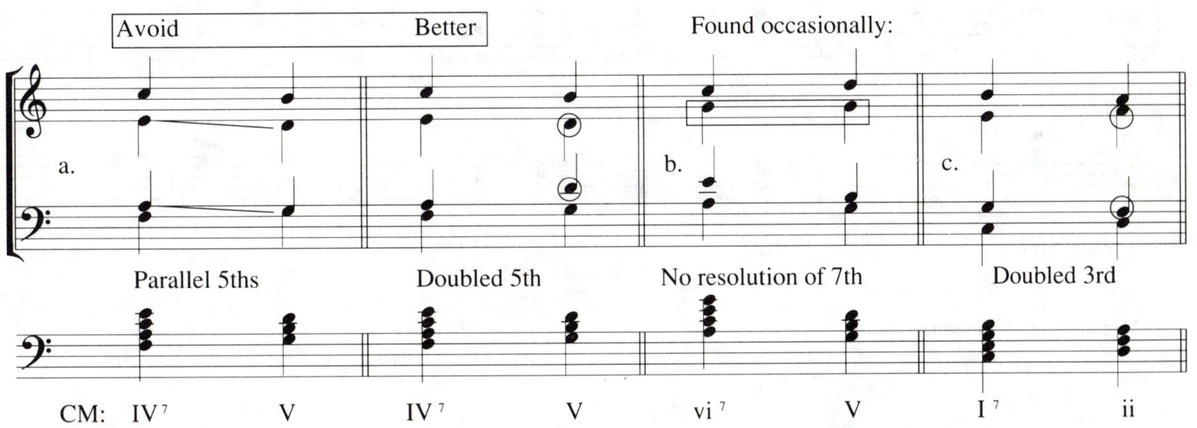

Resolution of 7th Factor

Circle progressions permit the 7th of a nondominant 7th chord to resolve down one scale step to the 3rd factor of the next chord:

Figure 11.3

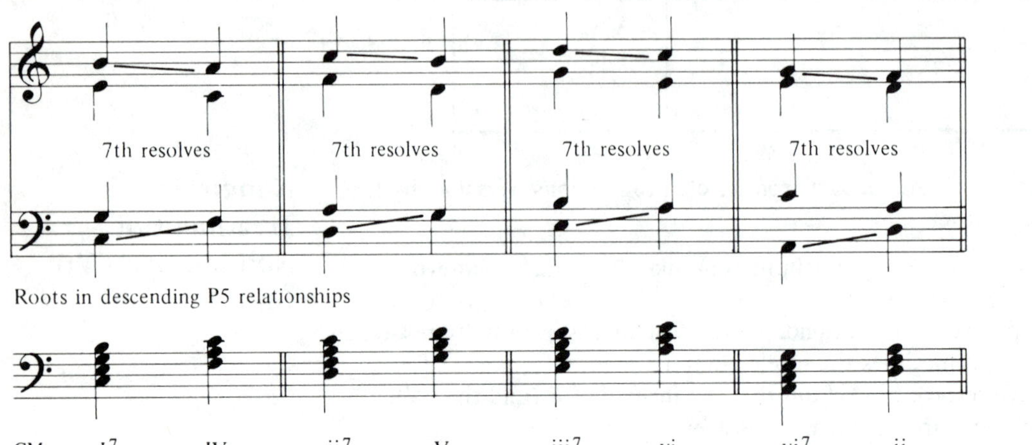

In inversion, likewise, tonic, supertonic, mediant, and submediant 7th chords are typically found in circle progressions:

Figure 11.4

*Resolution of seventh

The following are typical examples from music literature:

Figure 11.5

Bach: *Lass, O Herr, dein Ohr sich neigen* (Bow Thine Ear, O Lord), BWV 372

Handel: Harpsichord Suite no. 6 in F-Sharp Minor (Allegro)

Partwriting Nondominant 7th Chords

The following statement continues the list of stylistic practices on pages 123–129, 164 and 174. A complete list of all stylistic practices is found in Appendix C.

14. Resolve the 7th factor of nondominant 7th chords one diatonic scale degree down to the 3rd of the next chord (in circle progressions). Otherwise resolve the 7th factor down one step if its resolution is a part of the following chord.

(Workbook-Anthology Assignments 11.1–11.12, pp. 121–134)

History

Renaissance Period (1450–1600)

As with dominant and leading-tone 7th chords, vertical sonorities, resembling nondominant 7th chords, may be found. But such "chords" are the result of passing dissonance and are not a part of the harmony.

Baroque Period (1600–1750)

With the advent of functional harmony at the beginning of this period, nondominant 7th chords, although sparse at the outset, grew in numbers to become an integral part of baroque musical style. The following is a typical example of nondominant 7th chord usage in the Baroque period:

Figure 11.6

Bach: *O Ewigkeit, Du Donnerwort* (Oh Eternity, Thou Word of Thunder) BWV 20

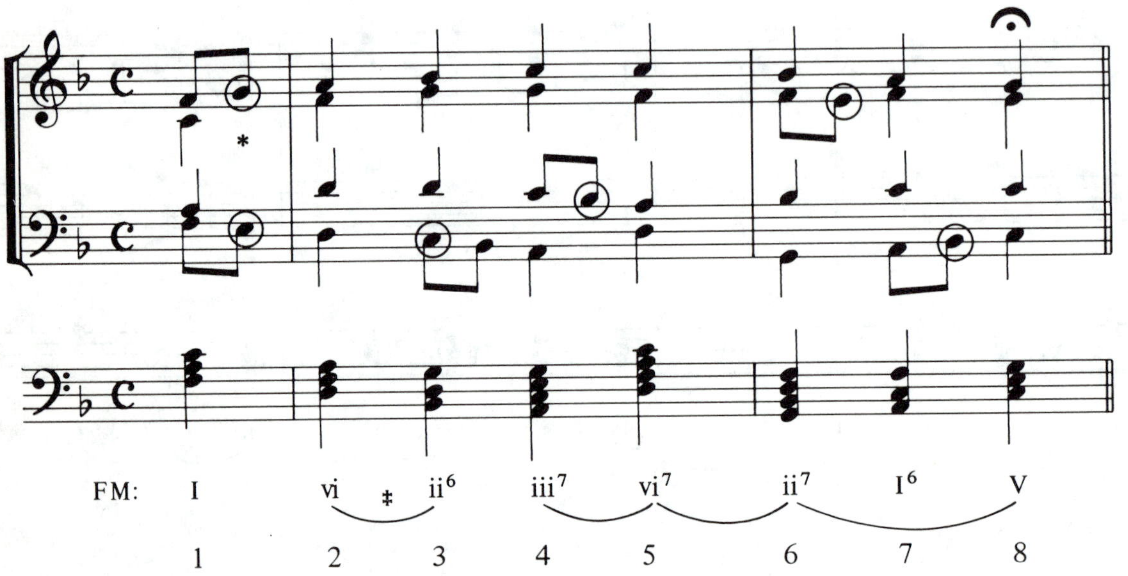

*Circles indicate nonharmonic tones.
‡Slurs indicate circle progressions.

Classical Period (1750–1825)

Continuing the trend passed on from the Baroque period, nondominant 7th chords are found in large numbers by all major composers of the Classical period.

Romantic Period (1825–1900)

With the increased use of altered chords (chords containing non-diatonic notes), nondominant 7th chords, especially those in circle progressions, became somewhat less common. From a song written by Anton Rubenstein (a famous pianist of the period), this excerpt (figure 11.7) illustrates a **IV⁷** that resolves eventually to $\mathbf{V^4_2}$, but is delayed by a **ii⁶**. Two positions of the supertonic 7th chord that fit neatly into circle (**ii V I**) patterns are also present. Measures three through five contain a repeated note (F) in the piano accompaniment that becomes a dissonant pedal tone in measure 4.

Figure 11.7

A. Rubenstein: *Gelb Rollt mir zu Füssen* (Golden at my Feet)

Post-Romantic and Impressionistic Period (1875–1920)

While some aspects of functional harmony were still used in this period, the chord qualities of nondominant 7th chords, if not always the accompanying circle of fifths progressions, were preserved in large numbers. In figure 11.8, Ravel includes three nondominant 7th chords (and two nondominant 9th chords) in a setting that includes a long circle progression in the aeolian mode (F G A♭ B♭ C D♭ E♭ F).

Figure 11.8

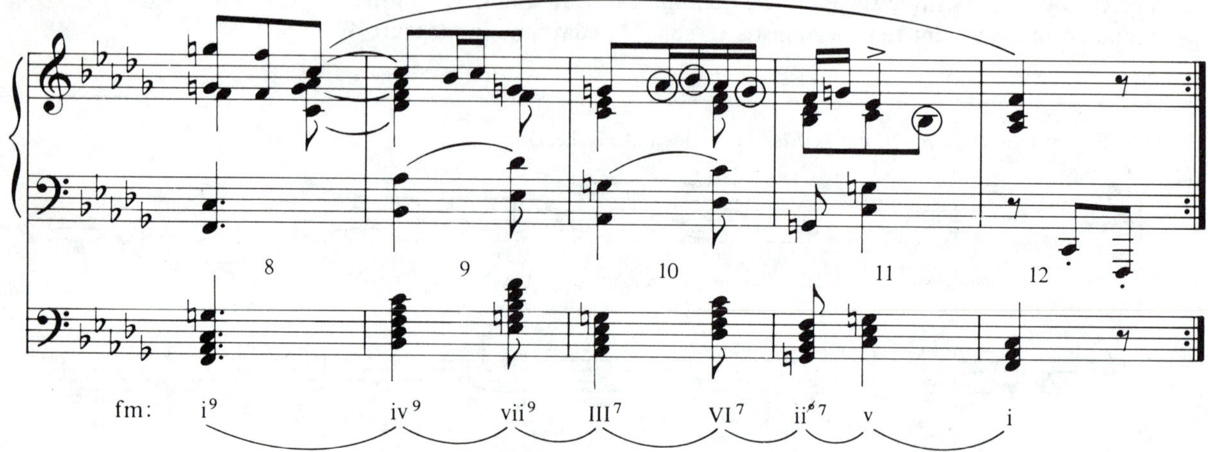

Contemporary Period (1920–Present)

Except for those composers making conscious use of traditional materials, non-dominant 7th chords, as functional harmonies, ceased to exist.

Jazz and Popular Music (1900–Present)

Nondominant 7th chords, a legacy from the Romantic period, are found in large numbers in jazz and popular music. An example is shown in figure 11.9.

Figure 11.9

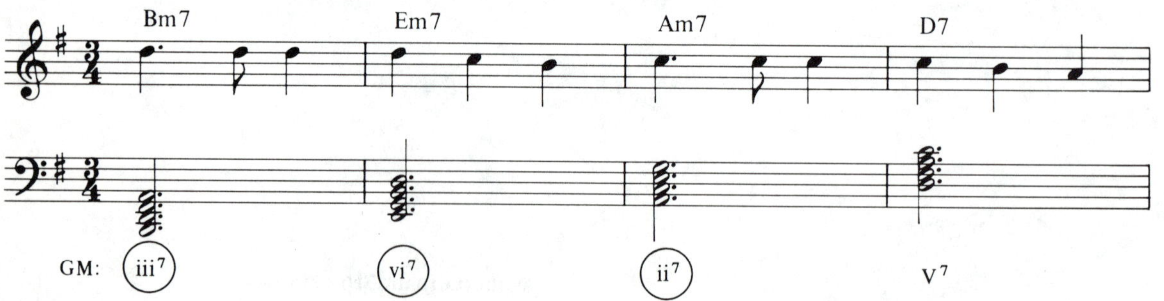

REVIEW

1. Study the chart of diatonic 7th chords in figure 11.1 (page 182). While this chart appears quite complicated, observe that there is considerable duplication among the various scales. For example, the super-tonic 7th chord is a minor 7th chord in major and the ascending minor scales, and a half-diminished 7th chord in the natural and harmonic forms of the minor. Learn the roman-numeral symbols for each of the nondominant 7th chords.
2. Most nondominant 7th chords progress in a circle pattern. What chord will usually follow the supertonic 7th chord? The mediant 7th chord? The subdominant 7th chord? The submediant 7th chord? The tonic 7th chord?
3. Play the examples of nondominant 7th chord progressions in figures 11.3 and 11.4 (page 184), observing the common pattern in the circle progressions involving the nondominant 7th chords in root position (figure 11.3).
4. Write a mediant 7th chord in a major key in four parts. Resolve it in a circle progression to the submediant 7th chord using Stylistic Practice 14. Continue the progression by resolving each 7th chord to another 7th chord in the circle pattern. Play the resulting progression at the piano. Repeat this pattern in minor, choosing the chords from the various forms of the scale that sound best to your ear.
5. Study the section on **Noncircle Treatment of Nondominant 7th Chords** of the nondominant 7th chords on page 183. Do you observe any common pattern among these noncircle resolutions? Play the examples that illustrate each of these progressions (figure 11.2).
6. Find examples of nondominant 7th chords in music. Do these examples follow Stylistic Practice 14?

Test Yourself 11

1. The chorale setting above contains a number of partwriting errors. Check each progression and describe any errors. There may be no errors, one error, or more than one error in any progression.

a. ______________________________
b. ______________________________
c. ______________________________
d. ______________________________
e. ______________________________
f. ______________________________
g. ______________________________
h. ______________________________
i. ______________________________

a. DM: b. fm: c. AM: d. E♭M: e. bm: f. A♭M:

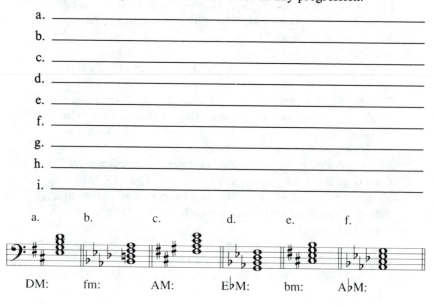

2. Each chord above is a nondominant 7th chord in the given key. Give the proper roman numeral for the chord. If the chord is resolved in a circle progression, what chord would follow?

a. Roman numeral: _____ Roman numeral of following chord: _____
b. Roman numeral: _____ Roman numeral of following chord: _____
c. Roman numeral: _____ Roman numeral of following chord: _____
d. Roman numeral: _____ Roman numeral of following chord: _____
e. Roman numeral: _____ Roman numeral of following chord: _____
f. Roman numeral: _____ Roman numeral of following chord: _____

CHAPTER 12

Modulation

Modulation
Pivot Chord
Common Chord Modulation
Phrase Modulation
Chromatic Modulation
Enharmonic Modulation
Modulation in Period Construction
Closely Related Keys
Macro Analysis

Exposition

Modulation

Modulation is a process by which a shift of tonal center is achieved. The term applies to those occasions in music when one established tonal center gives way to another.

Closely Related Keys

Most modulations occur between *closely related keys,* which are those keys that differ by no more than one accidental in the key signature. If the original key is C major, the closely related keys are G major and F major, and the relative minors of each of the three keys: A minor, E minor, and D minor. If the original key is A minor, the closely related keys are E minor and D minor, and their relative majors: C major, G major, and F major.

An easy way to understand modulation is to observe the ebb and flow of circle progressions. Up to this chapter, circle progressions have consistently remained diatonic, that is, they have remained within the limits of a single tonal center.

Figure 12.1

Full-Circle Progression—Diatonic

Handel: Chaconne in G Major (with 20/21 Variations)

Var. 11

gm: i iv^6 VII III^6

VI $ii^{\circ 6}$ V i^6

The *Tonal Profile* shown above illustrates uninterrupted movement toward tonic and contains circle progressions only. Note that the entire passage contains only the diatonic tones of G minor.

Now, look carefully at figure 12.2. In this illustration the first series of circle progression moves **vi** $\mathbf{ii^6}$ $\mathbf{V^7}$ **I,** then repeats the $\mathbf{ii^6}$ and $\mathbf{V^7}$—all in D major. However, both sets of circle progressions in the second phrase conclude with the A-major triad, the chord preceding it is an E^7 chord and acts as a dominant 7th, and G♯ is exclusively found from measure 6 on. All of this evidence points toward a modulation from D major to A major—a fact that will be quite evident when the excerpt is heard.

Figure 12.2

Mozart: Piano Sonata in D Major, K. 284 (3rd Movement)

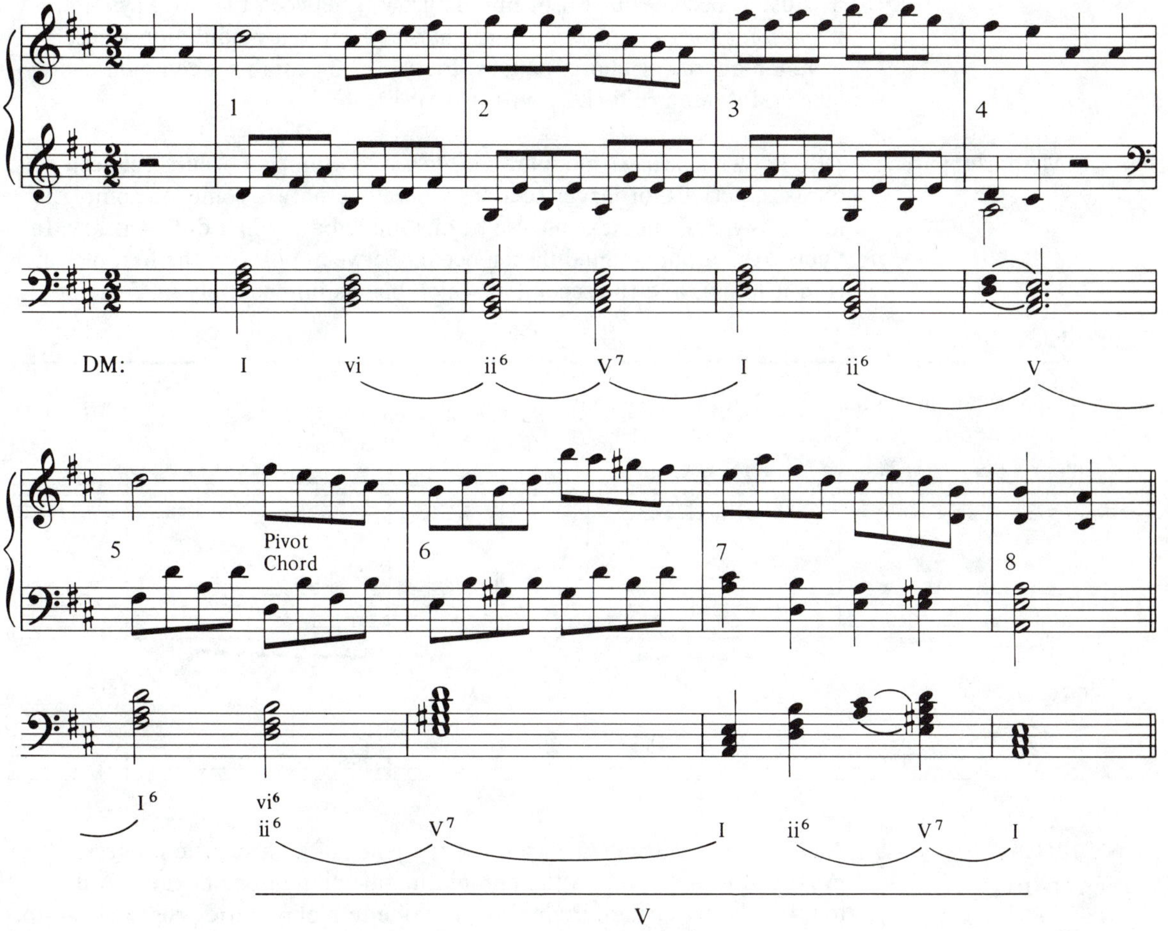

1 2 3 4

DM: I vi ii^6 V^7 I ii^6 V

5 Pivot Chord 6 7 8

I^6 vi^6 ii^6 V^7 I ii^6 V^7 I

V

Tonal Profile

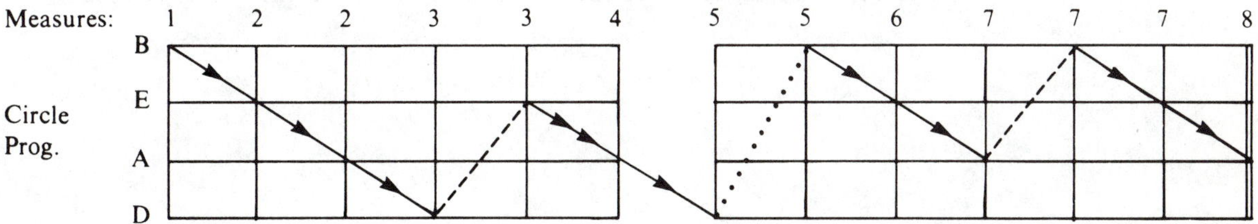

Common Chord Modulation

A *common chord,* meaning a chord that is common to each of two keys, offers a smooth introduction to the new key since it is diatonic to both the old and the new key. This common chord is often called a *pivot chord* because it becomes a sort of middle ground between the two keys. *Common chord modulation* is the name given to a modulation where a common chord (or chords) exists. Figure 12.2 contains a common chord—labeled in measure 5 (DM: vi^6 = AM: ii^6).

Phrase Modulation

Also known as *direct* modulation, *phrase modulation* occurs between phrases, periods, or larger sections where one phrase comes to completion in one key, and the next phrase begins immediately in a different key. In figure 12.3 a phrase modulation occurs between phrases, the first of which is in E minor, and the second of which begins immediately in C major.

Figure 12.3

Mozart: Piano Sonata in A Major, K. 331 (3rd Movement)

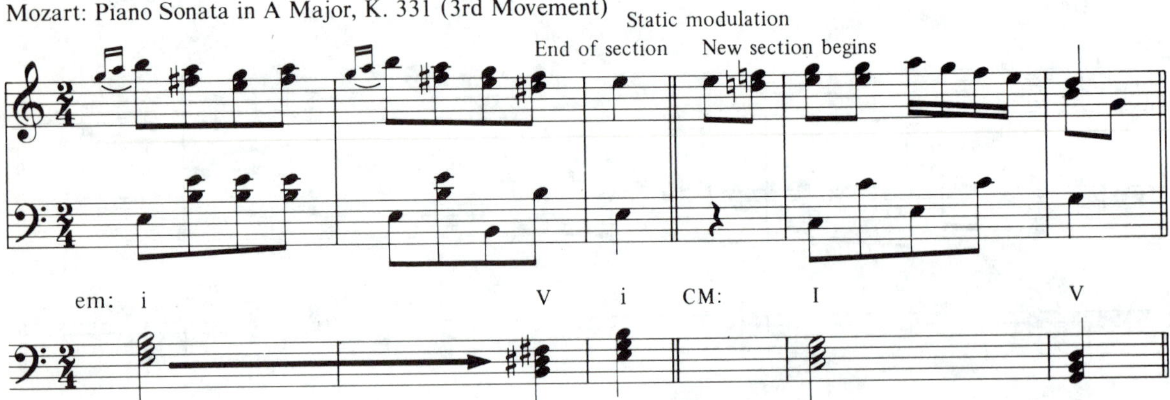

Chromatic Modulation

A *chromatic modulation* occurs at the point of a chromatic progression (a progression that involves the chromatic inflection of one of the chord tones). The letter name remains the same in a chromatic progression—for example, in the following Bach Chorale. At chord 2 the tenor is C, but in the next chord, at 3, the C becomes C♯. Chromatic modulations often occur in passages where the two keys involved are not closely related.

Figure 12.4

Bach: *Du grosser Schmerzensmann* (Thou Great Man of Sorrow) BWV 300 (Transposed)

Chromatic modulation

Enharmonic Modulation

Enharmonic modulation is a rare type of modulation in which enharmonic spellings are employed. Figure 12.5 demonstrates how a diminished 7th chord can be respelled (while maintaining the same sound) to effect a modulation. The root of the first diminished 7th is F♯ (F♯ A C E♭), normally resolving to a Gm triad, but by changing the E♭ to D♯ (enharmonic) the diminished 7th resolves to an Em triad.

Figure 12.5

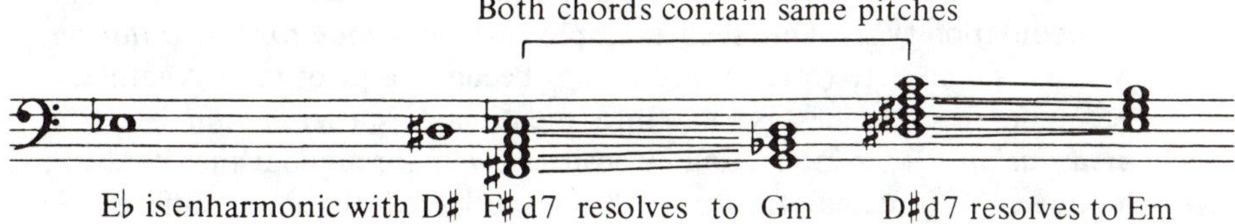

Figure 12.6 illustrates how this progression occurs in music literature.

Figure 12.6

Beethoven: Piano Sonata in C minor, op. 13 (*Pathétique*) (1st movement)

Enharmonic modulations are also employed by composers when there is an enharmonic key with fewer accidentals. As an example, suppose a composition contained a modulation from E♭ minor to A♭ minor. The key signature of A♭ minor is seven flats, but the equivalent sharp key, G♯ minor, has only five sharps. For less difficult score reading, G♯ minor is often selected.

Other Modulation Types

Music of the tonal period contains a number of unusual or rare examples of modulation types. One such example is the *common tone modulation* where a single note (often heard alone) becomes a pivot tone. Another, occurring in sequences, is sometimes mentioned as a *sequential modulation.* Other interesting curiosities occur throughout the literature of music, but the analytical procedures you have learned are sufficient for the understanding of any modulation—common or rare.

Modulations in Period Construction

Chapter 5 (page 87) sets the parameters for identifying phrases and periods in music. With the introduction of modulation (not discussed in Chapter 5), some further information may be helpful.

In two-phrase periods:

1. Either phrase may contain a modulation.
2. Either phrase may cadence in a different key.
3. The basic definition of a period remains—the cadence at the end of the second phrase must be stronger (usually perfect authentic) than at the end of the first.

The following parallel period (figure 12.7) begins in D major but ends in A major. Only the first measure of each phrase is the same.

In figure 12.8, the second phrase repeats the first phrase, transposed up a step.

Figure 12.7

Mozart: Piano Sonata in D Major, K. 284 (3rd movement)

Figure 12.8

Grieg: The Last Spring, op. 34, no. 2

Figure 12.9 illustrates a contrasting period where the second phrase is in the key of the dominant:

Meas.	Phrase	Melody	Type	Key	Symbol	Form
1–4	1		Half	AM	a	Contrasting
5–8	2	Contrasting to phrase 1	Perfect Authentic	EM	b	Period

Figure 12.9

Explanation of the Haydn Piano Sonata analysis:

1. Nonharmonic tones are circled.
2. Measure 3—Although all six notes of beat one (2/4 meter) indicate a tonic (**I^6**) triad, the second beat could also be construed to form harmony.
3. The line (below the analysis) drawn from measures 4 through 8 is called an *extended line* and simply informs us that this section is being analyzed in the key of *the dominant* (the key of E major).
4. Measure 5—The chord analysis is omitted because the chord itself is in second inversion and the voice leading shows it to be nothing more than an upper neighbor for the tonic (E major) chord on either side of it—measures 4 and 6. Another analyst might, justifiably, include it as functional harmony.
5. The slurs connecting certain chords let us know that these are circle progressions and are of considerable importance, for they determine the direction of the music at all times. In measures 4 through 8 the slurs indicate a basic harmony of **I IV V I**—one of the most common progressions in all of music.

Analytical Symbols for Modulations

1. Traditional Analysis: If you are analyzing a short excerpt and wish to examine every detail of voice leading:

   Common chord modulation—Select the common chord and analyze it in both keys:

   C Major: I ii^6 V I [vi^6
   G Major: [ii^6 V I

   or

   CM: I ii^6 V I [vi^6
   GM: [ii^6 V I

   Other types of modulation—Name the new key and adjust chord analysis accordingly:

   G Major: I V I A Minor: V^6 i V i

   or

   GM: I V I am: V^6 i

2. Macro Analysis: If you are analyzing an extended composition and wish to show the larger relationships:

   All types of modulation—Place an extended line beneath the analysis symbols, and indicate (below the extended line) the relationship of the new key to the original key of the composition. If the new key note is not diatonic in the original key, indicate the alteration from the diatonic note with an accidental to the left of the roman numeral. For example, a modulation from A♭ major to B minor would be indicated with ♮ii under the extended line. The ii indicates the second scale degree of A♭ major, and the natural signifies that the pitch is raised by a half step (B♮ instead of B♭). Absence of an extended line signifies a return to the original key.

To illustrate a common chord if desired:

CM: I ii^6 V [I
IV ii^6 V I
V

Otherwise:

GM: I V I V^6 i V i
ii

Remember that *traditional* and *macro* analyses are fundamentally the same—the only difference is in emphasis. Traditional analysis emphasizes minute detail, while macro analysis often starts with traditional, but highlights breadth and overall structure by eliminating details. (See Appendix F for a discussion of macro analysis).

(Workbook-Anthology Assignments 12.1–12.4, pp. 135–141, and 12.10–12.11, p. 147)

Harmonizing Melodies That Modulate

The same procedure should be followed for melodies that modulate as for those that do not. This procedure is described in chapter 8, "Harmonic Progression." To illustrate the technique, two phrases of the chorale tune *Keinen hat Gott verlassen* (God Has Forsaken No One) are harmonized to show each step of the process.

1. Determine the harmonic rhythm, and write out the possible harmonizations beneath the melody.
2. Analyze the cadences for all possible formulas (authentic, deceptive, half, and plagal) in all possible keys. Since this is a chorale melody, it lends itself best to modulations of the closely related type. It may be assumed for the moment that the melody could be harmonized in G major, E minor, or a combination of both.

Original Key	**Closely Related Keys***
G Major	D Major, C Major, E Minor, B Minor, A Minor
E Minor	D Major, C Major, G Major, B Minor, A Minor

*Closely related keys are those major and minor keys whose key signatures differ from that of the original key by no more than one accidental.

Figure 12.10

Keinen hat Gott verlassen
(God Has Forsaken No One)

Chorale

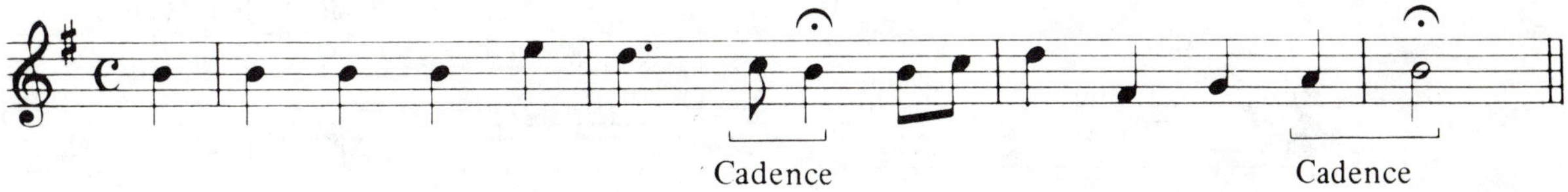

Cadence   Cadence

The first cadence supports any of the following formulas. It should be pointed out, however, that the cadence in E minor is without the raised 7th scale degree and will sound somewhat modal in character.

Three possibilities for the first cadence:

Figure 12.11

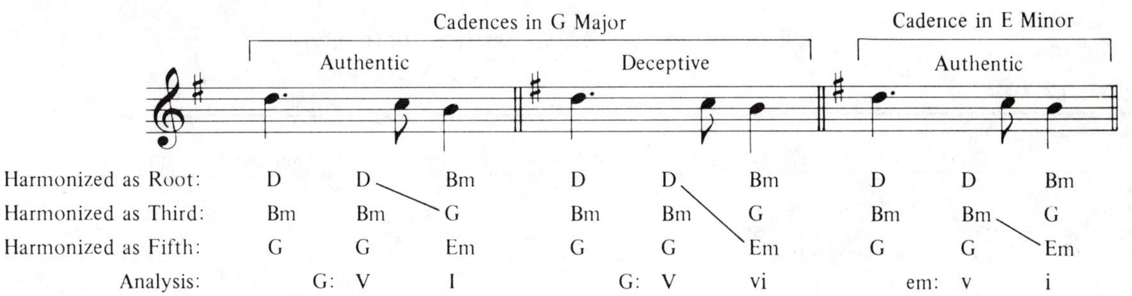

These same cadences in four-part harmony:

Figure 12.12

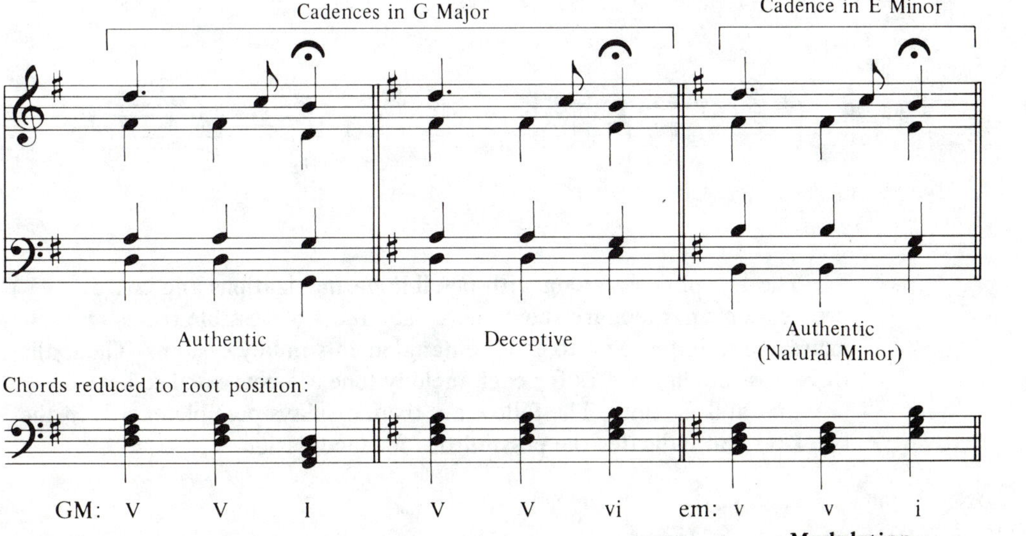

Five possibilities for the second cadence:

Figure 12.13

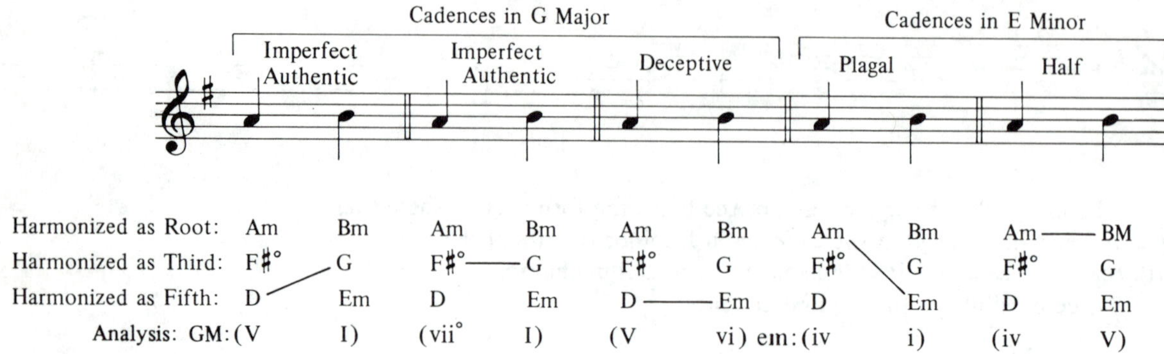

These same cadences in four-part harmony:

Figure 12.14

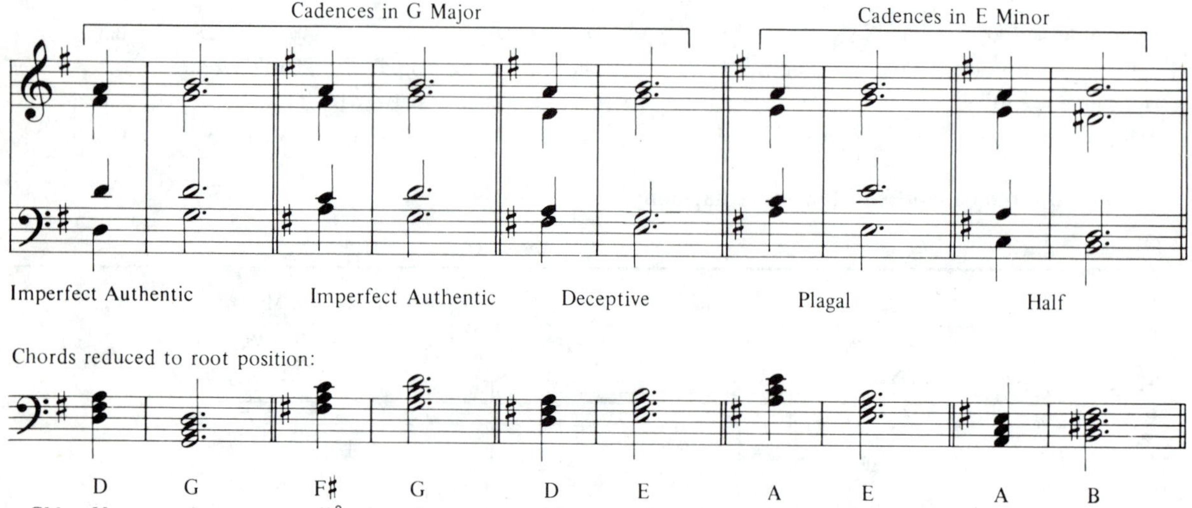

The two phrases, along with possible harmonizations and circle progressions marked, are shown here. The roots of possible triads are expressed in letters first to avoid entanglements in key systems. Then, all three possible harmonies for each melody tone are converted to keys of G major and E minor. The following, then, displays possible chords in the two keys and indicates the possibilities for modulation.

Figure 12.15

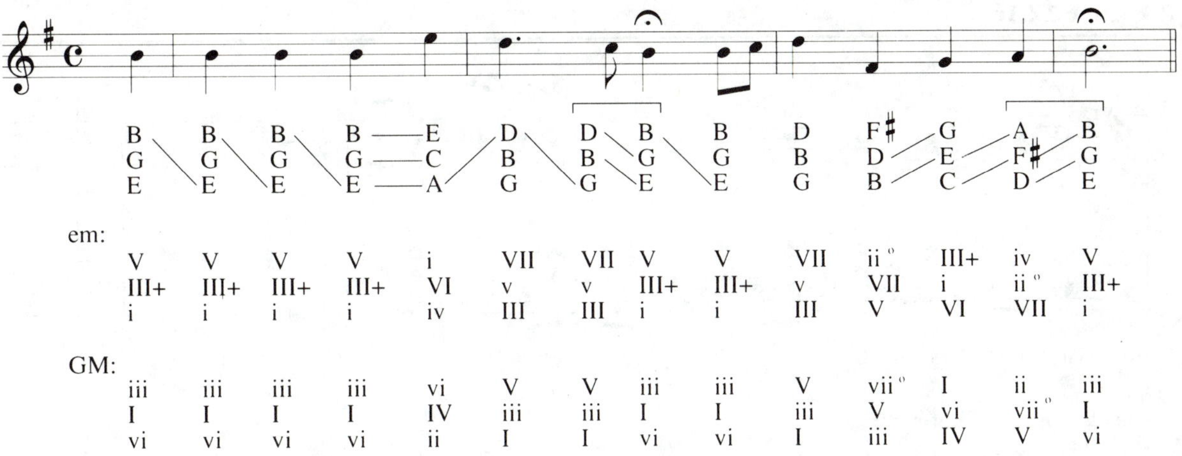

3. Play the chorale melody on the piano and accompany it (using block chords) with several combinations from the above possibilities. When a selection has been made, follow the procedures described in Chapter 8, "Harmonic Progression," fashioning a compatible bass line, adding the remaining voices, and finally inserting appropriate nonharmonic tones. The following suggestions will assist in making good choices:
   a. Remember that the descending P5 progression involving dominant and tonic harmony is important in establishing a key, and should be included in a set of progressions designed to identify and substantiate a new tonal center.
   b. For the present it is desirable to include at least one chord common to both keys just before the new key is to be initiated.
   c. Start your selection of chords with the cadence and work backwards, if necessary, to establish a smooth set of progressions.

From the previous information, two harmonizations were made by students. The first conceives the entire melody in G major while the second begins in E minor, modulates to G major, then returns to E minor:

Student harmonization of the chorale melody:

Figure 12.16

Another student harmonization of the chorale melody:

Figure 12.17

Finally, the harmonization of these two phrases by J. S. Bach is presented for comparison:

Figure 12.18

Bach: *Keinen hat Gott verlassen* (God Has Forsaken No One) BWV 369

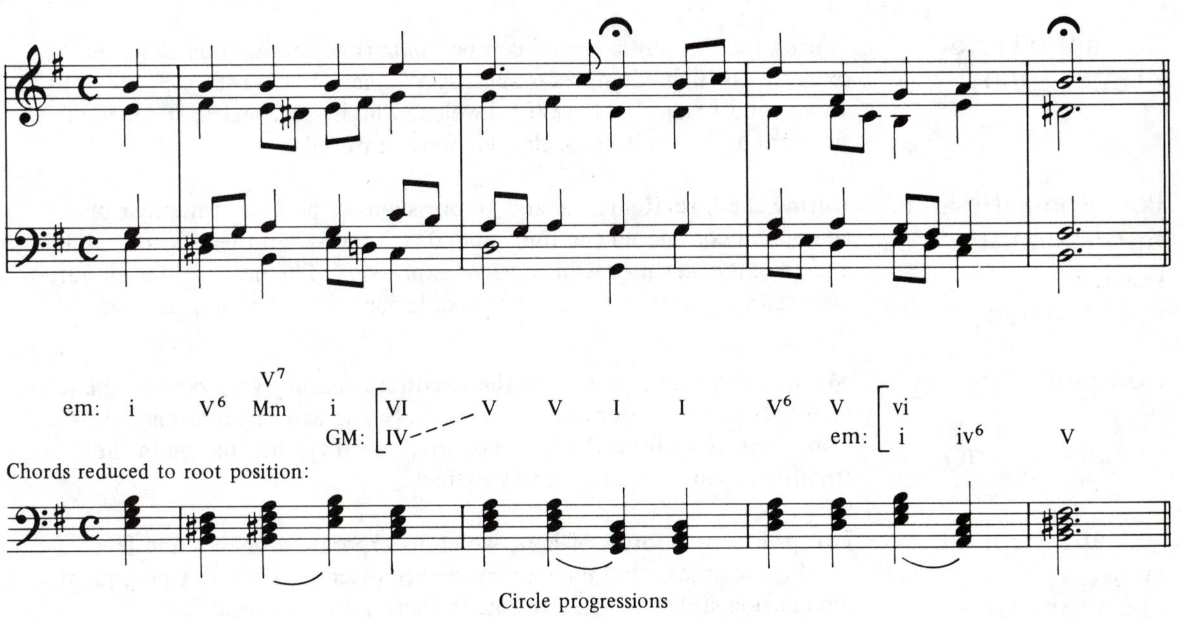

(Workbook-Anthology Assignments 12.5–12.9, pp. 141–147, and 12.12, p. 48)

History

Renaissance Period (1450–1600)

Most compositions of the Renaissance period are based on modal systems (Dorian, Phrygian, Lydian, Mixolydian, and Aeolian), and therefore did not contain modulations in the tonal sense.

Baroque Period (1600–1750)

Simple modulations to closely related keys began to develop in the early Baroque period. Joachim Burmeister (1564–1629), in his treatise, *Musica poetica* (The Poetics of Music), was one of the first theorists to distinguish between major and minor modes. Composers were reluctant to wander far from the original tonic of a composition because the prevailing system of tuning caused serious tuning problems. By 1700, with the improvements in the tuning system, modulation was an integral part of the musical style.

Classical Period (1750–1825)	Modulation became somewhat more venturesome during the Classical period. During the last twenty-five years (1800–1825) of the period, composers such as Beethoven (1770–1827) and Haydn (1732–1809), edged past the limits of modulation as set forth in the Baroque period. Modulations to distant keys (beyond closely related) became more common.
Romantic Period (1825–1900)	During the Romantic period composers carried modulation to its most extreme position. Composers such as Wagner (1813–1883), Franck (1822–1890), and Liszt (1811–1886) developed highly chromatic styles in which frequent and unusual modulations were featured.
Post-Romantic and Impressionistic Period (1875–1920)	During the Post-Romantic and Impressionistic periods, a number of composers considered the tight bounds of traditional tonality too confining and sought other means of musical expression. The nearly three-hundred-year span of tonality (including modulation) was coming to an end.
Contemporary Period (1920–Present)	Much of the music written in the twentieth century goes beyond the tonal system based on major and minor keys. So, as experimentation led composers away from the limits of strict tonality, modulation in the traditional sense became nearly extinct.
Jazz and Popular Music (1900–Present)	Except for some forms of jazz, which incorporate atonality and free tonality, both jazz and popular music are essentially tonal. Consequently, modulation still plays a large role in these types of music.

REVIEW

1. Select a major or minor triad. List all major and minor keys in which that triad appears. (For example, the C-major triad appears in: CM, FM, GM, am, fm, em). The triad can serve as a pivot chord in a common chord modulation between any two keys. Select two keys on the list and analyze the selected triad in both keys.
2. Turn to the Bach Chorale settings in the *Workbook/Anthology*. Examine the beginning and end of each phrase to determine the key(s) at both points. If the key is different at the end of the phrase than at the beginning, complete a roman-numeral analysis to determine the point of modulation. Is the modulation a common chord or chromatic modulation? (If you are not sure of the difference, see figures 12.2 and 12.4, which illustrate each type.) Are there any examples of phrase modulation in the chorales? What is the difference between a phrase modulation and a common chord modulation?
3. The diminished 7th chords are favorite vehicles for enharmonic modulation, since they may be spelled in a variety of ways. Select a diminished 7th chord and write at least four enharmonic spellings. For each spelling determine the key in which it would be the leading-tone 7th chord. This chord can function as a pivot chord between any two of those keys.

Test Yourself 12

1. Write all possible diatonic pivot chords between the given keys:
   a. Example: B♭ major and F major

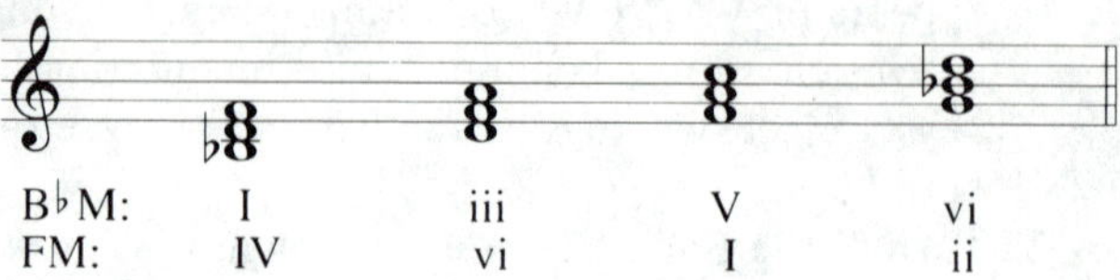

   b. D major and G major
   c. F♯ natural minor and A major
   d. E natural minor and C major
   e. F natural minor and Db major
   f. B major and D♯ natural minor
   g. G♯ harmonic minor and B major
   h. G harmonic minor and D harmonic minor
   i. E major and F♯ natural minor
2. Provide a complete harmonic analysis for each chorale phrase. The example shows the proper way to analyze the pivot chord and subsequent modulation. Use the same procedure in your own analyses.

Example:

a.
____:
b.
____:
c.
____:
d.
____:

CHAPTER 13

Secondary Dominants and Leading-Tone Chords

Secondary Dominants
Secondary Leading-Tone Chords
Altered Chords
Tonicized Chord
Part Writing
Nondiatonic Tone

Exposition

Secondary Dominants

Secondary dominants are diatonic chords that are altered to sound like dominants. This means changing minor triads to make them major and changing 7th chords to make them major-minor. While the *primary dominant* in C major is **G B D (V),** any other major or minor triad **(ii iii IV vi)** in C major may also have its own dominant—called a *secondary dominant*. In figure 13.1 (a), the **vi** triad is preceded by **iii,** but in example (aa), **vi** is preceded by its own dominant. The **iii** triad is transformed into a secondary dominant simply by making it a major triad **(E G♯ B),** so it sounds like a dominant in A minor.

Figure 13.1

Diatonic progressions:

Same progressions with secondary dominants:

Characteristics of Secondary Dominants

1. To be a secondary dominant, a chord must be either a major triad or a major-minor 7th chord. When you see the slash (/), substitute the word "of." **V/V** becomes **V of V.**
2. Secondary dominants are called *altered chords* because they contain *nondiatonic tones,* tones that are not found in the prevailing key. Secondary dominants are created out of diatonic chords that have been changed to make them major or major-minor 7th chords.

3. Secondary dominants, because they are temporarily raised to the status of dominant, naturally resolve to their temporary tonic, just as primary dominants (**V**) resolve to tonic (**I**). Thus, secondary dominants often move in circle progressions—**V/vi** to **vi**, **V/ii** to **ii**, and **V/V** to **V**.
4. In circle progressions, the chord to which secondary dominants progress is called a *tonicized chord*. When **V/ii** progresses to **ii**, the **ii** triad is the tonicized chord.
5. Secondary dominants may occasionally follow other secondary dominants. (See figure 13.2.)

Figure 13.2

Diatonic circle of fifths progressions:

Same diatonic chords changed to secondary dominants:

6. Just as primary dominants may be inverted, so also may secondary dominants.

Figure 13.3

Secondary dominant triad and 7th chords in root position:

Chords reduced to simple position:

Secondary dominants in inversion:

7. The secondary dominant triad of **IV** is simply the tonic **(I)**, so **I** is not called a secondary dominant (no altered pitches). However, $\mathbf{V^7/IV}$ (in C major, C E G B♭) does contain an altered note, so it is listed as a secondary dominant.

Figure 13.4

The voice leading of secondary dominant chords is the same as for primary dominant chords. For voice leading of the dominant triad, see Chapter 7, pages 123–128, or Appendix B. The appropriate voice-leading practices for primary dominant 7th chords are reprinted here for convenience:

Part Writing Secondary Dominant Chords

Voice Leading for the V^7 (Interpret as $V^7/\_\_$).

10. Resolve the 7th of the V^7 chord down one scale degree in the same voice.

11. All four factors of the V^7 are usually present.

But, for smoothness of voice leading, the fifth may be omitted and the root doubled.

Figure 13.5

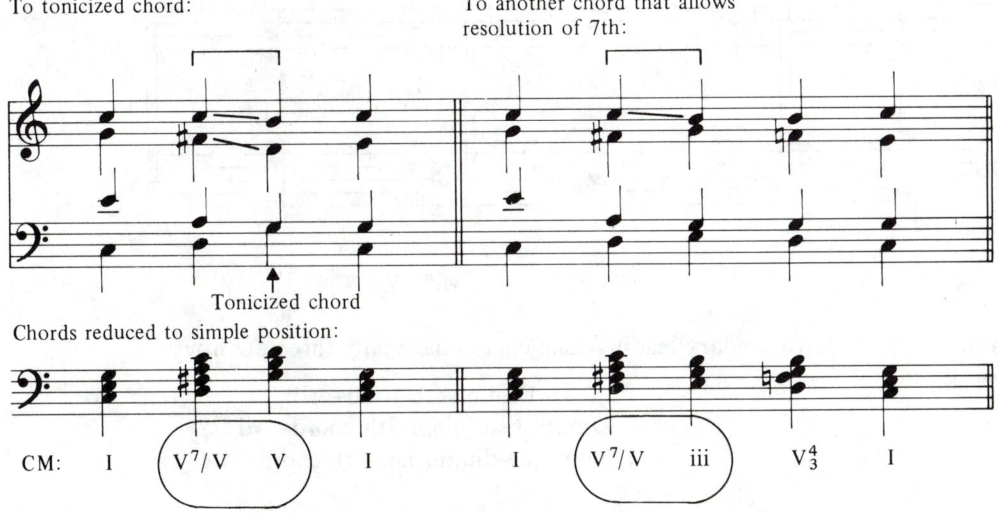

Secondary Leading-Tone Chords

Because leading-tone chords are often used as dominant substitutes (see Chapter 10), they also may function as temporary leading-tone chords—leading-tone sounding chords in a key other than the prevailing key. The primary leading-tone triad in CM is B D F (vii°), but any major or minor triad (**ii iii IV vi**) in C major may have its own leading-tone triad or 7th chord—called a *secondary leading-tone chord.* In figure 13.6 (a), the **vi** triad is preceded by **V**^{7}, but in example (aa), **vi** is preceded by its own leading-tone 7th chord. The **V**^{7} is transformed into a secondary leading-tone 7th chord simply by making it a diminished 7th chord (G♯ B D F), so it sounds like a leading-tone 7th chord (in A minor). Same progressions with secondary leading-tone chords:

Figure 13.6

Diatonic progressions:

Same progressions with secondary leading-tone chords:

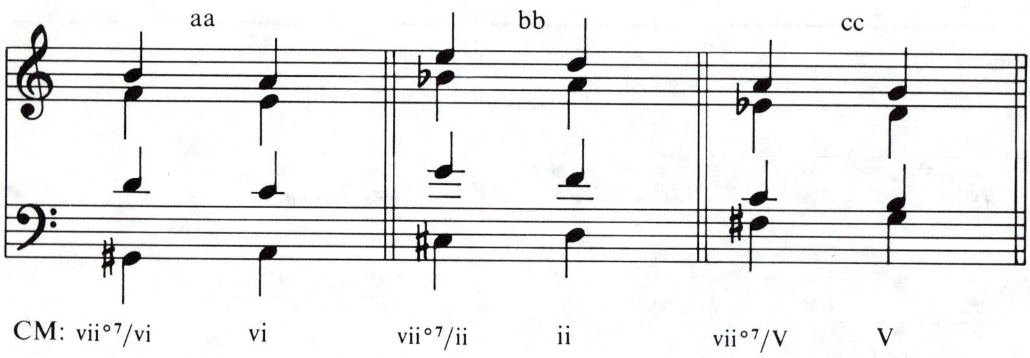

Characteristics of Secondary Leading-Tone Chords

1. Secondary leading-tone chords have only three qualities:

Diminished triad—**vii°**/
Diminished minor 7th chord—**vii**^{ø7}/
Diminished-diminished 7th chord—**vii**$^{°7}$/

2. Like secondary dominants, secondary leading-tone chords are called *altered* chords because they contain *nondiatonic* tones. Secondary leading-tone chords are created out of diatonic chords that have been changed to make them diminished, diminished-minor, or diminished-diminished.

Figure 13.7

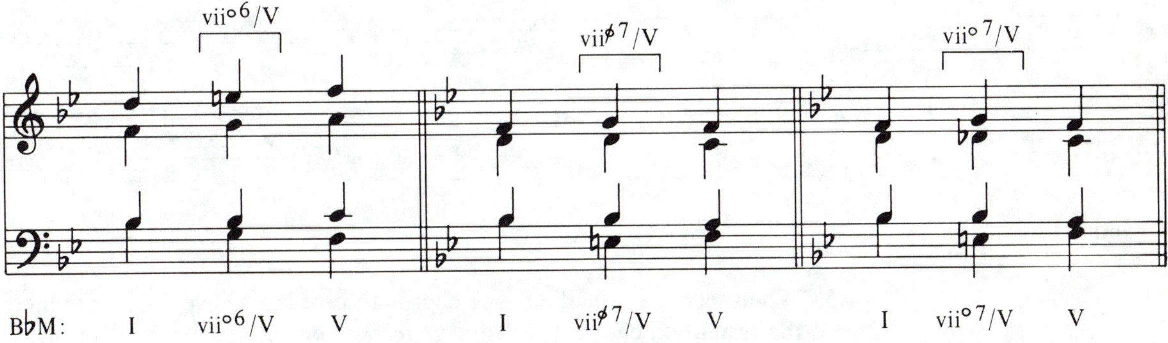

3. Because they are temporarily raised to the status of leading-tone chords, these chords naturally resolve to their temporary tonic, just as primary leading-tone chords resolve to their tonic. Thus, secondary leading-tone chords do not normally move in circle progressions, but resolve to a major or minor triad whose root is a half step above that of the secondary leading-tone chord.

Chord	Resolution
vii°7/ii	ii
vii°7/iii	iii
vii°7/IV	IV
vii°7/V	V
vii°7/vi	vi

4. Secondary leading-tone chords create a leading-tone relationship with diatonic major and minor triads:

In major keys:	**ii**	**iii**	**IV**	**V**	**vi**	
In minor keys:		**III**	**iv**	**V**	**VI**	**VII**

Figure 13.8

5. When secondary leading-tone chords resolve in a conventional manner, the resolution chord is called a *tonicized chord*. When **vii°7/V** resolves to **V**, the **V** triad is called a *tonicized chord*.
6. Secondary leading-tone chords are occasionally followed by other leading-tone chords. (See figure 13.9: chord 2 proceeds to another diminished 7th chord.) In these cases, conventional resolution is often impossible.

Figure 13.9

Part Writing Secondary Leading-Tone Chords

The voice leading of secondary leading-tone chords is the same as for primary leading-tone chords. The appropriate voice-leading practices for primary leading-tone chords are reprinted here for convenience:

Voice leading for the **vii°6**: (Interpret as **vii°6**/__)

7. **Special for vii°6. No established voice-leading pattern, but double bass note, avoid skips of a tritone, and move all voices with as much stepwise movement as possible.** (See Chapter 7 or Appendix C.)

Voice Leading for **vii°7** and **viiø7**:
(Interpret as **vii°7**/ and **viiø7**/.)

12. **Resolve the 7th of the vii°7 or viiø7 (and inversions) down one diatonic scale degree.** (Interpret "tonic" as *tonicized chord.*) (See Chapter 10 or Appendix C.)
13. **Resolve the tritone (root to 5th) inward if a d5th and outward if an A4th. However, it is not possible to do so in all situations.** (See Chapter 10 or Appendix C.)

Figure 13.10

(Workbook-Anthology Assignments 13.1 and 13.2, pp. 149–150)

History

Until the Baroque period and the development of functional harmony, secondary dominants and leading-tone chords as such did not exist.

Renaissance Period (1450–1600)

Baroque Period (1600–1750)

Secondary dominants and leading-tone chords developed during this period. Cautious use and conservative part writing of these chords marked the style of Baroque-period usage. Examples of secondary dominant and leading-tone triads (**V/** and **vii^{o6}/**) are more plentiful during this 150-year span than during any other period. Illustrated in figure 13.11 and figure 13.12 are both
V^6/V and **vii^{o6}/V.**

What would be the analysis of chord 6 without the A sharp?

Figure 13.11

Bach: *Wahrlich, ich sage euch* (Truly I Say Unto You) BWV 86

How would you analyze the nonharmonic tones at 1, 2, and 3 in figure 13.12?

1. unaccented appogiaturas
2. upper-neighboring tones

Figure 13.12

Purcell: Harpsichord Suite 8 in F Major, Z.669

Classical Period (1750–1825)

In the Classical period, as a natural development of the Baroque period, secondary dominant and leading-tone chords are found in somewhat greater frequency, and the application is less conservative. Progression of these chords to their tonicized resolutions constitutes by far the largest number of examples, but occasional nontraditional utilizations begin to appear.

Figure 13.13 shows representative examples of secondary dominant and leading-tone chords in the Classical period.

Figure 13.13

Romantic Period (1825–1900)

During the Romantic period secondary dominant and leading-tone 7th chords increased in frequency, especially those that are 7th chords. Partwriting became more daring (wider skips and 7th factors not always resolved.) Figure 13.14 illustrates successive secondary dominants.

Figure 13.15 illustrates a **vii°7/iii** that does not resolve to its tonicized chord:

Figure 13.14

Chopin: Polonaise, op. 26, no. 1

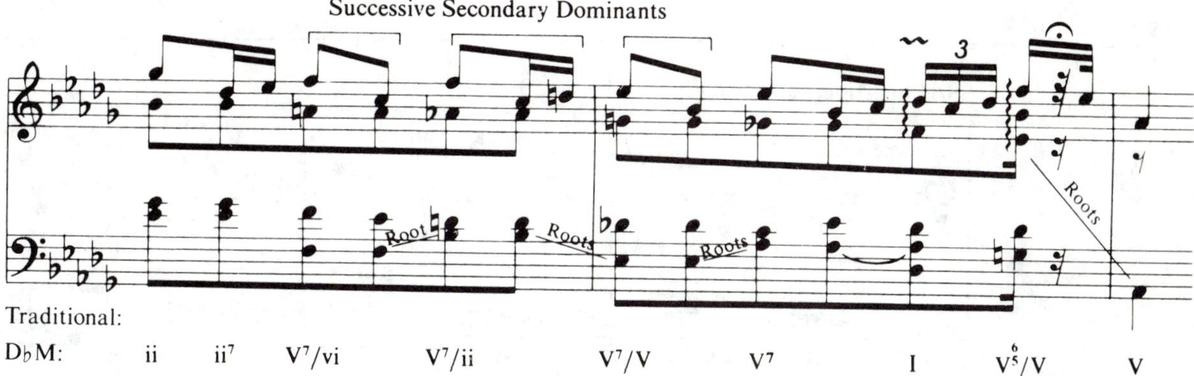

Chords shown in root position:

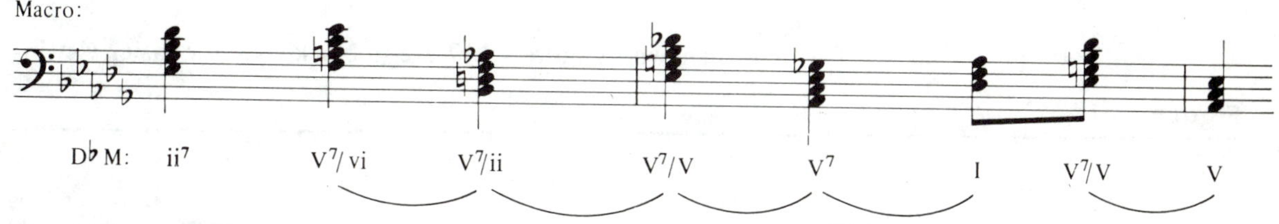

Figure 13.15

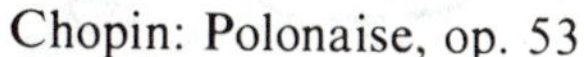
Chopin: Polonaise, op. 53

Figure 13.16 illustrates a half-diminished secondary leading-tone chord. It is somewhat less familiar than the more common diminished-diminished secondary leading-tone chord.

Figure 13.16

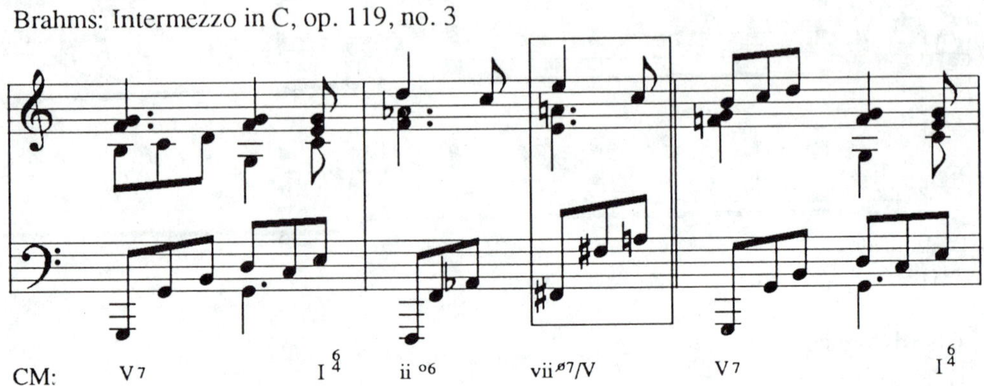

The chords shown in figure 13.17 are in block style for easier viewing.

Figure 13.17

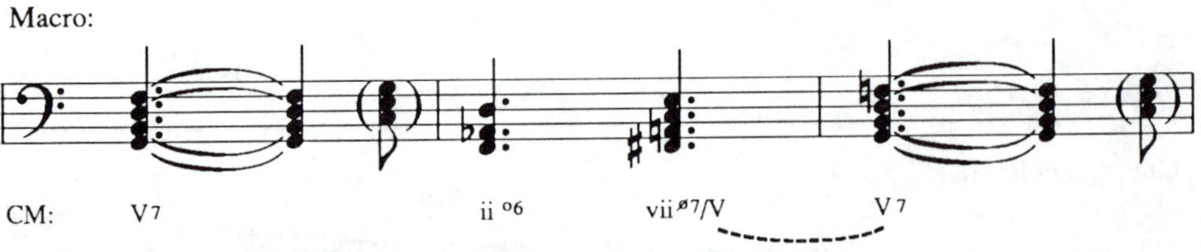

Figure 13.17 is primarily a decorated dominant 7th chord. Decorations are: $\mathbf{I}_4^6$, ii°⁶, and **vii**ø7/**V.**

Post-Romantic and Impressionistic Period (1875–1920)

Because functional harmony began to wane during this period, secondary dominant and leading-tone chord functions became less and less common. Figure 13.18 illustrates the use of a secondary dominant, which offers a fleeting suggestion of F♯ minor, a key not closely related to G major.

Figure 13.18

Source: Debussy: *Minstrels,* copyright © 1910, Durand et cie. Elkan-Vogel, Inc., sole representative, United States.

Secondary dominant and leading-tone chords are not a part of most twentieth century styles.

Contemporary Period (1920–Present)

Jazz and Popular Music (1900–Present)

One of the cornerstones of popular song accompaniments is the secondary dominant. These chords appear in abundance in popular songs and may occur singly or in successions of circle progressions. Jazz, excluding some avant-garde styles, also makes considerable use of secondary dominants. Secondary leading-tone chords are used only occasionally in popular songs and even less in jazz. A study of *four-chord formulas,* so common to the jazz and popular style, would be appropriate at this point.

Four-chord formulas (sequence of four chords) are a particular compositional device of jazz and popular music. Groups of four chords, played as a unit, are often used as a stylized accompaniment for popular songs, and as the basis for jazz improvisations. Some four-chord formulas consist entirely of secondary dominant 7th chords (examples: $\mathbf{C^7}$ $\mathbf{A^7}$ $\mathbf{D^7}$ $\mathbf{G^7}$), while others are a mixture of nondominant and secondary dominant 7ths. Some of the typical four-chord formulas are:

TYPICAL CHORD FORMULAS

Analysis Symbols				Popular Music Symbols in Key of C			
I^7	vi^7	ii^7	V^7	Cmaj7	Am7	Dm7	G7
V^7/IV	V^7/ii	V^7/V	V^7	C7	A7	D7	G7
I^7	$\flat iii^7$	ii^7	$\flat II^7_m$	Cmaj7	E♭m7	Dm7	D♭7
I	$vii^{\circ 7}/ii$	ii^7	V^7	C	C♯°	Dm7	G7
iii^7	vi^7	ii^7	V^7	Em7	Am7	Dm7	G7
iii^7	$\flat iii^7$	ii^7	$\flat II^7_m$	Em7	E♭m7	Dm7	D♭7
V^7/IV	$\flat VII^7_m$	$\flat VI^7_m$	V^7	C^7	B♭7	A♭7	G7
V^7/IV	$\flat III^7_m$	$\flat VI^7_m$	V^7	C^7	E♭7	A♭7	G7

Four-Chord Formulas in Succession

Often the harmonic structure of a phrase consists of a succession of four-chord formulas. When used in this manner, the patterns impart a distinct orderliness and logic to the music that is immediately perceived by the listener. This eight-measure phrase, composed by a student, illustrates two different four-chord formulas:

Figure 13.19

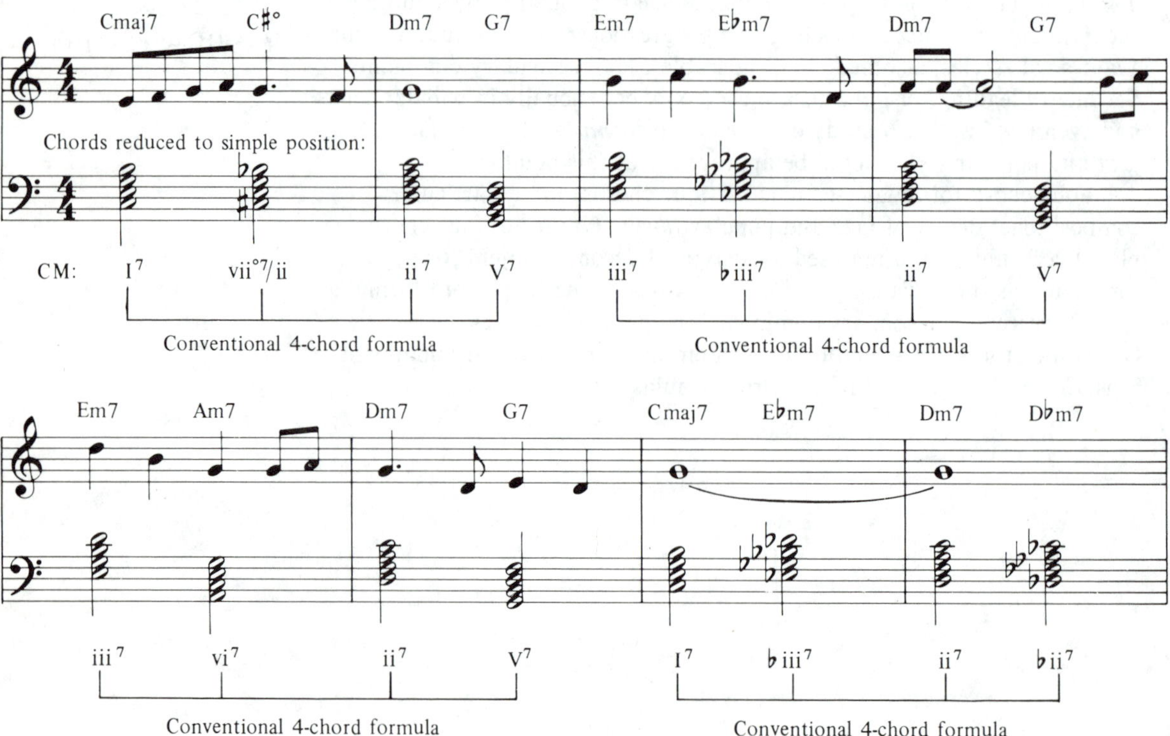

Repeated Four-Chord Formulas

Occasionally, a single four-chord formula provides the harmony for an entire popular song. Although only a brief excerpt, figure 13.20 shows how a conventional four-chord formula is repeated in a popular song:

Figure 13.20

R. Rodgers: "Mountain Greenery," copyright in 1926 by Harms, Inc. Copyrighted, renewed by Warner Bros. Music.

One innovation relating to the dominant 7th in the popular and jazz styles is the use of a *tritone substitution.* A major-minor 7th chord in a circle of P5ths progression may be replaced by the major-minor 7th chord an augmented 4th below.

Figure 13.21 shows a harmonic accompaniment using the circle progressions exclusively:

Figure 13.21

A harmonic accompaniment using circle-of-P5ths pattern exclusively:

Figure 13.22 shows the same accompaniment pattern except for the substitute chord, the root of which lies a tritone above or below:

Figure 13.22

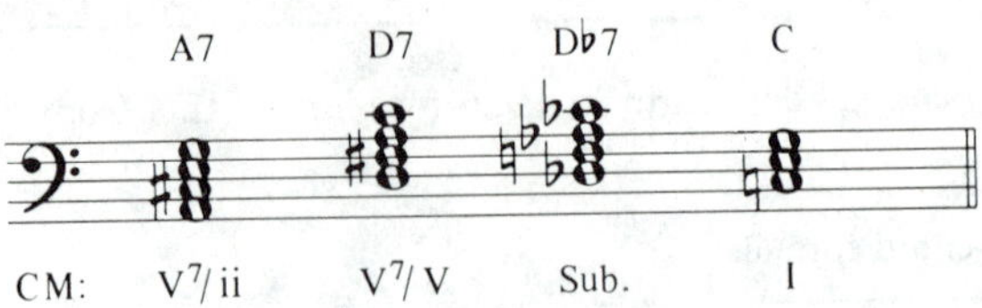

Figures 13.23 and 13.24 demonstrate harmonic substitutions that transform a circle progression into a chromatic-descending progression:

Figure 13.23

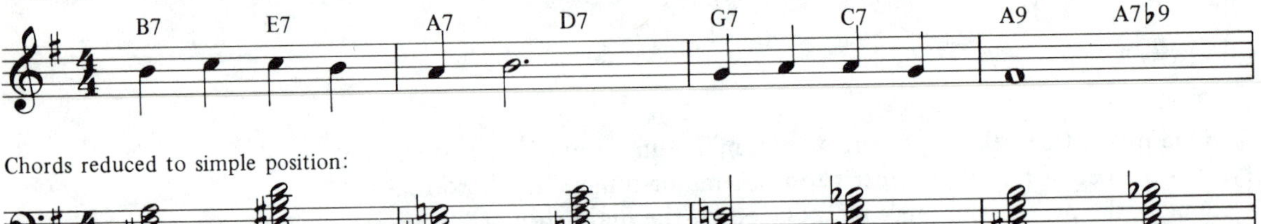

Chords reduced to simple position:

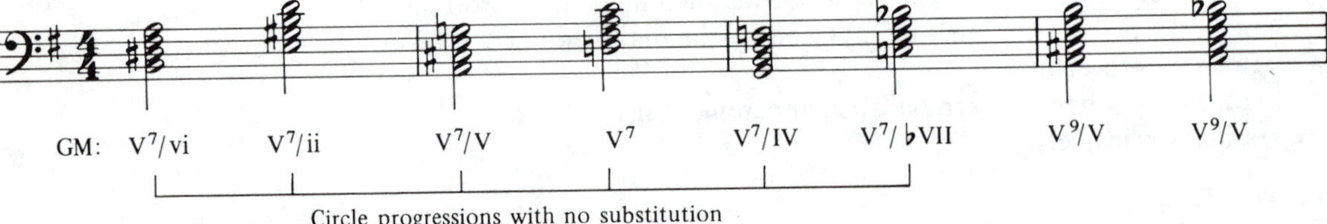

The same composition with substitutions:

Figure 13.24

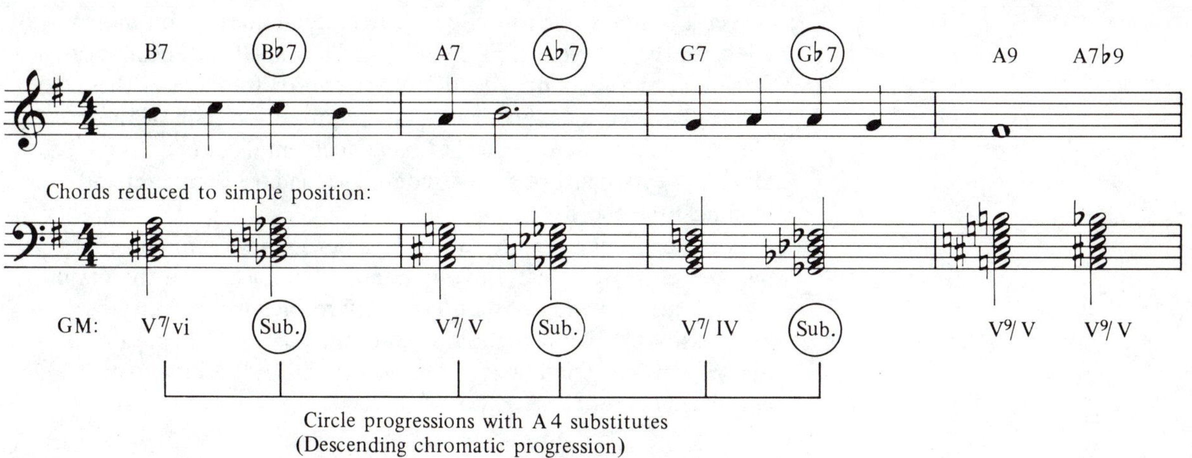

(Workbook-Anthology Assignments 13.3–13.18, pp. 150–169)

REVIEW

1. Select a major key and write all the diatonic major and minor triads in that key (I, ii, iii, IV, V, vi). Now spell the secondary dominant and secondary leading-tone chords for each of these triads. Take note of the accidentals required for each of these chords. Only those chords that have accidentals outside the original key signature are considered secondary dominants or leading-tone chords.
2. Any major-minor 7th chord can be a secondary dominant in a number of keys. Select a major-minor 7th chord, spell the major and the minor triad it would normally resolve to (in a circle progression). List all the major and minor keys that contain the major or minor triad above. Analyze the given major-minor 7th chord in each of those keys.

   Example:

   Major-minor 7th chord: **G B D F** (G7)

   Resolves to: **C E G** (C) or **C E♭ G** (Cm)

   Keys containing C chord: CM, GM, FM, am, fm, dm, em.

   Keys containing Cm chord: B♭M, A♭M, E♭M, cm, gm.

   Analyses of G7 chord:

   CM: V7 GM: V^7/IV FM: V^7/V am: V^7/III
   fm: V^7/V em: V^7/VI

   B♭M: V^7/ii A♭M: V^7/iii E♭M: V^7/vi cm: V^7 gm: V^7/iv

3. Select a diminished 7th chord, spell the minor triad it would normally resolve to, then list the keys containing that minor triad. Analyze the given diminished 7th chord in each of those keys.

   Example:

   Diminished 7th chord: **B D F A♭** (Bdim)

   Resolves to: **C E♭ G** (Cm)

   Keys containing Cm chord: B♭M, A♭M, E♭M, cm, gm.

   Analyses of Bdim chord:

   B♭M: $vii^{\circ 7}$/ii A♭M: $vii^{\circ 7}$/iii E♭M: $vii^{\circ 7}$/vi cm: $vii^{\circ 7}$
   gm: $vii^{\circ 7}$/iv

Test Yourself 13

1. A secondary dominant or leading-tone chord is analyzed in different keys, depending on the function of the chord to which it progresses. Assume in all cases that the chord following the given chord is the most common resolution of that chord. Name the key of the chord using the analysis given. Note the example.

Example:

vii°7/V in the key of *D major-minor*

vii°7/ii in the key of *G major*

vii°7/iv in the key of *e minor*

vii°7/VI in the key of *c♯ minor*

vii°7/iii in the key of *F major*

a.

V^6_5/V in the key of _____

V^6_5/ii in the key of _____

V^6_5/iv in the key of _____

V^6_5/vi in the key of _____

V^6_5/iii in the key of _____

b.

V^6/ii in the key of _____

V^6/VI in the key of _____

V^6/iii in the key of _____

V^6/V in the key of _____

V^6/IV in the key of _____

c.

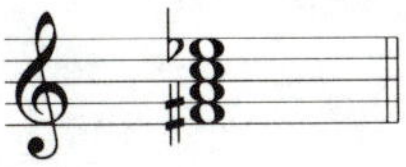

vii°7/iv in the key of _____

vii°7/iii in the key of _____

vii°7/V in the key of _____

vii°7/ii in the key of _____

vii°7/VI in the key of _____

2. Copy the given chords below on a separate piece of paper. Write the normal resolution for each secondary dominant or leading-tone 7th chord in four-part harmony, being careful to properly resolve the tritones and 7ths according to the voice-leading practices listed on pages 215 and 219. Name the key and provide a roman-numeral analysis of the resolution chord. Note the example:

PART 3

Form

Form refers to the larger shape of the composition. Coherent form is the result of the careful arrangement of all the elements of the composition, which enables the listener to recognize materials that are new and those that were presented earlier and follow the logic of the composition. A complete study of musical form would go far beyond the limits of this book, but we will introduce two important formal designs, upon which many of the larger forms are based: *two-part* or *binary* form and *three-part* or *ternary* form. These two forms and the larger forms that developed from them account for the structural plan of most music in the "common practice" period.

You already know the smaller elements of form—phrases and periods, and we will see how larger formal designs have been created from these elements.

CHAPTER

14

Two-Part (Binary) Form

Formal Divisions
Closed Form
Open Form
Simple Forms
Compound Forms
Two-Part (Binary) Form
Rounded Binary Form
Incipient Three-Part Form
Bar Form

Exposition

Form in music is the result of the interaction of all the structural elements. You are already familiar with the smaller elements of form: phrases and periods, but in this chapter we will begin to consider the form of complete compositions.

Formal Divisions

A piece of music can generally be divided into two or more major sections, and the boundaries between these sections are called *formal divisions.* Formal divisions are the result of strong harmonic and melodic cadences and rhythmic factors, such as rests, fermatas, longer note values, and so on. Changes in orchestration and texture may also contribute to the sense of formal division. The formal divisions define the sections of a composition, and these sections are labeled with capital letters: A, B, C, and so on. If a section of music is repeated, the same letter is used: A, A, B, B, and so on, and if it contains similar material, this is designated by adding primes to the previous letter: A, A′, A″, and so on.

Open versus Closed Formal Divisions

A section is designated as *closed* if it cadences on the tonic of the composition (the original tonic), and *open* if it cadences elsewhere. Open formal divisions commonly conclude with half cadences, or they may modulate to related keys, which requires a following section or sections to complete the tonal direction.

Simple versus Compound Forms

Smaller compositions are generally in one of the two *simple forms: two-part (binary) form,* or *three-part (ternary) form.* Larger works are often in *compound form,* in which the sections may themselves be complete binary or ternary forms.

Two-Part Form

Also called binary, the *two-part form* consists of two main sections. In its simplest configuration, the first part may consist of a period only, while in a more expanded construction a double period or larger section could comprise part A. The second part may also be composed in the same manner, but on frequent occasions the second part is longer than the first. In many binary forms the first section is open, concluding with a half cadence or moving to a related key, while the second section concludes with a perfect authentic cadence on the tonic. The antecedent-consequent period is a microcosm of the typical binary form (see figure 14.1).

Figure 14.1

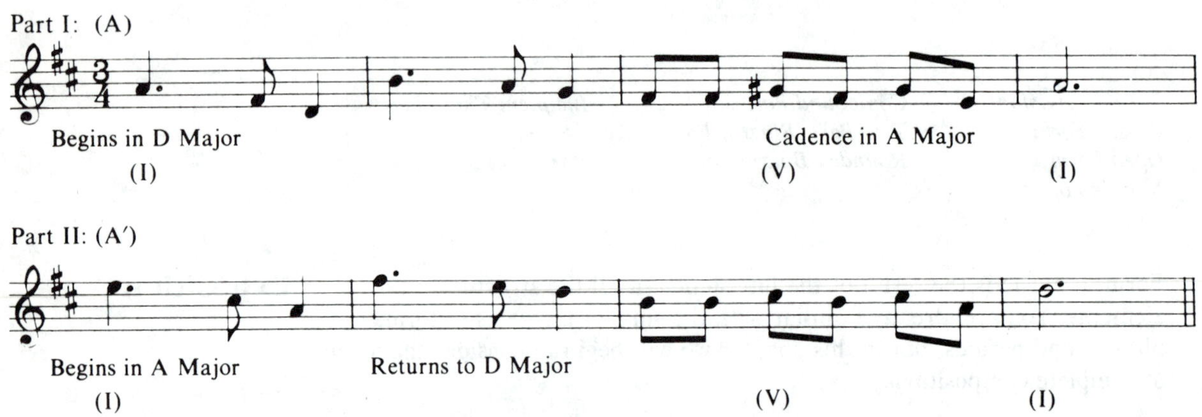

The two sections of a binary form are often repeated, as figure 14.2 illustrates. (Notice the open form of the structural divisions in this example.)

ANALYSIS OF BACH: PARTITA NO. 1 IN B-FLAT MAJOR

Measures	Key	Type of Cadence	Phrase Relationship	Formal Analysis
1–4	B♭ Major	Half	a	A
5–8	B♭ Major	Half	a	
9–12	g minor	Authentic	b	B
13–16	B♭ Major	Authentic	c	

Figure 14.2

Motive Y
5
6
7
8
Half cadence
Phrase b
Analysis: 5
6
7
8
IV
V
I6
V7
I
V
Part B
Motive X from Part A transposed P4 down
Motive Y from phrase b
9
10
11
12
Half cadence
13
Phrase a′
Analysis: 9
10
11
12
13
V
I6 4
V7
I
V
I
14
15
16
17
Perfect authentic cadence
18
Phrase c
Analysis: 14
15
16
17
18
V
I
I
V7
I
IV
V
I

Londonderry Air is an example of a binary form without repeated sections in which both sections are closed. The material of the second section is quite contrasting with the material of the first section.

ANALYSIS OF "LONDONDERRY AIR"

Measures	Key	Type of Cadence	Phrase Relationship	Formal Analysis
1–4	E♭ Major	Half	a	A
5–8	E♭ Major	Perfect authentic	a′	
9–12	E♭ Major	Half	b	B
13–16	E♭ Major	Perfect authentic	c	

Figure 14.3

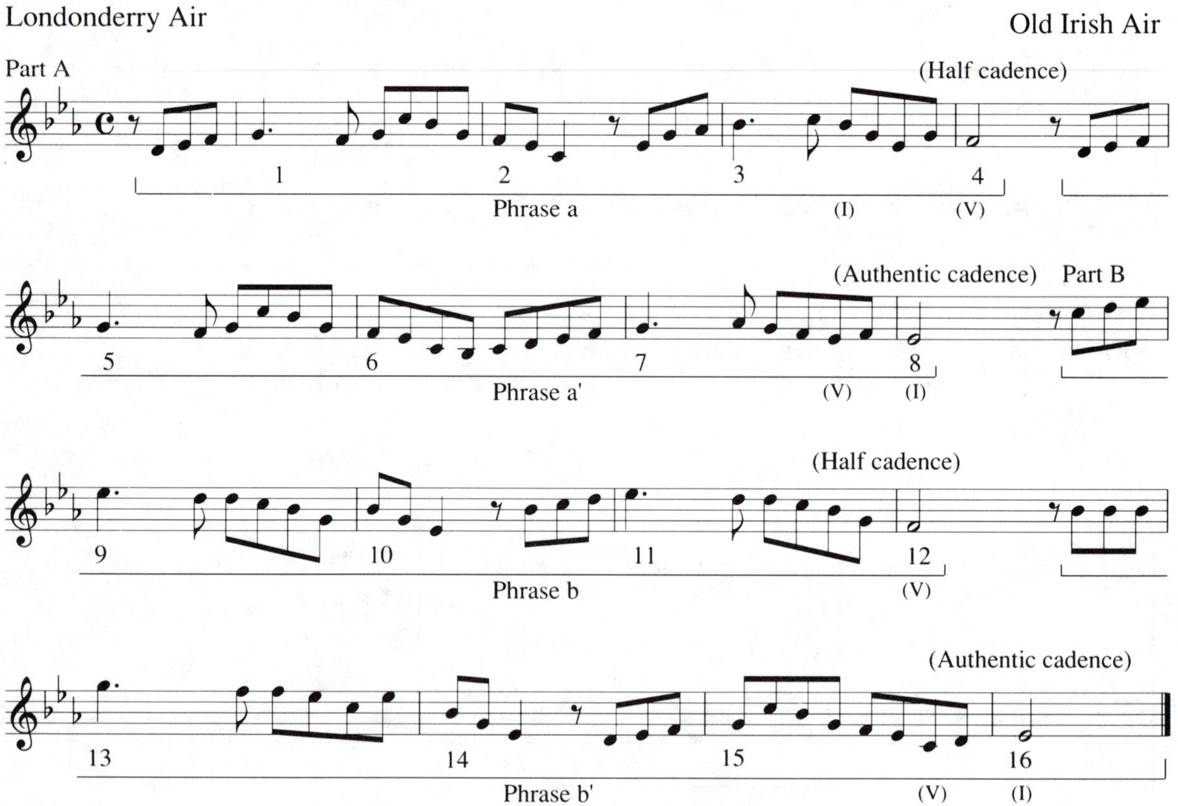

A type of two-part form very popular in the Baroque and Classical periods consisted of motivic material common to both the A and the B sections. Figure 14.4 typifies this treatment in the Classical period. It is essentially in homophonic texture (a single melody line with supporting accompaniment).

Figure 14.4

Haydn: Sonata in A Major, Hob. XV:5 (2nd Movement)

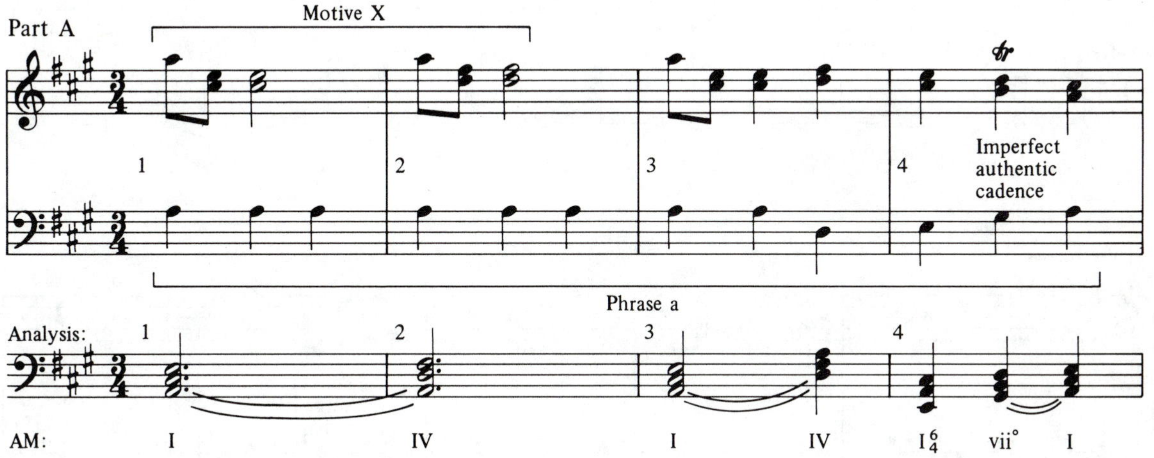

ANALYSIS OF HAYDN: SONATA IN A MAJOR

Measures	Key	Type of Cadence	Phrase Relationship	Formal Analysis
1–4	A Major	Imperfect authentic	a	A
5–8	A Major	Half	b	
9–12	A Major	Half	a′	B
13–18	A Major	Perfect authentic	c	

Note:

1. Phrase a′ is related to a in that it contains the same motive transposed.
2. The only perfect authentic cadence occurs at the end of the composition.

Figure 14.5 is an additional example of the two-part, or binary, form where both parts (A and B) utilize similar (but not exactly the same) material. This work by Bach is taken from one of the "English Suites" written for keyboard. Each suite is composed of a number of dances, all of which are in the same key. A prelude often introduces the dances. The dance types employed in the Baroque period include the allemande, courante, sarabande, gigue (jig), gavotte, bourree, minuet, and others. These had begun as popular dances, but by the time of the late Baroque period, they had gradually entered into the domain of art music.

The majority of dance movements are in binary form, and the following composition is a good illustration of the thematic unity so characteristic of the genre.

Figure 14.5

Bach: *Gavotte* from English Suite no. 3 in G minor, BWV 808

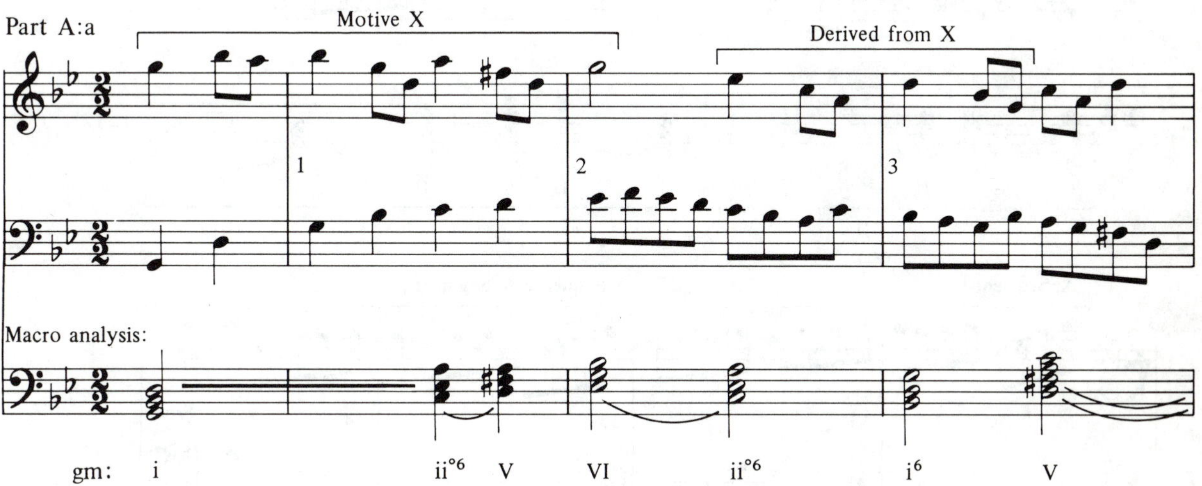

a′
Motive X
4
5
6
7
i
i
ii°6
V
VI
vii°6
V
vi
V7
III
1.
2.
Part B: b
Motive X
Sequence A,
8
8
9
10
Analysis:
8
9
10
I
I
I
IV
ii7
I
ii
III
VII
A, Segment 1
Sequence A, Segment 2
b′
11
12
13
14
From
Analysis:
11
12
13
Target
14
V7
I
(VII)
III
V7
i
v

Secondary Sequence
c
15
Motive X
16
17
18
Analysis:
15
16
17
Target
18
V
i
iv
V
i
iv⁷
v
Derives from Motive X
19
20
21
22
Pedal:
Analysis:
V⁷
i⁶₄
i
vii°⁷
iv
i
Secondary Sequence
d
23
24
25
26
Analysis:
23
24
25
26
i
V⁷
i
V⁷
i⁶
vii°⁷
i
V
i
i

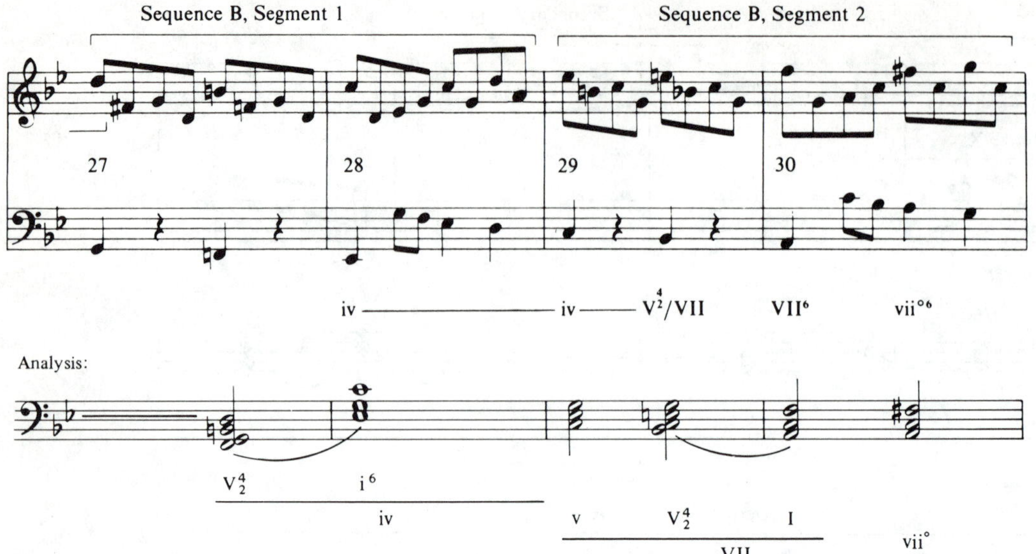
Sequence B, Segment 1
Sequence B, Segment 2
27
28
29
30
iv
iv
V4/2/VII
VII6
vii°6
Analysis:
V4/2
i6
iv
v
V4/2
I
VII
vii°

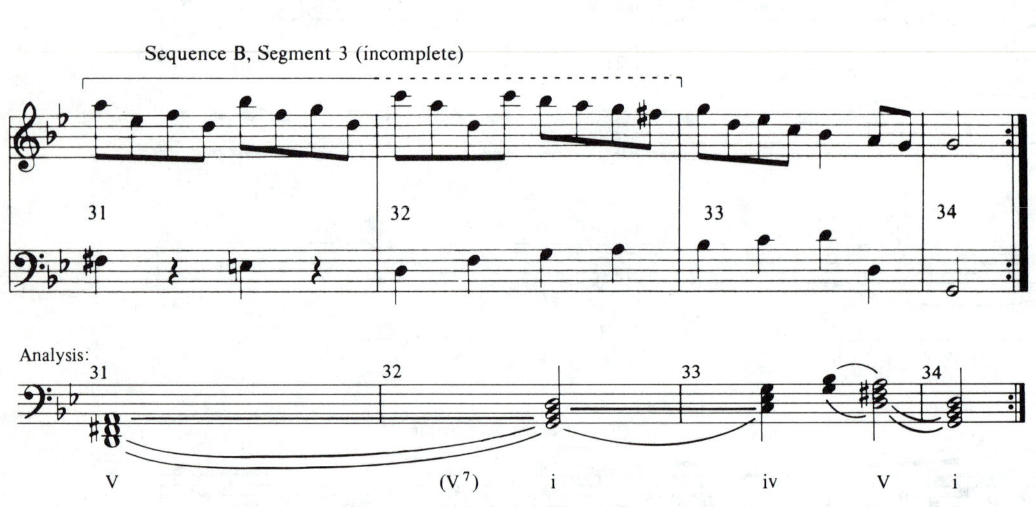
Sequence B, Segment 3 (incomplete)
31
32
33
34
Analysis:
31
32
33
34
V
(V7)
i
iv
V
i

ANALYSIS OF BACH: GAVOTTE

Measures	Key	Type of Cadence	Phrase Relationship	Formal Analysis
1–4	g minor	Imperfect authentic	a	A
4–8	g minor to B♭ Major	Perfect authentic	a′	
8–14	B♭ Major to d minor	Perfect authentic	b	B
14–18	d minor	Perfect authentic	b′	
18–26	d minor to g minor	Half	c	
26–34	g minor	Perfect authentic	d	

The Bach *Gavotte* is an excellent example of the style of tonal counterpoint (as opposed to modal counterpoint of the sixteenth century) found in the Baroque period. Here the counterpoint is governed by the functional harmony it implies. Although the composition lacks the organic intensity of a fugue or canon, it is essentially a polyphonic rather than homophonic work. Notice that the first section is in the usual open form.

Either motive X itself or derivatives of it appear frequently (six times) in part A or in part B. This is a compelling force for unification of the two parts and ensures organization in the composition. Motivic material appears only once in the lower voice (in measures 14–16). The lower voice for the most part simply provides supporting counterpoint for the upper voice, which contributes most of the elements of interest.

Two important sequences occur: one in measures 10–14 (sequence A), and the other in measures 27–33 (sequence B). Secondary sequences (sequences of less structural significance) are also found in measures 17 and 25.

The cadences in measures 4 and 26 are considered weak, since the melodic line allows only a brief pause at those moments and immediately picks up the next phrase. Thus, the force of the cadence is reduced.

Rounded Binary Form

The *rounded binary form* differs from true two-part or binary form in that the first section (A) is repeated (sometimes in part) at the end of the second (B) section, as you can see in figure 14.6. This form is sometimes called *incipient three-part form.*

Figure 14.6

Mozart: Piano Sonata in D Major, K. 284 (3rd Movement)

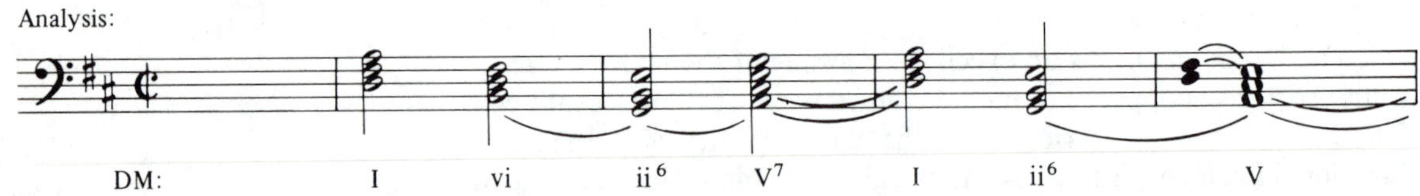

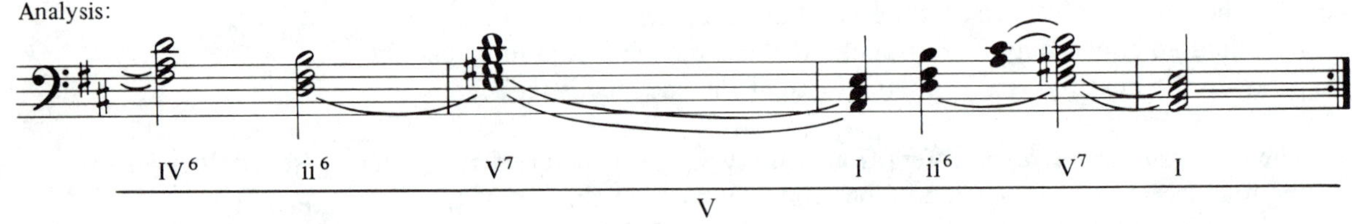

Analysis:

Analysis:

ANALYSIS OF MOZART: SONATA IN D MAJOR

Measures	Key	Type of Cadence	Phrase Relationship	Formal Analysis
1–4	DM	Half	a	A
5–8	AM	Perfect authentic	b	
9–13	DM	Half	c	BA
14–17	DM	Perfect authentic	a′	

(Workbook-Anthology Assignments 14.1–14.4, pp. 171–172)

History

Medieval and Middle Ages (500–1450)

The forerunner of two-part binary form was the *bar form.* This is a name given to a song form used by the Minnesingers (aristocratic poet-musicians from the twelfth to fourteenth centuries) and Meistersingers (middle-class, poet-musicians from the fourteenth to sixteenth centuries). Bar form consists of an A part (called *Stollen*) that is repeated and a B part (*Abgesang*) that is not repeated. As bar form developed, the B part began to contain either a section or all of the A part, and thus has a rounded binary character. Figure 14.7 is an example of the canzo, which resembles the bar form. It was written toward the end of the twelfth century and may have been performed as an unaccompanied solo song.

Renaissance Period (1450–1600)

The bar form continued into the Renaissance, although its use was not extensive. The two-part concept found its way into a variety of compositions of this period, among them the German part song, the Lutheran chorale, and the German lied.

Baroque Period (1600–1750)

It was during the Baroque period that the use of two-part form became most extensive. Suite movements of extended length (allemande, courante, sarabande, gigue, minuet, bourree, gavotte, etc.) were written using this construction, and only the basic elements of the older bar form remained.

Classical Period (1750–1825)

The Classical period, especially the early part, saw considerable use of the two-part form. From the concise shape of the baroque suite movements, the classical composers began to evolve embryonic development sections at the beginning of the second section, the theme (or themes) from the first section were repeated at the end of the second section in the original key, and the result was the sonata allegro form.

Figure 14.7

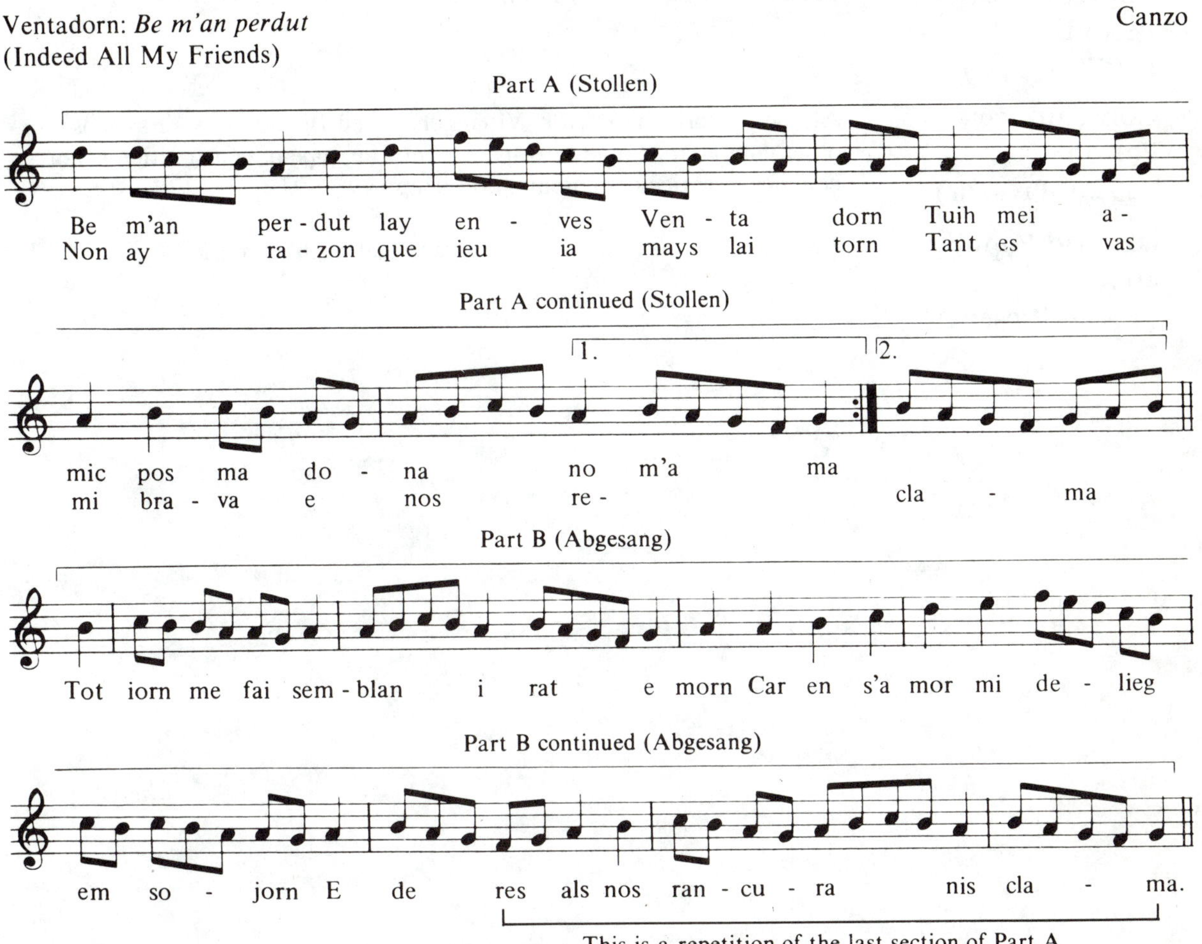

Romantic Period (1825–1900)

The use of the binary form continued through the Romantic period, although in greatly diminished numbers. Much greater freedom was taken in adapting the construction to nineteenth-century musical thought. Examples of binary form can be found in the works of Schubert, Berlioz, Mendelssohn, Bizet, and Schumann.

Post-Romantic and Impressionistic Period (1875–1920)

Although examples can be found during this period, the binary form was not an essential element in this era.

Contemporary Period (1920–Present)

Although works by Bartók, Villa-Lobos, and Britten, as well as those of other composers employ two-part form, this type of construction is not a common practice of contemporary composers.

Jazz and Popular Music (1900–Present)

Two-part form is seldom found in jazz and popular music.

REVIEW

Chapter 14 deals with larger areas of musical structure and will require a new approach to study. Previous chapters require fluency in spelling chords and knowledge of the specifics of voice leading, which can be practiced, whereas this chapter requires an understanding of larger concepts and can be reviewed in much the same way you would review the materials of other textbooks.

1. Play or listen to a recording of each of the compositions analyzed in this chapter. Carefully examine the analysis of each composition, including the analytical statements in the scores themselves and the summary analysis that follows. Make certain that you understand each analytical statement. If certain items are not clear to you, reread the pertinent section of the chapter, or look in previous chapters for an explanation. If you still have problems, discuss them with your instructor or a fellow student.
2. Define each term listed at the head of the chapter (page 237) in your own words. Compare your definition with the definition of the glossary and see if you can improve your definition. Consider how the terms can be applied to the compositions in the chapter.

Test Yourself 14

1. Examine measures 1–8 of figure 14.4 on pages 241–242. Would you describe the form of this section as open or closed? Why? What about the remaining section (measures 9–18)?
2. Examine measures 1–8 of figure 14.5 on pages 243–246. Would you describe the form of this section as open or closed? Why? What about the remaining section (measures 9–34)?
3. We have used the terms *phrase, period,* and *section* to designate the elements of form. Define each of these terms to make a clear distinction among them. Can a phrase ever be a period? Can a period ever be a section? Why or why not?
4. How does a rounded binary form differ from a binary form? How are they alike?

CHAPTER 15

Three-Part (Ternary) Form

Three-Part Form	*Expanded Three-Part Form*	*Refrain*
Ternary Form		*Bridge (Release)*

Exposition

Three-Part Form

A *three-part,* or *ternary form* is a sectional form consisting of three principal parts following the scheme A B A in which each section is a complete musical statement.

Part I	Part II	Part III
A	B	A
Statement	Contrast	Restatement

The "A" sections of three-part forms are typically closed in formal design (they cadence on the tonic). Three-part forms are found in a wide variety of sizes, from as small as three phrases to movements lasting several minutes. In this chapter we will concentrate on smaller examples of this form.

An independent, or complete, three-part form at the very lowest level (three-phrase) is somewhat rare. Figure 15.1 is an example of this construction:

Figure 15.1

Schumann: *Kinder Sonata* no. 1 from *Drei Clavier-Sonaten für die Jugend* (Three Piano Sonatas for the Young), op. 118

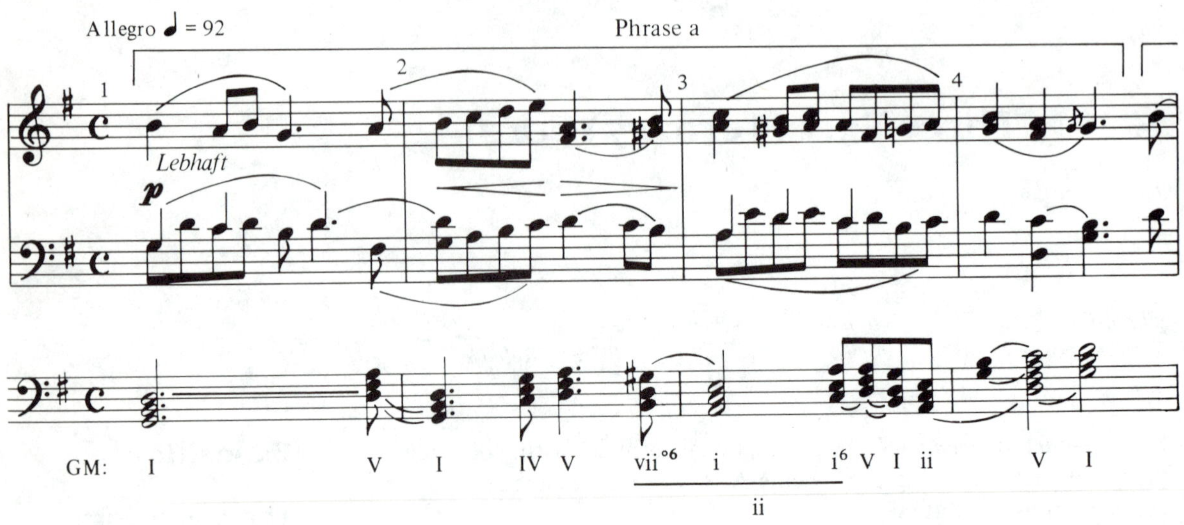

Notice that the first phrase has a cadence on the tonic, which is typical of the closed A section in three-part form.

The three-part form is one of the most prevalent small homophonic forms in the nineteenth century. In the usual pattern, both A sections are at least a period in length. The B section is usually at least a period in length, although it may sometimes be only a single phrase. The following is a typical example.

Figure 15.2

Chopin: Mazurka in C Major, op. 33, no. 3

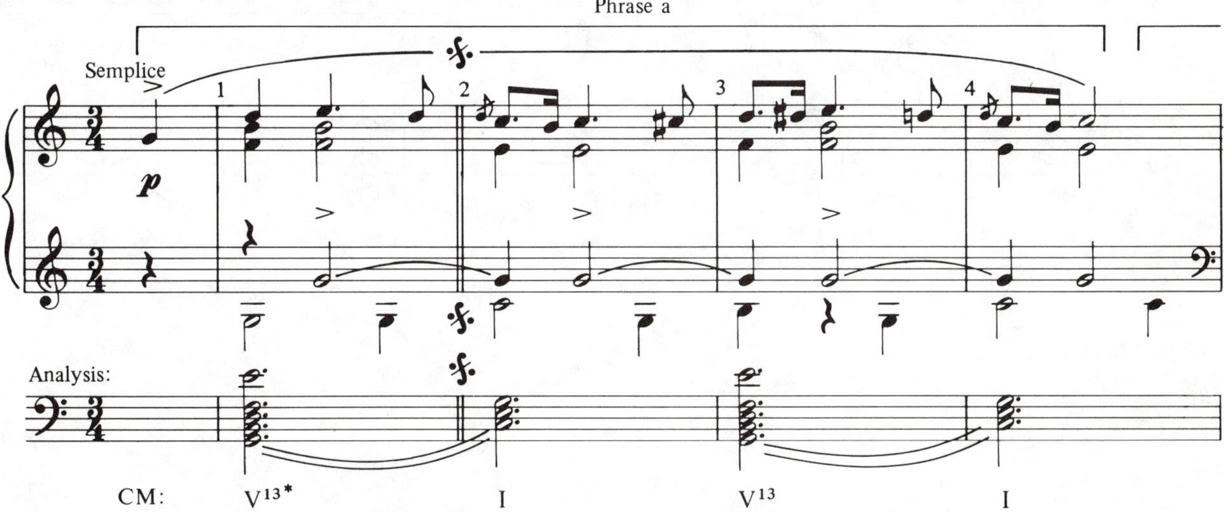

*See chapter 19 for discussion of 9th, 11th, and 13th chords.

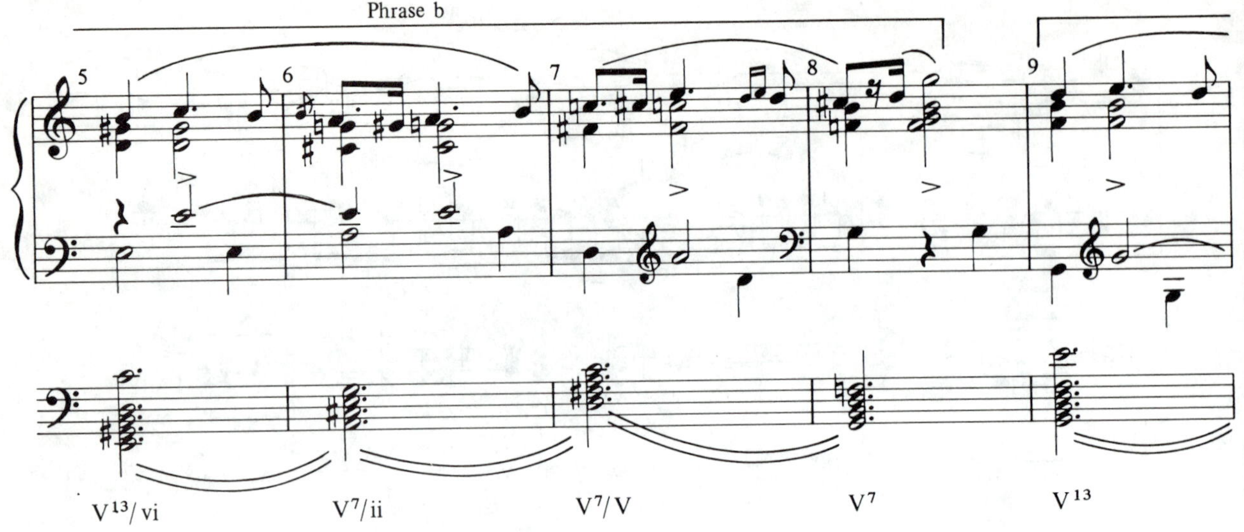
Phrase b
5
6
7
8
9
V 13/ vi
V7/ii
V7/ V
V7
V 13

Phrase a
Phrase c
10
11
12
13
14
I
V13
I
V 13/V
V 7

Phrase d
15
16
Fine
17
18
f
I
iv⁷
I
♭VI
Phrase e
19
20
21
22
23
V⁷
I
V⁹
I
V⁹
(♭VI)

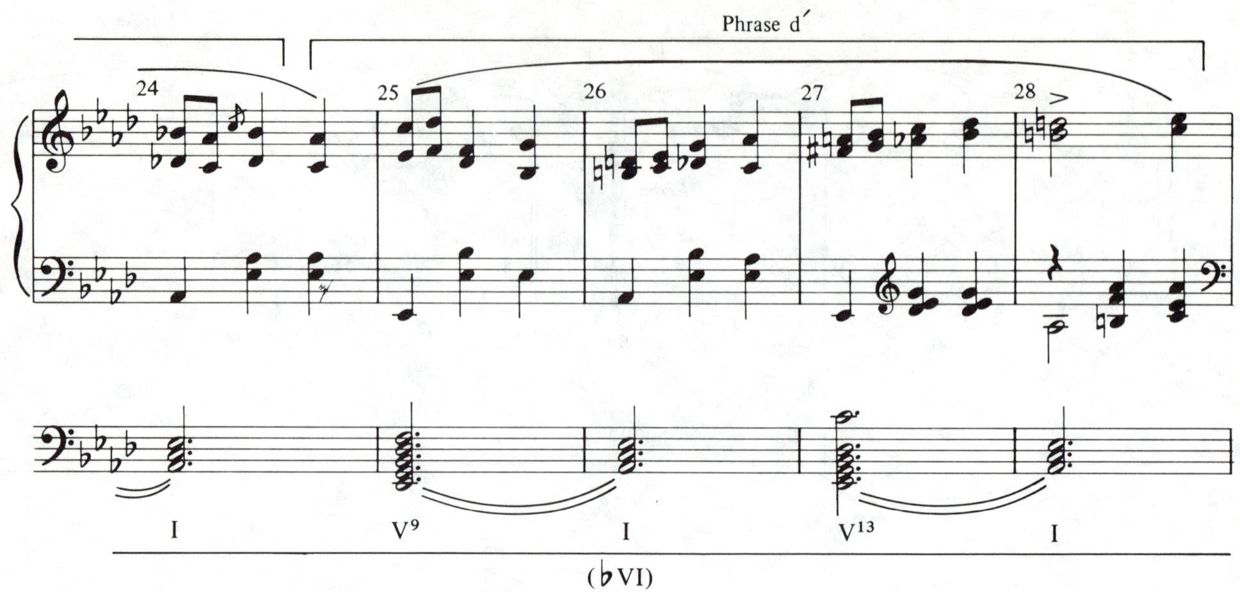
Phrase d´
24
25
26
27
28
I
V9
I
V13
I
(♭VI)

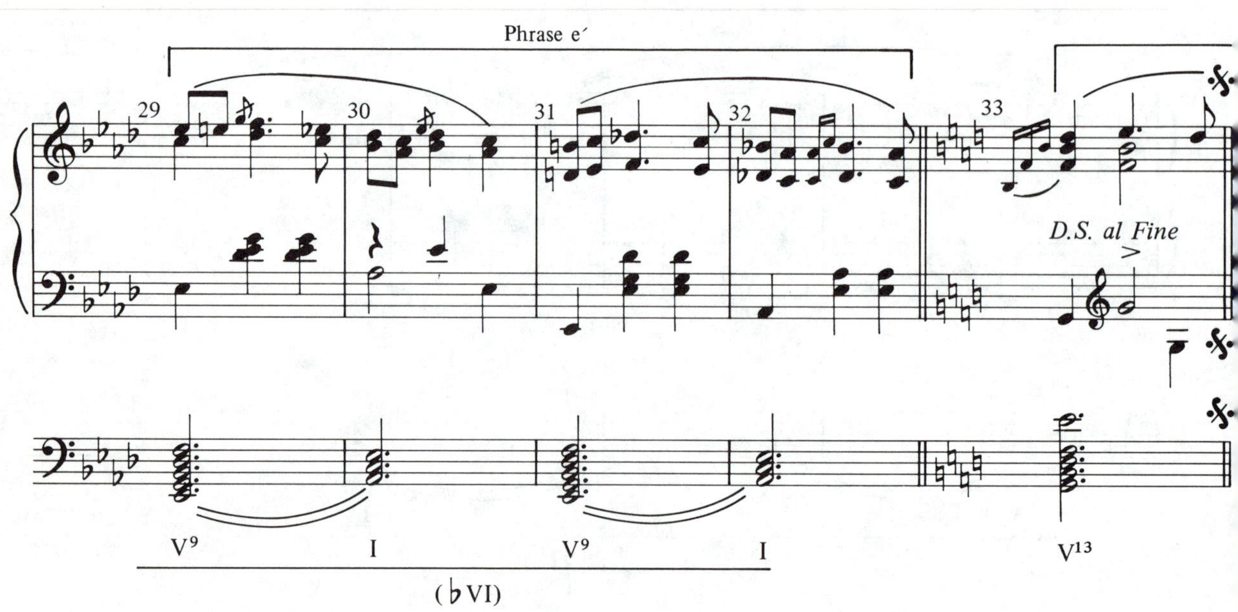
Phrase e´
29
30
31
32
33
D.S. al Fine
V9
I
V9
I
V13
(♭VI)

ANALYSIS OF CHOPIN: MAZURKA NO. 24

Measures	Key	Type of Cadence	Phrase	Part	Organization
1–4	CM	Perfect authentic	a		
5–8	CM	Half	b	A	Double period
9–12	CM	Perfect authentic	a		
13–16	CM	Perfect authentic	c		
17–20	A♭M	Imperfect authentic	d		
21–24	A♭M	Perfect authentic	e	B	Period repeated
25–28	A♭M	Imperfect authentic	d′		
29–32	A♭M	Perfect authentic	e′		
33+ Repetition of 2–16	CM	(See above)	(See above)	A	Double period

Figure 15.2 clearly illustrates the function of the B part in this form: to provide contrast with the A part and to create a need to return to the A part to complete the pattern. The degree of contrast between the A and B parts varies considerably from composition to composition. In some examples, the thematic material of B may be derived from that of A, resulting in a slight degree of contrast. In other examples, such as the Chopin Mazurka quoted above, the B may provide a sharp contrast with A.

Ternary Form Expanded

Repetition

The ternary form may be expanded by the use of repetitions of any section. The repeats may be made with double bars and repeat signs, or they may be written out for the composer to provide a different setting of the music when repeated. Such compositions are said to be in *expanded ternary form.*

Auxiliary Members

The three-part form may be expanded by the use of auxiliary members such as an introduction to precede the first A, a transition between the sections, or a coda after the final A part that serves to bring the composition to a close.

Suggested examples of the expanded three-part form:

Chopin: Mazurka in A minor, op. 17, no. 4
Chopin: Waltz in D-flat Major, op. 64, no. 1 (Minuet)
Prokofiev: Classical Symphony in D Major, op. 25, "Gavotte" (3rd Movement)
Mendelssohn: Songs without Words, op. 19, no. 3; op. 30, no. 2; op. 30, no. 4; op. 38, no. 4; op. 53, no. 1; op. 53, no. 3; op. 53, no. 5.

(Workbook-Anthology Assignments 15.1–15.6, p. 173)

History

Medieval and Middle Ages (500–1450)

The history of ternary design in Western music can be traced back to the liturgical chants of the early Christian church. The principle is present in chant settings of the *Kyrie eleison* (Lord Have Mercy) and the *Agnus Dei* (Lamb of God). It also appears in the structure of medieval secular song.

Figure 15.3

Kyrie eleison (in modern notation)

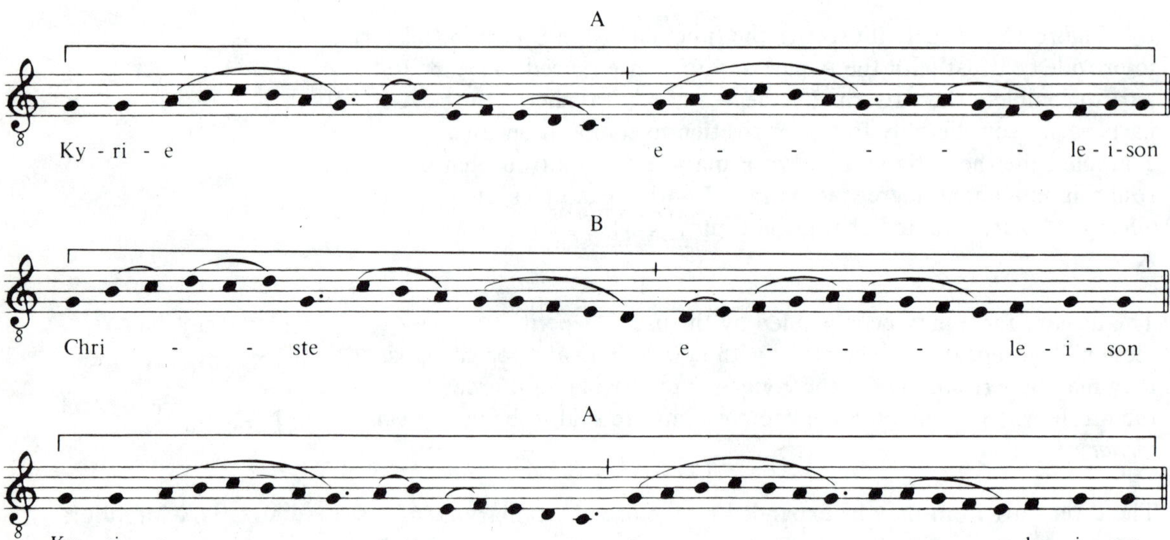

Josquin des Pres (1440?–1521) in *Faulte d'argent* (Lack of Money) observes the principle of ternary design, as do many composers of the sixteenth-century chansons (songs). The arias found in the seventeenth-century and early eighteenth-century operas, oratorios, and chamber cantatas utilize the principle in the form of the da capo (A B A) aria. In the baroque suite, the ternary design is achieved by alternating two dances, repeating the first after the second, e.g., Bourree I, II, I or Minuet I, II, I resulting in an A B A sequence.

Renaissance Period (1450–1600) and Baroque Period (1600–1750)

The minuet and trio in the symphonies and chamber music of the Classical period are an outgrowth of the baroque dance suite. The da capo aria, which was established in the Baroque period, continued as the best representative of ternary design in vocal music in the Classical period.

Classical Period (1750–1825)

The basic ternary design persisted through the nineteenth century in the character pieces of Schubert, Schumann, Mendelssohn, Chopin, and Brahms, to name only a few, and made its way into the twentieth century, notably in the shorter works of Debussy and Bartók.

Romantic, Post-Romantic and Impressionistic, and Contemporary Periods

The popular song is constructed of a verse and a chorus (refrain), although many songs consist only of a chorus. The chorus, which is usually of the most musical interest, is generally in ternary form with repeated first phrase. Typically, it is thirty-two measures long divided into four, eight-measure phrases. In the following illustrations, each letter indicates an eight-measure phrase:

Jazz and Popular Music (1900–Present)

Common Popular Chorus Forms

a a b a a a′ b a a a b a′ a a′ b a″

The "b" section of the popular song chorus is often called the *bridge* or *release.* The popular chorus form is often referred to as a *quaternary form,* since it usually consists of four phrases.

Figure 15.4 is a standard thirty-two bar popular song with the form: **a a b a′.**

Figure 15.4

Source: "Try to Remember"—Copyright © 1960 by Tom Jones & Harvey Schmidt. Chappell & Co., Inc., owner of publication and allied rights.

While the thirty-two bar chorus in ternary design is the most usual, a chorus may be of any reasonable length, and may be constructed in a great many other ways.

Other Popular Chorus Forms

a b c a   a b a b′   a b a c d   a b c a d e (etc.)

Phrase structure has become much freer in recent popular and rock music, and it is not at all unusual to see irregular phrase lengths in the music of such groups as the Beatles. The familiar song "Yesterday" (figure 15.5) begins with a seven-bar phrase; a bit of *text painting* on the word "suddenly," which seems to arrive one measure earlier than expected due to the shortened first phrase.

Figure 15.5

REVIEW

Chapter 15, like the previous chapter, deals with larger concepts of musical structure. This chapter can be studied in much the same way as Chapter 14.

1. Play or listen to a recording of each of the compositions analyzed in this chapter. Carefully examine the analysis of each composition, including the analytical statements in the scores themselves and the summary analysis that follows. Make certain that you understand each analytical statement. If certain items are not clear to you, reread the pertinent section of the chapter, or look in previous chapters for an explanation. If you still have problems, discuss them with your instructor or a fellow student.
2. Define each term listed at the head of the chapter (page 255) in your own words. Compare your definition with the definition in the Glossary and see if you can improve your definition. Consider how the terms can be applied to the compositions in the chapter.

Test Yourself 15

1. Examine measures 1–16 of figure 15.2 on page 257. Would you describe the form of this section as open or closed? Why?
2. Examine measures 17–32 of figure 15.2. Would you describe the form of this section as open or closed? Why?
3. Describe the function of the B section of a three-part (ternary) form.
4. In Chapter 14 a form called rounded binary form was discussed. How does the rounded binary form differ from a three-part (ternary) form?
5. A ternary form may be expanded in two ways: by repetition of a section or by the appearance of auxiliary formal members. Name three auxiliary members that may be added to the basic three-part design.

PART
4

Chromatic and Extended Harmony

In earlier chapters of this study we focused on tonal harmony based on the major and minor scales. You learned to construct harmonic progressions and harmonize melodies within the context of a single diatonic scale. With the introduction of modulation and secondary dominants, the tonal resources of other diatonic scales were added to your tonal palette and chromaticism was introduced. In this section we will further examine chromatic harmony, some of which represents incursions of the parallel minor scales into the major keys (the borrowed chords), as well as chromatic harmony of more distant origin (the *Neapolitan 6th* and the *augmented 6th chords*).

The chord vocabulary introduced in Chapters 19 and 20 represents the outer limits of tertian (third-based) harmony. These harmonic devices, which increase the dissonance level and chromaticism of the musical landscape, were much favored by composers in the nineteenth and twentieth centuries for their colorful and dramatic effects. The 9th, 11th, and 13th chords developed as logical extensions of the tertian system by piling additional thirds above the 7th chords, while altered dominants and chromatic mediants represent the triumph of chromaticism over the diatonic system. These harmonic devices will be presented in a four-part chorale setting for the most part, but they usually occur in music that goes beyond this basic texture.

It is tempting to assume that the history of music from the Renaissance period to the present shows a gradual progression from music that is purely diatonic to music that is purely chromatic, but the truth is far more complicated. If the tortured chromaticism of the music of Carlo Gesualdo (1561–1613) is compared with the purely diatonic elements found in certain works of Igor Stravinsky (1882–1971), it becomes clear that this assumption is an oversimplification. In fact, most of chromatic harmony was known to baroque composers, and it is the frequency of its use that tended to increase in the latter periods.

CHAPTER

16

Borrowed Chords

In Major Keys: ii°⁶ ii⌀7 iv ♭VI vii°⁷
In Minor Keys: I (Picardy)
Modal Mixture

Exposition

Borrowed chords are literally borrowed from a parallel major or minor key. Another term often used is *modal mixture.*

In Major Keys

Since the parallel minor key with its three scale forms provides a rich variety of triad and 7th chord colors, selections from this assortment are often borrowed for use in major keys. Although a large number of chords in the minor keys are available, the following five have received by far the greatest utilization by composers.

Figure 16.1

Five diatonic chords in D Major:

Same chords borrowed from parallel minor:

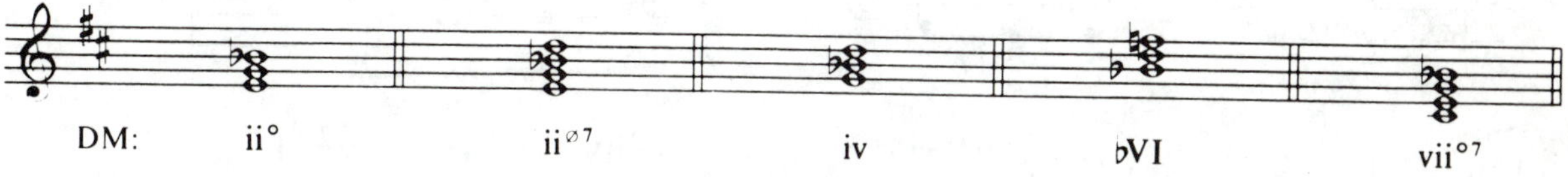

Position

Chord	Most Common	Others Possible
ii°	$ii^{\circ 6}$	—
$ii^{\varnothing 7}$	$ii^{\varnothing}{}^{6}_{5}$	$ii^{\varnothing 7}$ $ii^{\varnothing}{}^{4}_{3}$
iv	iv	iv^{6}
♭VI	♭VI	—
$vii^{\circ 7}$	$vii^{\circ}{}^{6}_{5}$	$vii^{\circ}{}^{4}_{3}$ $vii^{\circ}{}^{4}_{2}$

Mode

The chords just listed are borrowed from the parallel minor, which accounts for the alterations.

Progression

All borrowed chords progress in the same manner as the diatonic chords they replace, except for the ♭VI, which progresses to V or V^7.

Purpose

Borrowed chords are almost universally used as *color chords;* that is, they are employed to provide variety through the use of contrasting scale forms.

Figure 16.2 (from the song cycle, *Die Winterreise*—A Winter's Journey), in F Major, contains a borrowed $ii^{\circ 6}$ and a iv.

Figure 16.2

Schubert: *Das Wirtshaus* (The Inn), from *Winterreise* (Winter's Journey), op. 89, no. 21, D. 911

Figure 16.3 illustrates a $ii^{\varnothing 6}_{5}$ and a $vii^{\circ 4}_{3}$ borrowed from b flat minor.

Figure 16.3

Schubert: *Wanderers' Nachtlied* (Wanderers' Night Song) II, op. 93, no. 3, D. 768

Figure 16.4, an excerpt from Bach's *Vater Unser im Himmelreich,* shows a ♭VI borrowed from f minor.

Figure 16.4

Bach: *Vater unser im Himmelreich* (Our Father in Heaven), BWV 416

FM: V^6 I vi ii^6_5 V ♭VI

Borrowed chord

Borrowed Chords in Minor Keys

The only borrowed chord that occurs with any degree of frequency in minor keys is the *picardy third* (major tonic triad borrowed from major keys). The picardy third occurs almost exclusively in authentic cadences. A typical example occurs in *Jesu, meine Freude,* by Bach.

Figure 16.5

Picardy third:

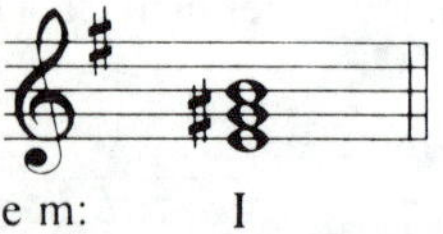

Bach: *Jesu, meine Freude* (Jesus, My Joy), BWV 227

Partwriting

Altered tones are seldom doubled.

General Guides:

Chord	**Double**	**Voice Leading (to V or V^7)**	**Illustration (Figure 16.6)**
$\text{ii}^{\circ 6}$	Bass note (not part of tritone)	Bass moves up—take upper three voices in contrary motion to bass.	**a and b**
$\text{ii}^{ø 6}_{5}$	Includes all factors	Bass moves up—take upper three voices in contrary motion to bass when moving to V; keep common tone when moving to V^7.	**c and d**
iv	Root	Bass moves up—take upper three voices in contrary motion to bass when moving to V or V^7.	**e**
♭VI	3rd factor (tonic)	Bass moves down—take at least two upper voices up. Leave doubled 3rd by contrary motion.	**f and g**
$\text{vii}^{\circ 7}$	Includes all factors	Bass moves up—take upper voices down.	**h**

Rule of Thumb for Borrowed Chords in Major Keys. Follow general guidelines for all borrowed chords as they appear in minor keys (diatonic).

Rule of Thumb for Borrowed Chords in Minor Keys. Follow general guidelines for I (picardy third) as the major tonic triad in major keys.

Figure 16.6

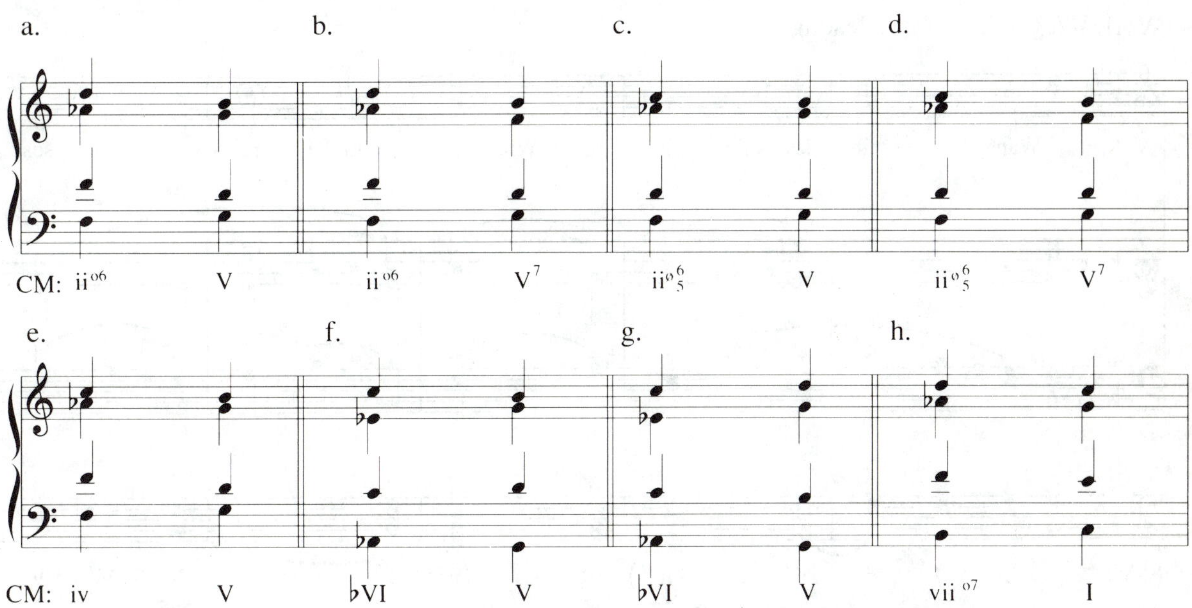

Mixing of the modes (major and minor) developed in the Baroque period and was considered a part of the general style.

The Classical period also includes borrowed chords. Their frequency and use is little changed from that of the Baroque period.

History

Baroque Period (1600–1750)

Classical Period (1750–1825)

Romantic and Post-Romantic Period (1825–1920)

The Romantic and Post-Romantic period saw a freer use of borrowed chords, including a chromatic approach and departure. The following excerpt by Hugo Wolf (1860–1903) shows the typical vi ii V (I) circle progression, but also includes two examples of the borrowed chord, $ii^{ø7}$.

Figure 16.7

REVIEW

1. Study figure 16.1, particularly the second line, where the most common borrowed chords in major keys are listed. Choose a major key and spell these five borrowed chords. Continue until you can easily spell any of these chords.
2. Study figure 16.6, which illustrates the most common progressions from each of the borrowed chords in major. Notice that all of the borrowed chords are commonly followed by the dominant chord except the vii°^{7}, which is followed by the tonic chord. Choose a major key and practice writing each of the borrowed chords in four parts and resolving it to the dominant chord or tonic, as appropriate. Continue practicing in various keys until you can easily resolve any of the common borrowed chords in major.
3. Play each of the progressions you have written in no. 2 above to familiarize yourself with the musical effect of the borrowed chords.

Test Yourself 16

The following are examples of the five most common borrowed chords (from minor keys to major keys). Copy each of the chords on a separate sheet of paper.

1. Analyze the borrowed chord. Analysis can be determined by determining the chord type (**ii°** is a diminished triad, **ii°⁷** is a diminished-diminished 7th chord, **iv** is a minor triad, **VI** is a major triad, and **vii**$^{\varnothing 7}$ is a diminished minor 7th chord.)
2. Name the key in which the example functions as *borrowed* chord.
3. Write the chord that normally follows the given chord (in four-part harmony).
4. Provide a roman-numeral analysis for both chords.

CHAPTER 17

Neapolitan 6th Chords

Exposition

The *Neapolitan 6th chord* is a major triad on the lowered second scale degree of a major or minor scale (figure 17.1).

Figure 17.1

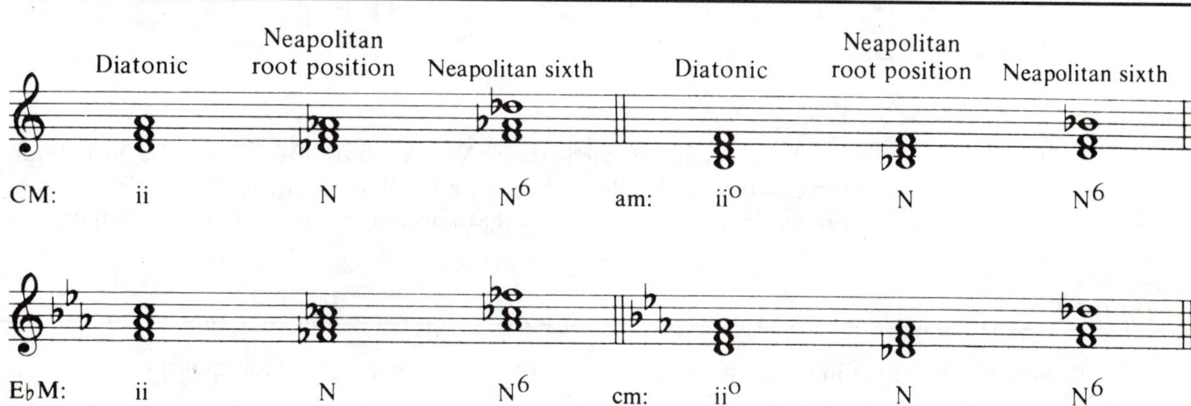

Position. The triad is generally found in first inversion—thus the name Neapolitan "sixth." Tradition has permitted this name to extend even to the root position of the chord.

Mode. The Neapolitan 6th chord is found more often in the minor than in the major mode. (See figure 17.2.)

Figure 17.2

Schubert: *Der Müller und der Bach* (The Miller and the Brook), from *Die schöne Müllerin* (The Beautiful Miller's Daughter), op. 25, no. 19, D. 795

Progression. Proceeds to the **V** or $\mathbf{V^7}$ most often. Thus, the Neapolitan 6th chord takes its place along with the **ii, ii°,** $\mathbf{I^6_4}$, $\mathbf{i^6_4}$, $\mathbf{V^7/V}$ and $\mathbf{vii^{o7}/V}$ as *predominant* chords—chords that normally progress to **V** or $\mathbf{V^7}$ (figure 17.3).

Figure 17.3

Beethoven: Piano Sonata in C-sharp minor (Moonlight), op. 27, no. 2 (1st Movement)

p

c♯m: V^6_5 i N^6 V

Other Chords Inserted between N⁶ and V. Frequently, to delay the dominant triad or 7th chord, other predominant chords are placed between the **N⁶** and the **V** or **V⁷** chords. The most common insertions are **I^6_4 (i^6_4)** or **vii°⁷/V**, or both.

Figure 17.4 shows an **N⁶** progressing to **V** through a **vii°⁷/V**.

Figure 17.4

Mozart: Fantasia in D Minor, K. 397

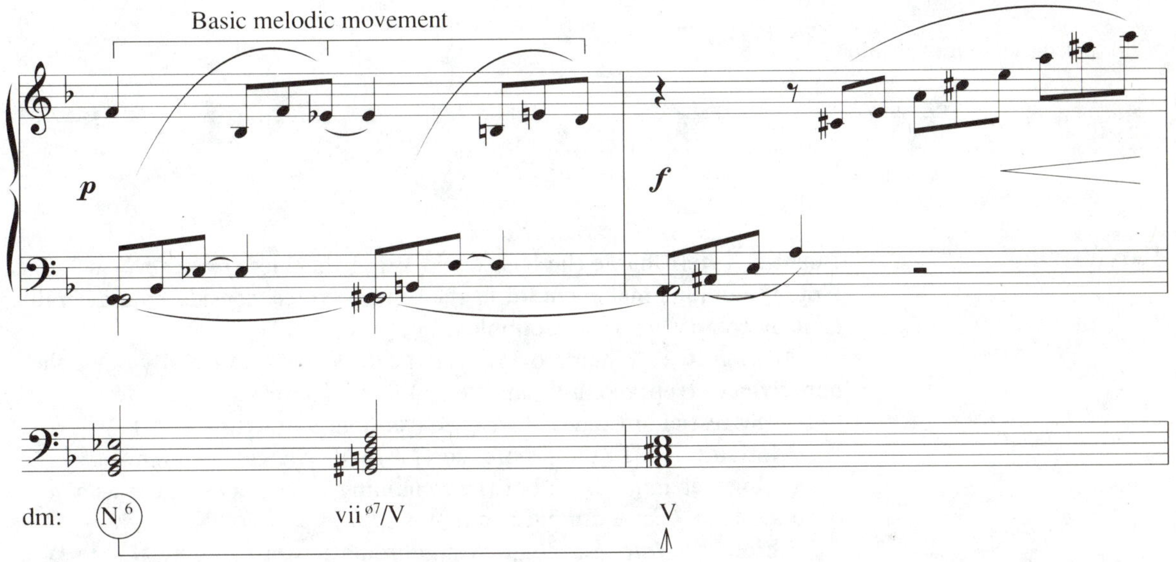

Some Exceptions.

a. **N⁶** is occasionally found in the major mode.
b. **N⁶** may sometimes be found in root position. (See figure 17.5.)
c. **N⁶**, especially in the Romantic period, may be preceded by **V⁷/N⁶**, thus the **N⁶** becomes a tonicized chord.
d. Somewhat rare is an **N⁶** that also contains a 7th factor.
e. An **N⁶** may, on occasion, be included in a passage consisting of nonfunctional harmony. During the Classical period the nonfunctional harmony often contained a series of first-inversion triads in parallel motion. (See figure 17.8.)

Figure 17.5

Partwriting

Doubled Note. Double the bass note (3rd of the chord) whenever possible. Note the unique melodic **d3rd** in the soprano voice, considered a desirable trait by composers. (See example *a* in figure 17.6.)

Motion to V. When moving from N^6 to **V,** you can usually move the upper voices (soprano, alto, and tenor) down (contrary motion to the bass) to the nearest chord tones of **V.** (See example *b* in figure 17.6.)

Motion to V^7. In the progression **N^6 to V^7** you can also move two voices down as in *b,* above but the remaining voice may be kept as a common tone. (See example *c* in figure 17.6.)

Chromatic Voice Leading. Avoid chromatic voice leading (**D♭** to **D** in example *d*) in any voice leaving N^6 in figure 17.6.

Caution: When N^6 proceeds to **I^6_4 or i^6_4,** watch out for parallel 5ths. Turn them upside down—into parallel 4ths. (See the two examples of *e* in figure 17.6.)

Figure 17.6

The Neapolitan 6th first appeared in the Baroque period and was treated very conservatively by composers of the time. Most often the **N⁶** was placed near a cadence point and was considered simply a substitute for the diatonic **ii** or **ii°**. (See figure 17.7.)

History

Baroque Period (1600–1750)

Figure 17.7

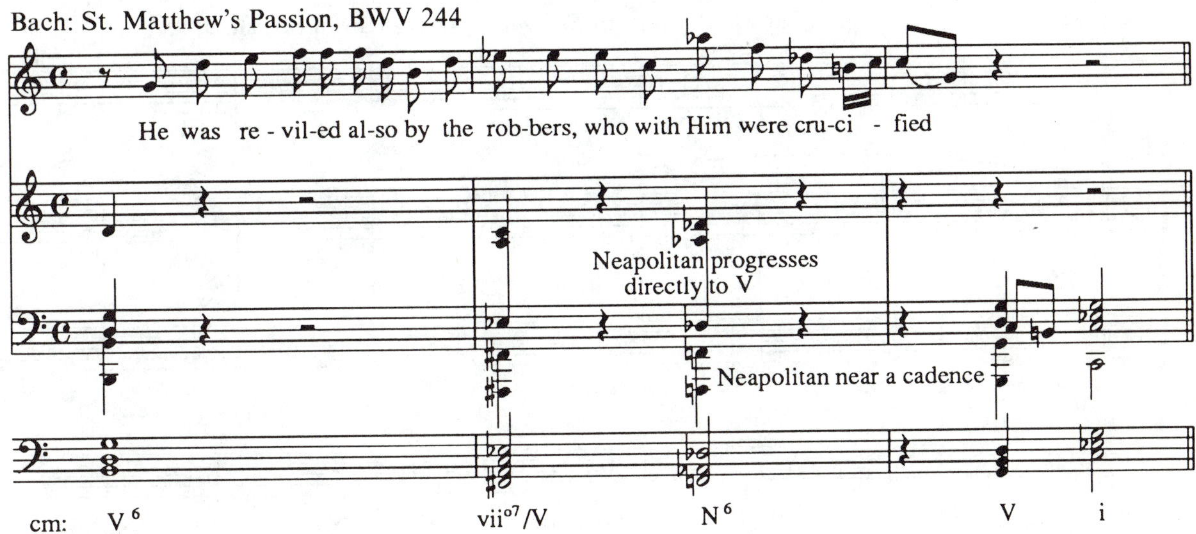

Classical Period (1750–1825)

In the Classical period nontraditional examples surface occasionally. The following passage, by Haydn, represents a series of nonfunctional first-inversion triads that descend in parallel motion. The **N⁶** is one of the chords in the series and takes part in the stepwise downward movement.

Figure 17.8

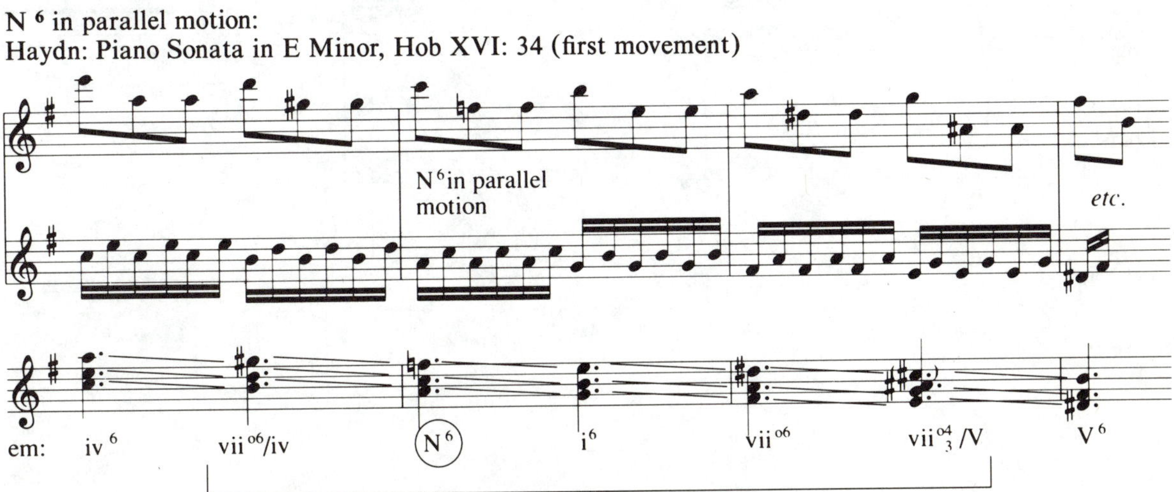

Romantic Period (1825–1900)

The use of the N^6 continued throughout the Romantic period and treatment broadened considerably. Most listeners hear the N^6 as a passing chord: $i^6 N^6 V^7/iv$. (See figure 17.9.) The i^6 and the V^7/iv share three notes in common.

Figure 17.9

Schubert: *Der Doppelgänger* (The Double), from *Schwanengesang* (Swan Song), D. 957, no. 13

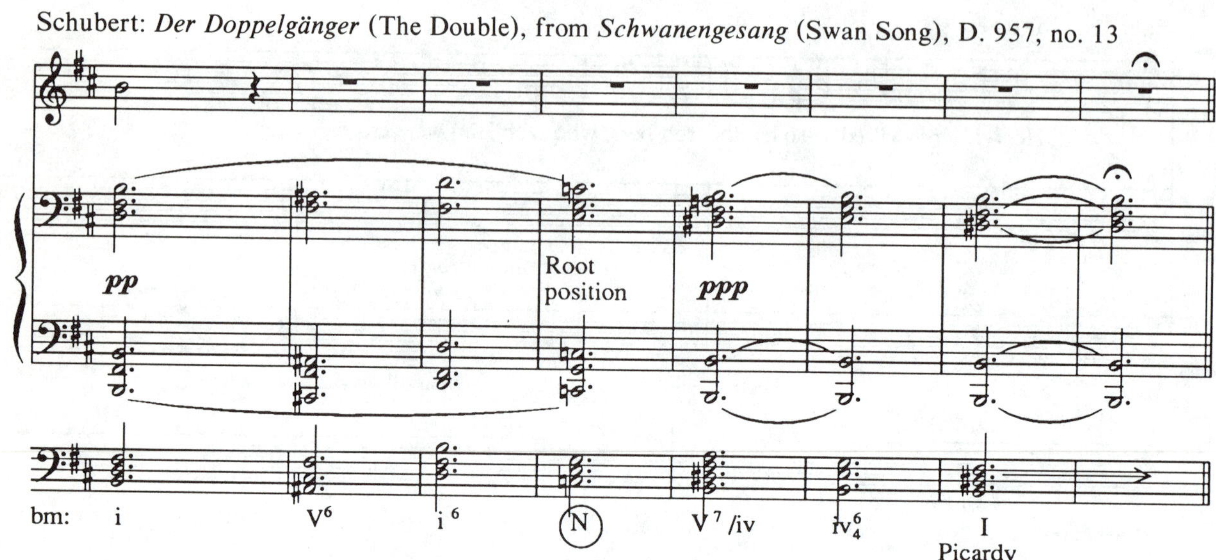

In figure 17.10, the N^6 occurs over a tonic pedal.

Figure 17.10

Rimsky-Korsakoff: Plenivshis rozoy, solovey (The Nightingale Charmed by the Rose), op. 2, no. 2

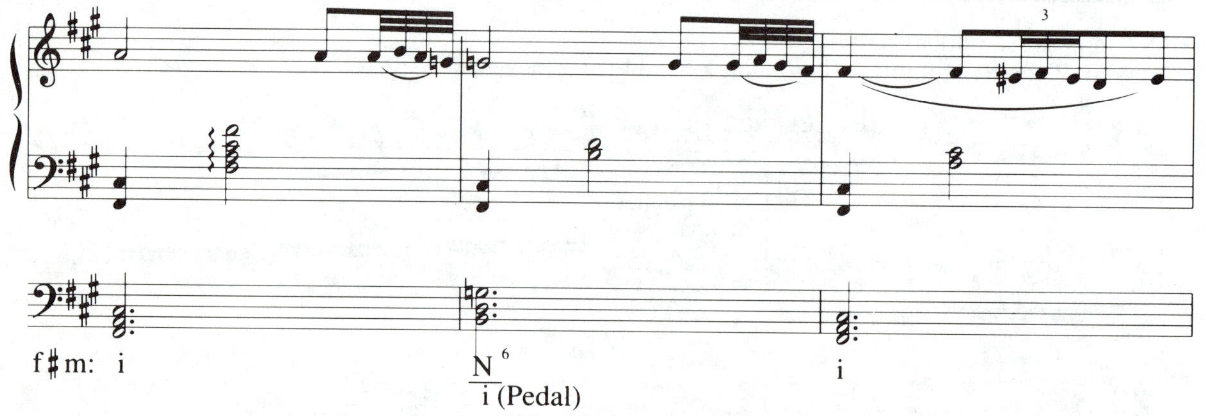

Post-Romantic and Impressionistic Period (1875–1920)

Because the N^6 is strictly a functional device of the Baroque, Classical, and Romantic periods, its presence in the Post-Romantic and Impressionistic period is much diminished. The composers of this transitional period occasionally returned to the idiom of the Romantic period for inspiration. The following example by Prokofieff, written circa 1910, reveals an N^6 with nearly traditional treatment.

Figure 17.11

Prokofieff: Moonlit Meadows (from Music for Children), op. 65, no. 12

REVIEW

1. Select a major triad and name the keys in which it would be the Neapolitan 6th chord (both major and minor). Continue practicing until you can quickly name the key.
2. Turn to the circle of fifths (figure 2.16 on page 37). For each key spell the Neapolitan 6th chord.
3. Study figure 17.6, which illustrates proper partwriting for the Neapolitan 6th chord. Practice writing and resolving the N^6 chord in a variety of major and minor keys using figure 17.6 as a guide. Pay particular attention to example e, which shows the way to avoid parallel 5ths in resolving the Neapolitan 6th to the tonic six-four.

Test Yourself 17

A. Each given triad in four-part harmony is the V chord in a minor key.

1. Determine the key (*minor*) and write it in the appropriate place.
2. Determine the Neapolitan 6th chord in this key and write it in four-part harmony so it leads smoothly to the V triad.
3. Place the analysis in the blanks beneath each chord (see measure 1, for example).

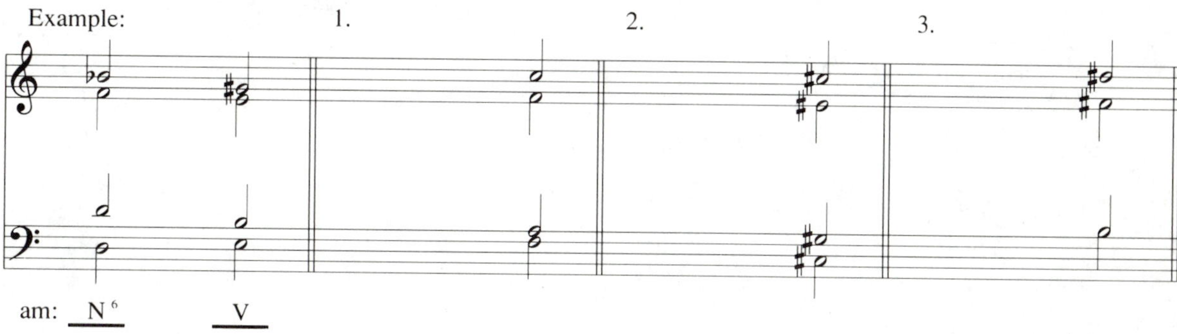

B. Complete in the same manner as A. the vii°⁷/V is added between the N⁶ and the V triad (see measure 1, for example).

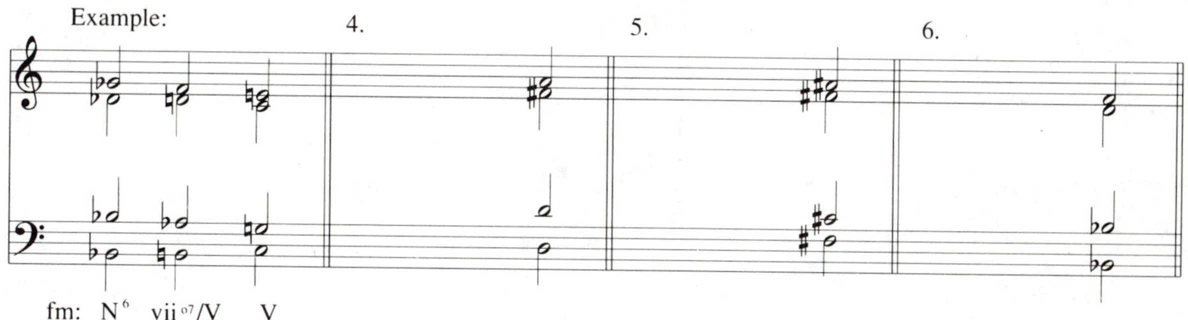

C. Complete in the same manner as A. The i_4^6 chord is added between the N^6 and the V triad (see measure 1, for example):

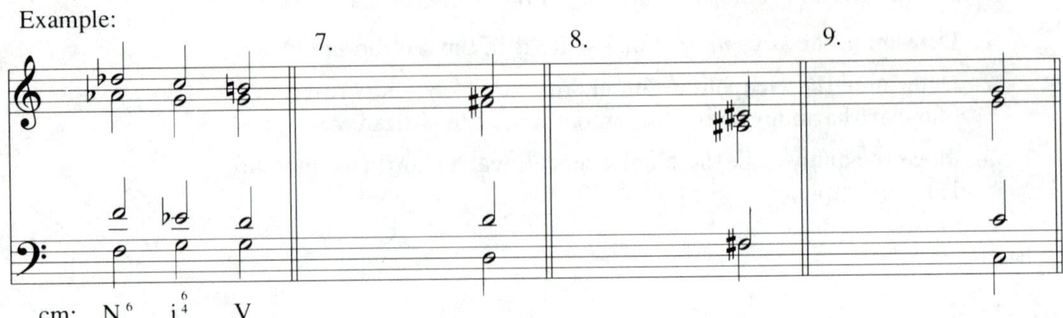

CHAPTER 18

Augmented 6th Chords

Italian 6th: It⁶ *French 6th: Fr⁶* *German 6th: Gr⁶*

Exposition

Augmented 6ths are chords that have been altered to include the interval of an augmented 6th. Although augmented 6ths could be seen as altered supertonic (ii°–ii) and subdominant (IV–iv) chords, their sound is unique and so different from the diatonic chords that they are given special analysis symbols: **It^6, Fr^6,** and **Gr^6.**

Three Types

Above the bass note (which is a major 3rd below the tonic) write:

Italian 6th: M3rd + **Aug. 6th** (total three notes)
French 6th: M3rd + **Aug. 4th** + Aug. 6th (total of four notes)
German 6th: M3rd + **Perf. 5th** + Aug. 6th (total of four notes)

Figure 18.1

Notes in Common. All three types have three notes in common:

Figure 18.2

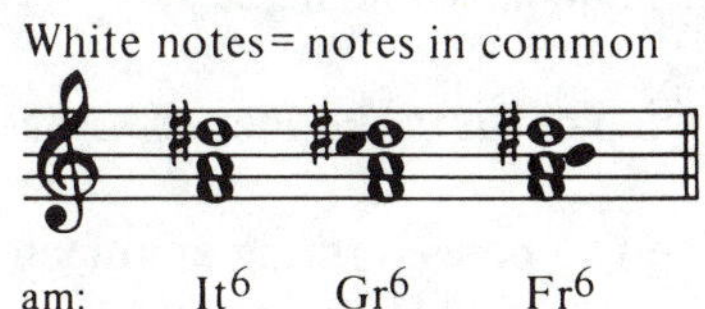

Bass Note Location. Another observation will assist in quick identification of most augmented 6th chords. The bass note (or lowest-sounding tone) is generally a major 3rd below the tonic in both major or minor keys. (Exceptions are noted later.)

Fourth Scale Degree. The fourth scale degree is raised in all three types.

Figure 18.3

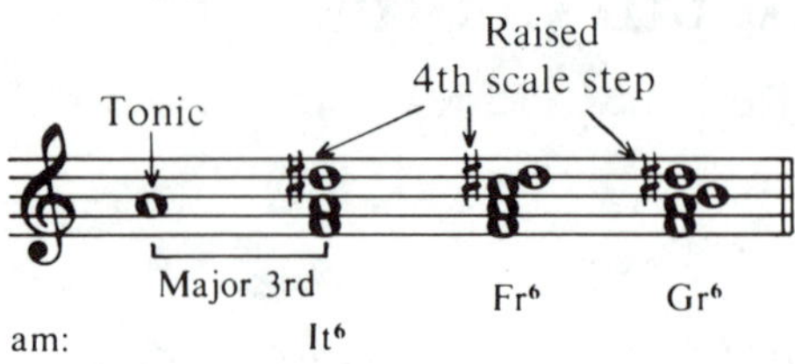

Progression

Italian 6th resolves to **V** directly or through $\mathbf{I}^6_4$

French 6th resolves to **V** directly or through $\mathbf{I}^6_4$

German 6th must resolve to **V** through $\mathbf{I}^6_4$ to avoid parallel 5ths

Figure 18.4

Exceptions

While by far the largest number of augmented 6th chords occur as described, some exceptions should be noted:

Different Position. Augmented 6th chords occur occasionally in positions other than those listed.

Bass Note on Other Scale Degrees. In rare instances the bass note of any augmented 6th chord may be a scale degree other than the customary one—major 3rd below tonic.

Augmented 6th Interval Inverted. Sometimes the augmented 6th interval is inverted, thus creating a diminished 3rd.

Notes Added. In extreme instances an augmented 6th chord may include notes other than those conventionally found.

Partwriting

Resolution. The bass note resolves a half-step down to the root of V. See figure 18.5e–g.

Augmented 6th Interval to Octave. The two notes forming augmented 6th interval resolve outward (contrary motion) by half-step to an octave. See figure 18.5a–g.

To I_4^6. The progression from augmented 6th chords to I_4^6 is only a partial resolution. The final resolution occurs when V is reached. See figure 18.5f.

Doubling. Neither of the two notes forming the augmented 6th interval is ever doubled. See figure 18.5e–g.

Double Tonic Scale Degree. In the Italian 6th, double the tonic scale degree (3rd above bass note).

Gr^6 to I_4^6 Only. To avoid parallel 5ths, Gr^6 proceeds to I_4^6 or i_4^6 instead of V. See figure 18.5a and b.

Two Spellings for Gr^6. The Gr^6 chord has two spellings. Figure 18.5a–d shows intervals above the bass note in C (minor and major):

Spelling of Gr^6 in **C minor: Ab C E♭ F♯ (progresses to i_4^6)**. See figure 18.5c and d.

Spelling of Gr^6 in **C major: Ab C D♯ F♯ (progresses to I_4^6)**. See figure 18.5g.

In **C minor** the E♭ progresses down to **D** (5th of V). But, in **C major** an E♭ progressing to **E** (of I_4^6) was considered poor spelling, so composers spelled **E♭** as **D♯.**

Figure 18.5

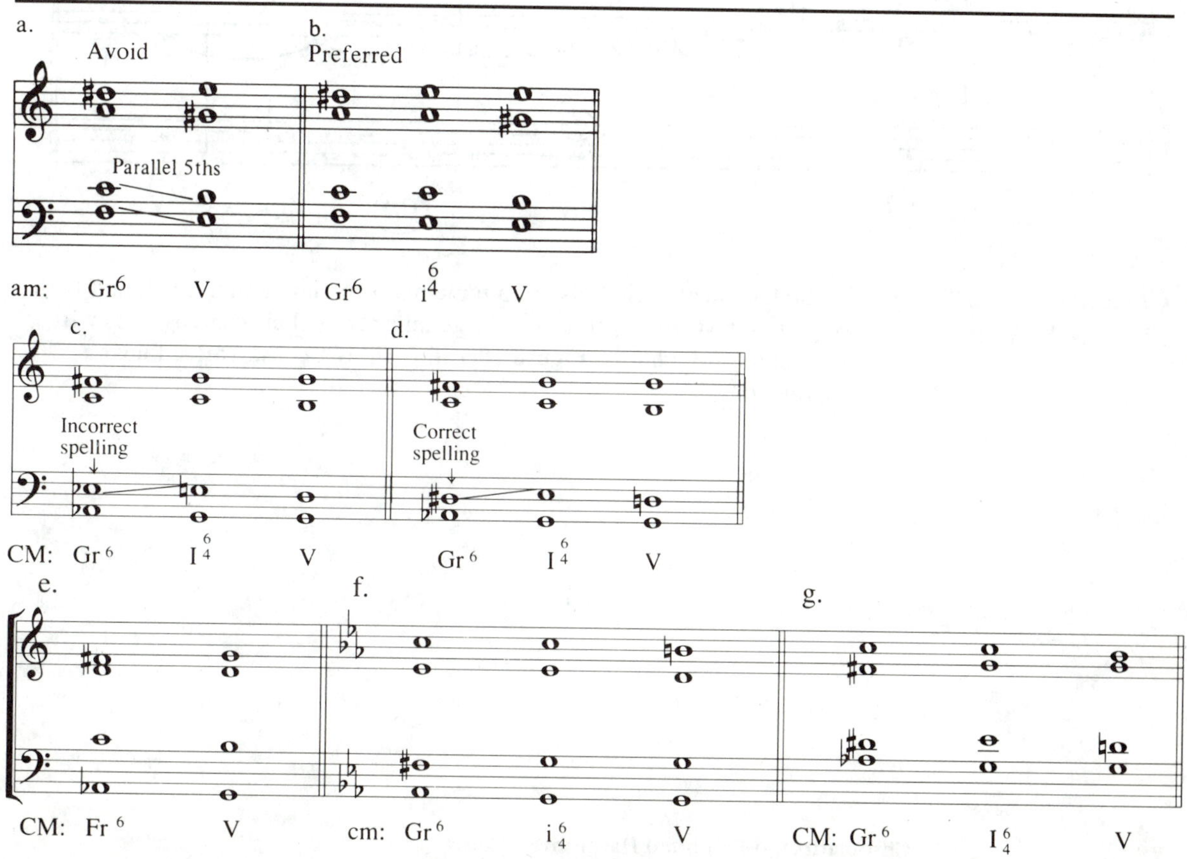

Stepwise Movement. Voice leading to and from an augmented 6th chord should be stepwise whenever possible—skips only when required. Augmented 6ths are basically linear and fall into the predominant classification—already populated by:

ii, ii°, ii^7, ii$^{\circ 7}$, I$^6_4$, i$^6_4$, N^6, V/V, V^7/V

History

Baroque Period (1600–1750)

Although rare examples appear prior to 1600, augmented 6th chords did not become a part of the general harmonic vocabulary until the Baroque period. Treatment of these chords was conservative, few exceptional examples can be found, and composers of the period tended to depart cautiously from diatonic harmony. The following example (figure 18.6) is excerpted from a toccata by Domenico Zipoli (1688–1726), a contemporary of Bach. Note the clever avoidance of parallel 5ths in the **Gr^6**.

Figure 18.6

Zipoli: *Toccata*

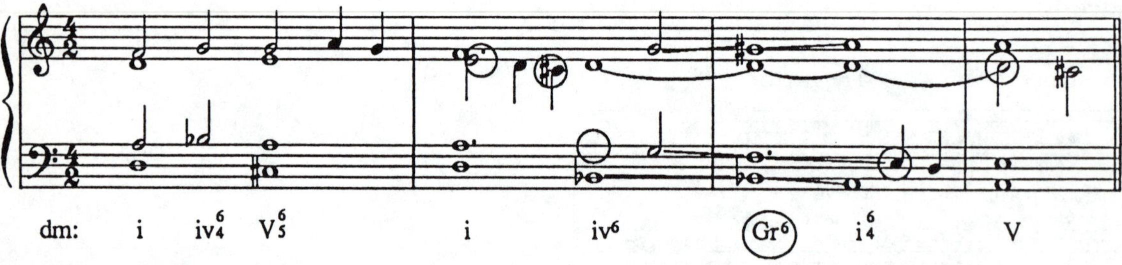

Classical Period (1750–1825)

In the Classical period, use of augmented 6th chords increased, and both Haydn and Mozart sprinkled a large number of their compositions with augmented 6th chords. Figure 18.7 illustrates a conservative linear approach.

Figure 18.7

Mozart: *Das Veilchen* (The Violet), K. 476

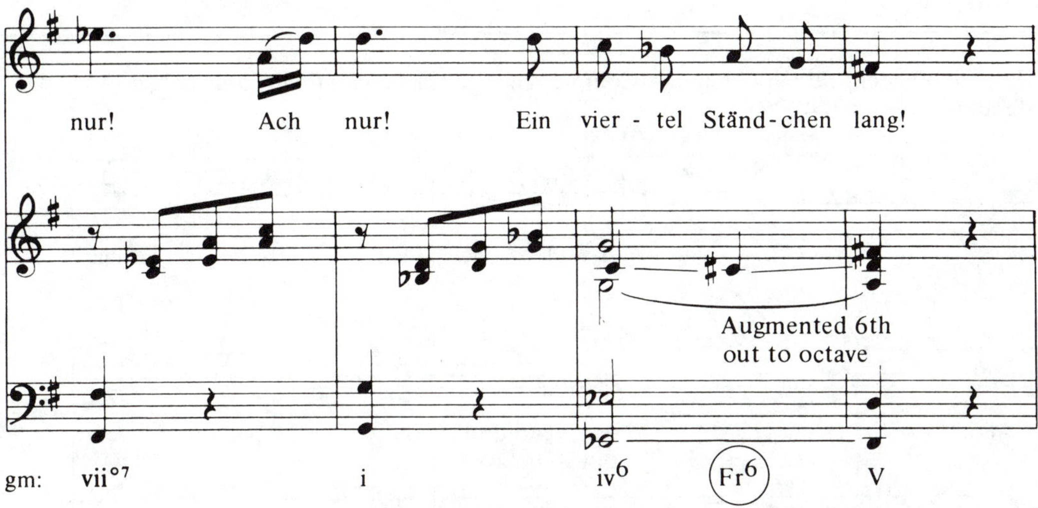

As with many altered chords, augmented 6ths reached their zenith during the Romantic period, where their use became more frequent, and handling of the chords became freer and more unpredictable. Figure 18.8 contains an augmented 6th chord in a different position, with the augmented 6th interval inverted into a diminished 3rd.

Romantic Period (1825–1900)

Figure 18.8

Chopin: Prelude, op. 28, no. 22

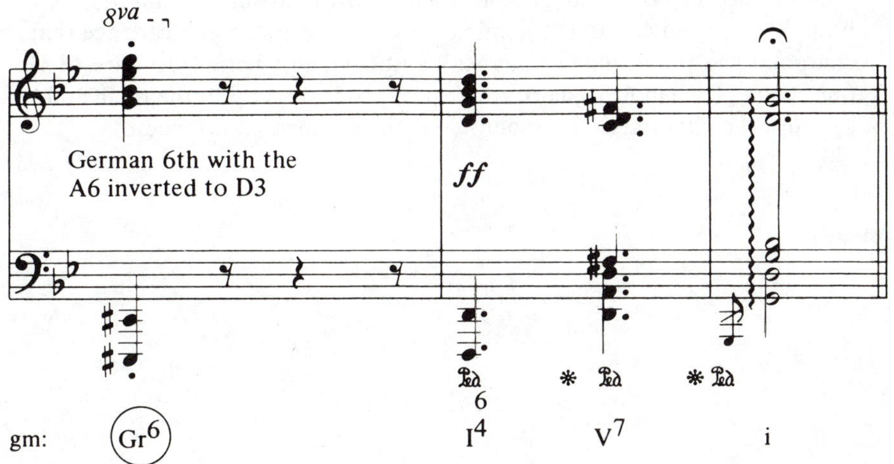

Figure 18.9 represents a traditional predominant string of chords ending in a half cadence. VI^7, Gr^6, and I^6_4 all precede the V triad and tend to build tension that is released when the V triad is eventually reached.

Figure 18.9

Schumann: Ich kann's nicht fassen (I Cannot Comprehend), from *Frauenlieben und Leben* (A Woman's Life and Loves), op. 42, no. 3

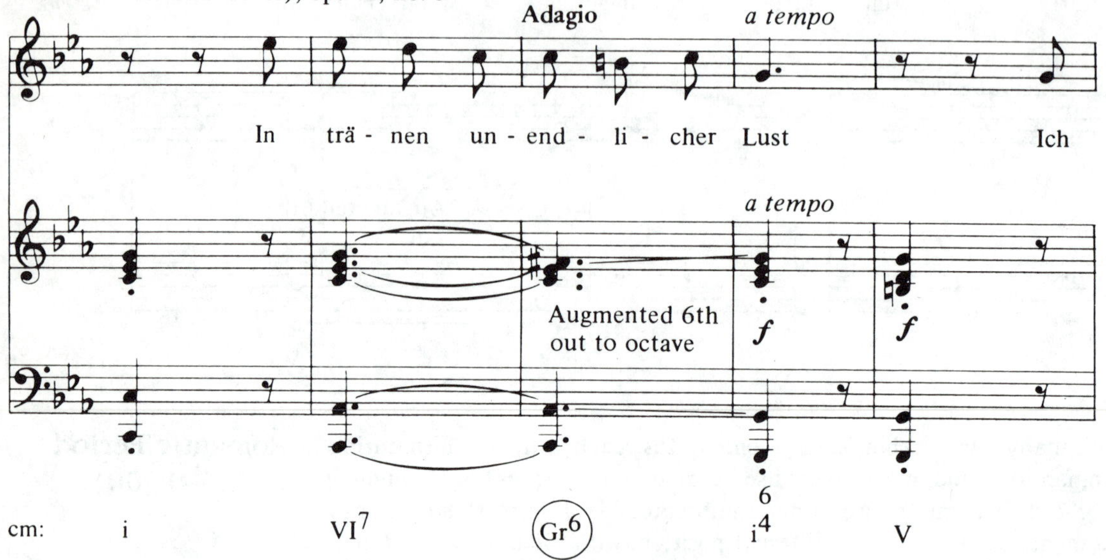

Post-Romantic and Impressionistic Period (1875–1920)

While there are a number of examples of chords containing the augmented sound in this period, few would be considered true augmented 6th chords. The advent of "floating" harmony, parallel chords, third relationship, and increasing employment of ostinato and pedal tones brought about an end to the dominant-tonic progression and cadence that characterized the Baroque, Classical, and Romantic periods. Figure 18.10 presents a German 6th sonority that progresses directly to the tonic and destroys the characteristic resolution of the augmented 6th chord.

Figure 18.10

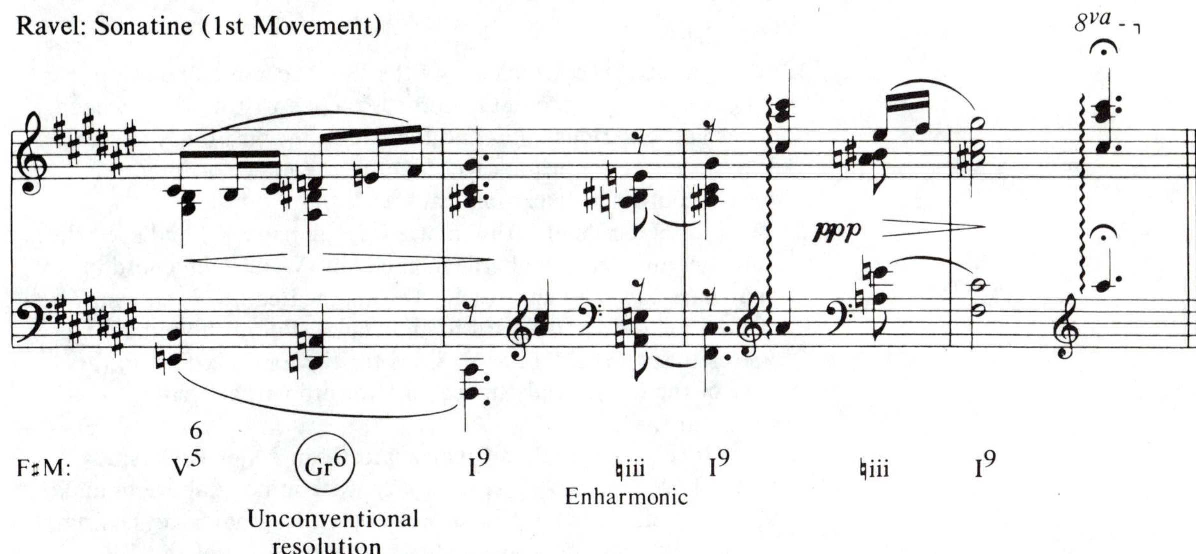

American Popular Music

Augmented 6th chords occur throughout popular music, especially in ragtime. Scott Joplin, one of the better-known composers and performers of ragtime, included a number of such chords in his own compositions. Note again the string of predominant chords—**ii^{6}**, **Gr^{6}**, and the tonic $^{6}_{4}$.

Figure 18.11

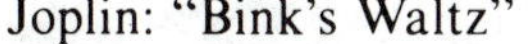

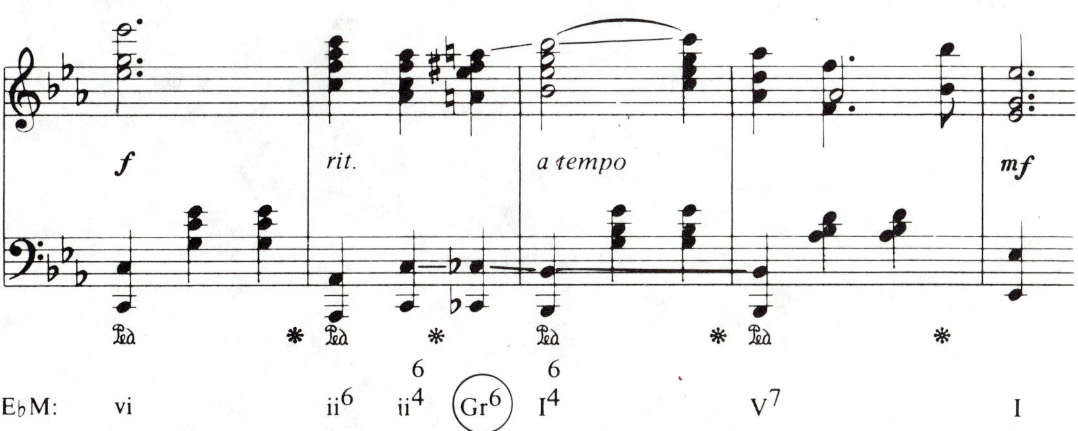

REVIEW

1. Study figure 18.2, which shows the three "common notes" among the augmented 6th chords. Practice writing the common notes above various notes and then add the extra tones to create the Gr^6 and Fr^6 in each case. Identify the major or minor key where you would likely find each chord.
2. Turn to the circle of fifths (figure 2.16 on page 37) and spell the three augmented 6th chords in each key. Write each chord in four-part harmony and resolve the augmented 6th in the most conventional way (outward to an octave). Fill in the remaining voices to spell the dominant chord (or the tonic six-four in the case of the Gr^6). Study figure 18.5 for proper partwriting procedures.
3. The Gr^6 chord is spelled enharmonically in major keys (study figure 18.5 c, d, and g). Check your work in no. 2 above to make sure that the Gr^6 chord is correctly spelled in major keys. If not, change the spelling to avoid chromatic resolution of the 5th above the bass in the Gr^6 chord.

Test Yourself 18

Each of the following chords is an augmented 6th chord in four-part harmony. Copy these chords on a separate piece of paper. Identify and label the augmented 6th chord (**It⁶, Gr⁶,** or **Fr⁶**). Identify the key in which the particular augmented 6th chord is most often found. Write a chord that represents the most conventional resolution of the given chord in four parts, using proper voice leading. Analyze the resolution chord.

CHAPTER 19

9th, 11th, and 13th Chords

V⁹ *V¹¹* *V¹³* *Nondominant 9th, 11th, and 13th Chords*

Exposition

9th Chord. A *9th chord* contains a 9th (octave + 2nd) above the root of a 7th chord.

7th Chord: C E G B♭ **9th Chord:** C E G B♭ **D**

11th Chord. An *11th chord* contains an 11th (octave + 4th) above the root of a 9th chord.

9th Chord: C E G B♭ D **11th Chord:** C E G B♭ D F

13th Chord. A *13th chord* contains a 13th (octave + 6th) above the root of an 11th chord.

11th Chord: C E G B♭ D F **13th Chord:** C E G B♭ D F A

Figure 19.1

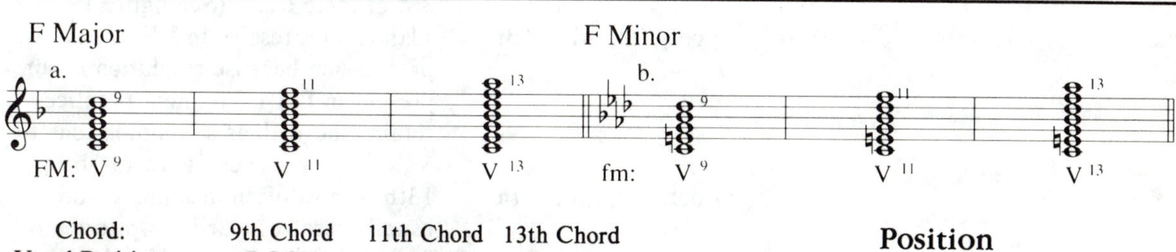

Position

Chord:	9th Chord	11th Chord	13th Chord
Usual Position:	ROOT	ROOT	ROOT

The 9th, 11th, and 13th chords tend to lose their identity when inverted, and thus are generally found in root position.

Mode

All three chords are found in both major and minor keys. Note that in major mode **V^{9}** and **V^{13}** contain a major 9th and major 13th (root to 9th and root to 13th), respectively, while in minor mode both are minor intervals. The 11th in **V^{11}** is unaffected by changes of mode. (See figure 19.1.)

Function Preference

Dominant (V) function is most often found—**V^{9} V^{11} V^{13}**. The chords also occur with other functions such as **I** and **IV.**

As Secondary Dominants

V^{9}, **V^{11}**, and **V^{13}** were also used by composers as secondary dominants—**V^{9}/V, V^{11}/V, V^{13}/V, V^{9}/ii, V^{11}/ii, V^{13}/ii,** etc.

Figure 19.2

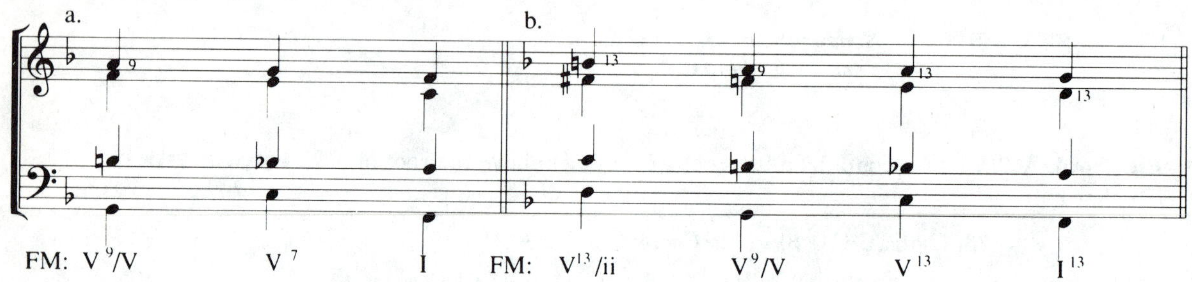

Progression

The addition of a 9th, 11th, or 13th to 7th chords does not change their function. As an example, **V^{13}** chords still resolve to **I** or **i; ii^{9}** chords normally progress to dominant (**V**) function, etc.

Partwriting 9th, 11th, and 13th Chords

Chord	**Most Common Factors Present**	**Voice-Leading Guides**
V^{9}	Root, 3rd, 7th, 9th	9th and 7th resolve down to 5th and 3rd of tonic triad. (See figure 19.3a.)
V^{11}	Root, 7th, 9th, 11th	11th cannot resolve in V^{11} to I or i progression because resolution is not present in I or i. Frequent practice retains the 11th as a common tone to V^{11} and I or i. (See figure 19.3b.)
V^{13}	Root, 3rd, 7th, 13th	13th is most often in soprano and usually resolves a 3rd down to tonic factor of I or i. 7th resolves down a step to 3rd of tonic triad. (See figure 19.3c.) If the tonic following V^{13} is a 9th chord, the 13th of V^{13} occasionally resolves to the 9th of I^{9}. (See figure 19.3d.)

Figure 19.3

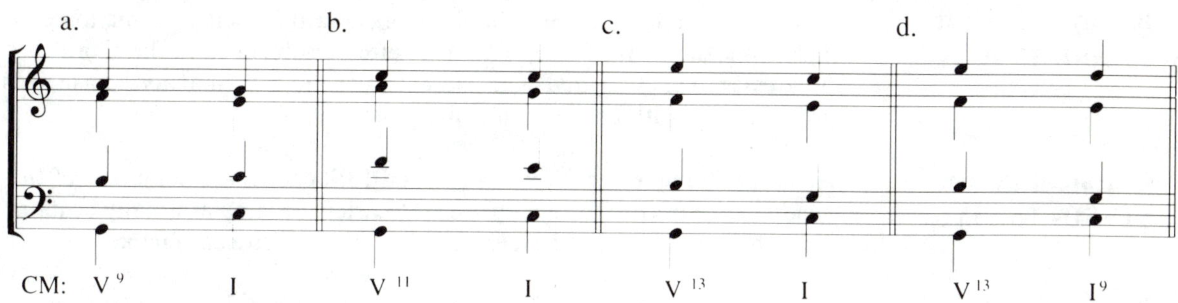

Chord Symbols

The 9th, 11th, and 13th chords are used extensively in jazz, in the harmonization of popular songs, in instrumental arrangements, and in lead sheets such as those in fake books. For each of these purposes, chord symbols are often employed to suggest preferred harmony. While there are many chord symbol systems, figure 19.4 illustrates those most frequently used.

Figure 19.4

History

Baroque Period (1600–1750)

True 9th, 11th, or 13th chords are rare in music of the Baroque period. However, especially in the late Baroque period, there are many instances where 9th-, 11th-, and 13th-chord factors appear as nonharmonic tones. The dissonance (9th, 11th, 13th) most often resolves before the chord progresses to another, and such examples are most often analyzed as triads or 7th chords with nonharmonic dissonance.

Classical Period (1750–1825)

As in the Baroque period, 9th, 11th, and 13th chords are not a part of the general style of the Classical period. Occasional examples usually contain a nearby resolution that lessens the effect of the dissonant factor.

Romantic Period (1825–1900)

It was the Romantic period that eventually solidified the 9th, 11th, and 13th factors as true chord tones. While still relatively rare, figure 19.5, by Schumann, illustrates a **V**^{13} that proceeds immediately to **I.** The 13th factor (**B**) moves down a 3rd to G (root) of the tonic triad.

Figure 19.5

Schumann: *Kleine Studie* (Short Study), from Album for the Young, op. 68, no. 14

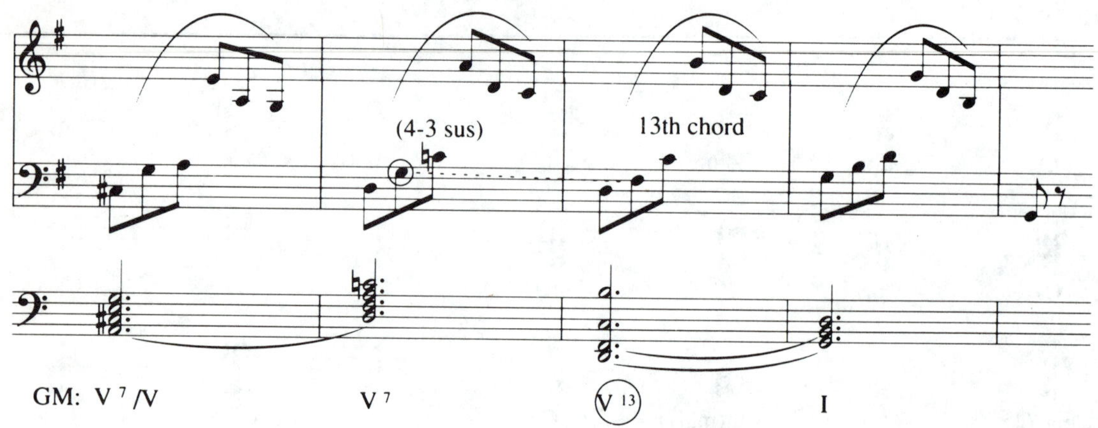

Another example, this one by Wagner (figure 19.6), was written (1859) only eleven years after the one just presented, by Schumann. In this illustration the 9th resolves before a change of harmony, but achieves the strength of a true chord factor through its duration (two measures).

Post-Romantic and Impressionistic Period (1875–1920)

From 1875 to 1920 9th, 11th, and 13th chords were regularly used. Figure 19.7, written in 1911 by Ravel, illustrates a **V**^{11} at a cadence point. The 11th (**C**) does not resolve down since it is a common tone with the tonic triad.

Figure 19.6

Wagner: *Tristan und Isolde,* Act II (voice part omitted)

Figure 19.7

Ravel: *Valses nobles et sentimentales* (Noble and Sentimental Waltzes)

Jazz and Blues

Figure 19.8 is from a composition written in 1901 by Scott Joplin. Although Joplin used most of the vocabulary of the late Romantic period, he used 9th chords somewhat sparingly.

Figure 19.8

Joplin: "The Augustine Club Waltz"

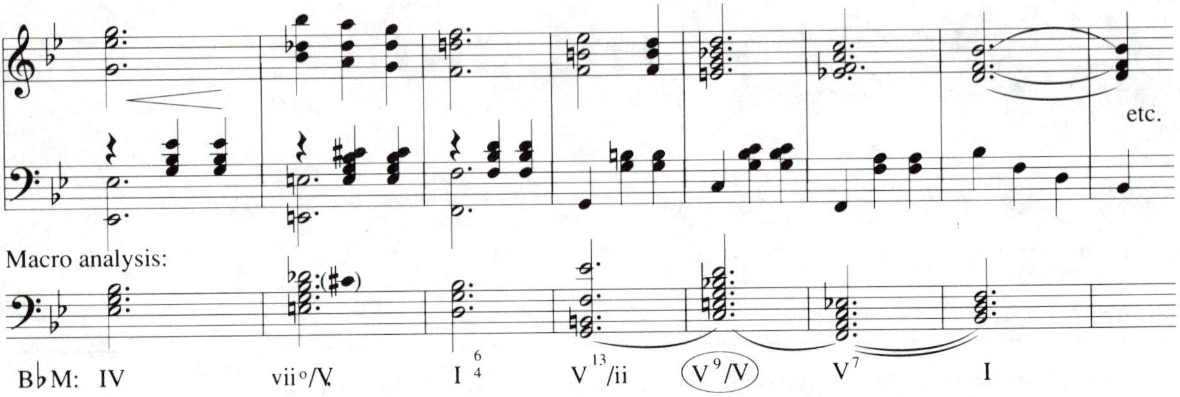

etc.

Macro analysis:

B♭M: IV vii°/V I $^{6}_{4}$ V^{13}/ii (V^{9}/V) V^{7} I

In subsequent jazz styles, the 9th chord became prevalent and was employed regularly in a full and sonorous harmonic style that made almost every chord into a 7th, 9th, 11th, 13th, or added-tone chord. The following is an illustration of a typical cadence found in the music of the 1950s.

Figure 19.9

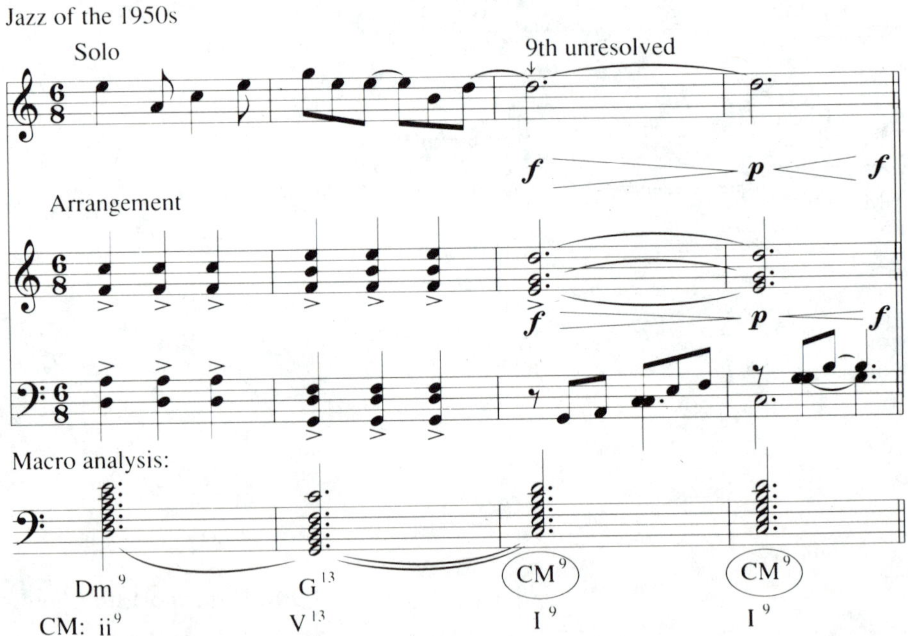

REVIEW

1. Spell the dominant 9th, 11th, and 13th chords in all major and minor keys. (Note that the 9th and 13th are major in the major keys and minor in the minor keys.)
2. Study the section labeled "Partwriting 9th, 11th, and 13th Chords" on page 300, and figure 19.3, which follows. Memorize the most common factors present in four-part settings of these chords, and the voice-leading guides for each chord. Write dominant 9th, 11th, and 13th chords in a number of major and minor keys in four-part harmony, and resolve each to its respective tonic triad using figure 19.3 as a guide.
3. If your instructor indicates that you should know the popular music chord symbols for the various 9th, 11th, and 13th chord qualities, study figure 19.4 by playing each chord on the piano and transposing that chord to different roots. Pay particular attention to the popular music chord symbol for each chord.

Test Yourself 19

Copy the following chords on a separate sheet of paper. All of these chords are dominant 9th, 11th, or 13th chords. Determine the key in which each chord would function as a dominant and give a proper roman-numeral analysis of the chord. Write a proper resolution to the tonic triad in that key.

CHAPTER 20

Altered Dominants and Chromatic Mediants

V^{+} $\quad V^{7}_{+}$ $\quad V5\flat$ $\quad V^{7}_{5\flat}$ $\quad v^{\varnothing 7}$

Exposition

Altered Dominants

Altered dominants are dominant (or secondary dominant) triads or 7th chords that contain a **raised or lowered 5th factor.** One altered dominant type ($v^{\varnothing 7}$) contains both lowered 3rd and 5th factors. Figure 20.1 illustrates the five altered dominant types in common use:

Figure 20.1

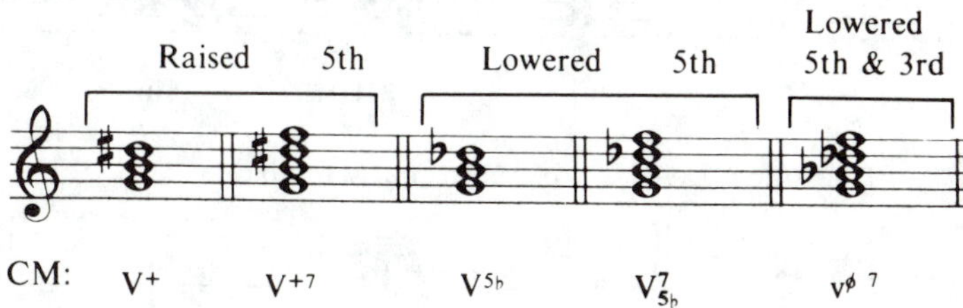

Position

Altered dominants are found most frequently in root position, but occasionally occur in any inversion.

Mode

The altered dominant with raised 5th does not occur in minor mode (raised 5th is enharmonic with 3rd scale degree), but the others may be found in major or minor keys.

Progression

Altered dominants, like diatonic dominants, proceed to tonic.

Secondary Dominants

Except for $v^{\varnothing 7}$, all altered dominants occur as secondary dominants.

Chromatic Mediants

Chromatic mediants in major keys:

III, ♭III or ♮III, and ♭iii or ♮iii
VI, ♭VI or ♮VI, and ♭vi or ♮vi

Chromatic mediants in minor keys:

iii, ♯III or ♮III, and ♯iii or ♮iii
vi, ♯VI or ♮VI, and ♯vi or ♮vi

Chromatic mediants are altered mediant and submediant major or minor triads (and 7th chords on occasion).

Figure 20.2

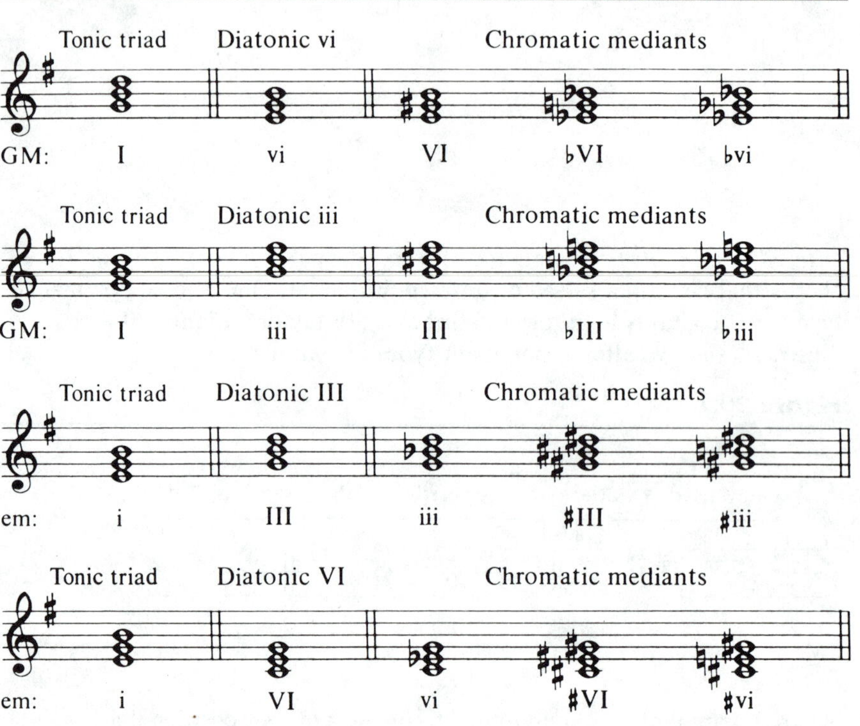

Similar Spellings

Some chromatic mediants are spelled the same as other altered chords:

Key	Chord	Other Function
Major	♭VI	Also a borrowed chord—from parallel minor (see Chapter 16)
Major	VI	Also secondary dominant of ii (see Chapter 13)
Major	III	Also secondary dominant of vi (see Chapter 13)

The analysis of these chords should reflect whatever function is evident from their relationship to surrounding harmony. Figure 20.3 illustrates correct analysis. In example a, an E-major triad (E G♯ B) resolves to a ii triad, leaving no doubt that the chord is a secondary dominant, while in example b the same E-major triad returns to the tonic triad, thus demonstrating the characteristics of a chromatic mediant.

Figure 20.3

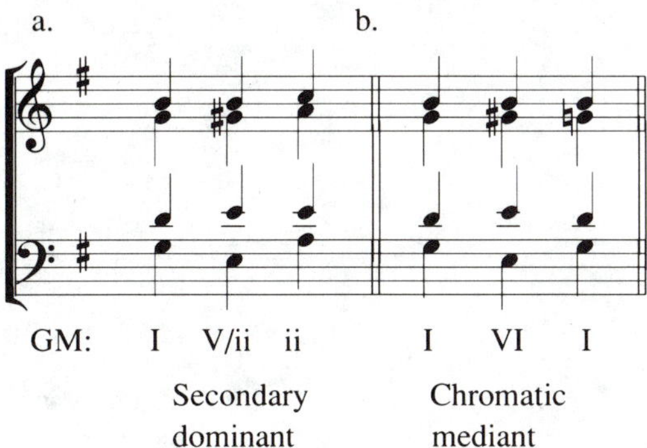

Position

Any position is possible, but root position is most frequent.

Mode

As seen in the preceding examples, chromatic mediants and submediants may appear in either major or minor keys.

Function Preference

Chromatic mediants are usually mediant or submediant chords that have been altered.

Progression

Chromatic mediants usually have a 3rd relationship (of chord roots) with tonic, and most often proceed from and to the tonic triad. Less often, the dominant (V) is the pivot around which chromatic mediants move. Sometimes chromatic mediants are preceded or followed by their own secondary dominant, and, in other instances, create a full-fledged modulation.

In the following illustrations:

a. Minor chromatic mediant
b. Major chromatic mediant
c. Major chromatic mediant
d. Major chromatic mediant with its secondary dominant

Figure 20.4

Partwriting Altered Dominants

Altered Tones. Take the altered 5th in the direction of the alteration—raised pitches up—lowered pitches down. See figure 20.5a–d.

7th Down. In altered dominant 7th chords, remember to resolve the 7th factor down one scale degree. This may result in either a doubled third or tripled root in the tonic triad that follows. (See figure 20.5a, b, and d.)

Never Double Altered Tones. Altered tones are almost never doubled. Note that the following illustrations contain no doubled altered tones. (See figure 20.5a–d.)

Figure 20.5

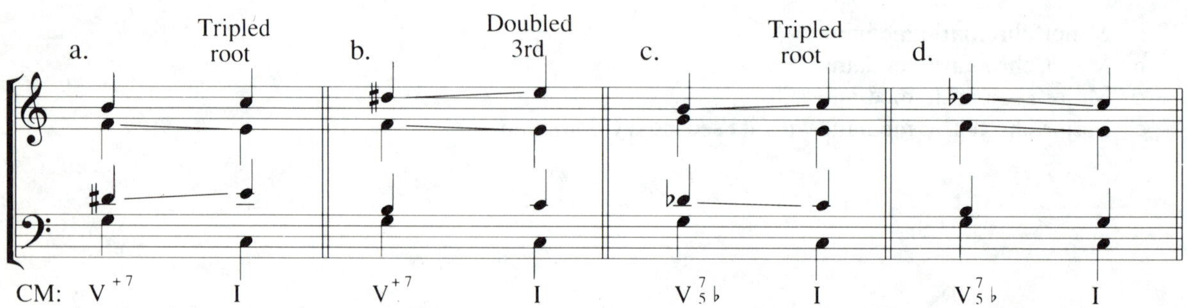

Partwriting Chromatic Mediants

General Guidelines

Chromatic Movement. Since chromatic mediants are reached by 3rd relationship progressions, chromatic movement, such as B to B♯, A to A♭, F♯ to F in melodic lines, is common.

Double Root. Chromatic mediants are either major or minor triads, so doubling patterns are often the same as for diatonic triads. Double the root whenever possible. (See figure 20.7.)

History

Baroque Period (1600–1750)

Both altered dominants and chromatic mediants were rare to nonexistent during this period.

Classical Period (1750–1825)

The frequency of altered dominants was low, but climbed in this period, and occasional examples of chromatic mediants or chromatic mediant key relationships occur now and then.

Romantic and Post-Romantic Periods

While altered dominants and chromatic mediants are not plentiful in any style period, a large percentage were written during the Romantic and Post-Romantic periods. Figure 20.6 is from the *Mörike Lieder* set of songs by Hugo Wolf (written 1888). In the five measures shown, there are three altered dominants.

Figure 20.6

Wolf: *Das verlassene Mägdlein* (The Forsaken Maiden), from *Gedichte von Eduard Mörike*

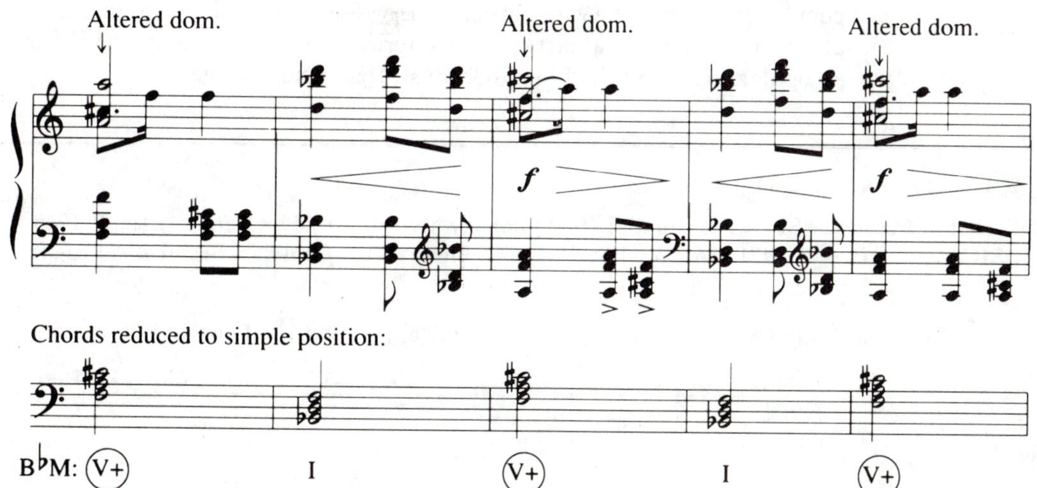

Figure 20.7 is from Brahms' Symphony no. 3 (published in 1883). A chromatic mediant (♭**VI**) in C major occurs in the third measure. In this instance the **A♭**-major triad is both a chromatic mediant (because it returns to a **C**-major triad immediately) and a borrowed chord (because it is borrowed from the parallel minor (**C** minor).

Figure 20.7

Brahms: Symphony no. 3 in F Major, op. 90 (2nd Movement)

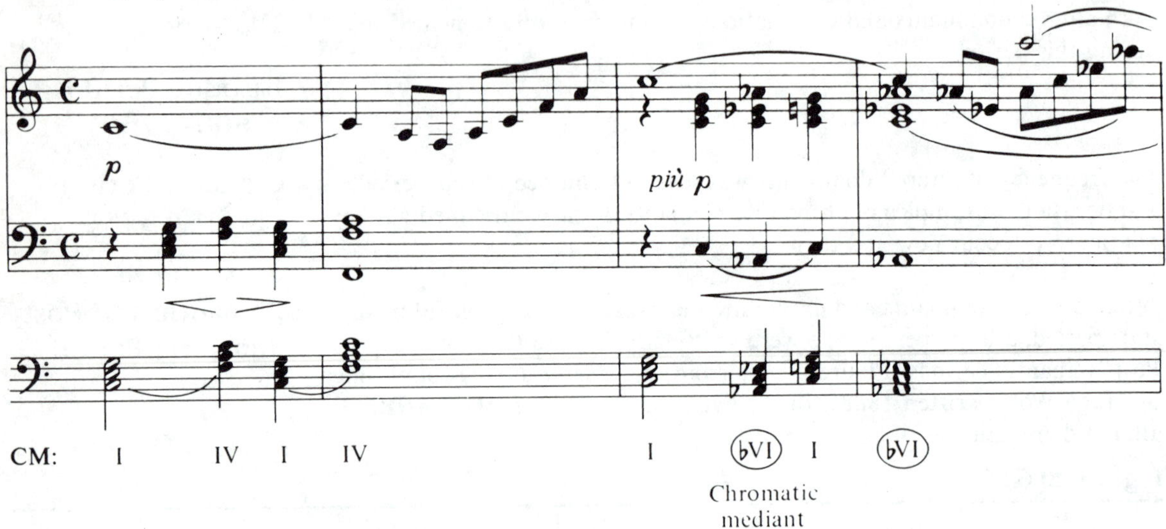

Jazz and Popular Music

Appearing in modest numbers, altered dominants were employed in popular music of the 1930s through the 1960s. Jazz artists also included altered dominants as a part of their improvisatory style. Figure 20.8, from a popular song published in 1943, illustrates typical usage.

Figure 20.8

Mercer and Arlen: "My Shining Hour"

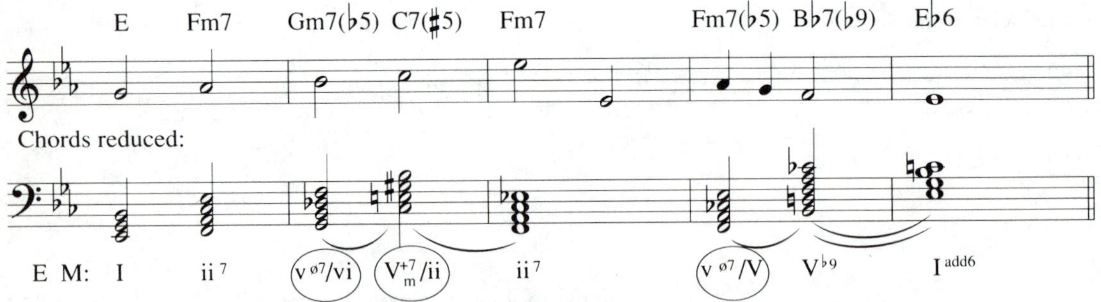

REVIEW

1. Study figure 20.1, which shows the five altered dominant chords in common use. Choose a major key, spell the dominant 7th chord, and then alter it to make each of the five chords illustrated in figure 20.1. Repeat this process in several other keys.
2. Study figure 20.5, which shows proper voice-leading of altered dominant chords. Write each of the chords you spelled in number 1 above in four parts and resolve it properly to the tonic chord. Use the section titled "Partwriting Altered Dominants" on page 310 for advice in proper voice leading.
3. Study figure 20.2, which illustrates the six chromatic mediants in the major keys and the minor keys (GM and em in the example). Choose a major key and spell all six chromatic mediant chords. Choose a minor key and spell the six chromatic mediant chords. Repeat this process in several other major and minor keys.
4. Chromatic mediants are most often approached or left by root motion of a 3rd, with chromatic motion in one or more parts. Study figure 20.4 to see these characteristics. Figure 20.3 illustrates the difference in function of the major triad on the 6th scale degree in major, which may be a secondary dominant of ii or a chromatic mediant, depending on the context. Study this example carefully. Can a similar situation exist with any of the other chromatic mediant chords?

Test Yourself 20

1. Each of the following chords falls into one or two of the categories listed below. Identify each chord using the letters a, b, c, d, e, or f from the list below. If a chord could fit into two categories, give both letters.

   a. 9th, 11th, or 13th chord

   b. Neapolitan 6th chord

   c. Augmented 6th chord

   d. Altered dominant

   e. Borrowed chord

   f. Secondary dominant

2. Write each of the six chromatic mediants in the following keys. The example illustrates the correct procedure.

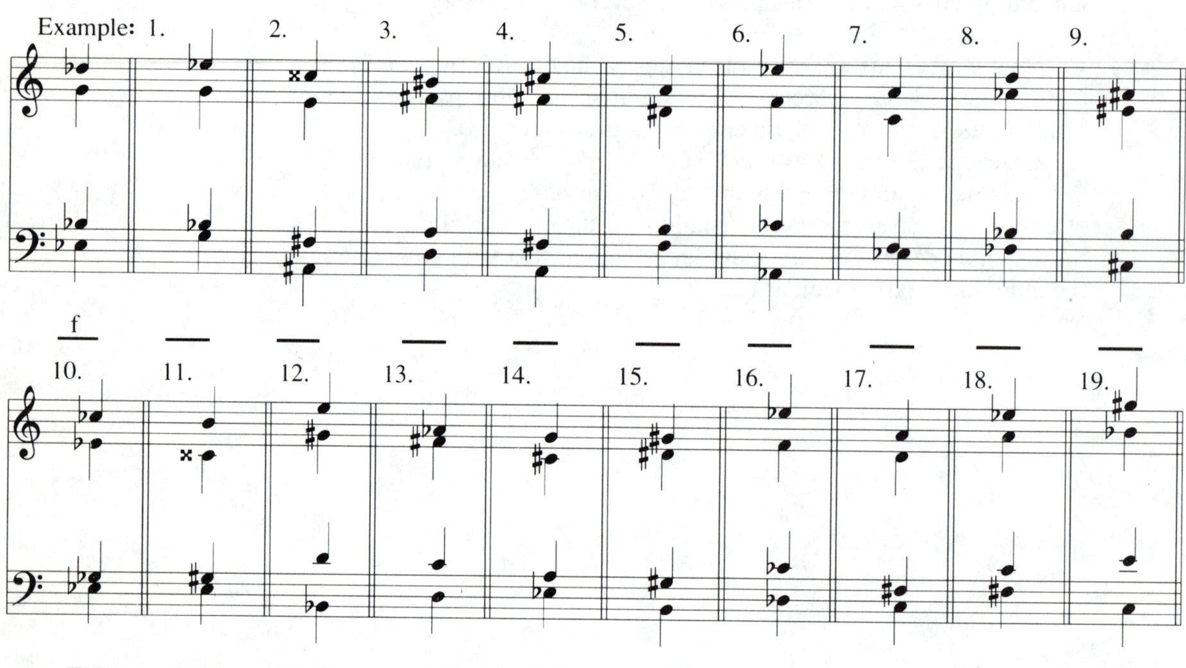

Example:
D Major: III ♮III ♮iii VI ♭VI ♭vi
20.
B♭ Major:
21.
C Minor:
22.
E Major:
23.
D♭ Major:
24.
B Minor:

PART 5

The Nineteenth and Twentieth Centuries

Romantic Period (1825–1900)

Music of the Romantic period was dominated by a wider range of emotional expression, more personal and individual styles, and more subjectivity. Musical forms, such as the sonata and symphony, became longer and more involved, but shorter forms, especially piano compositions, were also numerous. Harmony and orchestration expanded, as did sonorities in general.

The most substantial achievement of the Romantic period was in the development of complex harmonic techniques and an emphasis on instrumental color, which were used to create dramatic musical effects.

As against the classic ideals of organization, symmetry, control, and perfection within acknowledged limits, romanticism sought independence, movement, passion, and pursued the mysterious or exotic because its ideals could not be obtained. Romantic art was troubled by the spirit of longing and seeking after an unattainable goal.

Post-Romantic and Impressionistic Period (1875–1920)

The Post-Romantic composers developed and extended the musical style developed by the Romantic composers, resulting in a general weakening of the tonal basis of their music. As a movement among French painters, *impressionism* sought to eliminate the heroic subjects, the obsession with realistic detail, and the representational quality of romantic painting. In essence, the impressionist painter hoped to capture the impression a subject or object made on him rather than to paint its literal representation. So too, in music, composers such as Debussy aspired to renounce the clear phrase structure and goal-oriented harmonic idiom of the past, and replace them with a purposeful understatement and ambiguity that was evocative, but very different in effect from the romantic style. The impressionist composers abandoned traditional thematic development and became more concerned with the color or mood of a particular moment.

Contemporary Period (1920–Present)

The period from 1920 to the present has seen the development of great diversity of musical styles and techniques. Much of this development can be traced back to the upheavals caused by World War I (1914–1918) and World War II (1939–1945), which caused disruption of the established cultural institutions in Europe, and at the same time brought people of diverse cultural backgrounds together for the first time. The development of recording technology, radio and television transmission, and rapid transportation created a sense of world community in which all manifestations of human culture could freely intermingle. In more recent times technological advances have made possible the development of electronic and computer instruments for the composition and synthesis of music.

Popular song as now found in the United States evolved during this period. Some notable composers of popular song are George Gershwin, Cole Porter, Richard Rodgers, Irving Berlin, Vernon Duke, and Burt Bacharach. Popular songs by these and other composers were the dominant music with mass appeal until rock music became firmly entrenched in the 1960s.

Black American music is among the most notable expressions of religious, folk, and art music in the United States. The *blues* refers to a black-American song of sorrow. The blues, which arose from the black country and gospel music of the deep South, has not only been perpetuated as a unique style of its own, but has infused nearly all types of black music, some twentieth-century classical music, and the popular songs and rock music of the present day. Jazz, the general term for various music of black creation, has undergone many changes from its beginning and interpretations in its brief history, and its acceptance as a substantive art form has at last been accomplished.

Since the 1960s, rock music, which developed out of the traditions of the blues, jazz, and popular music, has become the dominant form of music with mass appeal.

CHAPTER 21

The Romantic Period (1825–1900)

Romanticism
Modal Mixture
Foreign Modulation
Nonfunctional Harmony
Chromatic Nonharmonic Tones
Enharmonic Spelling

Exposition

Romanticism is the term applied to much of the music written between 1825 and 1900. The period could be seen as little more than an extension of the Classical period, if you examine the more conservative works of composers such as Franz Schubert (1797–1828) and Johannes Brahms (1833–1897), or as a major change in style, if the more progressive works of composers such as Franz Liszt (1811–1886) and Richard Wagner (1813–1883) are considered. In spite of various national styles evident in the music of Frédéric Chopin (1810–1849), Alexander Borodin (1834–1887) and others, the music of the Romantic period was dominated by German composers.

Characteristics of Romanticism

Expanded Chord Vocabulary. The harmonic materials discussed in the previous chapters, including borrowed chords, 9th, 11th, and 13th chords, the Neapolitan 6th, augmented 6th chords, chromatic mediants, and altered dominant chords, were used much more frequently during the Romantic period.

Modal Mixture. The increasing use of borrowed chords resulted in a blending of the major and minor modes, sometimes to the point of modal ambiguity.

Figure 21.1

Schubert: Waltz, op. 9, no. 22, D. 365

Modulation. Romantic composers often imply several keys in rapid succession. This has the effect of decreasing the influence of the central tonic. Notice the sudden modulation after only one measure and the equally sudden return in measure 3 in figure 21.2. (See also figure 21.7 on page 323)

Figure 21.2

Chopin: Prelude, op. 28, no. 20

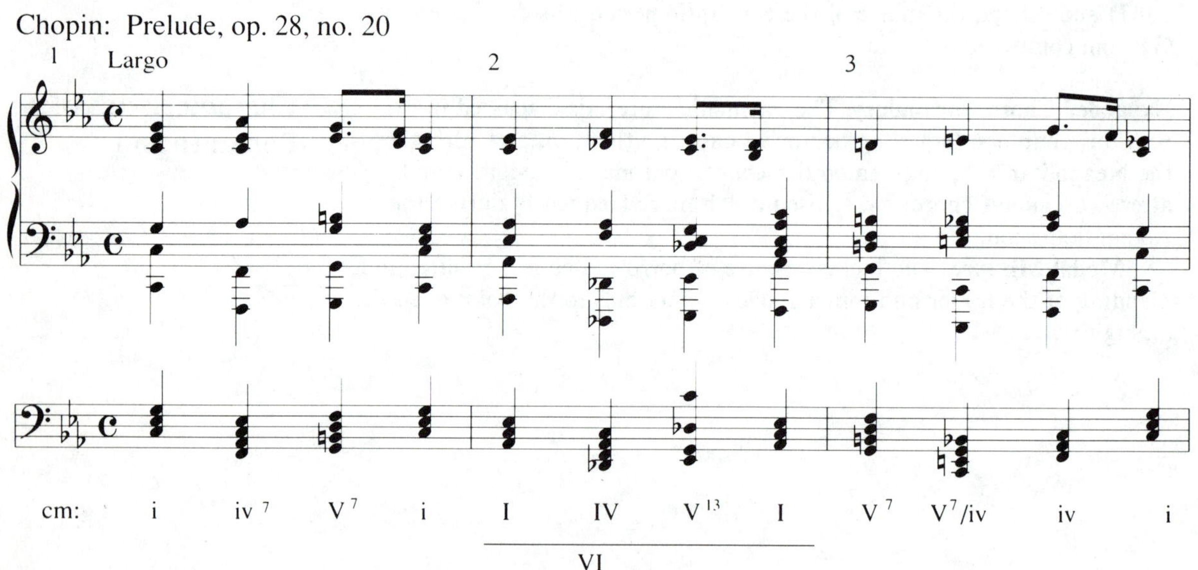

Foreign Modulation. The full spectrum of keys were exploited by nineteenth century composers, with modulations to keys quite distant from the tonic of the composition. These often necessitate enharmonic spelling of chords. The enharmonic relationship between the German 6th chord and the dominant 7th was a favorite device for modulation to foreign keys. In figure 21.3, notice that the German 6th chord in the first measure is respelled as a dominant 7th in the third measure and resolves in a circle progression.

Figure 21.3

Schumann: *Am leuchtenden Sommermorgen* (On a Shining Summer Morning), from *Dichterliebe* (Poet's Love), op. 48, no. 12

Unresolved Dissonance. Dissonant chords, which required resolution in earlier periods, were sometimes left unresolved by nineteenth-century composers. This was often exploited for its dramatic effect, as figure 21.4 illustrates.

Figure 21.4

Schubert: Symphony in B minor, D. 759 ("Unfinished") (1st Movement)

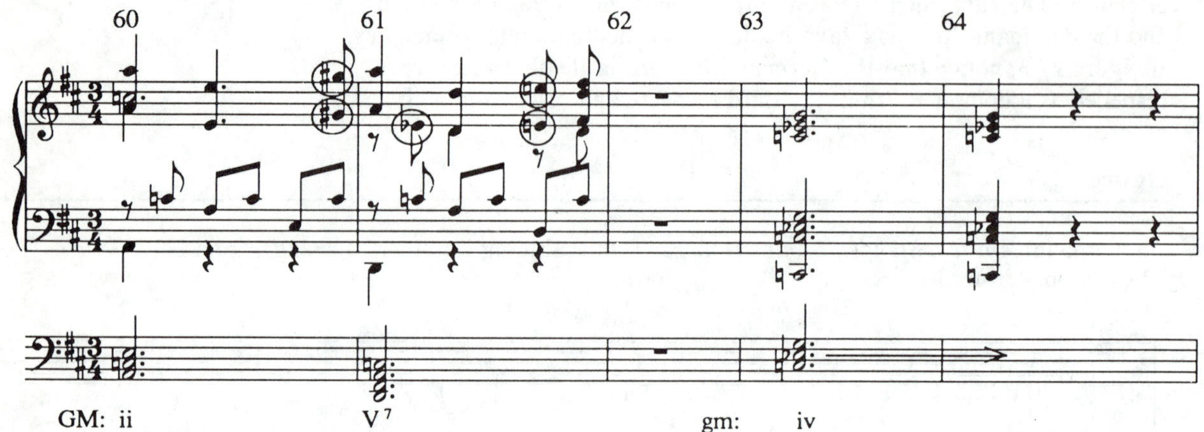

The tonic chord is clearly implied in measure 62 by the progression in the previous two measures (ii, V^7), and if this "missing chord" is filled in, a circle progression emerges. (See figure 21.5.)

Figure 21.5

Schubert: Symphony in B minor, D. 759 ("Unfinished") (1st Movement)

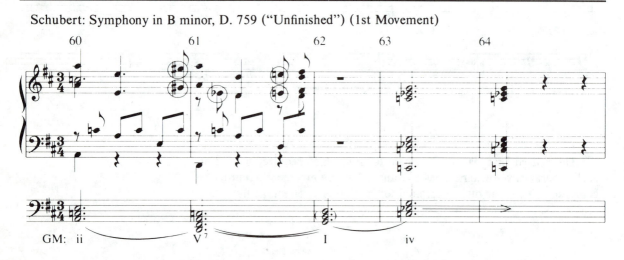

60 61 62 63 64

GM: ii V^7 I iv

Nonfunctional Harmony. On occasion, romantic composers abandoned functional harmony for short periods. These passages were often organized around a segment of the chromatic scale as figure 21.6 illustrates. The chords have been given roman numerals, but it is clear that they are not functionally related to each other. The passage is built around a descending chromatic pattern from the tonic in measure 5 to the dominant in measure 6.

Figure 21.6

Chopin: Prelude, op. 28, no. 20

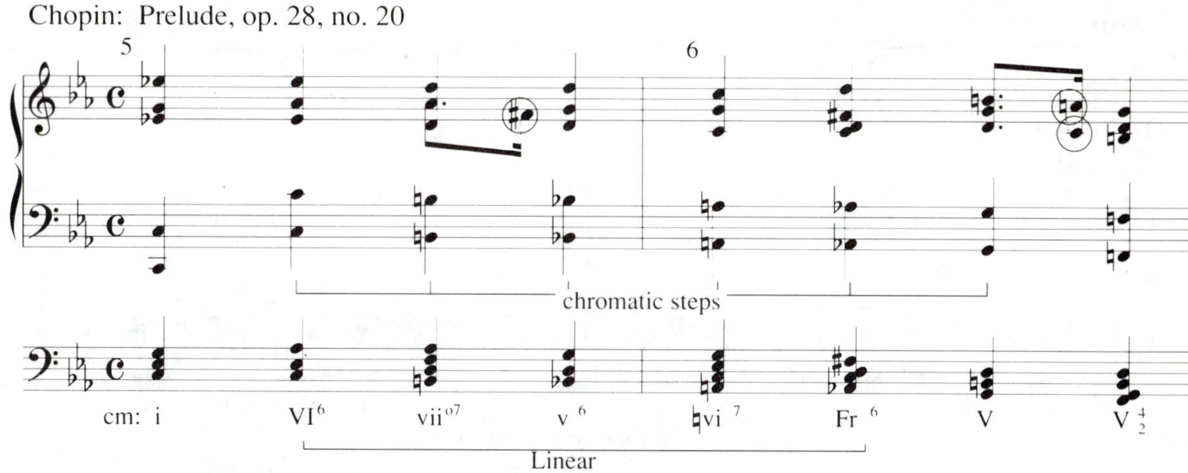

Chromaticism. The increased use of borrowed chords and augmented 6th chords along with modal mixture caused a general increase in chromaticism in the period. There also was an increase in the use of chromatic nonharmonic tones, particularly chromatic appoggiaturas and passing tones. Notice the chromatic appoggiaturas in measure 10 of figure 21.7.

Figure 21.7

Schumann: *Im wundershönen Monat Mai* (In the Wonderful Month of May), from *Dichterliebe* (Poet's Love), op. 48, no. 1

Chromatic passing tones are the central decorative devices in Chopin's Prelude (figure 21.8) occurring in nearly every measure of the work.

Figure 21.8

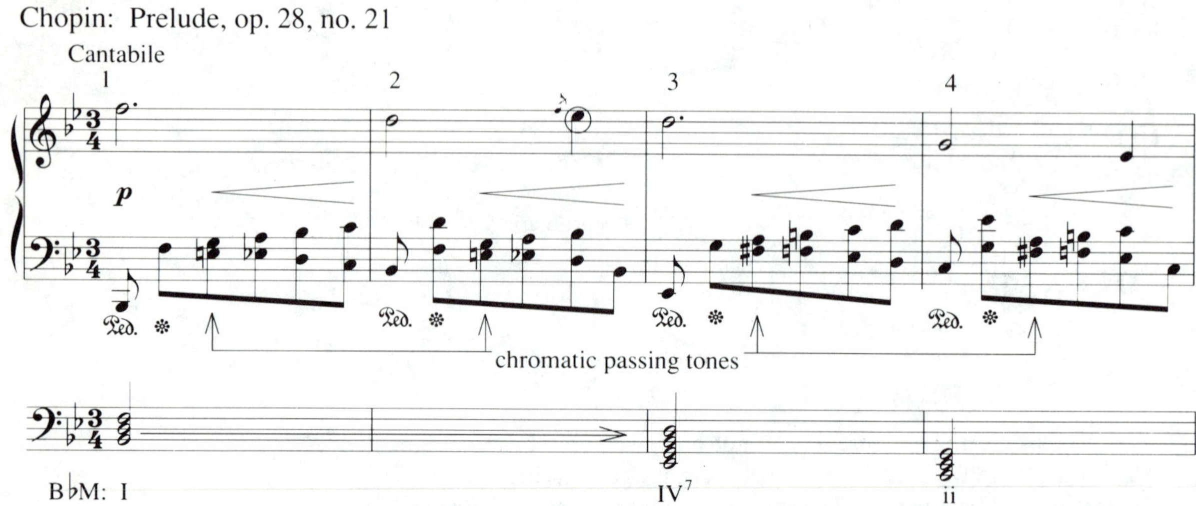

Increased Dissonance. More frequent use of 7th, 9th, 11th and 13th chords and augmented 6th chords increased the general level of dissonance in nineteenth-century music. Composers came to favor the accented dissonances more and more and these dissonances were often sustained much longer than their resolutions. In figure 21.9, notice the accented appoggiatura on the downbeat of measure 17 and the appoggiatura to the 9th of a dominant 9th chord in measure 16. These nonharmonic tones greatly increase the dissonance level of the passage.

Figure 21.9

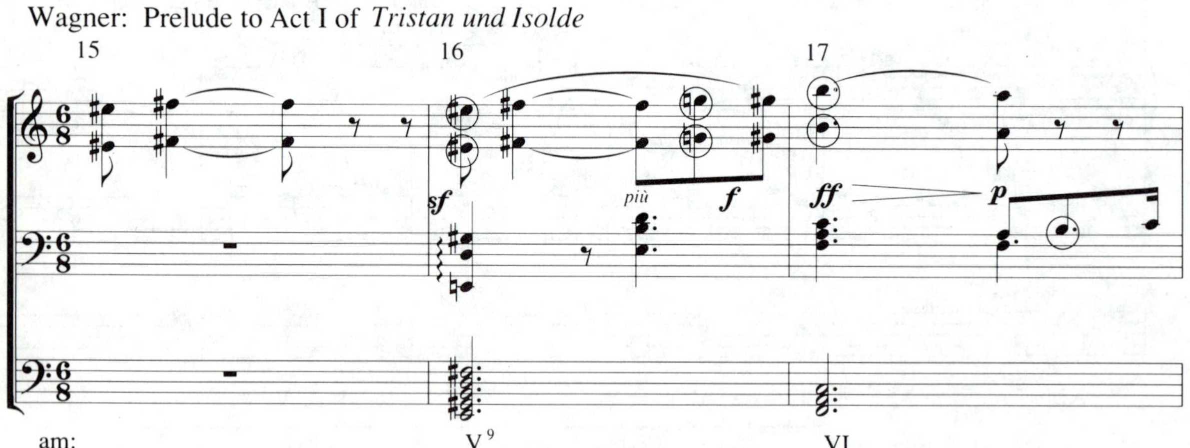

Enharmonic Spelling. The increased chromaticism of the nineteenth century complicated the notation of music, with the result that enharmonic spellings of chords and melodic lines became more frequent. (See measure 8 of Schumann's *Am leuchtenden Sommermorgen* on page 321 (figure 21.3), where the vocal part remains in flats while the accompaniment is written in sharps.) It is important that you develop skill in thinking enharmonically when analyzing the music of the nineteenth and twentieth centuries. The following examples of enharmonic spelling of chords by no means exhaust the possibilities, but they furnish models of what you will need to look out for in future analyses.

Diminished 7th Chords. Since all diminished 7th chords result from enharmonic spellings of three basic chords, composers often write them enharmonically.

Figure 21.10

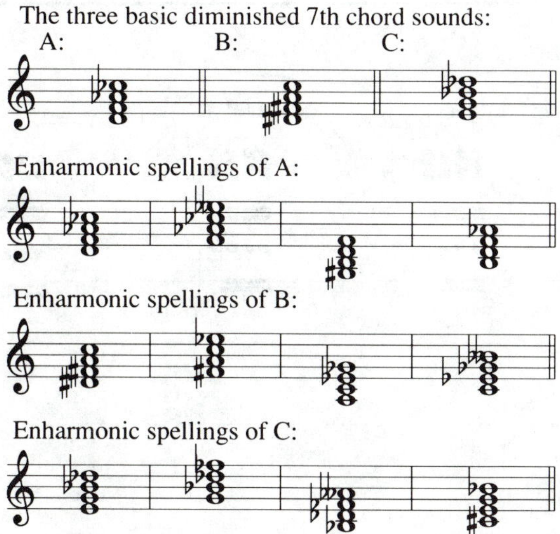

Any tone of a diminished 7th chord is a potential leading tone, and the chord may resolve to any of four roots. The chord may or may not be spelled to agree with its resolution, and enharmonic spelling must be considered in arriving at a correct analysis.

Figure 21.11

Figure 21.12 illustrates the enharmonic spelling of a diminished 7th chord to make a modulation from A minor to E-flat major.

Figure 21.12

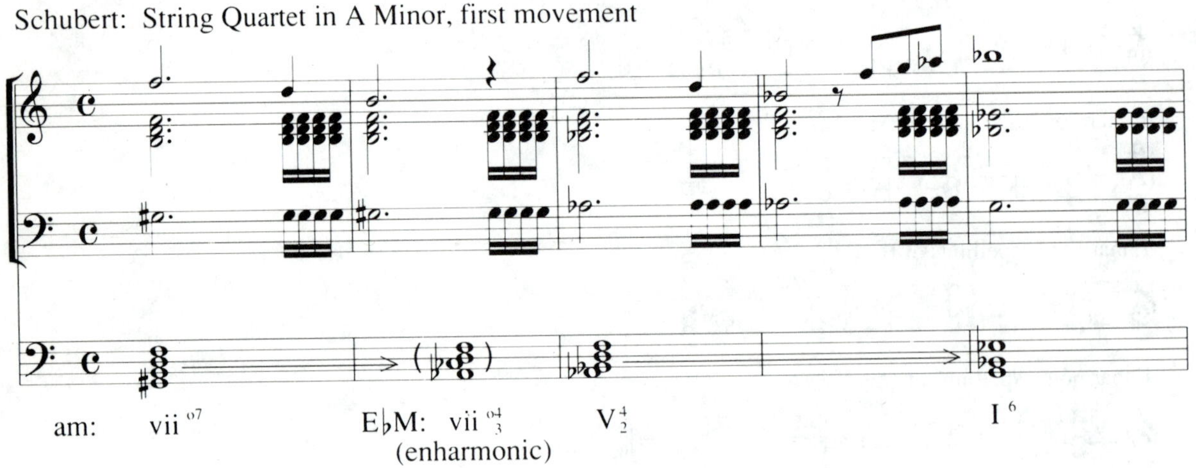

German 6th Chords. The enharmonic relationship between the Italian 6th and the German 6th chords and the dominant 7th led composers to spell these chords enharmonically. Be alert for dominant 7th chords where the root resolves downward by a half step. Most of these chords are functioning as German 6th chords. When the enharmonic relationship between dominant 7ths and the augmented 6th chords is used as a modulatory device (See figure 21.3 on page 321), the chord may be spelled correctly in one key, but not in the other.

Figure 21.13

REVIEW

1. Study figure 21.10 and 21.11 and observe the enharmonic spelling of the diminished 7th chords. Write out four resolutions of chords "B" in figure 21.10, using figure 21.11 as a model. Now do the same for chord "C" in figure 21.10.
2. Select a major or minor key. Spell the dominant 7th chord in that key. Now respell the same chord enharmonically as a German 6th chord (only the 7th of the chord will need to be spelled enharmonically). In what key would you normally find that German 6th chord? The chord you spelled could be used as a pivot chord between those two keys. Choose another key and repeat the process.
3. Select a major or minor key. Spell the German 6th chord in that key. Now respell the same chord enharmonically as a dominant 7th chord (only the augmented 6th will need to be spelled enharmonically to form a minor 7th). In what key would you find the dominant 7th chord? The chord you spelled could be used as a pivot chord between those two keys. Repeat the process choosing another key.
4. Form a chart of the results of numbers 2 and 3 above. Do you see a pattern in the keys that can be related through the enharmonic relationship of the German 6th and the dominant 7th?
5. The following is a list of pairs of keys that are quite distant from each other. For each pair find at least three common chords between the keys. Consider diminished 7th chords, German 6th chords, Neapolitans, borrowed chords, and enharmonic spelling of diatonic triads in each key.

a.	G major	A-flat major
b.	E major	B-flat major
c.	D minor	D-flat major
d.	F-sharp major	B-flat minor
e.	A minor	F-sharp major
f.	F major	C-sharp major

Test Yourself 21

Each of the following short excerpts contains a modulation in which the common chord is spelled enharmonically in one key. The enharmonic chord is marked by an asterisk in each excerpt. (There are two enharmonic chords in example 1. The second chord leads back to the original key.)

1. Determine the two keys involved.
2. Name the chord marked with an asterisk in both keys. (This will require an enharmonic spelling in one key.)

1. Chopin: Nocturne, op. 9, no. 1

2. Haydn: String Quartet, op. 54, no. 1, Hob. III: 43

3. Schubert: Waltz, op. 9, no. 14, D. 365

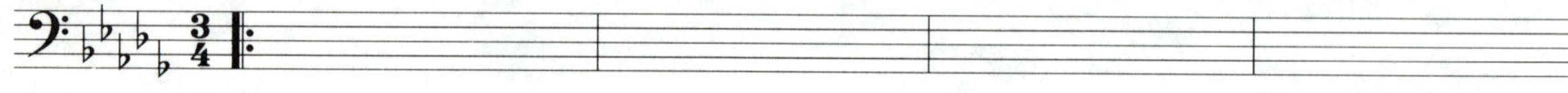

4. Schubert: *Das Fischermädchen* (The Fishermaiden) from *Schwangesang* (Swan Song), D. 957, no. 10

5. Chopin: Prelude, op. 28, no. 17

CHAPTER 22

The Post-Romantic, Impressionistic, and Related Styles

Post-Romanticism
Impressionism
Tonal Ambiguity
Nonfunctional Harmony
Weakened Cadence
Free Augmented Triads
Church Modes
Pentatonic Scale
Whole-Tone Scale
7th, 9th, 11th and 13th Chords
Chords of Addition and Omission
Quartal Chords
Traditional Cadences
Linear Cadence
3rd-Relationship Cadence
Altered Dominant or Tonic Cadences
Melodic Doubling at Various Intervals
Parallel Chords (Planing)

Exposition

Post-Romanticism. The term *Post-Romantic* is applied to the music of composers such as Hugo Wolf (1860–1903), Gustave Mahler (1860–1911), and Richard Strauss (1864–1949), who carried the musical style developed by the romantic composers (Richard Wagner in particular) to the outer limits of the tonal system based on the major and minor scales and functional harmony.

Impressionism. The term *impressionism* was first applied to a group of French painters, including Edouard Manet, Claude Monet, and Auguste Renoir. Their interest in light and color led to a style characterized by blurred images, which convey the "impression" of a scene instead of an actual representation. The term was first used in music to describe the work of Claude-Achille Debussy (1862–1918) and his followers, principally Maurice Ravel (1875–1937).

Characteristics of Post-Romanticism

Tonal Ambiguity. The Post-Romantic composers were greatly influenced by the music of Richard Wagner, who was able to sustain high levels of tension for long periods of time by avoiding resolution of the dominant function. Notice that each dominant 7th in figure 22.1 is followed by silence and not resolved in the expected way.

Figure 22.1

The use of chromatic harmony and nonharmonic tones, plus the absence of the tonic chord make this passage tonally ambiguous. In fact, this passage is one of the most discussed and analyzed passages in all Western music, and the analysis just presented is only one possible interpretation.

The following excerpt from a Wolf song (figure 22.2) creates tonal ambiguity at the outset of the song through thin textures, chromaticism, incomplete chords, and lack of strong moves toward the tonic. The music only arrives at a clear tonal center in measure 9 through a circle progression in the previous measure (V/V, V^7, i), and even here the tonic is somewhat obscured by nonharmonic tones.

Figure 22.2

Wolf: *Der Knabe und das Immlein* (The Boy and the Bee), from *Gedichte von Eduard Mörike*

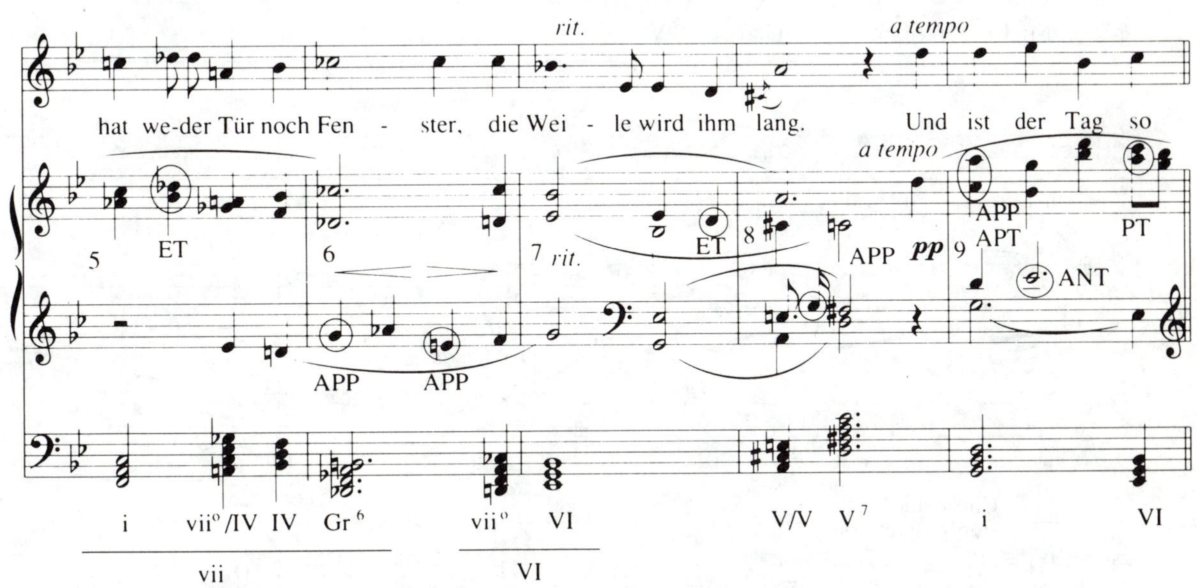

Nonfunctional Harmony. The post-romantic composers engaged in extended nonfunctional harmony (see page 322), often combined with foreign modulation to create tonal ambiguity. Figure 22.3 is the beginning of a passage that doesn't return to the tonic for sixteen measures. Notice the moves toward G major and D♭ major and the nonfunctional passage in measures 13–15 based on a chromatic scale.

Figure 22.3

Weakened Cadence. The tonic is sometimes in doubt during most of a composition in this period, but it normally returns at the end to create closure. At the end of a composition, strong cadences are often blurred by inserting other chords (particularly the V/IV) between the dominant and the tonic chord, as shown in figure 22.4. The authentic cadence was too obvious following the highly chromatic music of these composers.

Figure 22.4

Augmented Triads. The post-romantic composers added the augmented triad to their vocabulary of ambiguous chords. It appeared both as an altered dominant and as a nonfunctional chord. In the following passage nonfunctional augmented chords are treated with the same sliding chromaticism as the diminished 7th chord in earlier times.

Figure 22.5

Wolf: *Das verlassene Mägdelein* (The Forsaken Maiden), from *Gedichte von Eduard Mörike*

Characteristics of Impressionism and Related Styles

Debussy also felt the influence of Wagner, but his response was a conscious attempt to remove "Wagnerisms" from his music. In a letter to a friend during the composition of his opera *Pelléas et Mélisande,* he complained: "I was too hasty to crow over *Pelléas et Mélisande*. . . . The ghost of old Klingsor, alias *R. Wagner,* appeared at the turn of a measure, so I tore it all up. . ." Debussy created a unique musical style that has come to be called *impressionism*. It is a blend of elements borrowed from Eastern and Western music, as well as those of his own invention. Many composers in the early twentieth century were influenced by impressionism.

Church Modes. Composers of this time often utilize modal resources to create new and unusual melodic effects. "Chanty," from the group of piano compositions *Poems of the Sea* by Ernest Bloch (figure 22.6), illustrates the use of the Dorian mode.

Scale Resources

Figure 22.6

Dorian mode beginning on A

Bloch: "Chanty" from *Poems of the Sea*

Figure 22.7 illustrates the use of the Phyrgian mode beginning on A.

Figure 22.7

Respighi: *Trittico Botticelliano* (Botticelli Triptych)

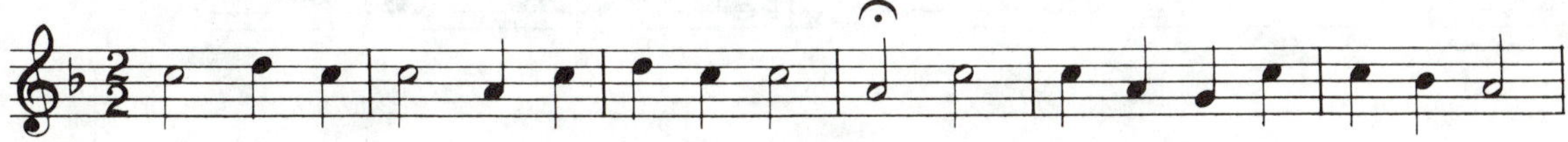

Pentatonic Scale. The pentatonic (five-tone) scale found frequent use in compositions of this period. Since it is a gapped scale (containing intervals larger than a whole step between adjacent tones), there are several possible forms available.

Figure 22.8 contains some of the more frequently used pentatonic scales.

Figure 22.8

Figure 22.9, from the Debussy Préludes, demonstrates the use of the pentatonic scale.

Figure 22.9

Pentatonic scale:

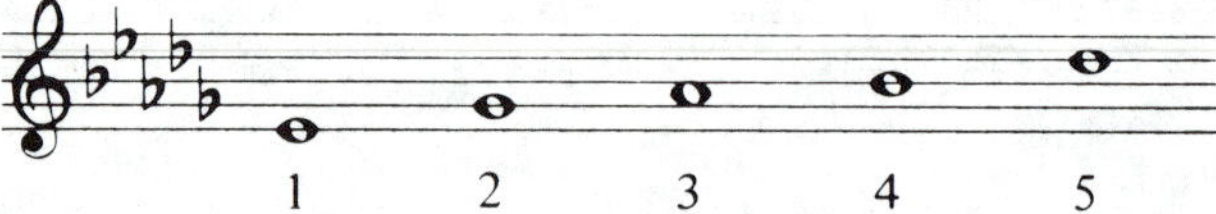

No. 2 from Preludes, Book I. Source: Debussy: *Voiles* (Sails), copyright © 1910, Durand et Cie. Elkan-Vogel, Inc., sole representative, United States.

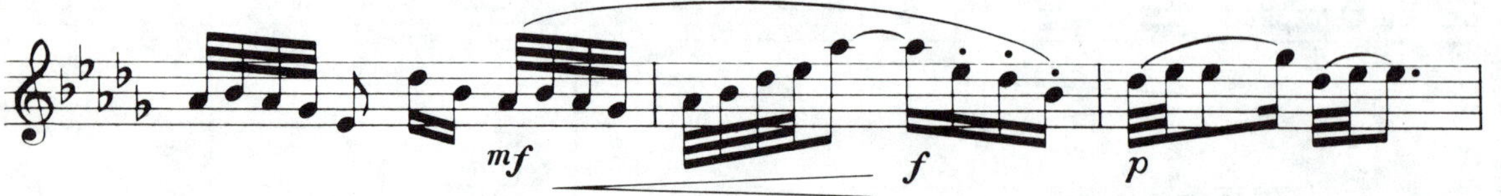

Whole-Tone Scale. The whole-tone scale is a scale in which each degree is a whole step from the next. The whole-tone scale has only six tones—it is a hexatonic scale. Only two different whole-tone scales are possible. An aggregate of the chromatic scale is formed by the two scales illustrated.

Figure 22.10 is a whole-tone scale utilizing the following tones (any pitch may be spelled enharmonically).

Figure 22.10

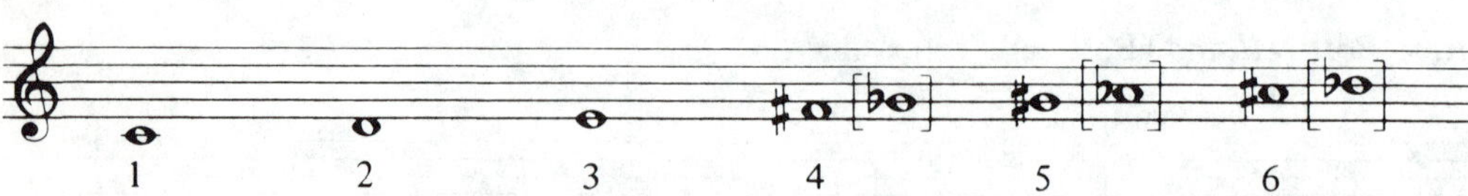

Figure 22.11 shows the remaining tones of the chromatic scale (any pitch may be spelled enharmonically).

Figure 22.11

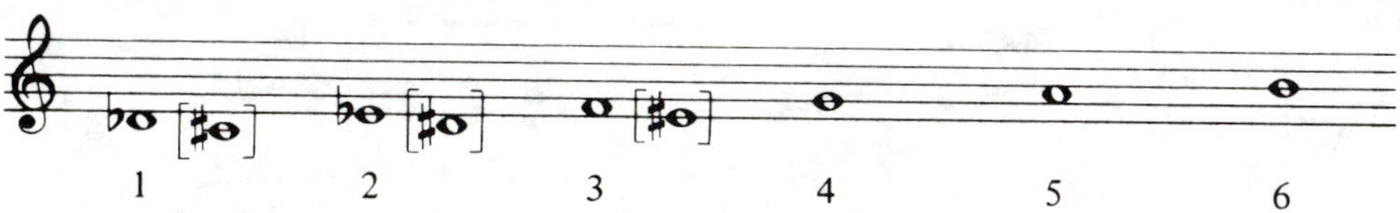

There are no P5ths or P4ths between any two degrees of the whole-tone scale. The whole-tone scale is not diatonic—it contains no key or tonal center, and may begin on any of the six tones.

Figure 22.12

No. 2 from Preludes, Book I. Source: Debussy: *Voiles* (Sails), copyright © 1910, Durand et Cie. Elkan-Vogel, Inc., sole representative, United States.

**Voiles* can also be translated as "Veils."

Chords

7th, 9th, 11th, and 13th Chords. The 7th, 9th, 11th, and 13th chords were employed with considerably greater frequency during the Impressionistic period, and with much less tendency to resolve the dissonant factors. Figure 22.13, from Ravel's *Sonatine* (1903), illustrates the use of 7th and 9th chords in succession. Note the circle of descending 5ths (ascending 4ths), a vestige of the Baroque, Classical, and Romantic periods.

Figure 22.13

Ravel: *Sonatine* (2nd Movement)

Successive circle progressions

Chords of Addition and Omission. Chords of addition and omission are chords with added or deleted tones. In order to enrich the sound of some sonorities, composers of the period often added a 6th, a 4th, or a 2nd to the traditional triad. Similarly, tones were, on occasion, deleted from chords, thus thinning the sound. Some common examples are found in figure 22.14.

Figure 22.14

Added 6th Added 4th Added 2nd Omitted 3rd Omitted 3rd

Chords with added tones often appear very similar to 9th, 11th, and 13th chords, but when the highest factor (9th, 11th, or 13th) is in a lower voice, the tendency is to hear it as an added tone (figure 22.15).

Figure 22.15

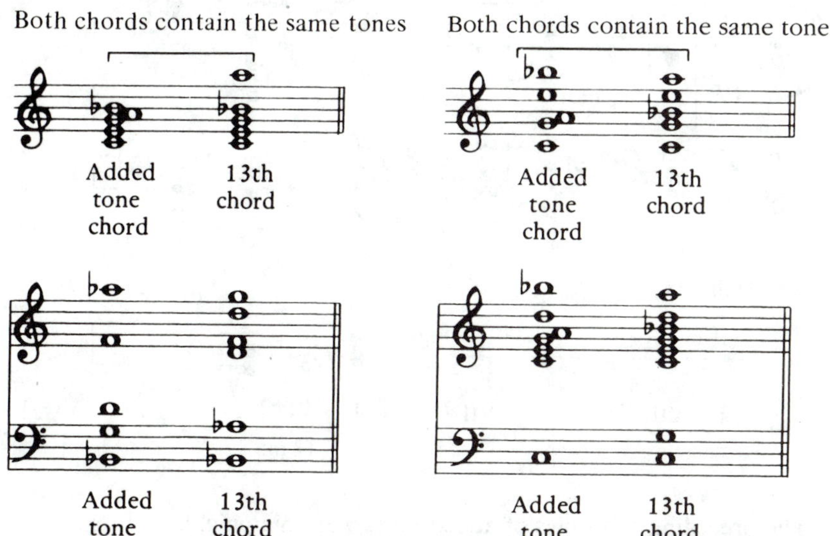

In this book we will use the word "no," plus the chord factor missing to indicate tones omitted from chords, and the word "add," plus the interval added for tones added to chords. For example, a chord with 2 missing third will be labeled (no 3), while a chord with an added 6th will be labeled (add 6).

The added 6th chord is especially prominent in figure 22.16.

Figure 22.16

Ravel: *Sonatine* (1st Movement)

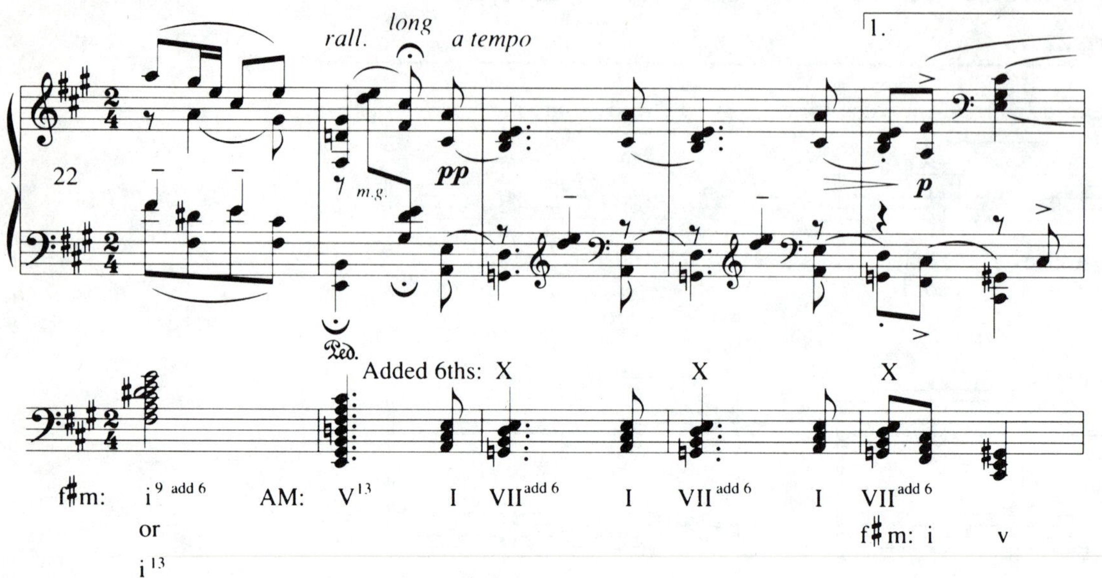

The preceding examples of added tones were diatonic, but chromatic added tones are also found. Such chromatic tones often produce double inflections of chord tones. Double inflection of the third of the chord produces a combination of major and minor, which is called a split 3rd. Figure 22.17 contains five chromatic added tones.

Figure 22.17

Ravel: *Valses nobles et sentimentales* (Noble and Sentimental Waltzes)

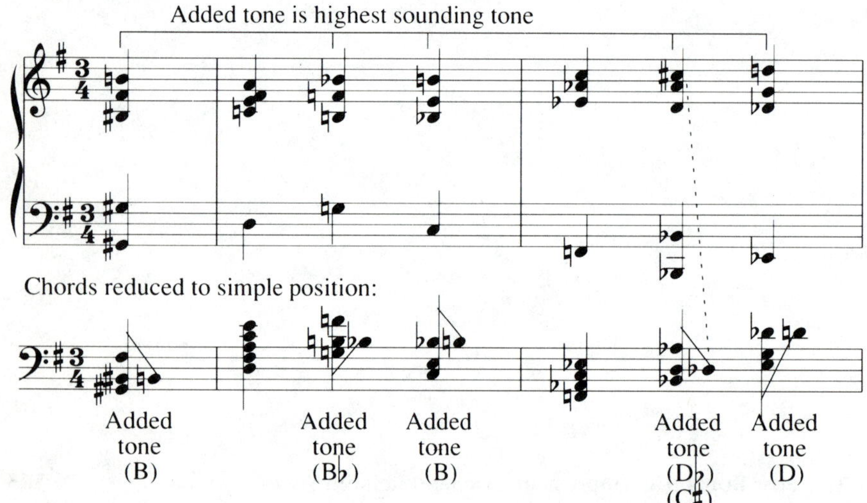

Figures 22.18 and 22.19 contain both *chords of omission* and *added tones.*

Figure 22.18

Debussy: *Soirée dans Grenade* (Evening in Granada) from *Estampes* (Prints)

Figure 22.19

Debussy: *Soirée dans Grenade* (Evening in Granada) from *Estampes* (Prints)

Quartal/Quintal Chords. Quartal chords are chords built in 4ths, while quintal chords are based on 5ths. Although by no means a common occurrence, quartal/quintal chords can be found in this style period. Two distinct types can be identified: "Consonant" and "Dissonant" quartal/quintal sonorities. *Consonant quartal/quintal chords* usually contain three to five factors built in P4ths (or P5ths), while *dissonant quartal/quintal chords* contain one or more A4ths (or d5ths), or five or more P4ths (or P5ths).

Figure 22.20

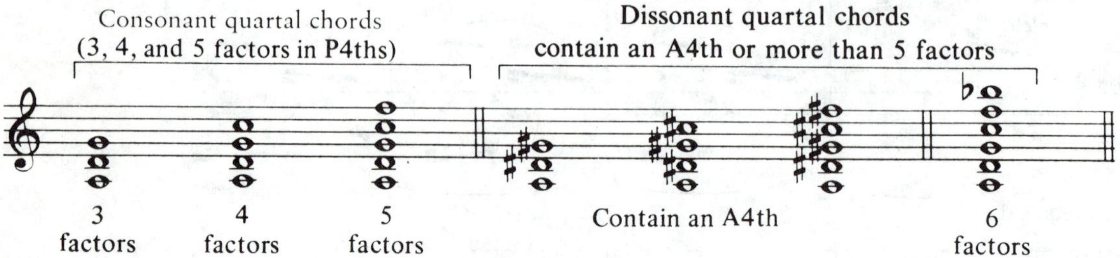

Quartal/quintal chords are not particularly common in impressionistic music, although they sometimes appear as parallel chords in nonfunctional harmony. Figure 22.21 illustrates such use.

Figure 22.21

No. 10 from Preludes, Book I. Source: Debussy: *La Cathedrale Engloutie* (The Engulfed Cathedral), copyright © 1910, Durand et Cie. Elkan-Vogel, Inc., sole representative, United States.

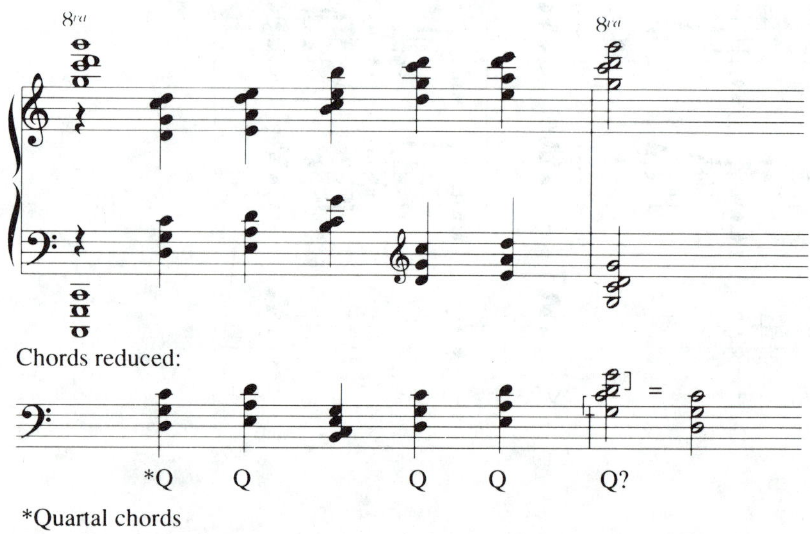

Traditional Cadences. A wide variety of cadences are found in this period, ranging from the traditional authentic cadence to the 3rd-relationship cadence. The traditional authentic cadence is frequently adorned with 7th, 9th, 11th, or 13th chords (figure 22.22).

Cadences

Figure 22.22

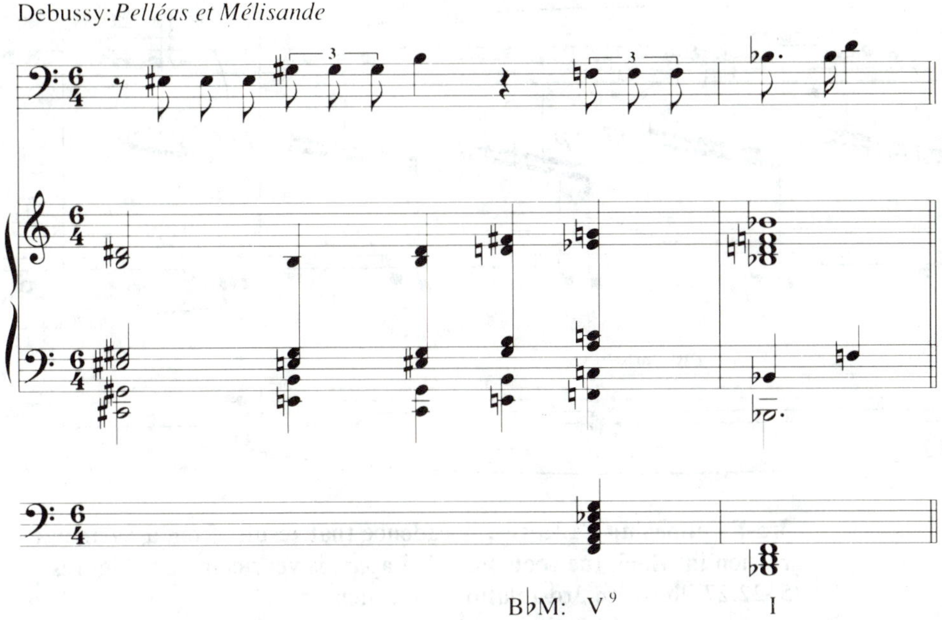

Linear Cadences. A *linear cadence* (or *line cadence*) consists of melodic lines that converge or diverge to form cadence points. These cadences are reminiscent of cadences in early music, before the development of the major-minor tonal system (figure 22.23).

Figure 22.23

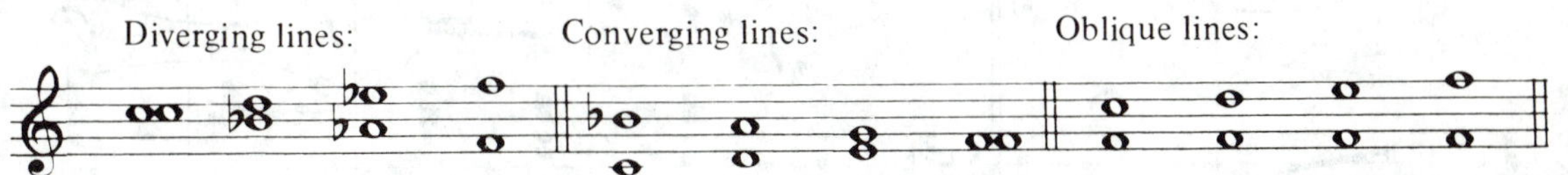

In figure 22.24, the final cadence results from oblique motion.

Figure 22.24

No. 3 from Preludes, Book I. Source: Debussy: *Le Vent dans la plaine* (The Wind on the Plain), copyright © 1910, Durand et Cie. Elkan-Vogel, Inc., sole representative, United States.

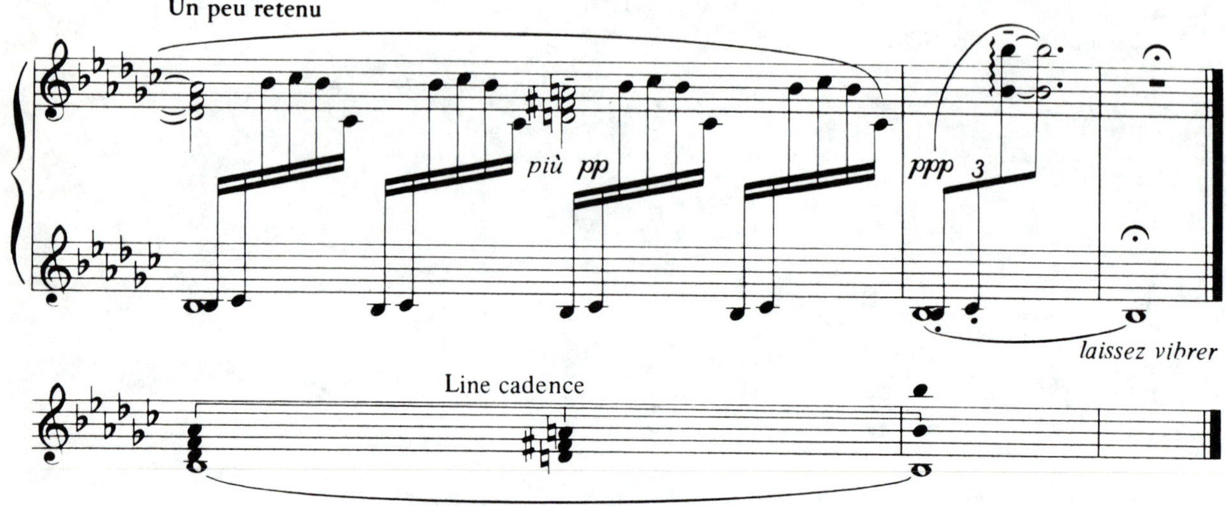

3rd-Relationship Cadences. A cadence that results from a harmonic progression in which the roots lie a 3rd apart is very common. Figures 22.25–22.27 illustrate 3rd-relationship cadences.

Figure 22.25

Ravel: *Sonatine* (2nd Movement)

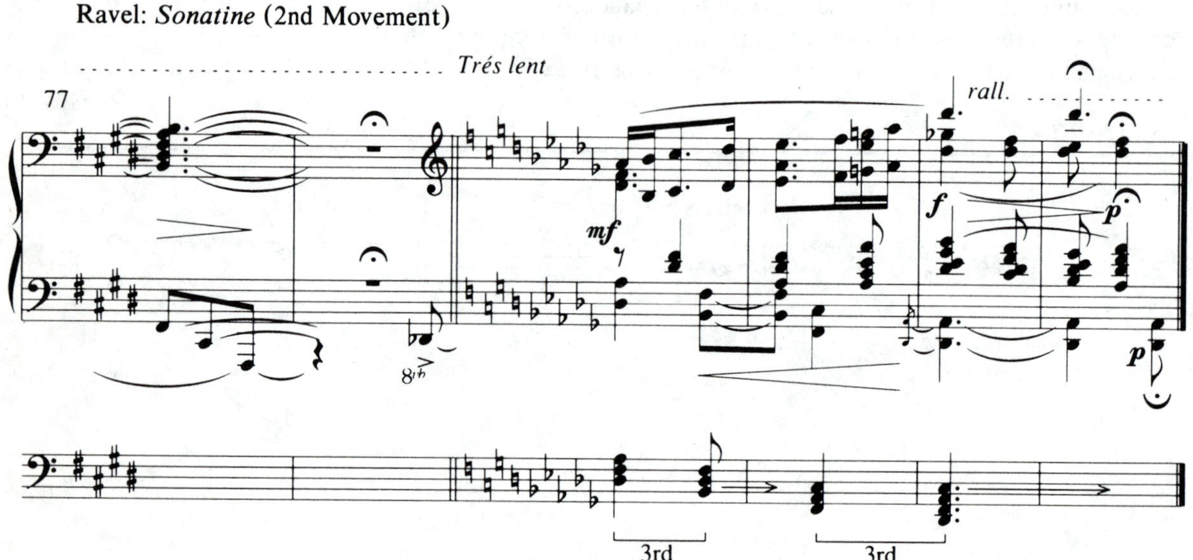

Figure 22.26

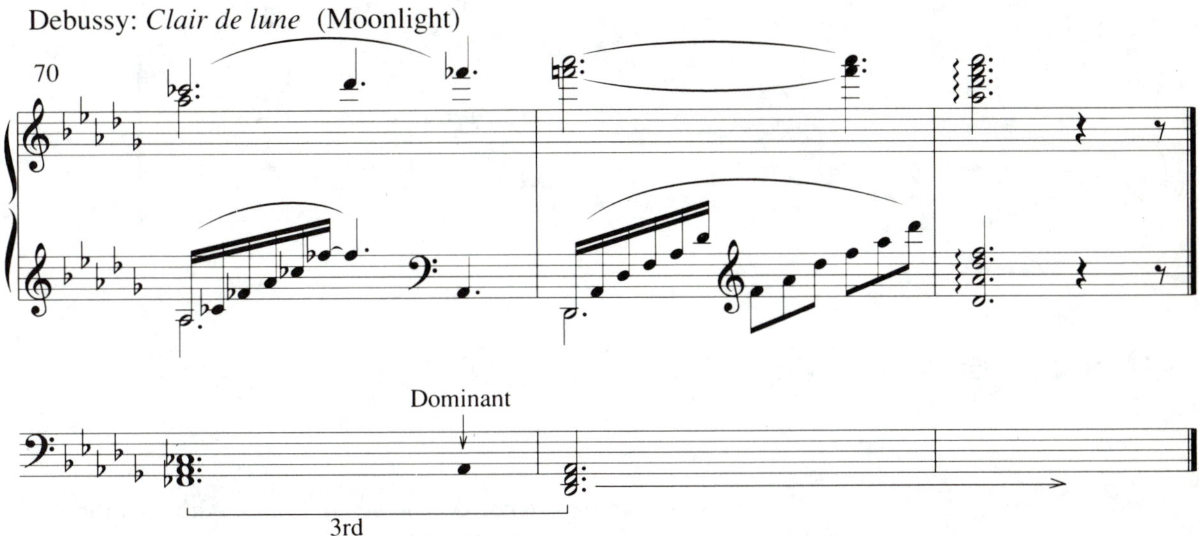

Figure 22.27

Cadences Containing Altered Dominants or Tonics. Although the authentic cadence of the late eighteenth and nineteenth centuries is sometimes found in its unaltered state in this style period, the dominant-tonic function is often camouflaged by chords to which additional factors have been added or from which they have been deleted. The final cadence from the second movement of *Suite Bergamasque* (figure 22.28) contains a dominant 7th chord with an added 4th. This chord thus contains elements of both dominant and tonic harmony.

Figure 22.28

Debussy: *Menuet* from *Suite* Bergamasque

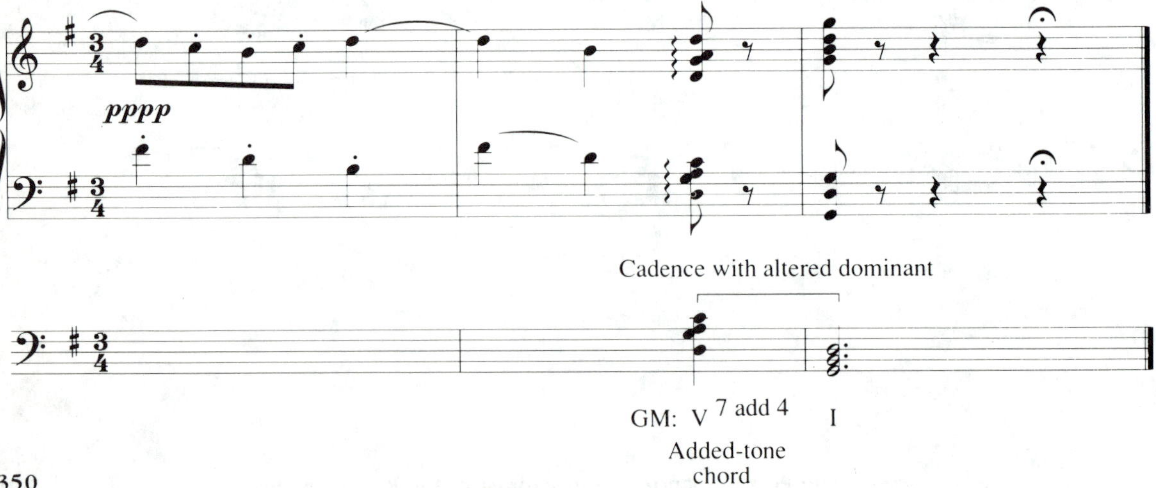

Other Cadences. A variety of other cadences are also a part of the late nineteenth- and early twentieth-century style. Most are simply variations of traditional cadences. Figure 22.29, the short piano composition "Gymnopedie" no. 2 (Greek ceremonial dance) by Eric Satie, written in 1888, ends with a dominant-tonic cadence in the mixolydian mode:

Figure 22.29

Melodic Doubling

Melodic Doubling at Various Intervals. Melodic doubling in parallel refers to the doubling of melodic lines to create parallel movement. The doubling may be simply the addition of a single tone at a fixed harmonic interval (figure 22.30).

Figure 22.30

Melody:

Same melody with melodic doubling:

While treated in a unique way in this period, melodic doubling is by no means the invention of twentieth-century composers. Such doubling has been in existence for many centuries and can be found in *fauxbourdon* and *English discant* of the fifteenth century (figure 22.31).

Figure 22.31

Fauxbourdon:

Dufay: Mass (circa 1465)

Figure 22.32 illustrates the use of melodic doubling at the interval of the 2nd.

Figure 22.32

No. 7 from Preludes, Book I. Source: Debussy: *Ce qu' a ve le vent de l'Ouest* (What the West Wind Saw), copyright © 1910, Durand et Cie. Elkan-Vogel, Inc., sole representative, United States.

Parallel Chords (Planing). Similar to melodic doubling, parallel chords are chords in which all factors or voices move in parallel motion. This motion is called *planing.* Generally, planing reduces or negates the effect of harmonic progression, but occasionally chords such as the tonic and dominant may create the sense of harmonic progression (figure 22.33).

Figure 22.33

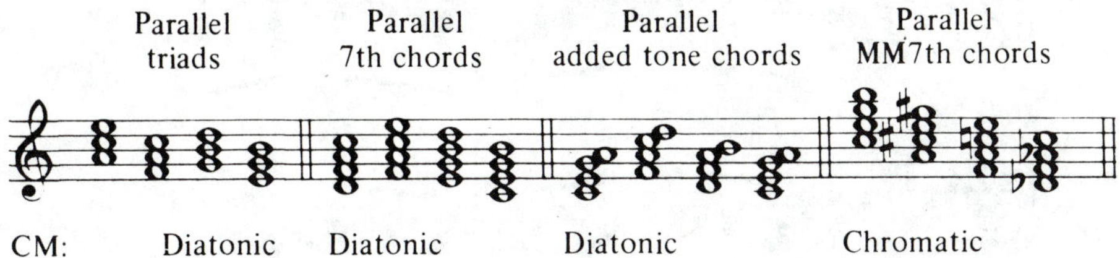

The following example of planing (figure 22.34) contains only Mm-7th chords:

Figure 22.34

Debussy: *Sarabande* from *Pour le Piano* (For the Piano)

Figure 22.35 contains mixed major and minor triads in first inversion:

Figure 22.35

Debussy: *Soirée dans Grenade* (Evening in Granada) from *Estampes* (Prints), for piano

Scale Vocabulary. In previous analyses the major or minor scales could be assumed to be the tonal basis, but no such assumption can be made with music of the late nineteenth and early twentieth centuries. Instead, the identification of the scale basis (major, minor, modal, chromatic, pentatonic or whole-tone) will be an important step in analysis. If the music is not based in some way on the major/minor tonal system, then traditional roman-numeral analysis is not likely to prove fruitful. (In some cases, however, modal materials can be successfully analyzed with roman numerals.)

Chord Vocabulary. The introduction of quartal chords raises questions concerning the interval basis of harmony. Roman-numeral analysis assumes a ***tertian*** system (a harmonic system based on thirds) and is not appropriate for quartal harmonic materials. Chords of addition and omission present new problems in chord labeling.

The following suggestions are intended to help you recognize and label the tonal materials you will encounter in studying the music of this period.

Suggested approach to analysis.

1. Establish the scale basis by examination of the music. If the music is chromatic, try to determine if the chromaticism is the result of functional chromatic harmony, or is nonfunctional. If the music seems diatonic, check first to see if it may be pentatonic. Since the

pentatonic scale is a subset of the diatonic scale, it is easily overlooked. If the music proves to be diatonic, check for modal versus major/minor basis.

2. Examine the harmonic vocabulary by looking at prominent chords. Check particularly for quartal/quintal sonorities.
3. If the music is major/minor or functional chromatic, then roman-numeral analysis is appropriate. Do a harmonic reduction on the blank staff below the music and complete a traditional or macro analysis below this staff.
4. If the music contains passages of nonfunctional harmony, do a harmonic reduction and identify each chord by quality, either with roman numerals or direct labeling (A^7, $D^{\circ 7}$, etc.). Check carefully for functional relationships that may be masked by enharmonic spellings.
5. If the music falls outside 3 and 4, do a harmonic reduction and resort to direct labeling of scales and chords.
6. Melodic and rhythmic analysis is little affected by the introduction of new tonal materials, and can be done in the usual way.

Specimen Analysis: *La Cathédrale Engloutie* by Debussy. This excerpt (figure 22.36) from a well-known work of Debussy should be examined as an example of the analysis of late nineteenth- and early twentieth-century music.

Figure 22.36

No. 10 from Preludes, Book I. Source: Debussy: *La Cathedrale Engloutie* (The Engulfed Cathedral), copyright © 1910, Durand et Cie. Elkan-Vogel, Inc., sole representative, United States.

8
9
10
11
12
(E Lydian)
(Melody against E pedal)
13
pp
8va
14
(sans nuances)
pp
15
(E Lydian)
C Major
E no 3
CM 7 Q Q Q Q Q Q Q Q
(C-G pedal established)
Peu à sortant de la brume
16
sempre pp
B Pentatonic (B C♯ D♯ F♯ G♯)
B
(added tones)

17
p marqué
pp
B add 6
18
p marqué
pp
(B pentatonic)
B add 6
19
p
marqué
E♭ Major
E♭
(added tones)

Augmentez progressivement (Sans presser)
20
(E♭ Major)
E♭
21
(E♭ Major)
E♭
8va
22
23
24
25
più f
C Major
Q
Dm 7 add 4
(CM: II 7 add 4)

21
(E♭ Major)
E♭
8va
22
23
24
25
più f
C Major
Q
Dm 7 add 4
(CM: II 7 add 4)
Sonore sans dureté
sff
26
27
28
ff
29
30
V
8vb
(C Major)
(Dm 7 add 4)
CM: V
I
C
Dm
G
F
Em
Dm
Dm
Am
Em
(Authentic cadence)
(V)

Un peu moins lent (Dans une expression allant grandissant)

31
32
33
34
35
C Major
C Mixolydian
F Dm C
C Am
B♭ Dm F
C Am
B♭ D F
36
37
38
39
40
(C Mixolydian)
C Major
Gm F Gm B♭
Gm Am
F
Dm Em
C
41
42
43
44
45
p
più p
pp
più pp
C Major
C Aeolian
Q (added tones)

8va
p
f
56
57
58
59
(C♯ Aeolian)
F♯m add 6
8va
ff
molto dim.
60
61
62
63
(C♯ Aeolian)
Chromatic
B add 2
F♯m add 6
B add 2
D♯ 7
C♯ 7
B 7
A7
C♯ 7
p
64
65
66
67
68
69
(half cadence)
(Chromatic)
(ambiguous)
C♯M: V7
V7/V
V7
V7/IV
V7

8va
ff
molto dim.
60
61
62
63
(C♯ Aeolian)
Chromatic
B add 2
F♯m add 6
B add 2
D♯ 7
C♯ 7
B 7
A7
C♯ 7
p
64
65
66
67
68
69
(half cadence)
(Chromatic)
(ambiguous)
C♯M: V7
V7/V
V7
V7/IV
V7
au Mouvt
Comme un écho de la phrase
entendu précédement
70
71
72
pp
pp
Flottant
et lourd
8vb
(Chromatic)
C Major
Q
C
Dm
continues as pedal until the end

73
74
75
8vb
(C Major)
G
F
Em
Dm
Dm
Am
Em
F
Dm
C
76
77
78
8vb
(C Major)
C Mixolydian
C
Am
B♭
Dm
F
C
Am
79
80
81
8vb
(C Mixolydian)
B♭
Dm
F
Gm
F
Gm
B♭
Gm
Am

Tonality and Overall Form. Like most other aspects of *La Cathédrale Engloutie,* the form is ambiguous when compared to the clear structure of eighteenth- and earlier nineteenth-century compositions. But that is not to say that form is completely lacking. Figure 22.37 shows the strong bass line that extends throughout the entire composition and the two-part form that emerges. Each section (A and B) contains two identifiable themes (a and b).

In addition, figure 22.37 reveals an overall tonal center of C. This is suggested by the pedal tone (C) and the two descents from dominant (G) to tonic (C), which encompass the entire return of theme b (measures 72–89). Thus, with a bare minimum of functional harmony, Debussy was able to create a fragile and tenuous tonal center. As if to hide or confuse this meager illusion, Debussy introduces third-relationship passages at measures 16–25 and measures 71–72.

Figure 22.37

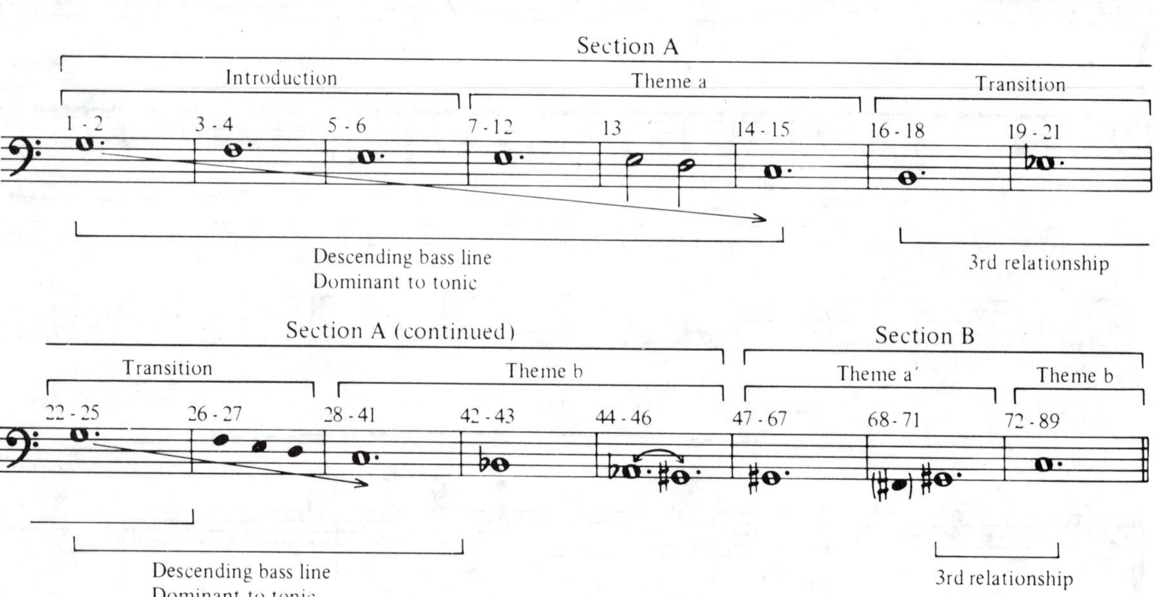

Chord Progressions. The effect of regularly recurring harmonic progressions is minimized in this composition. The reasons are:

1. The actual progressions occur at widely spaced intervals of at least two measures, and in one instance at a distance of thirteen measures. The harmonic rhythm is extremely slow.
2. Some of the harmonic progressions (such as from measures 18–19 and 21–22) contain chords whose roots lie in 3rd relationship to each other. When the thirds are ascending, the harmonic strength is weakened considerably.

Cadences. Traditional harmonic cadences are suggested, but seldom stated clearly as in earlier styles. (The authentic cadence at measures 27–28 is veiled with added-tone chords and a running figure in the lower voice.) The cadence points are as follows:

Measures	Cadence Type	Tonality	Chords
27–28	Authentic	C	V (implied) to I
39–40	Linear (parallel motion)	C	I (pedal)
64–66	Half	C♯	V^7/V to V^7
86–89*	Authentic (modified dominant)	C	V (or quartal) to I

*Not included in the excerpt.

Summary of late nineteenth- and early twentieth-century devices:

Device	Measures
Planing (parallelism)	28–41, 62–67, 72
Church modes (E Lydian or C♯ Dorian)	7–13, 47–54
Quintal chords and planing	14–15
Added 6th chord	16–18
Pentatonic scale	16–18
3rd relationship of chord roots	16–27
7th and 9th chords	19–21, 62–67
Chord with added 4th	23, 26
Quartal or quintal chords	42–45
Chord with added 2nd	60

REVIEW

1. Study the list of terms at the beginning of the chapter (page 333). Define each of the terms in your own words. Take a piece of paper and make three headings: **Post-Romanticism, Impressionism,** and **Both.** Place each term on the list under one heading, depending on the style to which that term refers. (Place a term in the **Both** column if it refers to a characteristic of both styles.)
2. Review the authentic form of the church modes (see figures 2.33 and 2.34 on page 45–46). Select a single note. Spell each of the modes beginning on that note. Repeat this process using a different note.
3. Study figure 22.8 on page 340, which shows four common pentatonic scales. Write these four pentatonic scales beginning on several different notes.
4. Spell the whole-tone scale beginning on several notes.
5. Study figure 22.20, which shows a number of consonant and dissonant quartal chords, all spelled beginning on **A.** Spell these chords beginning on several other notes.
6. Carefully examine the specimen analysis (figure 22.36) after listening to the work several times. See if you understand each analytical symbol.
7. Review the **Suggested Approach to Analysis** on page 354. This step-by-step procedure will help you by establishing an organized approach to analysis.

Test Yourself 22

Play the excerpt from Franck: Chorale for Organ no. 2 several times (or listen to a recording) and then answer each of the following questions:

1. Is the scale basis diatonic or chromatic?
2. Set up an analysis line on a separate sheet of staff paper. Show the key signature, time signature, and eight blank measures. Examine the harmonic vocabulary by writing each chord on the analysis line (the harmonic rhythm is given above the staff). Label each chord using popular music chord symbols. What is the most common chord quality in this excerpt?
3. List pairs of chords that could be functionally related to each other and give a key and possible roman numeral for each chord. Do any of these progressions result in the establishment of a tonal center?
4. Are there any progressions in which nonfunctional harmony is organized around a chromatic step progression?
5. Point out three places where accented nonharmonic tones increase the level of dissonance.

Franck: Chorale for Organ, no. 2, m. 39

The following are short excerpts from the works of impressionistic composers. Using the following list, identify elements in each excerpt that are characteristic of impressionistic style.

a. church modes
b. pentatonic scale
c. whole-tone scale
d. 9th, 11th, and 13th chords
e. chords of addition and omission
f. quartal/quintal chords
g. linear cadence
h. third-relationship cadence
i. melodic doubling at various intervals
j. parallel chords (planing)

1. Debussy: *La Cathedrale Engloutie* (The Engulfed Cathedral) no. 10 from Preludes, Book I

2. Debussy: *Pelléas et Mélisande,* Act I, Scene I.

3. Debussy: *Canope* (Canopic Jar) no. 10 from Preludes, Book II

4. Ravel: *L'Enfant et Les Sortilè ges* (The Child and His Fantasies)

5. Debussy: Nocturnes, *Fêtes*

CHAPTER

23

The Contemporary Period (1920–1945)

Primitivism	*Quartal Chords*	*Set Theory*
Neoclassicism	*Quintal Chords*	*Interval Classes*
Pandiatonicism	*Clusters*	*Set Types*
Polytonality	*Changing Meter*	*Inversion*
Dual Modality	*Asymmetric Meter*	*Retrograde Inversion*
Shifted Tonality	*Nonaccentual Rhythms*	*Normal Order*
Free Tonality	*Set*	*Best Normal Order*
Polychords		

Exposition

Contemporary Period. Concurrent with the surge of post-romantic and impressionistic music, several newer and quite different styles began to surface, which are generally grouped together as *contemporary music.* As the works of such composers as Debussy, Delius, Wolf, Fauré, and Richard Strauss were receiving their premieres, other composers such as Arnold Schoenberg (1874–1951), Charles Ives (1874–1954), Béla Bartók (1881–1945), and Igor Stravinsky (1882–1971) were writing music in distinctly different idioms. Some composers maintained tertian chord structures, but abandoned functional harmony, while others experimented with chords constructed in 4ths, 5ths, or combinations of several intervals. Some preserved tonality while others discarded it in favor of atonality. Experimentation ranged even to the tuning system itself, which led to the development of *microtonal* systems, which are based on more than twelve different pitches per octave. This chapter will deal with the music of Stravinsky, Bartók, and composers with similar styles, while the following chapter will concern itself with the work of Schoenberg and the other composers who evolved a music based on the *twelve-tone technique,* a compositional technique in which all pitches are related to a fixed ordering of the twelve tones of the chromatic scale.

Primitivism. *Primitivism* provided a contrast to the extremely refined and fragile music of composers such as Debussy and Ravel. Rhythm was the primary structural element of this music, and driving rhythms were combined with simple and clearly defined melodies, often of a folk nature, that operated within a narrow pitch range. Sharp percussive effects with thick chords and much parallel movement typified the style. Bartók's *Allegro Barbaro* (1911) and Stravinsky's *The Rite of Spring* (1913) represent examples of this movement, which flourished in the early years of the twentieth century.

Neoclassicism. The term *neoclassicism* refers to the music of composers such as Stravinsky and Hindemith, who sought to return to the classical values of symmetry and balance while maintaining the newer tonal materials of the twentieth century. This movement, which began just after World War I, was quite important through the first third of the twentieth century.

Characteristics of Contemporary Music

Tonal Basis

Pandiatonicism. *Pandiatonicism* is the use of the tones of a diatonic scale in such a way that each tone is stripped of its traditional function. Figure 23.1 demonstrates the use of pandiatonicism and exhibits the following characteristics:

1. Absence of functional harmony.
2. Use of all seven tones of the D-major scale.
3. Thick harmonies (several are five-factor chords.)
4. No chromaticism.

Figure 23.1

Stravinsky: Sonata for Two Pianos (2nd Movement, Var. I)

Polytonality. Polytonality is the use of two or more tonalities at the same time. (The simultaneous use of *two* tonalities is often called *bitonality.*) (See figure 23.2.)

Figure 23.2

Dual Modality. The simultaneous use of a pair of major and minor modes or combinations of Gregorian modes is called *dual modality.* Usually the two modes have the same tonic.

Figure 23.3

Bartók: "Major and Minor," no. 59 from *Mikrokosmos,* vol. 2
Copyright 1940 by Hawkes & Sons (London) Ltd. Renewed 1967. Boosey and Hawkes, Inc.

Treble clef notes: Dorian

Bass clef notes: Lydian

Shifted Tonality. Shifted tonality refers to a sudden change of tonality without preparation:

Figure 23.4

Prokofieff: Piano Sonata no. 8 in B-Flat Major, op. 84 (2nd Movement)

Copyright 1957 by MCA Music, a divison of MCA, Inc.

Free Tonality. Free tonality has the following characteristics:

1. No conventional mode or key is used.
2. A clear tonal center is present.
3. Any combination of the twelve tones of the octave may be used.
4. The traditional functioning of the diatonic tones of a key based on that same tonal center is minimized or avoided entirely.
5. The dominant-tonic relationship of key-centered tonality is absent.

In figure 23.5 all twelve tones (except G♮) are present, the tonality of F is achieved without a single dominant-tonic progression, and the Phrygian mode is suggested but not confirmed.

Figure 23.5

Hindemith: Piano Sonata no. 2 (1st Movement)

Chords reduced:

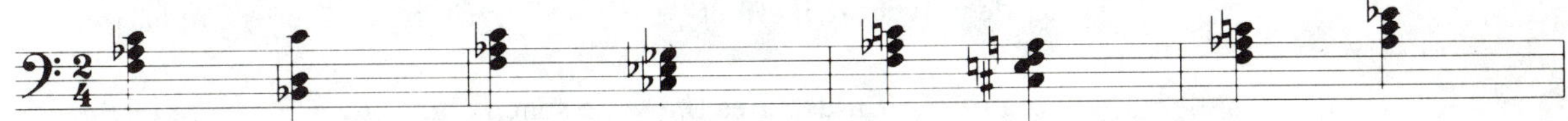

Harmony

Polychords. A *polychord* consists of two or more triads, 7th chords, or other chords sounded simultaneously and spaced far enough apart to make each recognizable as a separate structure. Two triads containing common tones and spaced a distance apart may not be perceived as separate structures if the combination of the two form a chord very familiar to us.

But, if the triads contain no common tones and are of sufficiently contrasting nature, fusion will not result and each triad will maintain its identity as shown in figure 23.6.

Figure 23.6

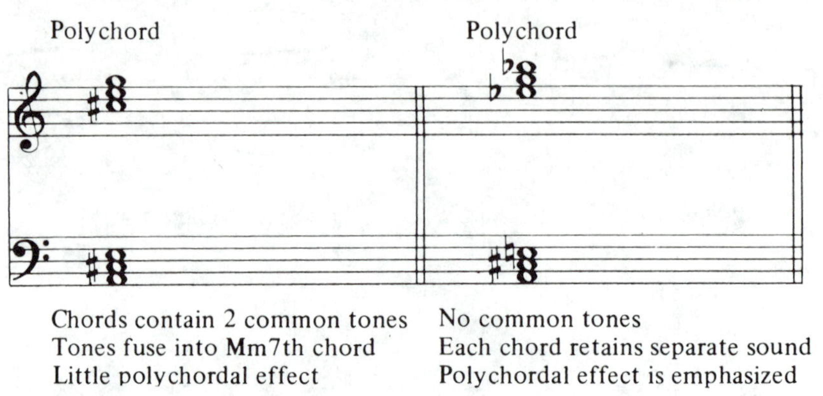

Figure 23.7 illustrates the wide spacing and diverse nature of the simultaneous chords making up *polychords:*

Figure 23.7

Schuman: No. 2 from Three Score Set
Three Score Set, by William Schuman. Copyright © 1943 G. Schirmer, Inc.

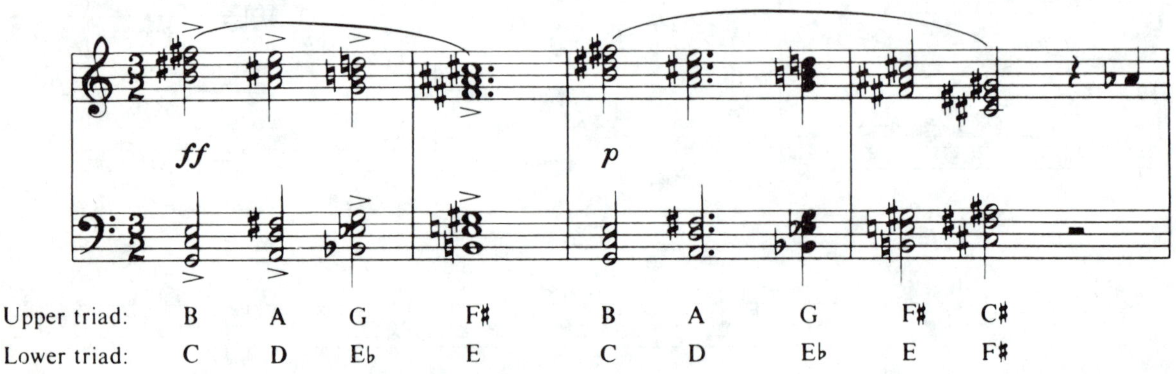

Quartal Chords. Quartal chords are common in contemporary music. Figure 23.8 contains pure quartal chords almost exclusively throughout the composition, which makes it a rare example of quartal chord treatment.

Figure 23.8

Ives: "The Cage" (no. 64 of 114 Songs)

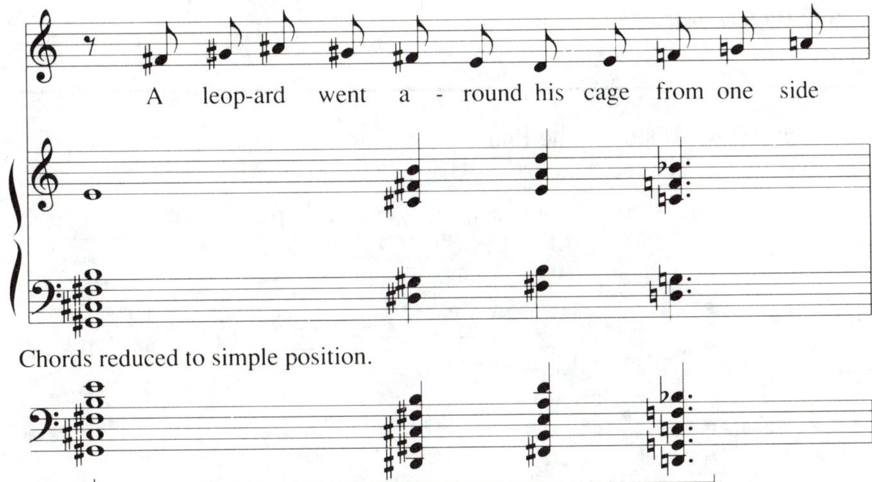

All are 5 factor consonant quartal chords

Frequently, quartal chords are not pure—that is, other intervals are included in the chord, thus creating a mixture of quartal and tertian harmony. The following excerpt (figure 23.9) from Alban Berg's first opera (1921) illustrates the intermixing of 3rds and 4ths. The parallel 4ths in contrary motion (treble against bass) create a counterpoint that adds to the interest of the composition.

Figure 23.9

Berg: "Marie's Lullaby" from *Wozzeck*

*Predominantly quartal

The following excerpt (figure 23.10) from a composition written in 1958 by Paul Pisk also illustrates the mixing of quartal with tertian (triadic) harmony. Note that the melody contains a motif made up of two intervals, the m2nd and the tritone. In its last two appearances in this excerpt, the m2nd is maintained, but the tritone gives way first to a P5th and then a M3rd:

Figure 23.10

Pisk: "Nocturnal Interlude" from New Music for the Piano

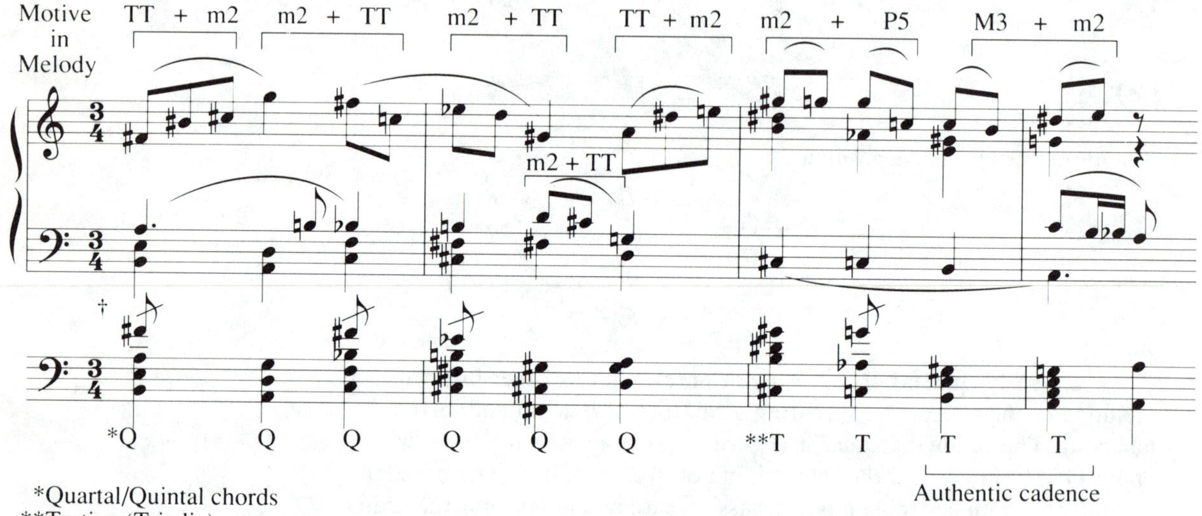

*Quartal/Quintal chords
**Tertian (Triadic)
†Grace notes are not part of the chords

Both quartal and tertian harmony often contain the same tones, each distinguished only by the arrangement of the chord factors. (See figure 23.11.)

Figure 23.11

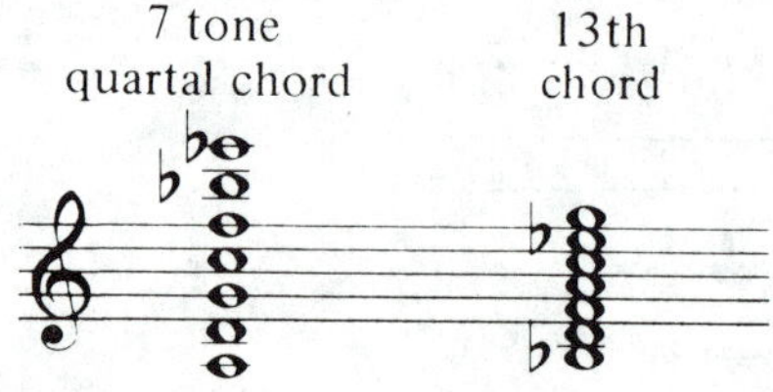

Both contain the same pitches

Clusters. Chords containing three or more factors of which each is no more than a whole step from its adjacent factor are called *clusters.* (See figure 23.12.)

Figure 23.12

Rhythm

Changing Meter. Meter changes from measure to measure within a composition show shifting rhythmic patterns more clearly than would a single governing meter. The signature is changed as often as necessary to clarify rhythms. Changing meter often occurs in music with *additive rhythm* (where the pulse is irregular in length, varying between groups of two and three regular divisions). (See figure 23.13.)

Figure 23.13

Stravinsky: Triumphal March of the Devil, from *L'Histoire du Soldat* (The Tale of the Soldier)

Asymmetric Meter. *Asymmetric meters,* also known as *irregular meters* or *combination meters,* are meters in which the beats are not grouped into units divisible by two or three. These meters are a common way of notating additive rhythm, particularly when there is a recurring pattern of beats. (See figure 23.14.)

Figure 23.14

Gillion: Suite no. 1

Nonaccentual Rhythms. *Nonaccentual rhythms* are characterized by the absence of dynamic accents, which focuses the listener's attention on agogic accents (accents by virtue of duration). (See figure 23.15.)

Figure 23.15

Lucerne: Dirge

Analysis of Contemporary Music

The diversity of style in the music of the twentieth century resists analysis using any single system. Several systems for analysis have been proposed, but none appear to be useful for all styles of music. In the face of such diversity it becomes important to choose analytical methods that reveal the underlying structure of a given work. Thus, the choice of analytical method becomes the first, and most important decision you must make when approaching the analysis of a contemporary composition. Two specimen analyses, one of the *Marche du Soldat* from Stravinksy's *L'Histoire du Soldat* (1918) and the other of "Chromatic Invention," no. 91 from *Mikrokosmos,* volume 3 by Béla Bartók, will illustrate two approaches to the analysis of twentieth-century music.

Marche du Soldat. L'Histoire du Soldat (The Soldier's Story), a work intended "to be read, played, and danced," was written in 1918 for a small touring theater company composed of a few actors, dancers, and a chamber (small) orchestra with soloists. Swiss author (C. F. Ramuz prepared the libretto, and since he was not a dramatist, he prepared a mimed narration (narrator and mime) supported by dancers and orchestra. Currently the work is sometimes performed without the staging.

Because the work is heterogeneous (consisting of many diverse elements) the analytical approach is largely descriptive.

Figure 23.16

Stravinsky: *Marche du Soldat* (Soldier's March) from *L' Histoire du Soldat* (The Tale of the Soldier)

Un sol - dat qui rentre chez lui.
Tramps a sol - dier with his load.
11
12
13
14
15
16
17
18
Bsn.
19
Cor.
p
(pizz.)
sf
20
21
3
Cor.
Trb.
f
22
23
A Lydian
Bitonal:
A (with chromaticism)
G Major
to ms. 31
Ostinato
to ms. 31
AM: I
II
I
DM:

Quinze jours
Ten days
Cl.
Cor.
(m.d.)
Cl.
de con - ge qu'il a,
leave he has to spend,
marche de - puis long temps dé -
Will his jour - ney nev - er
Vln.
Cl.
Bsn.
Vln.
D Major (some chromaticism) to ms. 46
(ostinato)
pedal
to ms. 42

jà.
end?
Cl.
Vln.
Cor.
Bsn.
Vln.
Cor.
Bsn.
Cl.
Vln.
Vln.
Bsn.
Cl.
Cor.
poco sf
ostinato to ms. 84

Cl.
45
46
47
Vln. pizz.
Cor.
Bsn.
A major (with chormaticism)
Bitonal:
G major
to ms. 60
Cl.
Cor. (Bsn. doubles 8ve lower)
48
49
50
51
Vln.
Trb.
52
53
54
55

"Chromatic Invention" no. 91 from *Mikrokosmos,* volume 3 by Béla Bartók. The series of compositions known as the *Mikrokosmos* is a group of 153 piano compositions in six volumes, graded from easy to difficult. They are often assigned as "teaching pieces," and illustrate in miniature form the compositional techniques Bartók used in his larger works. The *Mikrokosmos* was written in an eleven-year period (1926–1937).

Because this work is much more homogeneous in its materials than "The Soldier's March," it will be given an analysis based on set theory. These methods were developed by such theorists as René Leibowitz, Milton Babbitt, and Allen Forte to analyze compositions that are not based on the diatonic scales, but exhibit a great deal of internal consistency of musical materials.

Set Theory. *Set-theory* analysis is based on a collection of *pitch classes.* A *pitch class* is any particular pitch (such as C or F) in any octave. Thus, pitch class G refers to the pitch G regardless of the octave in which it may appear.

Set. The term *set* means a group of pitch classes such as C, D, and E. A set may contain any number of pitch classes from two through twelve:

Figure 23.17

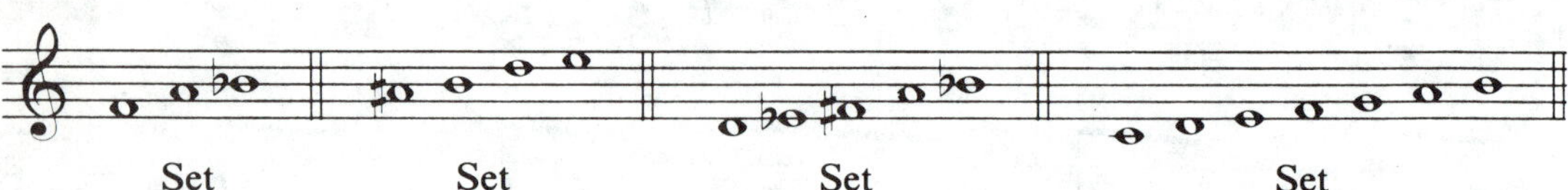

The advantage of the system as applied to this composition lies in its capacity to include groupings of pitch classes (sets) outside the traditional diatonic scales. (The diatonic scales may also be thought of as sets. See page 390.) As an example, the first five notes of the "Chromatic Invention" are A, G-sharp, E-flat, D, and G—notes that do not conform to any of the diatonic scale systems.

Interval Classes. These are six interval classes, indicated by the number of half-step intervals between the two pitch classes. Thus, "3" refers to the interval class that contains three half-steps—such as a minor 3rd or augmented 2nd.

Figure 23.18

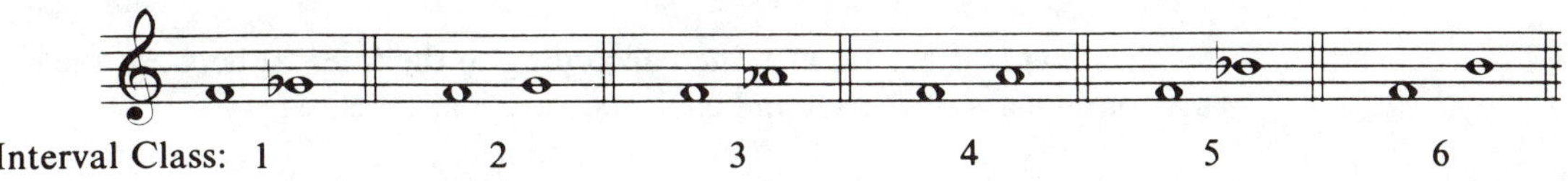

Intervals greater than six half-steps are placed in the same category as their inversion. Thus, a perfect 5th (seven half-steps) is an interval class "5" since its inversion, the perfect 4th, contains five half-steps:

Figure 23.19

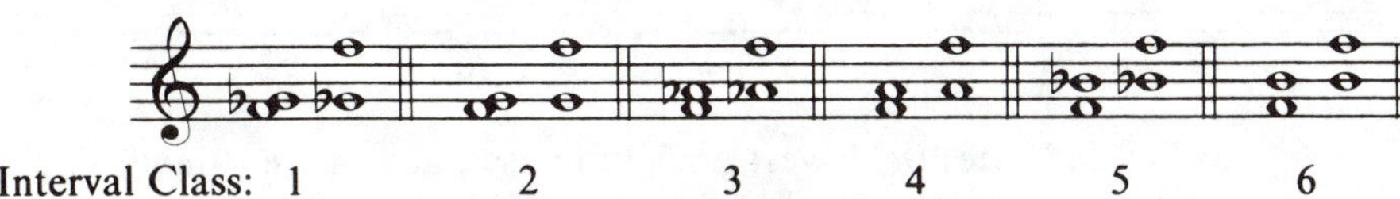

An interval class is determined strictly by its interval content and not by the spelling of the notes forming the interval:

Figure 23.20

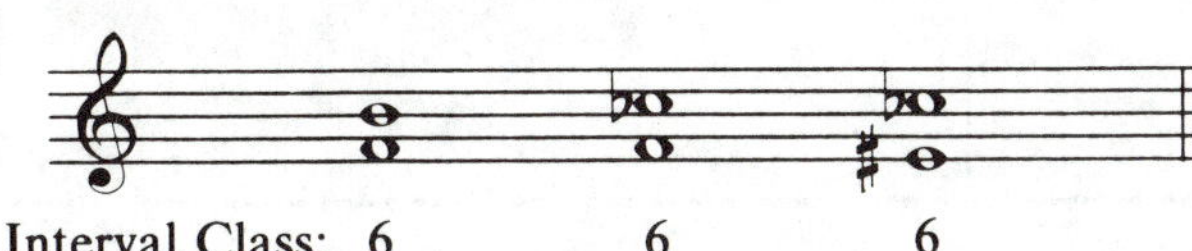

The following is a summation of interval classes:

INTERVAL CLASSES

Interval Class	Intervals Contained in This Class
0	P1
1	m2, M7, A1
2	M2, m7, A6, d3
3	m3, M6, A2, d7
4	M3, m6, d4, A5
5	P4, P5, A3, d6
6	A4, d5

Set Types. Sets are classified according to the interval between the first pitch class of the set and each successive pitch class.

Figure 23.21

Some typical sets:

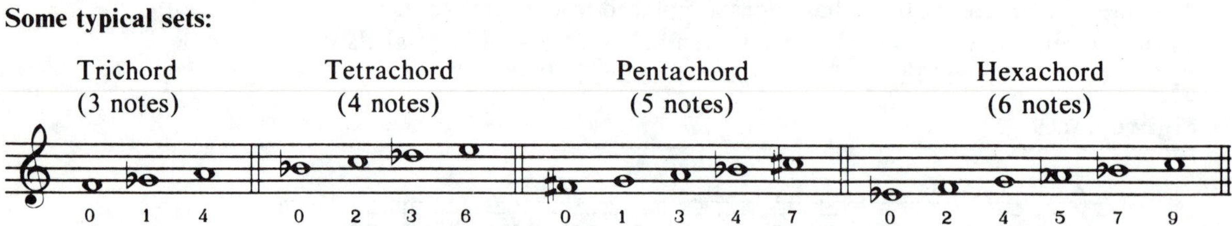

The "0" indicates the lowest pitch in the set, and the remaining pitches are named by the interval they form with the lowest pitch. For example, the **0 1 4** trichord contains:

Interval	From	To
0	F	F
1	F	G-flat
4	F	A

The major scale can be considered to be a heptachord (a seven-tone set).

Figure 23.22

Major scale:

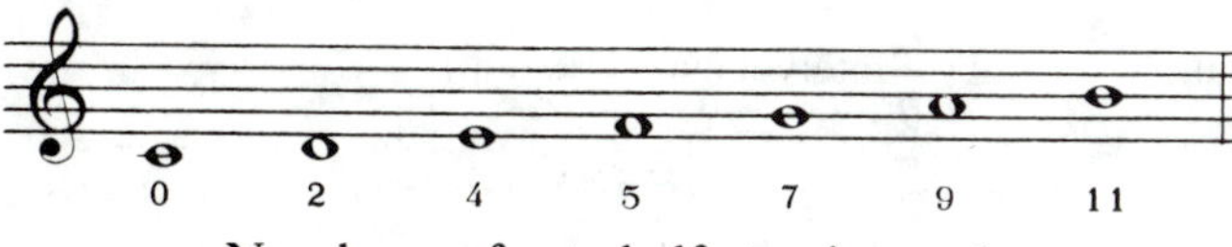

Numbers refer to half-step intervals above the first note (C)

Sets are usually written with the pitches in ascending order, but in compositions, they are often transposed or written in different orders. Below is the tetrachord **0 1 2 5** followed by the same set reordered and transposed:

Figure 23.23

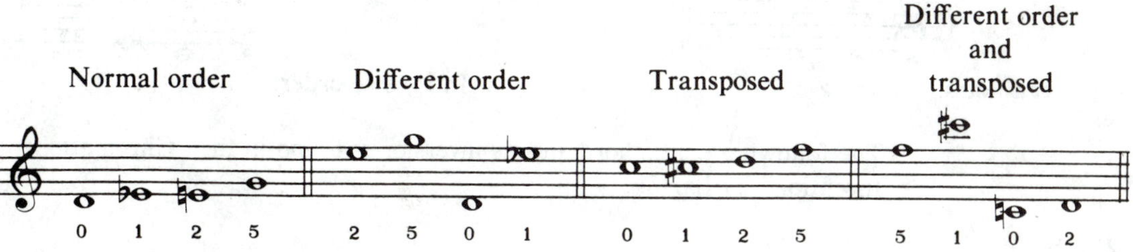

Inversion and Retrograde Inversion. Sets, like chords, can be inverted. In inversion, the original direction of the intervals is inverted, or turned upside down. In retrograde inversion, the intervals are not only inverted, but also stated backward. Consider the following three note sets:

Figure 23.24

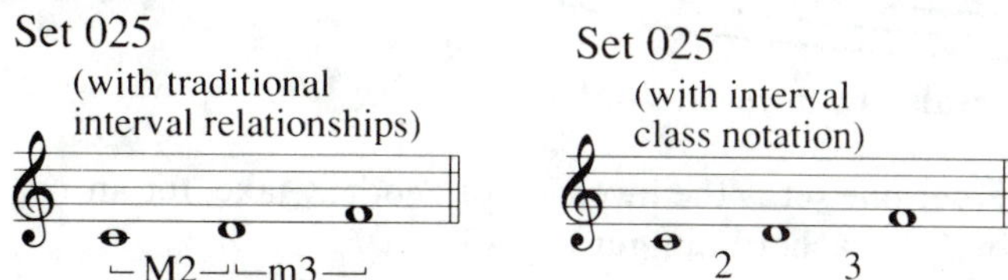

The inversion of this set would be:

Figure 23.25

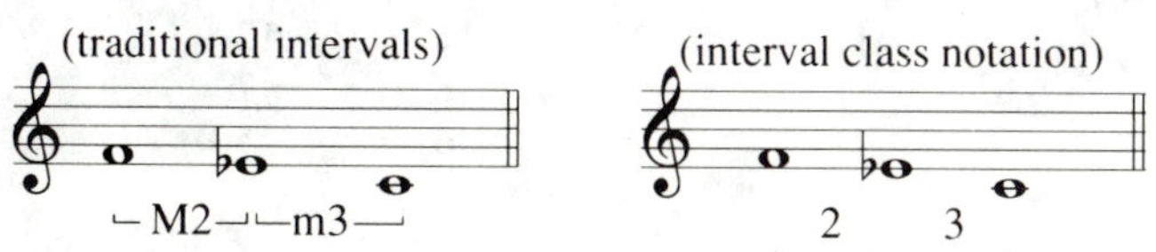

and the retrograde inversion would be:

Figure 23.26

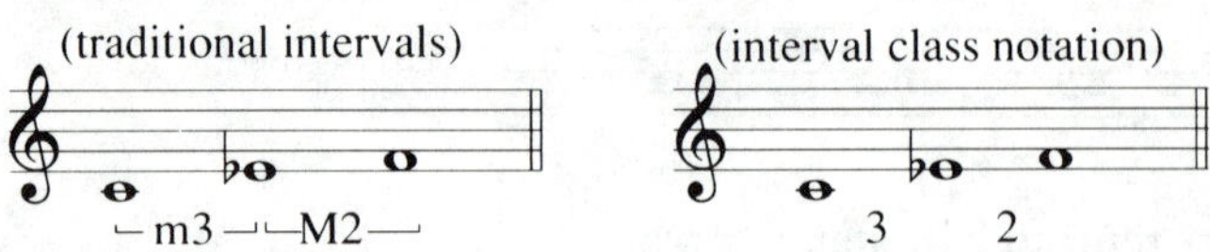

A retrograde inversion of a set is obtained by reversing the order of the intervals between adjacent notes of the set.

Figure 23.27

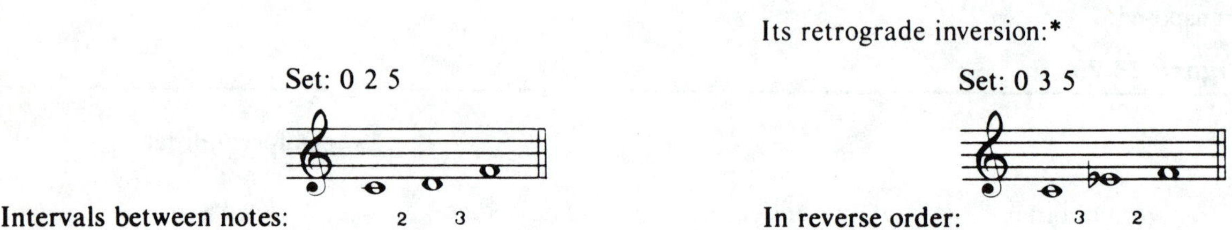

The following pentachord and its inversion is found in the "Chromatic Invention" by Bartók.

Figure 23.28

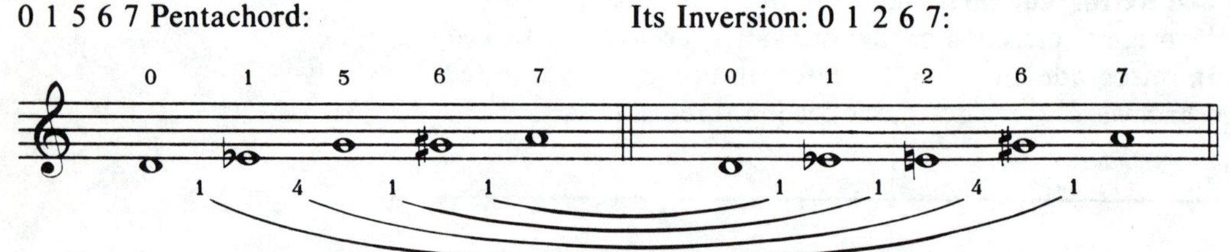

Each contains the same intervals but in reverse order

To find out whether one set is the inversion of another, take, for an example, the **0 1 5 6 7** pentachord in figure 23.28.

1. First, subtract all the numbers of the set from 12. This procedure will invert all the intervals, just as the inversion of a major 2nd (two half-steps) is a minor 7th (ten half-steps).

Inversion of 0 1 5 6 7

12	12	12	12	12
−0	−1	−5	−6	−7
12	11	7	6	5

2. These numbers represent the inversion, but they are confusing because the set does not begin with **"0"**. To convert the set to the lowest possible numbers, just subtract from all the numbers the lowest one. Here the lowest is **5**:

12	11	7	6	5
−5	−5	−5	−5	−5
7	6	2	1	0

3. Now, put the numbers in order from the lowest to highest, and the inversion of **0 1 5 6 7 = 0 1 2 6 7.**

Normal Order. As mentioned before, composers employ sets in a variety of configurations, and, to understand the compositional techniques employed, it is necessary to trace the derivation and development of such structures. The fundamental ordered form of a set is the *normal order.* To reduce a set to its normal order:

1. Begin with any note in the set and rearrange the remaining notes in ascending order within an octave. Change the order of the notes as needed.
2. At the end of the set add the first note an octave higher.

Figure 23.29

Set as it appears in a composition:

Set rearranged within an octave:

3. Bracket the largest interval.

Figure 23.30

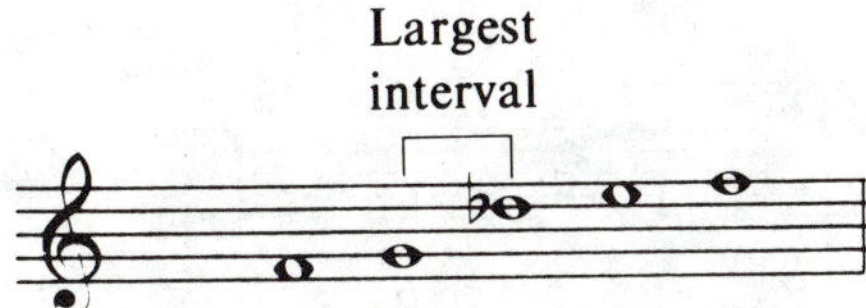

4. Begin the set with the second note of the bracketed interval and the set will be in its normal order.

Figure 23.31

Normal order:

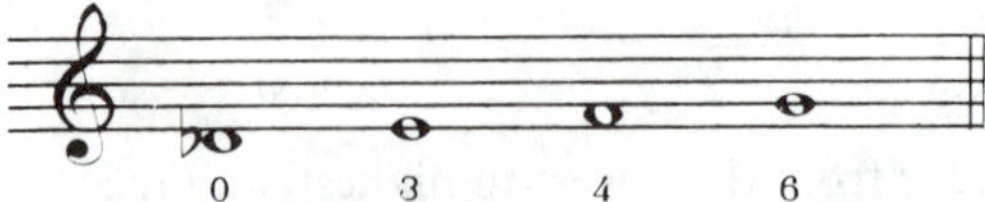

5. Occasionally a set will contain two larger intervals of the same size. Add the numbers (interval classes) of both possibilities. The *best normal order* is the arrangement with the lowest total (i.e., the most small intervals at the beginning of the set). (Another way of thinking of best normal order is the arrangement that is most densely packed to the left of the set.) When the set is in its normal order (or best normal order) and the first number is **0,** it is said to be in its *prime form.*

Figure 23.32

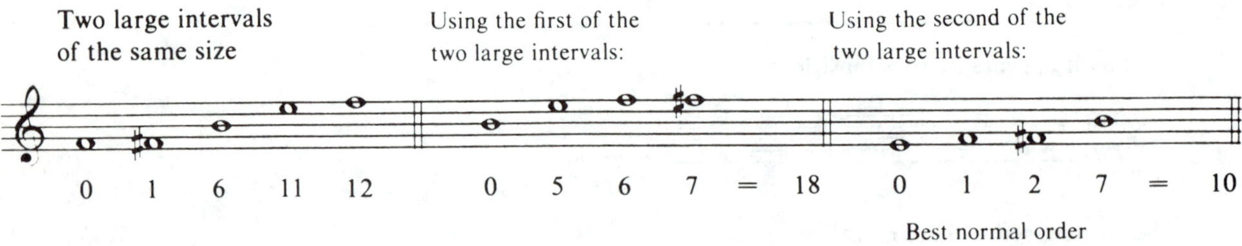

Figure 23.33 shows the distribution of the sets found in Bartók's "Chromatic Invention": the **0 1 5 6 7**; its inversion, the **0 1 2 6 7** set: and the **0 1 2** set:

Figure 23.33

Bartók: "Chromatic Invention" no. 91 from *Mikrokosmos,* vol. 3

REVIEW

1. Use the list of terms on page 373 as a test of your understanding of the materials of contemporary music. Define each term in your own words and check your definition with the definition in the book.
2. Write a number of polychords using major and minor triads at different intervals (use figures 23.6 and 23.7 as models). Test each at the piano to compare the levels of dissonance among your polychords.
3. Select four notes at random or choose a motive from a composition you are studying. Find the normal order (or best normal order) for this tetrachord (see figures 23.29–23.32). Now write the retrograde inversion of this set (see figures 23.24–23.27). Select other groups of three, four, and five notes for similar treatment. Play each set and its retrograde inversion to hear the similarity between them.
4. Study the specimen analyses (figures 23.16 and 23.33) carefully, making certain that you understand each label.

Test Yourself 23

The following are short excerpts from the works of contemporary composers. Identify elements in each excerpt that are characteristic of the contemporary period, using the following list:

a. pandiatonicism
b. polytonality
c. dual modality
d. shifted tonality
e. free tonality
f. polychords
g. quartal/quintal chords
h. clusters
i. changing meter
j. asymmetric meter
k. nonaccentual rhythms

Examine each of the following short melodic fragments and derive a set that includes all the pitch classes present in the melody. Place this set in its prime form.

1. Poulenc: "Laudamus Te" from Gloria

Très vif et joyeux ♩=124

ff ff

Lau- da - mus te Lau- da - mus te Lau-

ff ff

Lau- da - mus te Lau- da - mus te Lau-

ff ff

Lau- da - mus te Lau- da - mus te Lau-

ff ff

Lau- da - mus te Lau- da - mus te Lau-

Très vif et joyeux ♩=124

f ff

2. Ives: "Lincoln, the Great Commoner" (No. 11 of 114 Songs)

3. Bartók: Bagatelle I

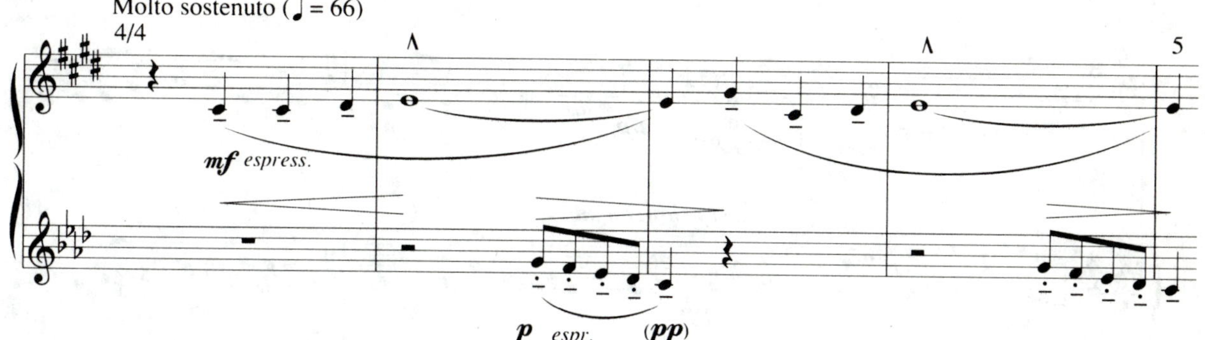

4. Honegger: Symphony no. 5, "Di tre re" (1st movement)

5. Ives: Second Sonata for Violin and Piano (3rd movement)
poco ten.
pizz.
ppp
pp
arco
Very slowly again
rit.
pp
Ped.
6.
7.
8.

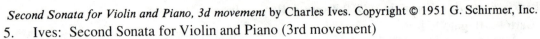

CHAPTER 24

Twelve-Tone Technique

Prime
Inversion
Retrograde
Retrograde Inversion
The Matrix
Row
Series
Set
Pitch Class
Segments

Exposition

Twelve-tone technique. *Twelve-tone technique* is a method of composition based on a fixed order of the twelve chromatic tones. It was developed by Arnold Schoenberg around 1920 as a means of providing a coherent basis for highly chromatic music. Of the technique Schoenberg said: "The method of composing with twelve tones grew out of necessity. In the last hundred years the concept of harmony has changed tremendously through the development of chromaticism. The idea that one basic tone, the root, dominated the construction of chords and regulated their succession—the concept of *tonality*—had to develop first into the concept of *extended tonality*. Very soon it became doubtful whether such a root still remained the center to which every harmony and harmonic succession must be referred. Furthermore, it became doubtful whether a tonic appearing at the beginning, at the end, or at any other point really had a constructive meaning." Schoenberg saw clearly that innovations of the Post-Romantic period had had the effect of weakening the constructive force of functional harmony, and sought a means to return order to music—to replace the lost power of tonal harmony to regulate the relationships among tones. He said, "After many unsuccessful attempts during a period of approximately twelve years, I laid the foundations for a new procedure in musical construction which seemed fitted to replace those structural differentiations provided formerly by tonal harmonies. I called this procedure the *Method of Composing with Twelve Tones Which Are Related Only with One Another.*"

Schoenberg provided the following guides for his twelve-tone technique (dodecaphonic composition):

Order. The set of all twelve tones contained within the octave in a particular order (tone row) forms the basis for the method. Except for immediate repetitions, there is no return to a particular tone until all the succeeding tones in the row have been sounded.

Register. The tones of the series (tone row) may appear in any octave.

Forms. The tone series may appear in any of the following four forms:

Symbol		Form	Description
P	=	Prime	The series as it is originally constructed.
R	=	Retrograde	The prime series sounded in reverse order.
I	=	Inversion	Starting with the first tone of the prime series, the direction (up or down) of each successive interval is inverted.
RI	=	Retrograde Inversion	The inversion of the series is sounded in reverse order.

Transposition. Any of the four forms of the series can be transposed. The prime form untransposed is $\mathbf{P^0}$, one-half step up is $\mathbf{P^1}$, another one-half step up P^2, etc. As a further illustration:

$\mathbf{P^8}$	=	Prime form of the series transposed up eight half-steps (m6th).
$\mathbf{RI^2}$	=	Retrograde inversion transposed up two half-steps (M2nd).
$\mathbf{I^{11}}$	=	Inverted series transposed up eleven half-steps (M7th).

Row, Series, or Set. The term "row" is a literal translation of the German word *Reihe.* Other terms such as "series" and "set" are used by later authors who believe that "row" denotes certain properties not in keeping with the true nature of the original German term. Despite controversies over subtleties in translation, "row" and "series" are used synonymously in this book.

Numbering. Earlier writers also numbered the series from 1–12, but later theorists adopted a 0–11 numbering system to facilitate mathematical calculation.

Pitch Class. *Pitch class* is another term frequently found in contemporary writing. This term is used in preference to "tone" or "pitch" since it is broader in meaning and includes a single pitch together with its octave duplications.

The Matrix. A *matrix* is a convenient analytical device for showing all forms and transpositions of a row. The matrix (described in detail later) was not invented by Schoenberg himself, but its use by later writers has made it a standard device for analysis of twelve-tone music.

As an example of twelve-tone technique, figure 24.1 will be given a detailed analysis.

Figure 24.1

Webern: *Wie bin ich froh!* (How Happy I Am!),
no. 1 from *Drei Lieder* (Three Songs), op. 25

tempo
leuch - tet so!
noch ü - ber -
rit. - - - tempo
blühn die Blu - men mir die Welt! noch ein -

RI²:
11 0 1 2 3 4 5 6 7 8 9
rit.
mal bin ich ganz ins Wer - den hin - ge - stellt
5 6 7 8 9 10 11
P⁰: 0 1 2 3 4
9
f
10
f
10 11
R⁰: 0 1 2
Sehr langsam (= ca. 42)
tempo I
pp
und bin auf Er - den.
9 10
4 5 6 7 8
ppp
f
9 10 11
p
11
12
R⁰

The Matrix. The following matrix (also called a *magic square*) will help to show the possible series forms and their transpositions (forty-eight possibilities in all). This particular matrix represents the series that is the basis of Webern's *Wie bin ich froh!*

	I^0	**I^{11}**	**I^8**	**I^{10}**	**I^9**	**I^6**	**I^3**	**I^7**	**I^2**	**I^5**	**I^4**	**I^1**	
P^0	F#	F	D	E	D#	C	A	C#	G#	B	A#	G	**R^0**
P^1	G	F#	D#	F	E	C#	A#	D	A	C	B	G#	**R^1**
P^4	A#	A	F#	G#	G	E	C#	F	C	D#	D	B	**R^4**
P^2	G#	G	E	F#	F	D	B	D#	A#	C#	C	A	**R^2**
P^3	A	G#	F	G	F#	D#	C	E	B	D	C#	A#	**R^3**
P^6	C	B	G#	A#	A	F#	D#	G	D	F	E	C#	**R^6**
P^9	D#	D	B	C#	C	A	F#	A#	F	G#	G	E	**R^9**
P^5	B	A#	G	A	G#	F	D	F#	C#	E	D#	C	**R^5**
P^{10}	E	D#	C	D	C#	A#	G	B	F#	A	G#	F	**R^{10}**
P^7	C#	C	A	B	A#	G	E	G#	D#	F#	F	D	**R^7**
P^8	D	C#	A#	C	B	G#	F	A	E	G	F#	D#	**R^8**
P^{11}	F	E	C#	D#	D	B	G#	C	G	A#	A	F#	**R^{11}**
	RI^0	**RI^{11}**	**RI^8**	**RI^{10}**	**RI^9**	**RI^6**	**RI^3**	**R^7**	**RI^2**	**RI^5**	**RI^4**	**RI^1**	

The matrix is created by first listing the **P^0** form along the top:

P^0	F#	F	D	E	D#	C	A	C#	G#	B	A#	G	**R^0**

Next list the inversion beginning with the first pitch of the original row down the left side of the chart:

	I^0												
P^0	F#	F	D	E	D#	C	A	C#	G#	B	A#	G	**R^0**
	G												
	A#												
	G#												
	A												
	C												
	D#												
	B												
	E												
	C#												
	D												
	F												

Label the left side of the chart beginning with $\mathbf{P^0}$ according to the number of half-steps each tone of the $\mathbf{I^0}$ series is above the first tone:

	$\mathbf{I^0}$												
$\mathbf{P^0}$	F #	F	D	E	D #	C	A	C #	G #	B	A #	G	$\mathbf{R^0}$
$\mathbf{P^1}$	G												
$\mathbf{P^4}$	A #												
$\mathbf{P^2}$	G #												
$\mathbf{P^3}$	A												
$\mathbf{P^6}$	C												
$\mathbf{P^9}$	D #												
$\mathbf{P^5}$	B												
$\mathbf{P^{10}}$	E												
$\mathbf{P^7}$	C #												
$\mathbf{P^8}$	D												
$\mathbf{P^{11}}$	F												

Now write the $\mathbf{P^1}$ series, which will be one half-step above the $\mathbf{P^0}$ series:

	$\mathbf{I^0}$											
$\mathbf{P^0}$	F #	F	D	E	D #	C	A	C #	G #	B	A #	G
$\mathbf{P^1}$	G	F #	D #	F	E	C #	A #	D	A	C	B	G #
$\mathbf{P^4}$	A #											
$\mathbf{P^2}$	G #											
$\mathbf{P^3}$	A											
$\mathbf{P^6}$	C											
$\mathbf{P^9}$	D #											
$\mathbf{P^5}$	B											
$\mathbf{P^{10}}$	E											
$\mathbf{P^7}$	C #											
$\mathbf{P^8}$	D											
$\mathbf{P^{11}}$	F											

Fill in the remaining transpositions in order (**P^2, P^3**, etc.). Each row will be one half-step above the row you have just completed:

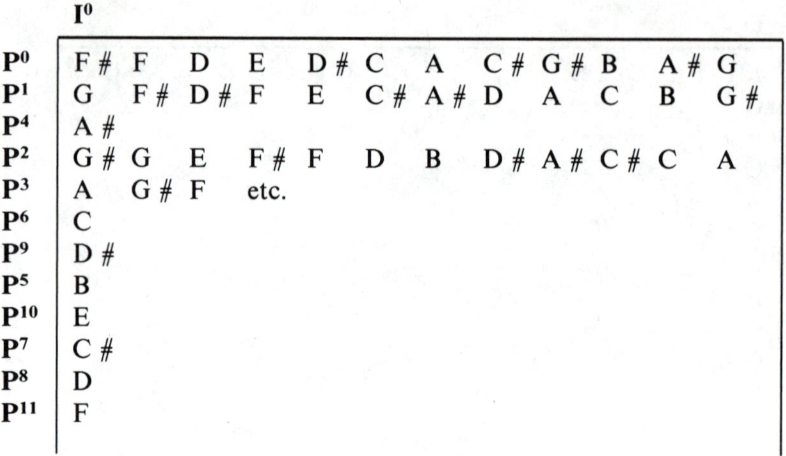

	I^0											
P^0	F#	F	D	E	D#	C	A	C#	G#	B	A#	G
P^1	G	F#	D#	F	E	C#	A#	D	A	C	B	G#
P^4	A#											
P^2	G#	G	E	F#	F	D	B	D#	A#	C#	C	A
P^3	A	G#	F	etc.								
P^6	C											
P^9	D#											
P^5	B											
P^{10}	E											
P^7	C#											
P^8	D											
P^{11}	F											

Finally, add the remaining labels (**I, R,** and **RI**) to complete the matrix.

	I^0	I^{11}	I^8	I^{10}	I^9	I^6	I^3	I^7	I^2	I^5	I^4	I^1	
P^0	F#	F	D	E	D#	C	A	C#	G#	B	A#	G	R^0
P^1	G	F#	D#	F	E	C#	A#	D	A	C	B	G#	R^1
P^4	A#	A	F#	G#	G	E	C#	F	C	D#	D	B	R^4
P^2	G#	G	E	F#	F	D	B	D#	A#	C#	C	A	R^2
P^3	A	G#	F	G	F#	D#	C	E	B	D	C#	A#	R^3
P^6	C	B	G#	A#	A	F#	D#	G	D	F	E	C#	R^6
P^9	D#	D	B	C#	C	A	F#	A#	F	G#	G	E	R^9
P^5	B	A#	G	A	G#	F	D	F#	C#	E	D#	C	R^5
P^{10}	E	D#	C	D	C#	A#	G	B	F#	A	G#	F	R^{10}
P^7	C#	C	A	B	A#	G	E	G#	D#	F#	F	D	R^7
P^8	D	C#	A#	C	B	G#	F	A	E	G	F#	D#	R^8
P^{11}	F	E	C#	D#	D	B	G#	C	G	A#	A	F#	R^{11}
	RI^0	RI^{11}	RI^8	RI^{10}	RI^9	RI^6	RI^3	RI^7	RI^2	RI^5	RI^4	RI^1	

For Prime Series (**P**): Read from Left to Right
For Inverted Series (**I**): Read Down
For Retrograde Series (**R**): Read from Right to Left
For Retrograde Inversion Series (**RI**): Read Up

Selected Forms and Transpositions. Webern selected the following series forms and transpositions (from the preceding matrix) for *Wie bin ich froh!*

Figure 24.2

Prime series untransposed (P^0):

Pitch class: 0 11 8 10 9 6 3 7 2 5 4 1

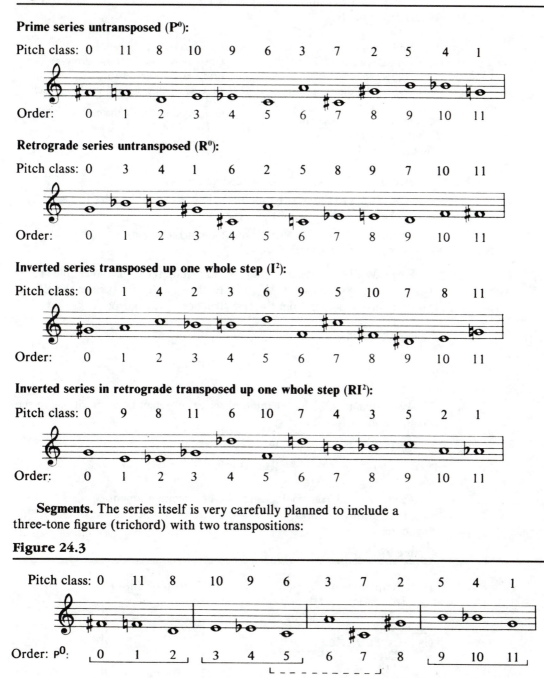

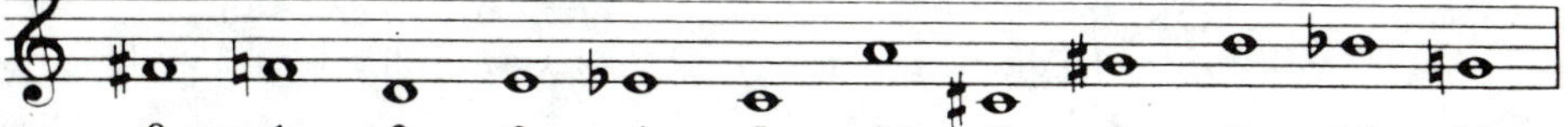

Order: 0 1 2 3 4 5 6 7 8 9 10 11

Retrograde series untransposed (R^0):

Pitch class: 0 3 4 1 6 2 5 8 9 7 10 11

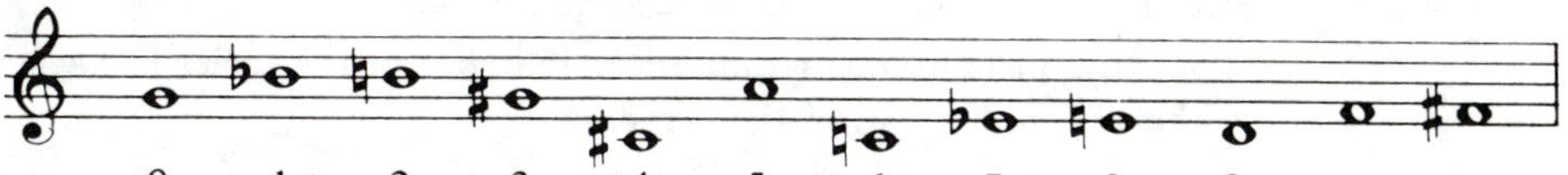

Order: 0 1 2 3 4 5 6 7 8 9 10 11

Inverted series transposed up one whole step (I^2):

Pitch class: 0 1 4 2 3 6 9 5 10 7 8 11

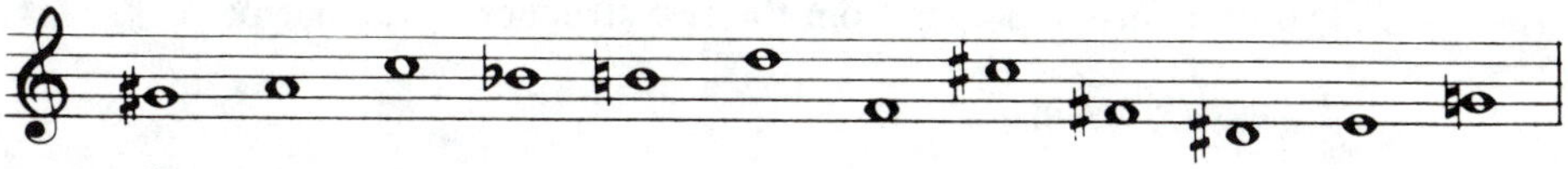

Order: 0 1 2 3 4 5 6 7 8 9 10 11

Inverted series in retrograde transposed up one whole step (RI^2):

Pitch class: 0 9 8 11 6 10 7 4 3 5 2 1

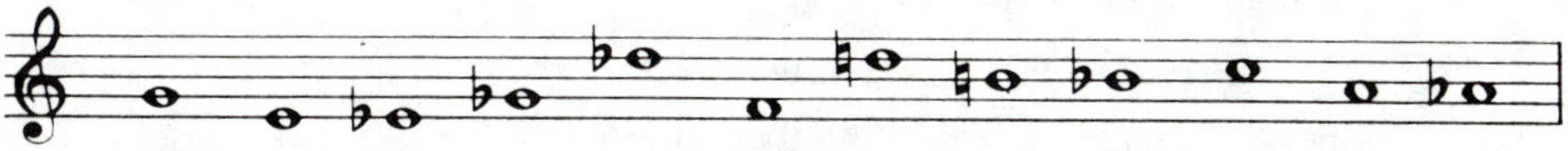

Order: 0 1 2 3 4 5 6 7 8 9 10 11

Segments. The series itself is very carefully planned to include a three-tone figure (trichord) with two transpositions:

Figure 24.3

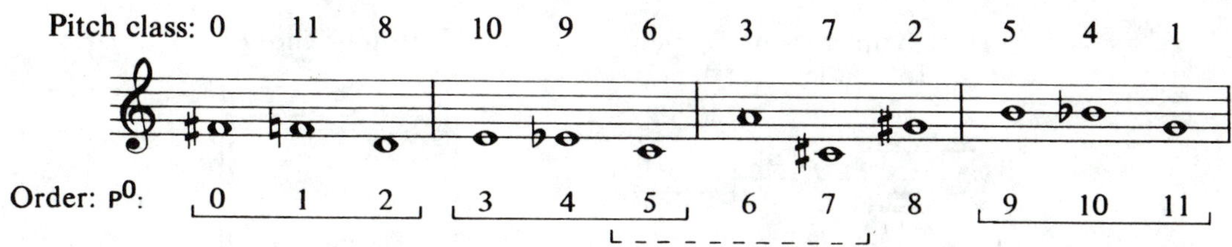

The Text. The composition is based on a poem of two strophes by Hildegard Jone.

Wie bin ich froh! noch einmal wird mir alles grün und leuchtet so! noch über blühn die Blumen mir die Welt! noch einmal bin ich ganz ins Werden hingestellt und bin auf Erden.	How happy I am! Once more all around me grows green and shimmers so Blossoms still cover the world for me! Once again I am at the center of Becoming and am on earth.

Strophes. The voice line is divided as follows:

First Strophe: The retrograde inversion (**RI**) of the series followed by the first four notes of the same.

Second Strophe: The retrograde of the original series followed by the complete retrograde inversion.

Form. While an internal balance and symmetry in the voice line is obtained through the use of **RI²**, then **R⁰**, and finally a return to the **RI²**, a two-part form emerges from the two strophes of the poem:

Strophe	Section	Measures
1	A	1–5
2	B	6–12

Accompaniment. The selection of series forms and transpositions in the accompaniment is as follows:

Strophe 1	Strophe 2
P^0 RI^2 P^0 RI^2	R^0 I^2 I^2 P^0 R^0

Rhythmic and Harmonic Figures. The accompaniment consists for the most part of three figures, two of which are rhythmic and the other harmonic:

Figure 24.4

The Sixteenth Note Triplet Figure. There is a direct relationship between the figures and the pitches contained in them. All sixteenth triplet figures are based on a minor 2nd + minor 3rd:

Figure 24.5

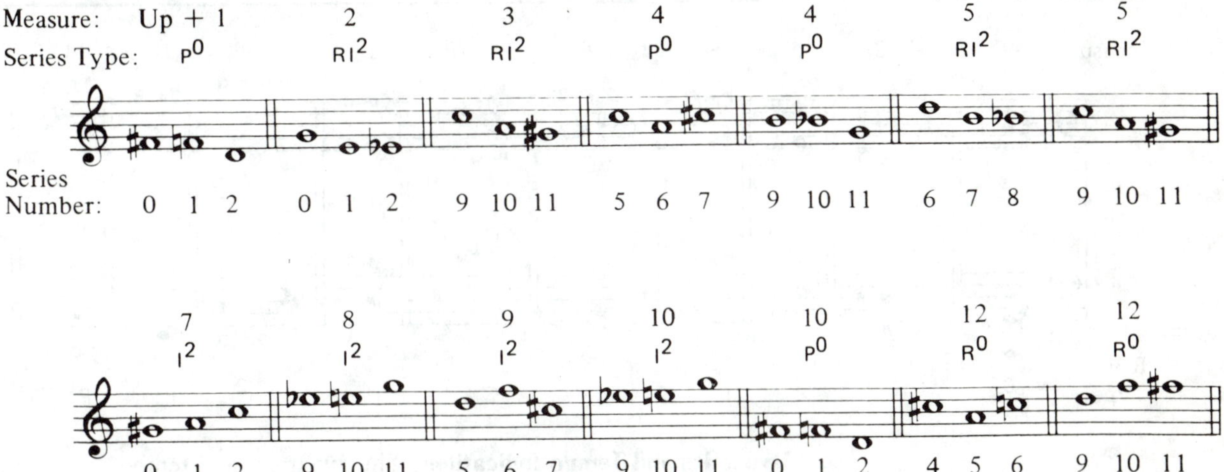

The Eighth-Note Figure. Most two-tone eighth-note figures are made up of half-step intervals, with the exception of two examples, indicated by an *.

Figure 24.6

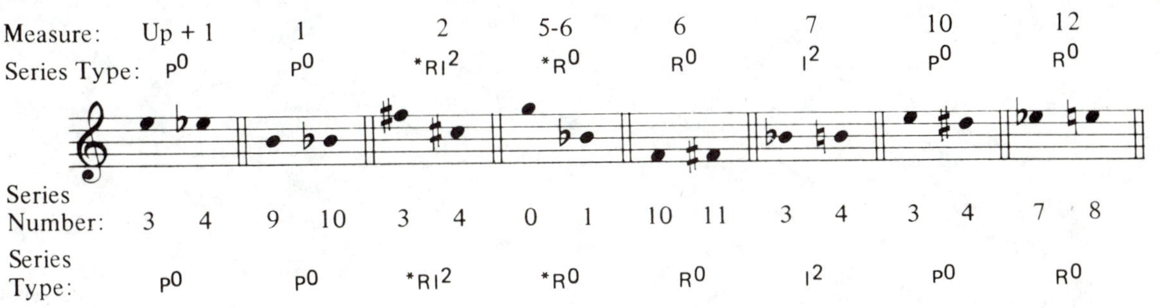

The Four-Tone Chord Figure. In most four-tone chord figures:

1. The lower two tones form a major 7th (exception, measure 2).
2. The upper two tones form a major 7th (three exceptions).

Figure 24.7

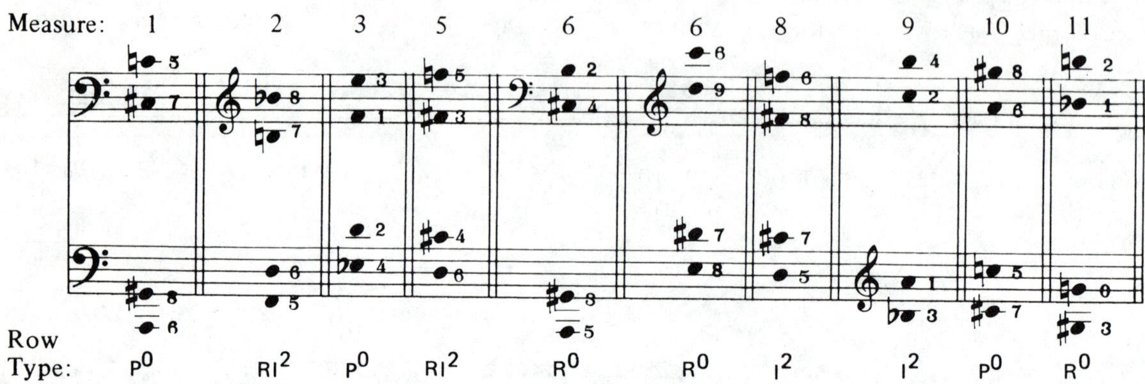

Dynamics and Tempo Indications. The dynamics and tempo indications follow this pattern:

1. The third line of each strophe is marked with a soft dynamic.
2. The first line of each strophe begins loud and ends soft.
3. For each strophe, accompaniment begins loud and ends soft.
4. The tempo is usually slowed at the end of each line or strophe.

REVIEW

1. Write a twelve-tone row of your own choosing. (Choose notes at random if you don't feel particularly creative.) Create a matrix for this row using the instructions on page 406. Write a melodic line using two forms of the row.
2. Study the specimen analysis (figure 24.1), making certain that you understand each analytical symbol.
3. Define each of the terms at the head of the chapter (page 401) in your own words. Check your definition with the definition in the chapter.

Test Yourself 24

The following composition is written in serial technique. Find the row (in the first five measures of the voice) and form a matrix. Do a serial analysis along the lines of the specimen analysis in this chapter (figure 24.1)

Dallapiccola: *Goethe-Lieder*, no. 2, for Mezzo-Soprano and E♭ Clarinet

* *La parte del Clar. picc. è scritta in suoni reali.*
(The E ♭ Clarinet part is written at sounding pitch.)

CHAPTER 25

Since 1945

Serialism
Indeterminacy
Electronic Music
Computer Music
Musique Concrète
Live Performance with Tape
Live Electronic Music
Voltage-Controlled Synthesizers
Computer-Assisted Composition
Computer Synthesis
Improvisation
Avant-Garde
Sound Mass
Extended Techniques
Rock 'n' Roll
Rock Music
Minimalism
Performance Art
MIDI Technology
Sampling Systems
New-Age Music
Space Music

The years since 1945 have witnessed the greatest stylistic changes and most extensive exploration of new techniques in the history of Western music. In the popular music field the most important development has been rock music. In art music, composers have explored new media and new compositional methods to a greater extent than at any other time. While it is still too early to make a definite judgment, it seems two distinct periods may be observed. These periods are distinguished not so much by style as by attitude.

Art Music: 1945–1970. The first of these two periods lasted from about 1945 to 1970. This era, dominated by the philosophy of the *avant-garde,* emphasized the exploration of new compositional techniques and placed a premium highly regarded innovation and experimentation. The primary paths of exploration were:

Serialism
Indeterminacy
Electronic and computer music
Sound mass
Extended vocal and instrumental techniques

Several of these new directions might be observed in a single work.

Serialism. *Serialism,* rooted in the years 1920–1945, is an extension of the twelve-tone technique of the Viennese atonalists, especially Anton Webern. As you saw in chapter 24, Webern's music is characterized not only by use of a pitch series, but also by carefully controlling the number of rhythmic motives in the piano accompaniment. It seems Webern was the primary inspiration for composers who chose to order or serialize other elements of music, such as rhythm, dynamics, articulations, and tone colors.

Perhaps the most important serialist is Milton Babbitt (b. 1916), who composed Three Compositions for Piano in 1947.

Figure 25.1

Babbitt: First Composition, mm. 1–6, from Three Compositions for Piano

Rhythmic and Dynamic Series. The rhythmic series Babbitt employs in this piece consists of the numbers 5 1 4 2. This series is used to articulate a rhythmic division in the statement of each hexachord. In the first measure, the lower voice is entirely in sixteenth notes until C is reached. C is the first long note and fifth pitch of the hexachord, hence the "5" (note brackets in illustration) of the rhythmic series 5 1 4 2. The single remaining note in this hexachordal statement represents "1" in this rhythmic series. The same 5 1 rhythmic grouping may be observed in the upper voice in measure 1, although the long note ending the first rhythmic subdivision of this hexachord is only an eighth's duration.

Diagram of Rhythmic Series

P (Prime)	5	1	4	2
R (Retrograde)	2	4	1	5
I (Inversion)	1	5	2	4
RI (Retrograde-inversion)	4	2	5	1

In the next measure, the sixteenth-note continuity of the hexachords of each voice is broken by a long note, the fourth in the hexachord. This produces a 4 2 grouping that completes the 5 1 4 2 statement, which is the **P** (Prime) form of the rhythmic series.

The **R** (Retrograde) form of the series (2 4 1 5) is found in the upper voice of measures 3 and 4. The **I** (Inversion) form (1 5 2 4), derived by subtracting each number of the P form from 6 (the number of pitches in a hexachord), appears in measures 5 and 6, lower voice. The **RI** (Retrograde-Inversion) form (4 2 5 1) occurs in measures 3 and 4, lower voice.

The dynamic series is much simpler, associating each form of the pitch set with a different dynamic*:

SET FORM	= DYNAMIC
P	Mezzo-Forte
R	Mezzo-Piano
I	Forte
RI	Piano

Babbitt's approaches to rhythmic and dynamic serialism are only some of the nonpitch elements that have been serialized. Composers have experimented with articulations, timbres, and numerous other aspects of music.

*This analysis owes a great deal to George Perle, *Serial Composition and Atonality* (Berkeley, University of California Press, 4th Edition, 1977), pp. 132–34, and David Cope, *New Directions in Music* (Dubuque, Iowa: Wm. C. Brown Publishers, 4th edition), pp. 42–44.

Indeterminacy. Another important concept explored by composers of this period is *indeterminacy,* sometimes also called *aleatory* or *chance* music. The following characteristics are essential to indeterminacy:

1. Some aspect or aspects of the composition, the performance, or both are beyond the composer's control.
2. Some musical decisions are unpredictable or left to chance.

The stage at which chance enters the music-making process varies from work to work.

John Cage. Always an innovator, the American composer John Cage (b. 1912) thoroughly explores methods by which chance may be incorporated into composition and performance. Cage's Music of Changes (1951), for piano, is traditionally notated, but was composed in an untraditional fashion. All musical decisions (pitches, rhythm, dynamics) were made by consulting the *I Ching* (pronounced 'e Jing'), an ancient Chinese method of soothsaying.

A very different type of indeterminacy is represented by figure 25.2, Cage's Aria (1958). This work for solo voice is composed in graphic notation. Vertical contoured lines represent relative pitch; horizontal contours give the relative durations. Each page was intended to last about thirty seconds. Eight different singing styles can be determined by the soloist. The black squares indicate other sounds of the performer's choice. Since each performer has the major responsibility for interpreting the precise meaning of the symbols, performances vary greatly. The singer also has the option of performing the work simultaneously with either of two other Cage compositions: Fontana Mix (1958), for magnetic tape or instruments, or Concert for Piano and Orchestra (1957–58).

Electronic and Computer Music. While efforts to create *electronic music* date back to the turn of the century, serious development came after World War II with the invention of plastic magnetic recording tape. Early composers worked primarily on tape, as opposed to live performance, and used either live or electronically generated sources.

Musique Concrète. Preferred by French composers, *musique concrète* used live sounds from the environment. Sounds were processed or modified by:

1. Splicing—cutting and rearranging the tape.
2. Playing the tape backwards.
3. Varying the speech and pitch of the tape.
4. Tape loops—cutting and splicing the tape in an endless loop.
5. Tape delay—a means of creating artificial echo by rerecording a sound multiple times.

These taping techniques ranged from simple reordering of familiar sounds to complete transformations.

Figure 25.2

Cage: Aria

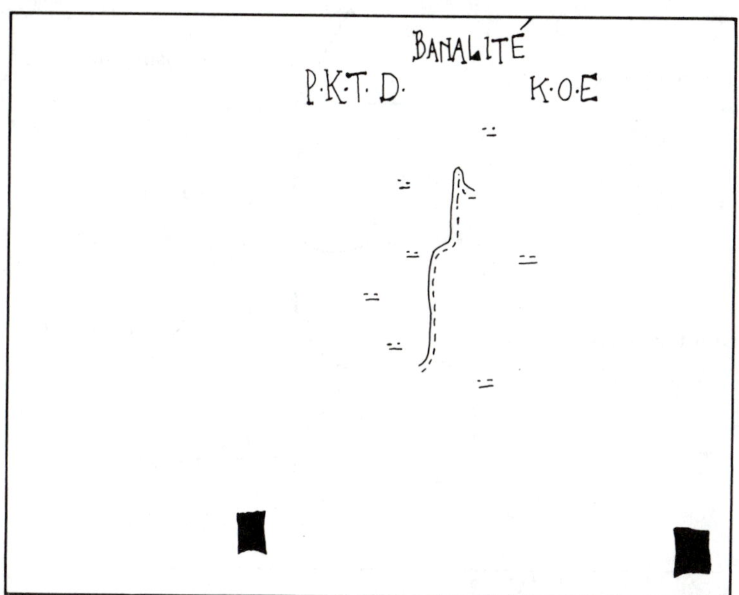

Electronic Music. The first German composers of electronic music generated sounds with equipment previously found in physics laboratories: oscillators, pulse generators, filters, and ring modulators. This music required even more splicing than the works of musique concréte.

Two of the greatest early masterpieces of electronic music combined both techniques. It is appropriate that one of these works, *Gesang der Jünglinge* (Song of the Youths in the Fiery Furnace) (1955–1956), is by the German Karlheinz Stockhausen (b. 1928), and that the other, *Poème Électronique* (1956–1958), was composed by the French-born American, Edgard Varése (1885–1965). (See figure 25.3.) Since a performance of either work consists of playing a tape recording, neither has a score in the conventional sense. An analytical transcription has been made of the Varése composition by David Cope. The work must be heard to understand the transcription.

Figure 25.3

Varèse: *Poème Électronique*

From David Cope, *New Directions in Music,* 5th ed. Copyright © 1989 Wm. C. Brown Publishers, Dubuque, Iowa. All Rights Reserved. Reprinted by permission.

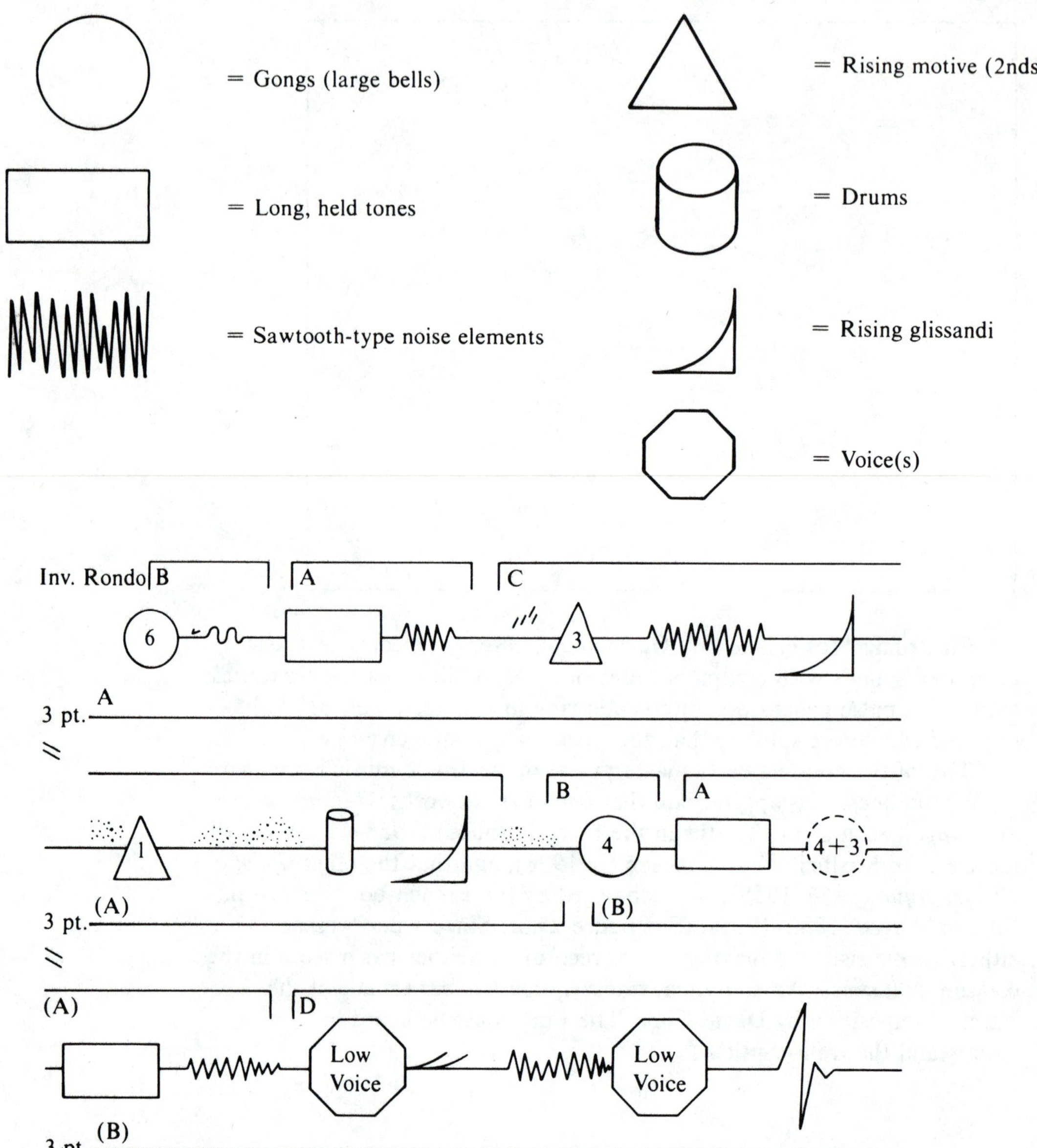

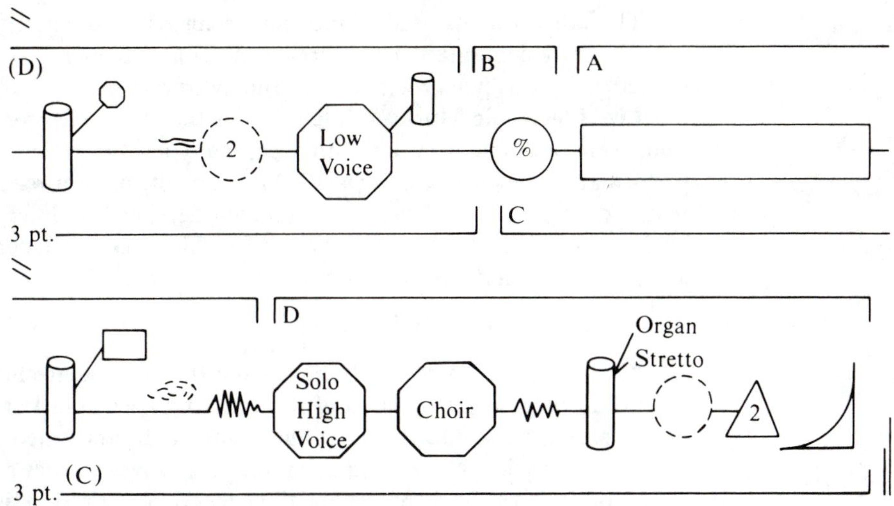

Live Performance with Tape. Any arbitrary limitations on the use of electronic media were short-lived. From the early years of electronic music, composers began to combine taped sounds with live instrumental or vocal performance. One of the greatest contributions to this genre is the series of six Synchronisms of the Argentinian-American Mario Davidovsky (b. 1934). (See figure 25.4.)

Figure 25.4

Davidovsky: No. 3 for Cello and Electronic Sound from Synchronisms

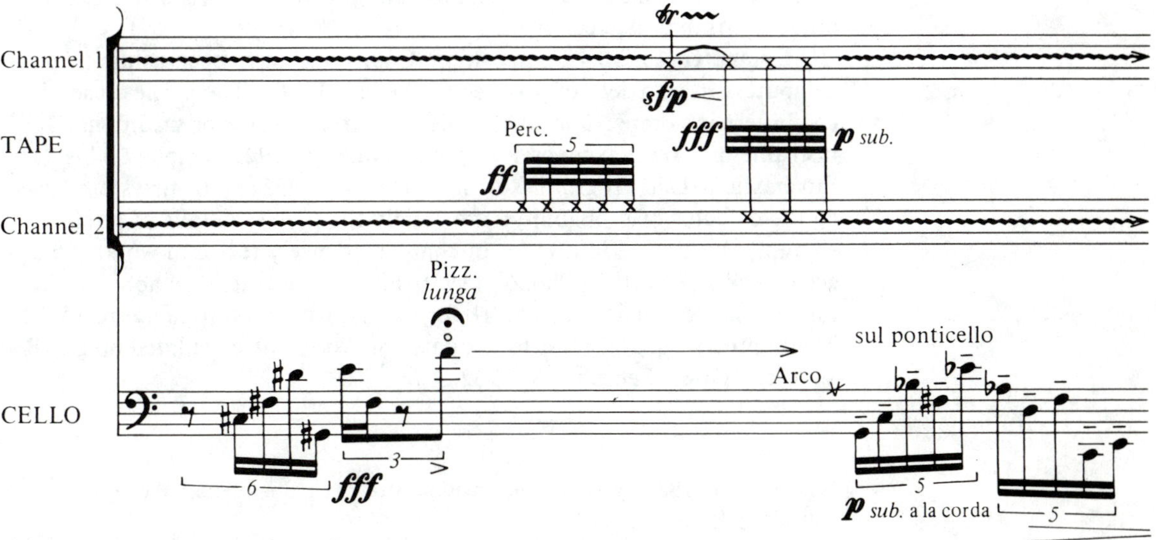

The taped sounds used in the Synchronisms were entirely electronically generated. The scores transcribe only as much of the tape as is needed for the synchronization of the instrumentalists.

Live Electronic Music. While it seems that most electronic music composers preferred to work with tape, many used electronics in live performance. Alvin Lucier's (b. 1931) "I am sitting in a room" (1970) required only a microphone, two tape recorders, an amplifier, and a loudspeaker. The text Lucier provided for this work is a technical description of what the audience hears.

Lucier: "I am sitting in a room"*

"I am sitting in a room different from the one you are in now.

"I am recording the sound of my speaking voice and I am going to play it back into the room again and again until the resonant frequencies of the room reinforce themselves so that any semblance of my speech, with perhaps the exception of rhythm, is destroyed.

"What you will hear, then, are the natural resonant frequencies of the room articulated by speech.

"I regard this activity not so much as a demonstration of a physical fact, but more as a way to smooth out any irregularities my speech might have."

Voltage-Controlled Synthesizers. The *voltage-controlled synthesizer,* introduced in the 1960s, generated and processed sound by a series of control voltages rather than manual settings. This allowed the composer to move instantaneously rather than gradually from one setting to another. If, for example, a composer desired a melody from a nonsynthesizer oscillator, each pitch would have to be recorded separately and then spliced together. On a voltage-controlled synthesizer, a melody could be played on an oscillator by a series of voltages from a keyboard or some other controlling device.

Computer-Assisted Composition. Composers have been using computers in a variety of ways since the late 1950s. The earliest use of computers in composition was an aid in writing works for traditional instruments. Greek composer Iannis Xenakis (b. 1922) employed his Stochastic Music Program (stochasticism is a mathematical system based on the calculus of probabilities) to supply the precise details of pitch, rhythm, and timbre in a series of complex, densely textured works. One such work is ST/10–1, 080262 (1956–62), whose title is an abbreviation for Stochastic Music, First Work for Ten Instruments. (See figure 25.5.) The numbers 080262 refer to the date the work was calculated on an IBM 7090 computer: February 8, 1962.

Figure 25.5

ST/10-1, 080262
Dediée à Konstantin Simonovitch et à son ensemble de musique contemporaine de Paris

JW=1
4+4/8
= 40↔60↔80 MM
Cl Sib
B/Cl Sib
Cor I
Cor II
Harpe
Cong
Tom
Temple-Bl
Wood-Bl
V1
V2
Alt.
V/c

Computer Synthesis. A more popular application of computer technology is *sound synthesis.* Electronic or traditional instrumental sounds can be generated by a computer in either of two ways. The American composer Charles Dodge (b. 1942) created a series of works featuring the electronic simulation of singing and speaking voices. (See figure 25.6.)

Figure 25.6

Dodge: In Celebration (based on the poem by Mark Strand)

Improvisation. *Improvisation* is the spontaneous realization of any or all aspects of a composition and has been employed throughout most of Western music history. Beethoven's concerts, for instance, often featured his improvisations. Today, the most familiar forms of improvisation are those used in jazz performance.

Improvisation differs from other types of indeterminacy in that the composer predetermines a desired musical effect rather than detailing the notation. The performer is free to spontaneously interpret any or all of the composition.

William Duckworth's (b. 1943) "Pitch City" (1969) provides a completed twelve-tone matrix with four "paths" from corners to center. (See figure 25.7.) Performers on four unspecified wind instruments improvise durations, choose their own octaves, and play from the corners of the matrix to the center.

For Pauline Oliveros (b. 1932), spontaneity is a philosophy, the benefits of which transcend the performed sounds. She breaks with many long-held notions of what a composition can or cannot do. As a result of her democratic philosophy, she creates music accessible to all. Sonic Meditations I, "Teach Yourself to Fly," is an example of a therapeutic, relaxing work in which anyone—not just trained musicians—can participate.

Pauline Oliveros, Sonic Meditations I, "Teach Yourself to Fly." Copyright 1974 Smith Publications, Baltimore, Maryland.

> Any number of persons sit in a circle facing the center. Illuminate the space with dim blue light. Begin by simply observing your own breathing. Always be an observer. Gradually allow your breathing to become audible, then gradually introduce your voice. Allow your vocal chords to vibrate in any mode that occurs naturally. Allow the intensity to increase very slowly. Continue as long as possible naturally, and until all others are quiet, always observing your own breath cycle. Variation: Translate voice to an instrument.

Figure 25.7

Duckworth: "Pitch City"

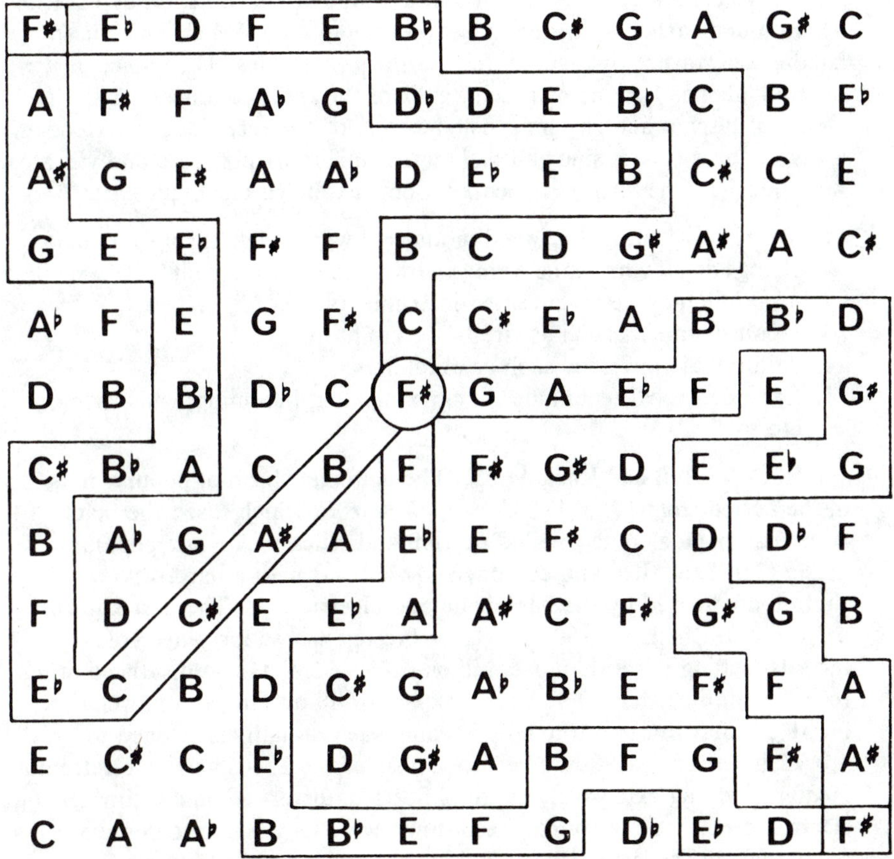

Sound Mass. *Sound mass* denotes a texture of such density and complexity that the musical effect resides in the whole, rather than the delineation of individual parts. A listener need not, and often cannot, easily distinguish between shifts in pitch, timbre, and dynamics.

Chord clusters, which have been used since the beginning of this century, form a large part of the tonal language of sound-mass compositions. Some works also employ the many-voiced rhythmically intricate, highly chromatic counterpoint known as *mikropolyphonie.*

One of the best-known sound-mass compositions, the Threnody in Memory of Victims of Hiroshima for fifty-two strings (1960) by the Polish composer Krzysztof Penderecki (b. 1933), uses both clusters and mikropolyphonie. (See figure 25.8.)

Extended Techniques. Throughout this century composers have explored new instrumental and vocal timbral possibilities. This search for innovative techniques is an extension of a type of instrumental exploration begun much earlier in this century, most notably by Webern, who used handpicked, rather than standard, chamber ensembles. The choice of instruments has become as much a part of the creative process as the choice of pitches and rhythms. The labeling of any technique as extended is always provisional, since all techniques, including pizzicato and vibrato, were unusual when it first appeared. Some extended techniques are:

1. Western instruments played in unusual ways, such as muting piano strings or playing piano strings with a metal instrument.
2. Unfamiliar or newly invented instruments.
3. Noninstruments such as sirens or auto horns.
4. Additional apparatus such as amplifiers.
5. Extended vocal techniques: tongue clicking, humming, whispering, etc.

Rock 'n' Roll and Rock Music. The dominant form of popular music in the period from 1955–1960 was *rock 'n' roll,* which fused the black-American popular music called rhythm and blues with white popular music (Tin Pan Alley and country and western) with a hard-driving rhythm dominated by the bass drum and electric bass. The best-known performer of the late 1950s was Elvis Presley, whose forty-five gold records (selling more than one million copies each) far outdistanced other rock 'n' roll musicians. The term "rock 'n' roll" became an umbrella term for all popular music of the late 50s and was gradually shortened to "rock" in the early 1960s. The *rock* music of the 1960s was an electronic medium, relying extensively on amplification, distortion, and ultimately on electronic synthesis of sound. Recording technology began to dominate rock music in the latter 1960s, and many bands curtailed live performance in favor of issuing albums. The best-known rock group of the latter part of the 1960s was the Beatles, whose album *Sgt. Pepper's Lonely Hearts Club*

Figure 25.8

Penderecki: *Threnos Den Opfern von Hiroschima*
(Threnody to the Victims of Hiroshima)

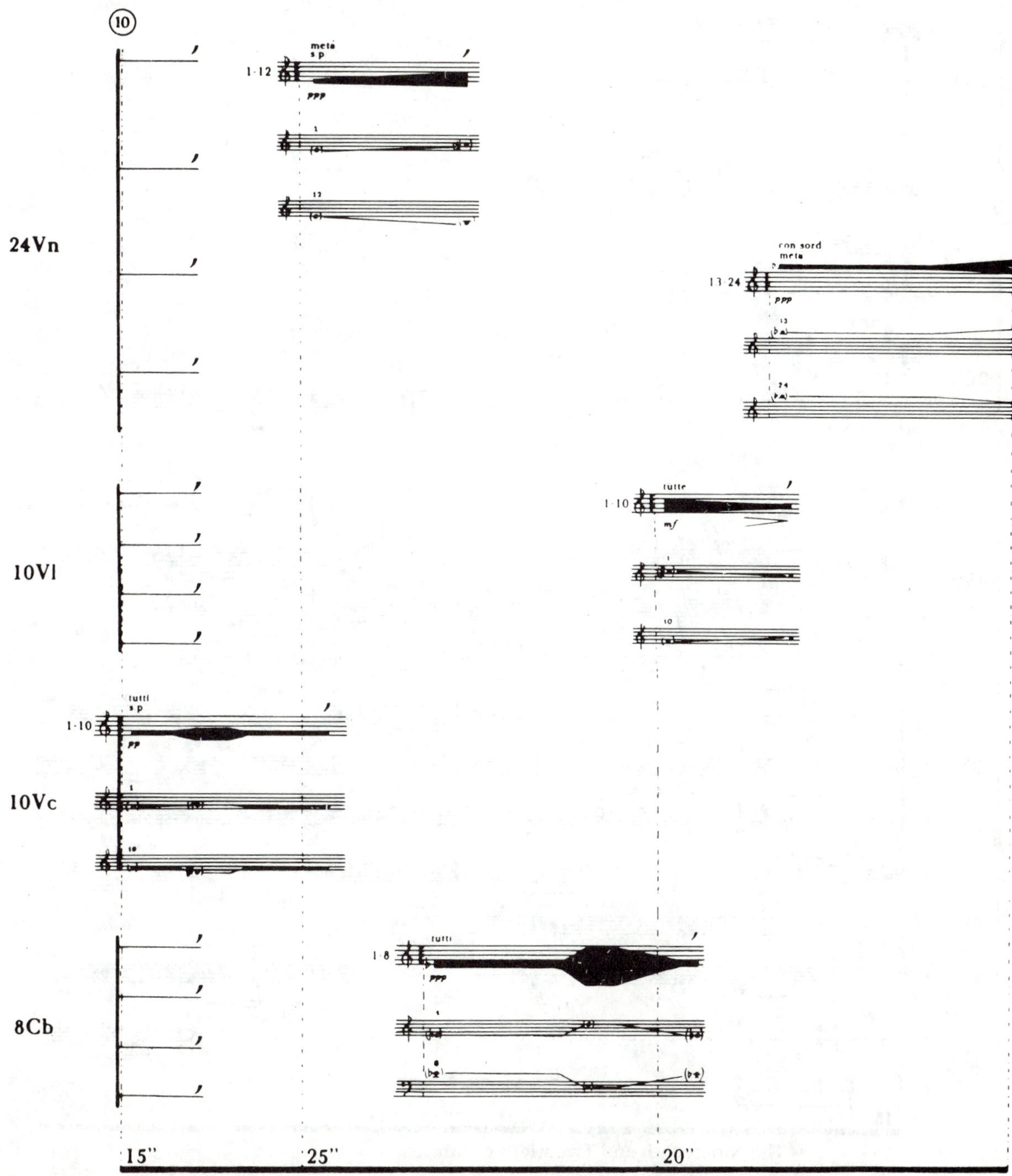

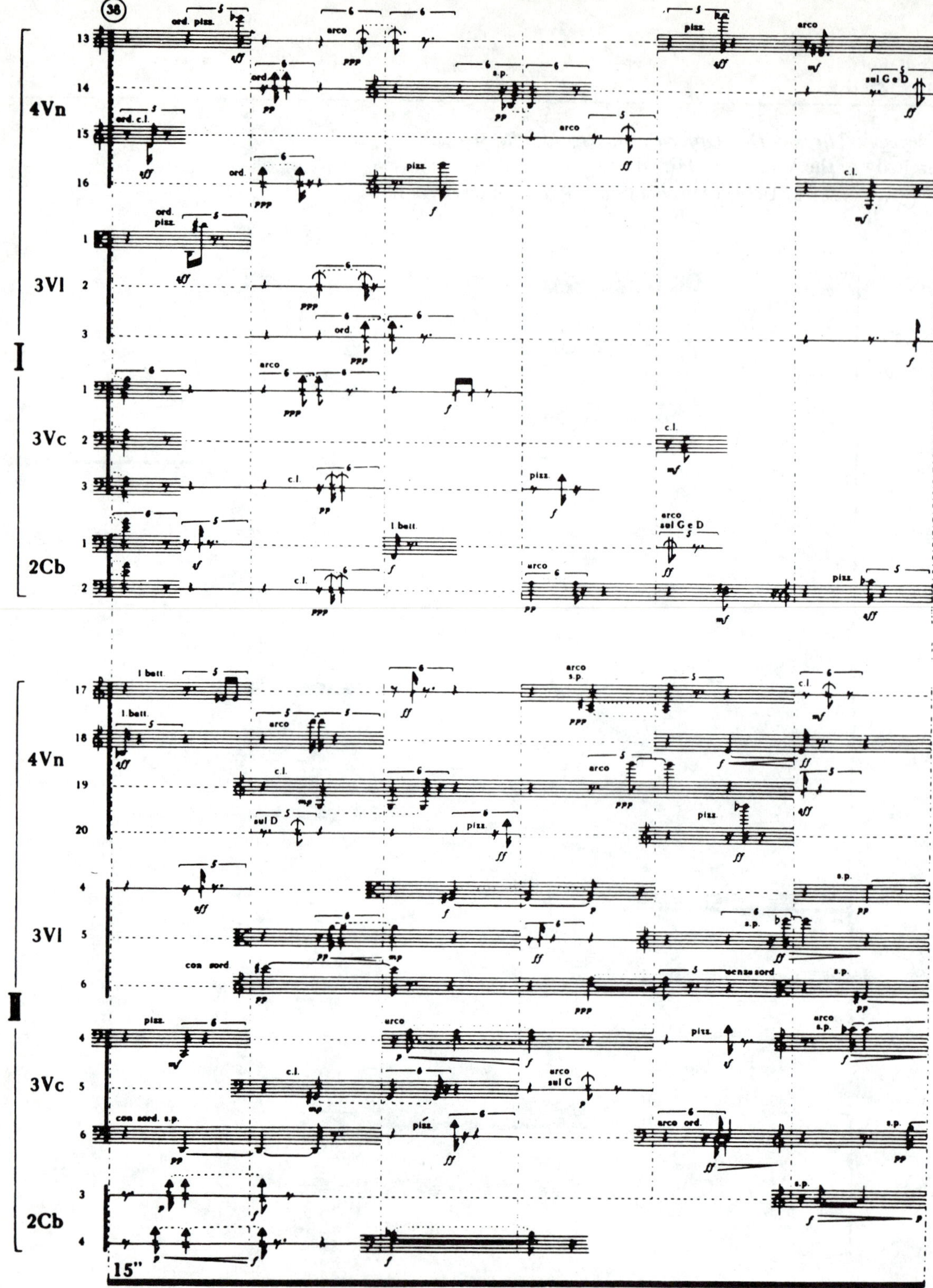

38
4Vn
3Vl
3Vc
2Cb
I
ord. pizz.
arco
pizz.
ord.
c.l.
s.p.
sul G e D
ord. c.l.
l batt.
sul D
con sord
senza sord
con sord. s.p.
arco ord.
sul G
15"

Figure 25.9

Reich: Four Organs (measure 1–4)

Steve Reich. *Writings About Music.* The Nova Scotia Series. The Nova Scotia College of Art and Design, Halifax, 1974.

The maraca part consists of steady unbroken eighth notes played throughout the piece thus:

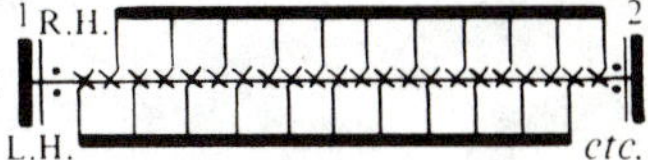

Since the maracas must be clearly heard over the four organs, it is suggested that two pairs be used, one pair in each hand.

♪ = *ca.* 200

Organ 1 — ***f*** 3 + 8

Organ 2 — ***f*** 3 + 8

Organ 3 — ***f*** 3 + 8

Organ 4 — ***f*** 3 + 8

Band (1967), which incorporated sophisticated studio techniques and many extra musicians (including the London Symphony Orchestra), set the tone for the age.

Music Since 1970. While none of the new musical trends of the years 1945–1970 have disappeared, it is apparent that at about 1970 a shift in attitude took place. This musical philosophy, called *post-modernism,* represents the idea that music can transcend the expectations and limitations of Western tradition. Like the *avant-garde,* post-modernists experiment, but innovation is not considered as much of a value in its own right as a tool to produce meaningful results. Using the cultural creations of all eras and all places, post-modernist composers create unusual and fascinating combinations. They also borrow quotations from earlier music and mix styles in what is called *eclecticism.*

No discussion of post-modernism or eclecticism can be complete without reference to Luciano Berio (Italian, b. 1925). His early post-modern five-movement masterpiece, *Sinfonia* (1968), uses a barrage of quotations from Bach, Ravel, Mahler, Stockhausen, and his own work. The vocalists sing in jazz syllables, or scat, and speak a collage of texts as eclectic as the music itself.

New Trends. Several new styles and genres have emerged in the post-modern era. One feature that unites all these approaches is their accessibility. The audiences who often felt shut out by the *avant-garde* can comprehend and enjoy these new styles.

Minimalism. *Minimalism* is the gradual process of unfolding a very limited body of motivic material, often with an unprecedentedly high degree of literal repetition. While the motivic material may be anything, it is most often simple, tonal or modal, and largely diatonic. Many minimal works owe a great deal to the influences of African and Asian music.

Steve Reich (American, b. 1936) is one of the most important of the Minimalists. His "Four Organs" for four electric organs and maracas (1970) consists entirely of a single chord, the individual tones of which are gradually augmented, while maracas keep a steady eighth-note pulse. (See Figure 25.9.)

Performance Art. *Performance art* is art that is performed, as opposed to object art such as painting and sculpture. It is, like opera, a multimedia genre that may involve costumes, staging, movement or dance, video, words, and, of course, music. Laurie Anderson (American, b. 1947) is trained, as are many performance artists, in the visual arts; however, she is now known mostly as a composer/performer and has wide followings among both concert and rock music listeners. Anderson's compositions are intended specifically for her own performances, no two of which are alike. Her music tends to be modal, minimal, rhythmically driving in the manner of rock music, and she frequently uses ostinato. Besides singing and playing the violin, Anderson also performs with various kinds of electronic devices.

MIDI Technology. In the early 1980s digital technology was increasingly applied to portable keyboard synthesizers, culminating in the establishment of an industry standard for connecting digital musical instruments called MIDI (Music Instrument Digital Interface). This development has facilitated the interfacing of personal computers with digital keyboards, and much software now exists for creating, editing, storing, and manipulation of musical information in computer-readable form. The implications of MIDI networks involving synthesis equipment, computers, and analog or digital recording technology on the future direction of music are now being explored, but the impact has already been felt on commercial music applications, in instructional applications, and in music publishing. Computer-assisted composition has largely shifted from large "main-frame" computer systems to MIDI networks, putting this technology in the hands of individual composers.

Sampling Systems. An outgrowth of digital recording technology, *sampling systems* produce their sounds by recording and playing back acoustic sounds. This makes possible the electronic simulation of all acoustic instruments. The full potential of this technology was first explored in commercial music, but these systems have made their way to the concert hall in recent years.

Post-1970 Rock. By the early 1970s the term *rock* was used for all popular music, regardless of style. During the 1970s and 1980s rock has come to mean a popular music with a basic instrumentation consisting of electric guitars, bass, keyboards and drums. (These instruments have been gradually augmented or replaced by digital instruments with the advent of MIDI instrumentation.) Much of this music was sophisticated and complex, derived in part from the style of the late Beatles albums. A blending of jazz and rock began in the 1970s, resulting in a style called *fusion.* In the latter 1970s new types of rock (punk and new wave) represented a return to the simplicity and directness of the earlier styles. The advent of *music videos* and MTV and other video programs in the 1980s marked a radical departure for all commercial popular music, and popular music is more and more conceived in visual as well as aural terms.

New Age Music/Space Music. In the 1980s elements of minimalism, jazz, and electronic music were fused into a genre that has come to be called *new age music* or *space music.* This largely instrumental music is characterized by a static or very slow harmonic rhythm, and an interest in complex textures with sensuous appeal that has relaxation or reflection as its goal. Minimalist composers such as Phillip Glass, Terry Riley, and Harold Budd; jazz composers such as Keith Jarrett, Paul Winter, and Pat Metheny; experimentalists such as David Hykes; commercial musicians such as Chip Davis (Mannheim Steamroller, Fresh Aire); and electronic composers such as Wendy Carlos and Kitaro have contributed to this eclectic popular music.

Conclusions. Today's music is rich in diversity. For the time being, it appears that the rigorous experimentation of the *avant-garde* has yielded the center stage to post-modernism, a philosophy that tolerates not only the uncompromisingly original, but also innovative combinations of the following:

Tradition and invention
Tonality and atonality
Eastern and Western music
Popular and high cultures
Trained and untrained musicians.

Audiences enjoy the new music and composers enjoy the attention. While no one can predict which recent developments will retain their importance in the future, we can all be grateful for the enormous variety of music that is available to us now. Today a high degree of artistic freedom is encouraged, and products of that freedom are in abundant evidence.

REVIEW

1. Review the list of terms at the head of the chapter and make a definition of each in your own words. Check your definition with the definition in the chapter.
2. Try to find recordings of works by the composers mentioned in this chapter and familiarize yourself with their music.

Since the material of this chapter is general information, no self-test is provided.

APPENDIX A

Introduction to Sound

Sound
Vibration
Compression
Rarefaction
Frequency
Pitch
Tone
Intensity
Duration
Meter
Rhythm
Timbre
Harmonic Series
Partials
Fundamental

The basic materials of music are sound and time. Every time you play on your instrument or sing you are producing sounds, so it is important to understand this basic material. Sound has four identifiable characteristics or properties: *pitch, intensity, duration,* and *timbre.* No matter how complicated the composition, the composer and the performer have only these four variables with which to work. The following definitions are important to your understanding of the nature of sound.

Sound

Sound is the sensation perceived by the organs of hearing when vibrations (sound waves) are produced in the air.

Vibration

Vibration is the periodic motion of an elastic body. When you play an instrument, parts of the instrument (such as strings, sounding board) and the air inside and around the instrument vibrate.

Compression and Rarefaction

These terms refer to the alternation of increased (*compression*) and decreased (*rarefaction*) pressure in the air caused by an activated (vibrating) surface or air column. One complete cycle of compression and rarefaction produces a vibration, or sound wave.

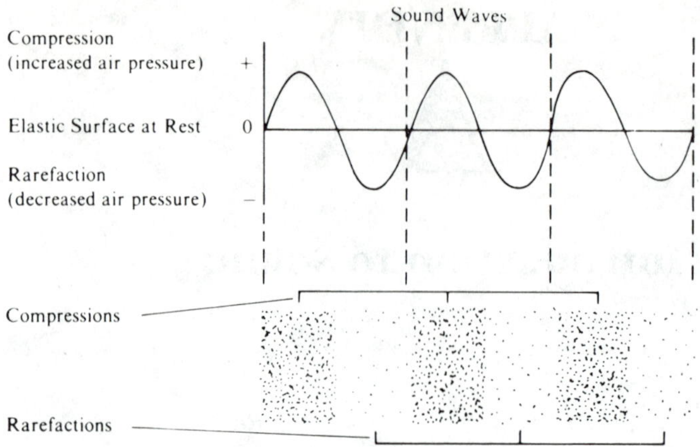

Frequency

Frequency refers to the number of compression-rarefaction cycles that occur per unit of time, usually one second. Audible sounds for the human ear range from 20 to 20,000 cycles per second (Hz.). (See page 438).

The Four Properties of Sound

The four properties of sound are described in the following musical terms.

Pitch

Pitch is the highness or lowness of a sound. Variations in frequency are what we hear as variations in pitch: the greater the number of sound waves produced per second by the vibration of an elastic body, the higher the sound we hear; the fewer sound waves per second, the lower the sound.

Tone

A *tone* is a musical sound of definite pitch.

Intensity

Intensity (amplitude) is heard as the loudness or softness of a pitch. In acoustics (the science of sound), intensity is the amount of energy affecting the vibrating body, and the physicist measures intensity on a scale from 0 to 130 in units called *decibels.* In musical notation gradations of intensity are indicated with the following Italian words and their abbreviations:

Italian Word	Symbol	Translation	Average Decibels
Pianissimo	**pp**	Very soft	40
Piano	**p**	Soft	50
Mezzo piano	**mp**	Moderately soft	60
Mezzo forte	**mf**	Moderately loud	70
Forte	**f**	Loud	80
Fortissimo	**ff**	Very loud	100

Duration

Duration is the length of time a pitch, or tone, is sounded. For patterns of duration the following terms are used: *meter* and *rhythm.*

Meter

Meter describes regularly recurring pulses of equal duration, generally grouped into patterns of two, three, four, or more with the first pulse in each group accented. These patterns of strong (–) and weak (~) pulses are called *beats*. For example:

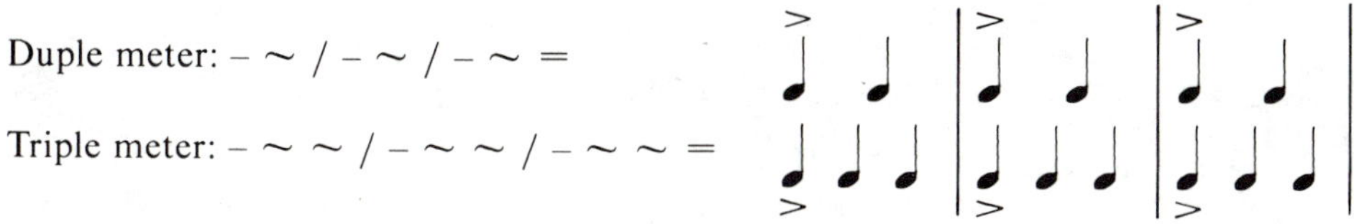

Duple (two-beat) *meter* and *triple* (three-beat) *meter* are the two basic meters. All other meters result from some combination of these two.

Rhythm

Overlaying or operating within the meter, *rhythm* is a pattern of *uneven* durations. While the steady beats of the meter combine to form measures, a rhythm may be a pattern of almost any length.

Timbre

Timbre is the tone quality or color of a sound. It is the property of sound that permits us, for instance, to distinguish between the sound of a clarinet and the sound of an oboe.

This individual quality of sound is determined by the shape of the vibrating body, its material (metal, wood, human tissue), and the method used to put it in motion (striking, bowing, blowing, plucking). It is also the result of the human ear's perceiving a series of tones called the harmonic series, which is produced by all instruments.

Harmonic Series

A *harmonic series* includes the various pitches produced simultaneously by a vibrating body. This physical phenomenon results because the body vibrates in sections as well as in a single unit. A string, for example, vibrates along its entire length as well as in halves, thirds, quarters, etc.

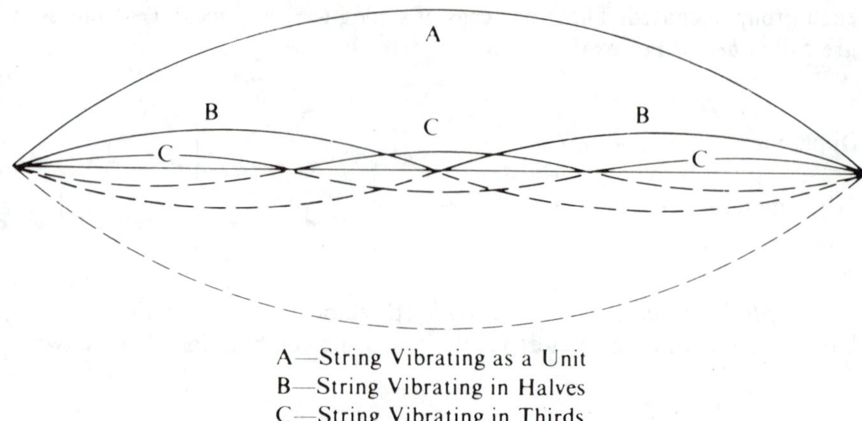

A—String Vibrating as a Unit
B—String Vibrating in Halves
C—String Vibrating in Thirds

The pitches produced simultaneously by the vibrating sections are called *partials, overtones,* or *harmonics*. The first partial, often called the *fundamental,* and the series of partials produced simultaneously by the vibrating body constitute a musical tone. Since the fundamental is the lowest frequency and is also perceived as the loudest, the ear identifies it as the specific pitch of the musical tone.

Although the harmonic series theoretically goes to infinity, there are practical limits; the human ear is insensitive to frequencies above 20,000 Hz. (Hz. is the abbreviation for Hertz, a standard measurement of frequency expressed in cycles per second.) The following illustration carries the harmonic series to the sixteenth partial:

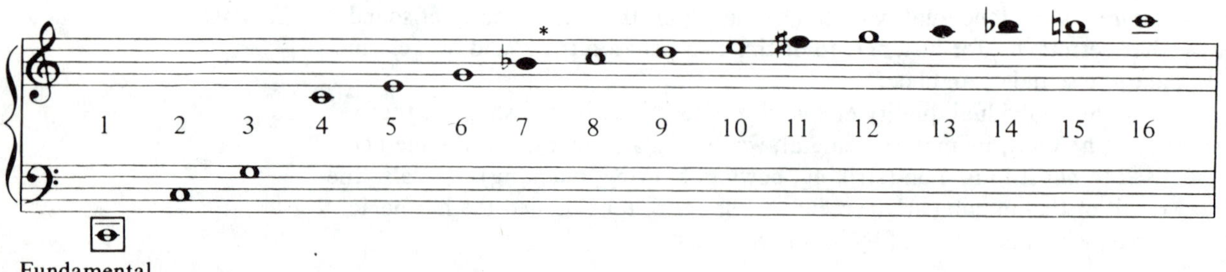

The individual partials that make up a musical tone are not distinguished separately, but are heard by the human ear as a blend that characterizes timbre.

If you are familiar with brass instruments you will notice that this series looks very similar to the series of tones playable without utilizing valves or slides. The brass instruments are capable of playing the various pitches in the harmonic series. An instrument like the clarinet tends to favor the odd-numbered partials (1, 3, 5, 7, 9, and so on) due to its nature and the makeup of its vibrating air column. This suppression of the even partials is what gives the clarinet its particular tone quality.

Summary

Music is an art of sound and time, and the basic characteristics of musical tone—pitch, duration, intensity, and timbre—are fundamental elements. The principal concern in this book is to determine how musical tones interact with each other to produce music.

*Black notes indicate those partials that cannot be represented accurately by notes in our pitch system.

APPENDIX B

Historical Overview

For purposes of style identification, the history of music is divided into style periods. The music within a particular style period is thought to share certain common traits, although there is a great deal of variety in the music within each style period. The following brief summary will introduce the style periods and place them in the context of European and American history.

Renaissance Period (1450–1600)

The term "renaissance" refers historically to the era of the rebirth of culture and intellectual curiosity that followed the Dark Ages. It began (1450) about the time that Christopher Columbus (1446–1506) was a child; its middle period saw the rise of the Protestant Reformation movement spurred by Martin Luther (1483–1546). It reached its zenith at about the time of Shakespeare (1564–1616). The overriding function of music in the Renaissance period was sacred; that is, to contribute to worship. Although greatly overshadowed by the sacred music of the period, secular works did exist and were an important part of the literature at that time.

Vocal music was far more common than instrumental music during the Renaissance period, and it was during this period that choral music became fully established. Choruses came into being shortly before the beginning of the Renaissance period, but did not reach full flower until well into the era. Choruses of the time were usually small groups of perhaps twelve to fifteen singers, whereas today a chorus may include several hundred. Through much of history, the choral group has been divided into four parts—the familiar soprano, alto, tenor, and bass—and referred to as a "mixed" chorus. Late Renaissance period music often required a fifth part, either a second soprano or a second tenor. Works for six-, eight-, and even sixteen-part choruses were not exceptional. Choruses were frequently accompanied by instrumental groups that usually doubled the voice parts. Most often in chapels, however, the groups sang *a cappella,* or unaccompanied.

Baroque Period (1600–1750)

The Baroque period consisted of many changes. Baroque period composers arranged for the words of sung texts to be more easily heard. They preferred new tonality systems to the modality of the Renaissance period. Instrumental music came of age and began to assume more importance than vocal music for the first time in history. Improvisation of music was a common practice, particularly in the performance of accompaniments (see figured bass in chapter 4) and in the performance of opera singers, who were expected to improvise embellishments at certain points in their arias.

Rameau, in his *Traite de l'Harmonie* (1722), sought to prove the invertibility of chords and designed an entire system of harmony that recognized the progression of triads and other sonorities. Furthermore, the older systems of tuning (just and meantone) found a new competitor in equal temperament, a system that allowed more freedom for modulation and a method of tuning that would eventually supersede all others in the ensuing century.

The Baroque period paralleled the rise of our own country from a wilderness to an established system of colonies. Shakespeare was still alive at the period's beginning and George Washington (1732–1799) was a young man at its close.

Classical Period (1750–1825)

This period encompassed the lives of many of our best-known composers whose works are still performed regularly in concert halls throughout the world. Haydn, Mozart, and Beethoven, giants of the music world, were included in this artistically wealthy period. The balance shifted even more in favor of instrumental music, although sacred and secular vocal music continued to be written. Chamber music, orchestral and other instrumental works gained the ascendancy. The sonata and the symphony developed during the Classical period and the string quartet took the place of the older trio sonata. The piano-forte (our modern piano), invented about 1710 by Christofori, became a popular household instrument. The improvisatory attitude toward performance died out, except in a few instances like the cadenzas in concertos. In the Classical period the orchestral literature grew in size and importance, and the orchestra itself acquired more color and flexibility. Clarinets became permanent fixtures along with flutes, oboes, and bassoons.

The early Classical period saw the American Revolution and the formation of the United States.

Romantic Period (1825–1900)

In the United States, the Romantic period began with the presidency of Andrew Jackson and ended with that of McKinley. A wrenching civil war tore at the basic fibers of the country, most of the states west of the Mississippi were admitted to the union, railroads spanned the country, and big business became a dominant force in our country for the first time.

Music of this period was dominated by a wider range of emotional expression, more personal and individual styles, and more subjectivity. Musical forms, such as the sonata and symphony, became longer and more involved, but shorter forms, especially piano compositions, were also numerous. Harmony and orchestration expanded, as did sonorities in general.

The most substantial achievement of the Romantic period was in the development of complex harmonic techniques and an emphasis on instrumental color, which were used to create dramatic musical effects.

As opposed to the classic ideals of organization, symmetry, control, and perfection within acknowledged limits, romanticism sought independence, movement, passion, and pursued the mysterious or exotic because its ideals could not be obtained. Romantic art was troubled by the spirit of longing and seeking after an unattainable goal.

Post-Romantic and Impressionistic Period (1875–1920)

This period in the United States began with the reconstruction days after the Civil War, and ended at about the time of World War I. The Spanish-American War (1898) was fought, and Theodore Roosevelt (1901–1909) and Woodrow Wilson (1913–1921) were president.

As a movement among French painters, impressionism sought to eliminate the heroic subjects, the obsession with realistic detail, and the representational quality of romantic painting. In essence, the impressionist painter hoped to capture the impression a subject or object made on him rather than to paint its literal representation. So too, in music, composers such as Debussy aspired to renounce the clear phrase structure and goal-oriented harmonic idiom of the past, and replace them with a purposeful understatement and ambiguity that was evocative, but very different in effect from the romantic style. The impressionist composers abandoned traditional thematic development and became more concerned with the color or mood of a particular moment.

Contemporary Period (1920–Present)

The period from 1920 to the present has seen the development of great diversity of musical styles and techniques. Much of this development can be traced back to the upheavals caused by World War I (1914–1918) and World War II (1939–1945), which caused disruption of the established cultural institutions in Europe and at the same time brought peoples of diverse cultural backgrounds together for the first time. The development of recording technology, radio and television transmission, and rapid transportation created a sense of world community in which all manifestations of human culture could freely intermingle. In more recent times technological advances have made possible the development of electronic and computer instruments for the composition and synthesis of music.

Jazz and Popular Music (1900–Present)

Popular song as now found in the United States evolved near the beginning of the twentieth century. Some notable composers of popular song are George Gershwin, Cole Porter, Richard Rodgers, Irving Berlin, Vernon Duke, and Burt Bacharach. Popular songs by these and other composers were the dominant music with mass appeal until rock music became firmly entrenched in the 1960s.

Black-American music is among the most notable expressions of religious, folk, and art music in the United States. The *blues* refers to a black-American song of sorrow. The blues, which arose from the black gospel and country music of the deep South, has not only been perpetuated as a unique style of its own, but has infused and inspired nearly all types of black-American music, some twentieth-century classical music, and the popular songs and rock music of the present day. Jazz, the general term for various music of black creation, has undergone many changes from its beginning and interpretations in its brief history, and its acceptance as a substantive art form has at last been accomplished.

Since the 1960s, rock music, which developed out of the traditions of the blues, jazz, and popular music, has become the dominant form of music with mass appeal.

APPENDIX C

Summary of Part-Writing Practices

Stylistic Practices

These refer to special part-writing situations that occur often.

Triads:

1. **Root Position.** When two roots lie a P5th or P4th apart, keep the common tone and move the remaining two upper voices stepwise to the chord tones of the next triad. Double the root in these triads.
2. **Root Position.** When two roots lie a P5th or P4th apart, and especially when the soprano voice descends one step (like from scale steps 2 to 1), do not keep the common tone. Move all three upper voices in similar motion to the nearest chord tone. Double the root in these triads.
3. **Root Position.** When roots lie a third apart, keep both common tones and move the remaining voice stepwise. Double the root in these triads.
4. **Root Position.** When roots lie a second apart, move the three upper voices in contrary motion to the bass, and make sure that each voice moves to the nearest chord tone of the next chord. Generally double the root in these triads, but in the progression **V** to **vi** or **VI,** double the third factor of the **vi** or **VI** triad.
5. **Any Position—Repeated Chords.** Maintain proper doubling, and avoid unstylistic departures, but otherwise, an exchange of chord factors among voices is acceptable. Change of position is common.
6. **First Inversion.** There are no established voice-leading patterns. Double any triad factor that facilitates smooth voice leading. Favored notes are the soprano (most common) and bass. Never double leading tone. Avoid unstylistic departures.
7. **Special for $\mathbf{vii^{o6}}$.** No established voice-leading pattern, but double bass note, avoid skips of a tritone, move all voices with as much stepwise movement as possible.

8. **Special for $\mathbf{ii^{\circ 6}}$**. No established voice-leading pattern, but double bass note or root, avoid skips of a tritone, and move all voices with as much stepwise movement as possible.
9. **Second Inversion.** No established voice-leading pattern, but double bass note and use only the four types of $^6_4$ chords described in chapter 7.

Dominant 7th Chords:

10. Resolve the 7th of the $\mathbf{V^7}$ chord down one scale degree in the same voice. In the few instances where the resolution tone is not present, either keep the 7th as a common tone or move it by the smallest melodic interval possible.
11. All four factors of the $\mathbf{V^7}$ are usually present. But, for smoothness of voice leading, the 5th may be omitted and the root doubled.

Leading-Tone 7th Chords:

12. Resolve the 7th of the $\mathbf{vii^{\circ 7}}$ or $\mathbf{vii^{\varnothing 7}}$ (and inversions) one diatonic scale degree down to the tonic.
13. Resolve the tritone (root to 5th) inward if a d5th and outward if an A4th. However, it is not possible to do so in all situations.

Nondominant 7th Chords:

14. Resolve the 7th of nondominant 7th chords one diatonic scale degree down to the 3rd of the next chord (in circle progressions). Otherwise, resolve the 7th down one step if its resolution is a part of the following chord.

Borrowed Chords:

15. Altered tones are seldom doubled. Otherwise, follow the guidelines for all borrowed chords as they appear in the parallel minor or major keys.

Neapolitan 6th Chord:

16. Double the bass note (3rd of chord) whenever possible. Move the upper voices in contrary motion with the bass and avoid chromatic voice leading in leaving the $\mathbf{N^6}$. When $\mathbf{N^6}$ proceeds to $\mathbf{I^6_4}$, watch out for parallel 5ths.

Augmented 6th Chords:

17. Resolve the augmented 6th interval outward (in contrary motion) by a half-step to an octave. Neither of the two tones forming the augmented 6th interval is ever doubled. In the Italian 6th, double the 3rd above the base note.
18. To avoid parallel 5ths, $\mathbf{Gr^6}$ proceeds to $\mathbf{I^6_4}$ or $\mathbf{i^6_4}$ instead of **V.**

19. In major keys, when the German 6th progresses to $\mathbf{I}_4^6$, the P5 above the bass is spelled as a doubly augmented 4th to avoid chromatic spelling of the resolution (upward to the 3rd of the tonic chord).

9th, 11th, and 13th Chords:

20. For $\mathbf{V}^9$, the root, 3rd, 7th, and 9th are usually present. The 7th and 9th resolve down to the 3rd and 5th of the tonic triad.
21. For $\mathbf{V}^{11}$, the root, 7th, 9th, and 11th are usually present. The 11th is retained as a common tone (tonic note), while the 7th and 9th resolve down to the 3rd and 5th of the tonic triad.
22. For $\mathbf{V}^{13}$, the root, 3rd, 7th, and 13th are usually present. The 13th is usually in the soprano and resolves a 3rd downward to the tonic factor of **I** or **i.** The 7th resolves down by step to the 3rd of the tonic triad.

Altered Dominant Chords:

23. Take the altered 5th in the direction of the alteration—raised pitches up—lowered pitches down. Remember to resolve the 7th of the chord downward by step, even if it results in a nonstandard doubling of the tonic triad. Altered tones are almost never doubled.

Chromatic Mediant Chords:

24. Double the root of chromatic mediants, even if this results in doubling an altered tone. Resolve as smoothly as possible, even if chromatic voice leading results.

Unstylistic Departures—Inviolate. These apply to **all** voice-leading situations including **stylistic practices** and override all other considerations.

Inviolate (never broken):

1. Always avoid parallel P8ths, P5ths, and P1s (unisons).
2. Never double the leading tone (7th) of the scale.
3. Always keep all four voices within their range.
4. Always avoid the melodic A2nd and A4th.

Unstylistic Departures—Occasionally Broken. Under most voice-leading conditions these should be followed but may be broken occasionally for expressive voice leading or other musical considerations.

Occasionally broken:

5. Keep voices in order: soprano, alto, tenor, bass.
6. Spacing between adjacent three upper voices should not exceed an octave.

7. Overlapping should be avoided. (See illustration on page 131.)
8. Avoid hidden parallels. (See illustration on page 131.)
9. Parallel unequal fifths. OK, but use sparingly.
10. Diminished and Augmented melodic skips. d5th and d4th OK sometimes, but A2nd and A4th, never.
11. When in an outer voice (soprano or bass), the leading tone should progress upward to tonic.

SUMMARY OF DOUBING PRACTICES

Major Keys: Minor Keys:	I i		ii		 ii$^{\circ 6}$		iii		 III		IV		 iv		V V		vi		 VI		vii$^{\circ 6}$ vii$^{\circ 6}$	
Choice:	1	2	1	2	1	2	1	2	1	2	1	2	1	2	1	2	1	2	1	2	1	2
Root Pos:	R	-	R	-	-	-	R	-	R	-	R	-	R	-	R	-	R	3	3	R	-	-
1st Inv:	S	B	S	B	B	-	S	B	S	B	S	B	S	B	*S	R	S	3	3	R	B	-
2nd Inv:	B	-	-	-	-	-	-	-	-	-	B	-	B	-	B	-	-	-	-	-	-	-

*Never double 3rd of V triad (7th scale degree)

Legend: (R = Root, S = Soprano, B = Bass, 3 = 3rd of triad)
- = Either no preferred practice, or does not apply

As a rule of thumb: (May be broken occasionally for better melodic line.)

DOUBLE	**(IN) POSITION AND CHORD TYPE**
Root	Root position major and minor triads.
Soprano or Bass	First-inversion major and minor triads.
Bass Note	Second-inversion major and minor triads.
Bass Note	First-inversion diminished triads (**vii$^{\circ 6}$** and **ii$^{\circ 6}$**).

APPENDIX D

Popular Music Chord Symbols

Comprehensive List of Chords Found in Popular Music

Following is a comprehensive list of chords found in popular song accompaniments. All are based on C, but may be transposed to any other tone:

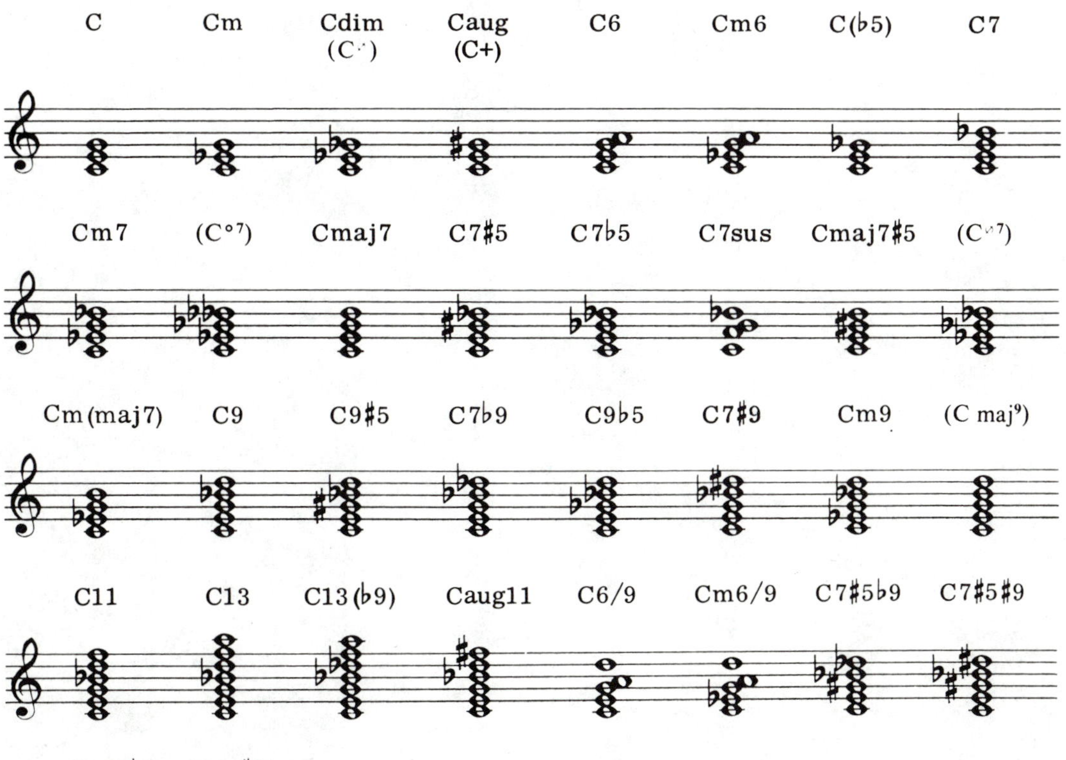

APPENDIX E

Instrument Ranges, Transpositions, and Foreign Names

In the charts on the following pages, the instruments are of two types.

Nontransposing Instruments

Nontransposing instruments produce a pitch that is the same as the written pitch. In the chart, the nontransposing instruments are those that have the actual sound "as written."

Transposing Instruments

Transposing instruments produce a pitch other than the written pitch. In the following chart, the actual transposition is given for instruments of this type. Most transposing instruments developed from traditions of the past, and to convert these instruments to nontransposing instruments would not be feasible since it would require rewriting a large part of the literature of music and retraining performers on the transposing instruments.

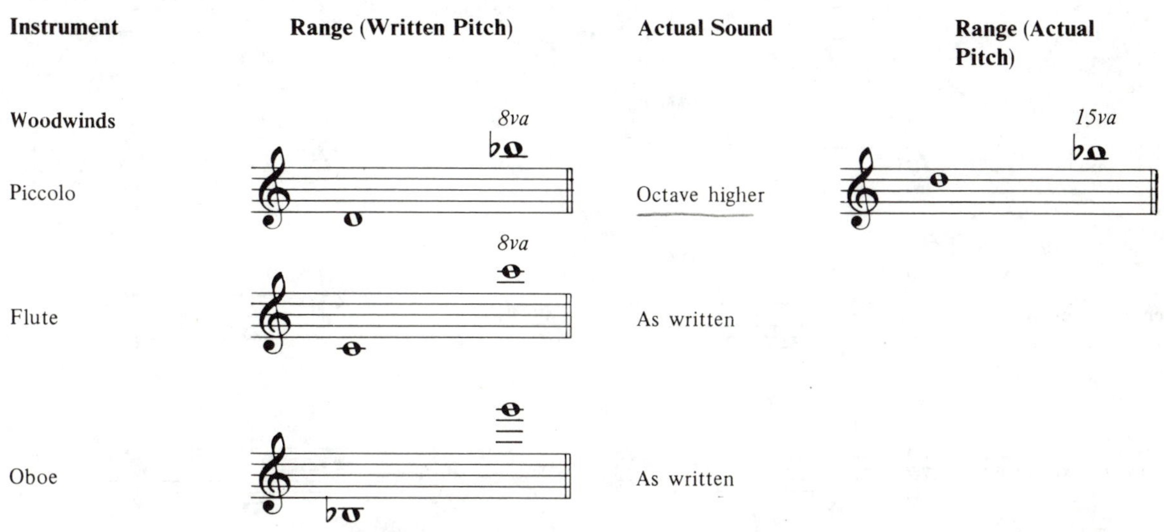

Instrument
Range (Written Pitch)
Actual Sound
Range (Actual Pitch)
Woodwinds
Piccolo
8va
Octave higher
15va
Flute
8va
As written
Oboe
As written

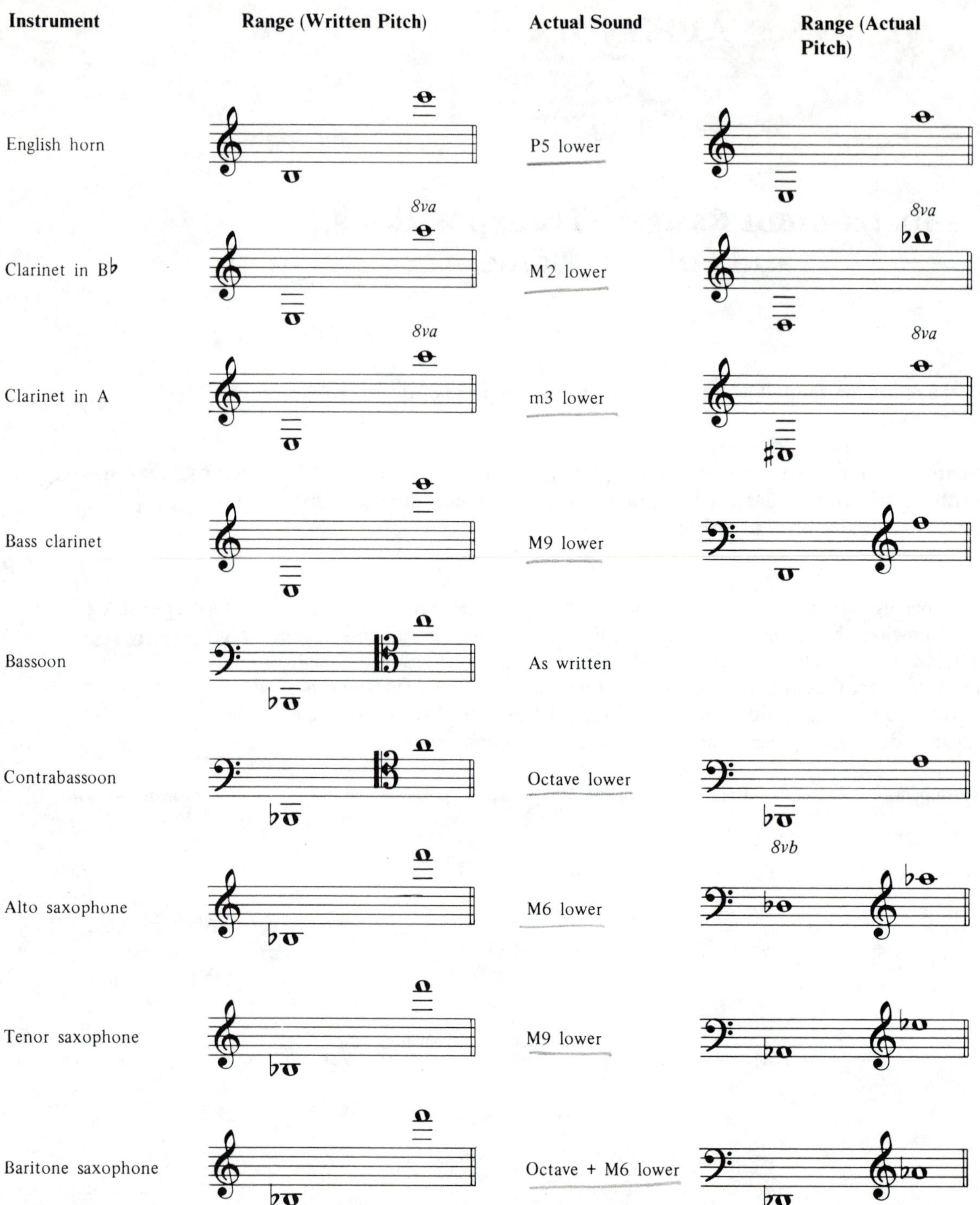
Instrument
Range (Written Pitch)
Actual Sound
Range (Actual Pitch)
English horn
P5 lower
Clarinet in B♭
8va
M2 lower
8va
Clarinet in A
8va
m3 lower
8va
Bass clarinet
M9 lower
Bassoon
As written
Contrabassoon
Octave lower
Alto saxophone
M6 lower
8vb
Tenor saxophone
M9 lower
Baritone saxophone
Octave + M6 lower

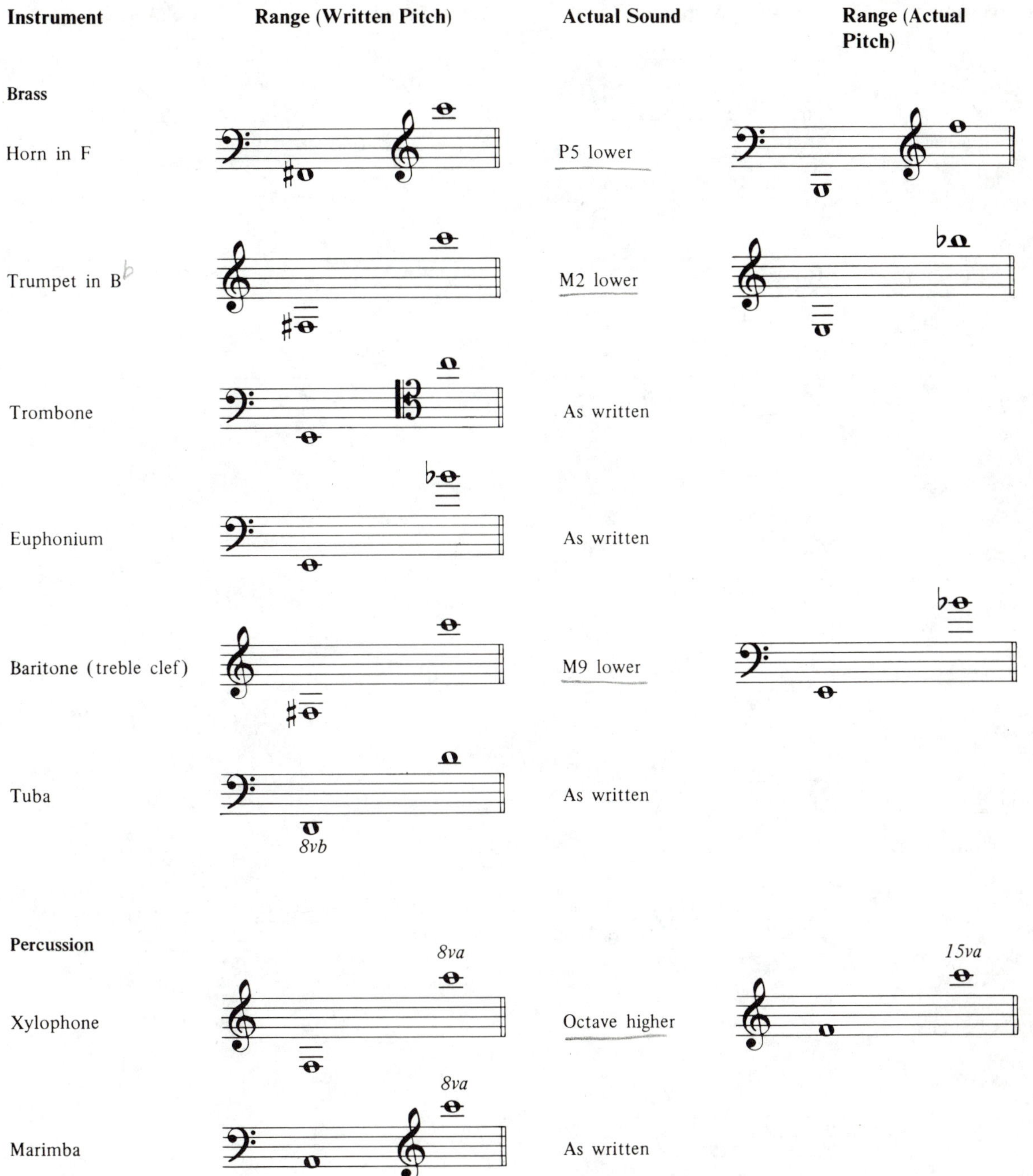

Instrument	Range (Written Pitch)	Actual Sound	Range (Actual Pitch)
Brass			
Horn in F		P5 lower	
Trumpet in B		M2 lower	
Trombone		As written	
Euphonium		As written	
Baritone (treble clef)		M9 lower	
Tuba	8vb	As written	
Percussion			
Xylophone	8va	Octave higher	15va
Marimba	8va	As written	

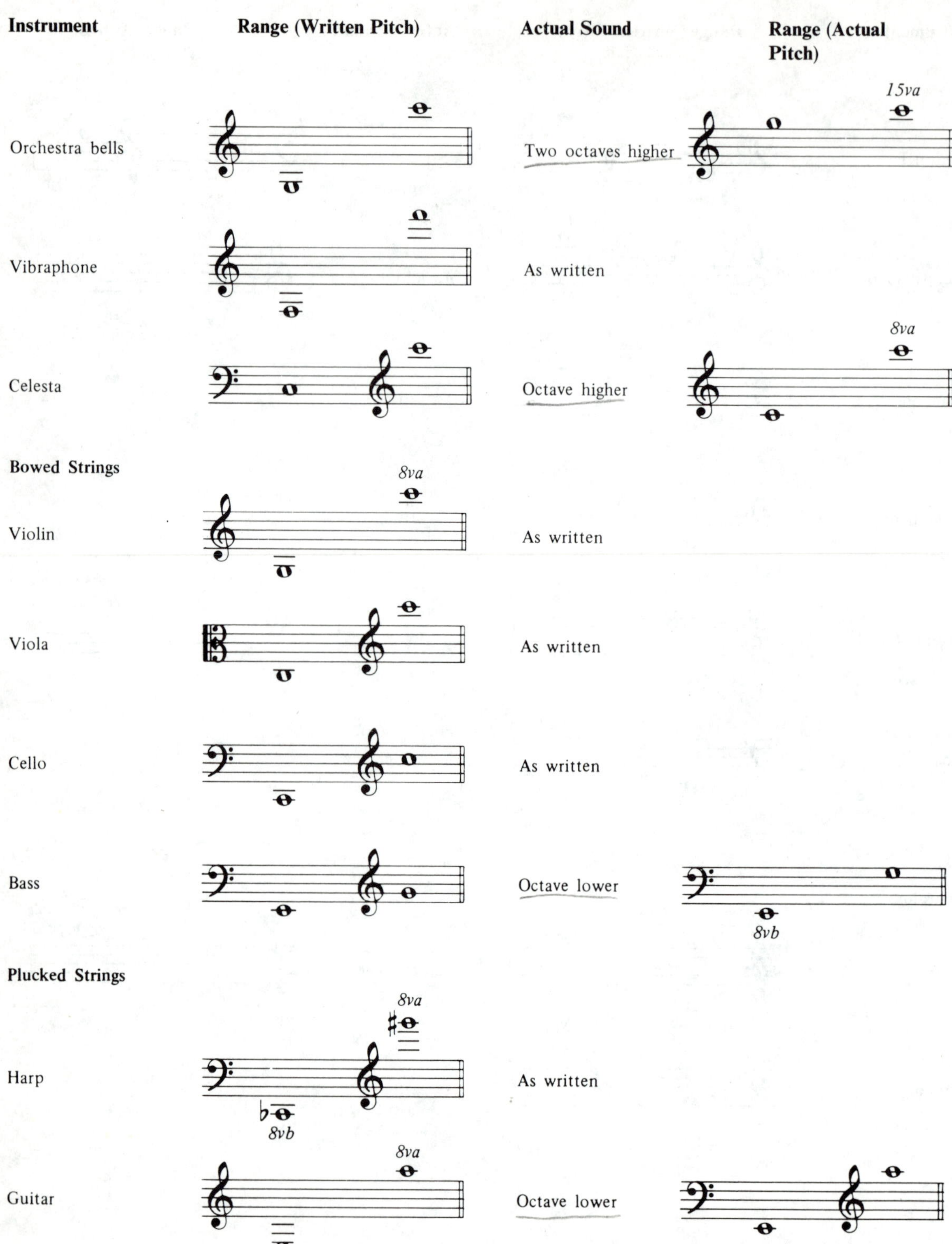
Instrument
Range (Written Pitch)
Actual Sound
Range (Actual Pitch)
Orchestra bells
Two octaves higher
15va
Vibraphone
As written
Celesta
Octave higher
8va
Bowed Strings
Violin
8va
As written
Viola
As written
Cello
As written
Bass
Octave lower
8vb
Plucked Strings
Harp
8va
8vb
As written
Guitar
8va
Octave lower

Foreign Names for Instruments

Since the many scores we will study are in Italian, French, and German, it is important that you know the names of all the common instruments in these languages. A reference list follows:

English	Italian	French	German
Woodwinds:			
Piccolo	Flauto Piccolo	Petite Flûte	Kleine Flöte
Flute	Flauto	Flûte	Flöte
Oboe	Oboe	Hautbois	Hoboe
English Horn	Corno Inglese	Cor Anglais	Englisch Horn
Clarinet	Clarinetto	Clarinette	Klarinette
Bass Clarinet	Clarinetto Basso	Clarinette Basse	Bassklarinette
Bassoon	Faggoto	Basson	Fagott
Saxophone	Sassofono	Saxophone	Saxophon
Brass:			
Horn	Corno	Cor	Horn
Trumpet	Tromba	Trompette	Trompete
Trombone	Trombone	Trombone	Posaune
Euphonium	Eufonio	Basse à Pistons	Baryton
Tuba	Tuba	Tuba	Basstuba
Percussion:			
Timpani	Timpani	Timbales	Pauken
Xylophone	Silofono (Xilofono)	Xylophone	Xylophon
Marimba	Marimba	Marimba	Marimba
Orchestra Bells	Campanelli	Jeu de Timbres	Glockenspiel
Vibraphone	Vibrafono	Vibraphone	Vibraphon
Tubular Chimes	Campane	Cloches	Glocken
Celesta	Celesta	Célesta	Celesta
Snare Drum	Tamburo	Tambour	Kleine Trommel
Bass Drum	Gran Cassa	Grosse Caisse	Grosse Trommel
Cymbals	Piatti	Cymbales	Becken
Triangle	Triangolo	Triangle	Triangel
Tam-tam	Tam-tam	Tam-tam	Tam-tam
Bowed Strings:			
Violin	Violino	Violon	Violine
Viola	Viola	Alto	Bratsche
Cello	Violoncello	Violoncelle	Violoncell
Bass	Contrabasso	Contre Basse	Kontrabass
Plucked Strings:			
Harp	Arpa	Harpe	Harfe
Guitar	Chitarra	Guitare	Gitarre

APPENDIX F

Macro Analysis: An Alternative Analytical System

Definition

Macro analysis is a reductive system that facilitates analysis of the important musical events of a composition. While based on a thorough analysis of smaller details, especially voice leading, macro analysis builds on these secondary configurations to reveal the larger structures so vital to a full understanding of a composition.

Important Aspects

Calculates Forward Motion. Forward motion creates tension, a striving to reach a goal or *target,* which is most satisfactorily achieved when the dominant chord (**V**) moves to the tonic (**I**). Thus, all tonal music is primarily a movement toward a target, the tonic (**I**). When the tonic is reached in the interior of a composition, forward motion is dissipated, and the surge toward another target is initiated.

Based on Circle Progressions. Most theorists agree that the circle progression **V** to **I** represents the most important forward motion (motion toward a perceived destination) in all of tonal music (1600–1900). The next in effectiveness is the progression **ii** to **V,** and following that, in decreasing strength, is **vi** to **ii, iii** to **vi,** and **vii°** to **iii.** A complete circle consists of **IV vii° iii vi ii V I,** although **IV** to **vii°** is seldom used in major keys because the roots of the two chords form a tritone. In macro analysis, circle-of-fifths progressions are charted through the use of slurs.

The Importance of Voice Leading. In the process of extracting circle progressions, it is very important to observe the voice leading that determines harmony. Sometimes certain types of voice leading, especially similar and parallel motion, may weaken the effect of chord progressions. In other instances voice leading purposely creates ambiguity in choosing the harmony that will be perceived by the ear. Trying to determine whether a chord is **vii°^{7}** or **V^7** is a good example. No macro analysis is valid unless the details of voice leading have been thoroughly investigated.

Prolonged Circle Progressions. A literal traditional analysis often hides a more sophisticated basic structure. Sometimes phrases or sections of a composition are organized around a series of circle progressions where the series members are not always adjacent. In the following illustration the **vi** triad is *prolonged* (duration of influence is extended) by **V^7/vi,** the **ii** triad is prolonged by the **IV** triad, and the **V** triad is prolonged by the two I$^6_4$ chords and the **vii°^{7}/V.**

Traditional:	I vi	V^7/vi vi IV	ii^6 I$^6_4$	vii°^{7}/V I$^6_4$V I
Macro:	I vi	V^7/vivi IV	ii	vii°^{7}/V V I

Elisions in Circle Progressions. On occasion, one chord of a circle progression is *elided* (omitted).

	Actual Progression	**Showing Elision**
Baroque Practice:	vi V I	Elided vi (ii)-V I
Post-Romantic Practice:	vi^7 ii^7 I	Elided vi^7 ii^7 (V^9) I

In the Baroque, Classical, and Romantic periods elided chords were usually **iii, vi,** or **ii** chords, while in the Post-Romantic period the **V** chord itself was not exempt from being elided.

Procedure

No Roman-Numeral Analysis for Now. To begin a macro analysis, avoid the urge to write chord symbols. Doing so at this time may cause you to miss many of the advantages macro analysis offers. Pay particular attention to the details of voice leading, for if your appraisal of the minute details is faulty, the macro analysis will also be flawed.

Add Chord Symbols

Chords on Single Bass Clef Staff or Use Chord Symbols. Write down the chords (**not** roman-numeral analysis). Chords may be represented in any of three ways:

1. Write on the bass clef staff in root position (example, p. 459).
2. Write on the bass clef staff in whatever position they are found in the score (example, p. 460).
3. Ignore the staff and write chord symbols below the score (example, p. 462).

Ask your instructor which procedure you should follow.

Nonharmonic Tones. Make sure you recognize all nonharmonic tones and do not include them in your macro analysis. Circle nonharmonic tones if you have trouble recognizing them.

Observe Harmonic Rhythm. Determine the prevailing harmonic rhythm before you determine the chords. Do not select harmony that changes so frequently that there is little likelihood of it being grasped at performance tempo. Although there are exceptions, a basic harmonic rhythm is seldom altered drastically in the interior of a phrase or section.

Successions of the Same Chord. Sometimes a chord progresses to the same chord in the same or different position. In such instances, enter one chord on the single staff and add an arrow (———→) to indicate the duration of the harmony.

Special Handling of $^6_4$ Chords. Because of their unstable nature, most second-inversion chords, especially those of the cadential type, may be indicated with black note heads to show the **6** and the **4** resolving to the **5** and **3** of the **V** chord. Correct analysis of a second-inversion triad is shown on the following page.

Haydn: Piano Sonata, Hob. XVI:41 (2nd Movement)

Add Slurs

Begin Macro Analysis. After you have entered all of the chords using one of the methods described on page 458, connect, with *slurs,* those adjacent chords that form *circle progressions*—**iii** to **vi, vi** to **ii, ii** to **V,** or **V** to **I** (see page 457 for full discussion).

Stepwise Linear Motion. Occasionally, you will encounter short passages that contain no circle progressions and include stepwise motion in either or both of the outer voices. These are instances where linear motion transcends harmonic progression. In the following example *(a)* by Beethoven, chord no. 4 is a diminished 7th chord that normally resolves to an *f*-minor triad, but in this instance does not resolve at all but progresses to another diminished 7th chord (at no. 5). The same example (at *b*) shows the two outer voices and the strong linear influence to continue the converging direction forcing chord no. 4 to abandon a conventional resolution.

a.

Beethoven: Piano Sonata, op. 110 (2nd Movement)

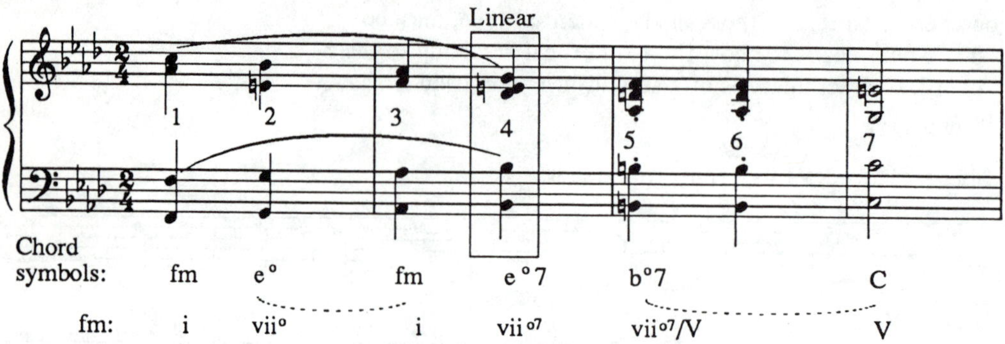

b.

In the following example by Haydn a series of chords (first-inversion triads) move in similar or parallel motion (measures 5 and 6). Since their sliding movement negates functional harmony, place a bracket above or below the passage to label these as primarily **linear** in nature. Analyze only the first and last chord in the series. Usually the sliding movement begins or ends with **I, VI,** or **V.**

Haydn: Piano Sonata, Hob. XVI:13 (Minuet)

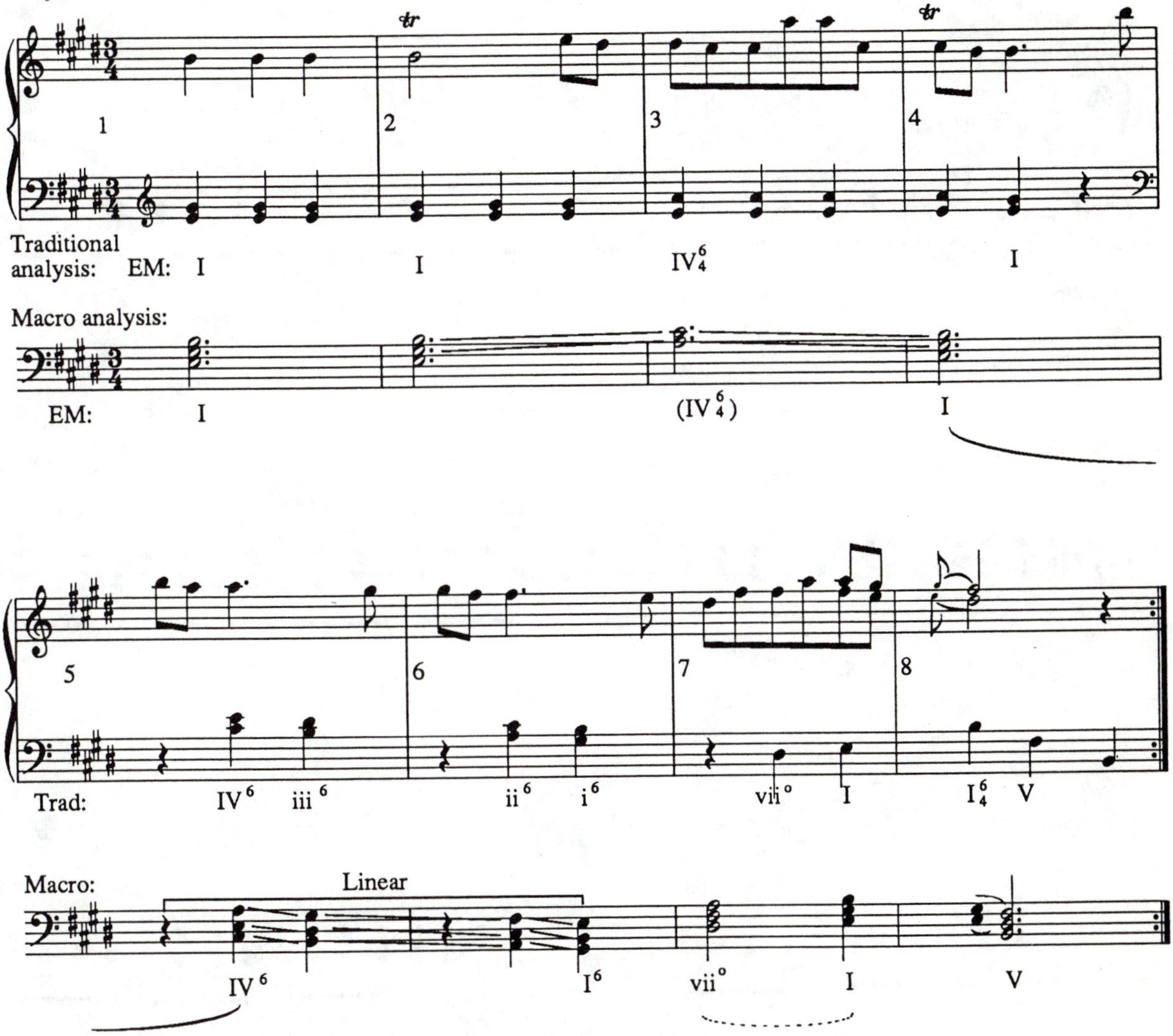

Traditional analysis: EM: I I IV^6_4 I

Macro analysis:

EM: I (IV^6_4) I

Trad: IV^6 iii^6 ii^6 i^6 vii° I I^6_4 V

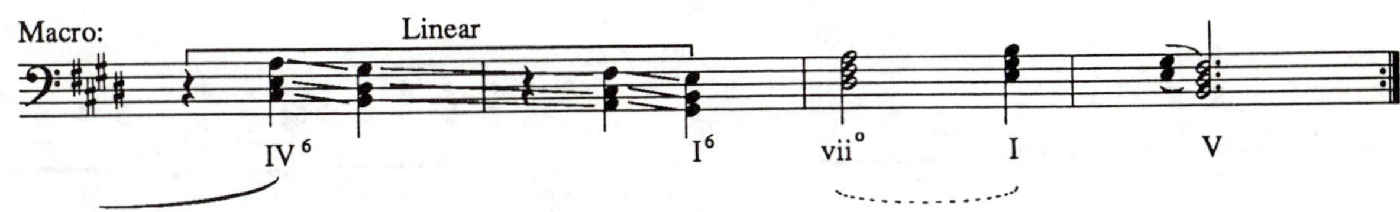

While the previous example by Beethoven illustrates a single linear chord, and the example of linear motion in the Haydn excerpt is completed in two measures, the following excerpt, by Chopin, extends linear motion by ten measures (measures 2–12). Here, the lowest voice continues downward primarily by half steps, while the uppermost voice makes its way as well in the same general direction. With the exception of one weak secondary leading-tone progression (measure 8, beat 4), this period of linear descent (measures 2–12), is virtually free of circle progressions. Note that the linear passage begins and ends on a dominant 7th chord in **e** minor. Within the passage, none of the chords, including three dominant 7th chords and seven diminished 7th chords, resolve conventionally.

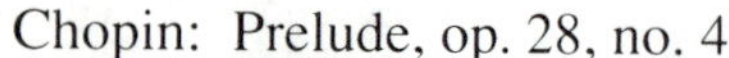

Chopin: Prelude, op. 28, no. 4

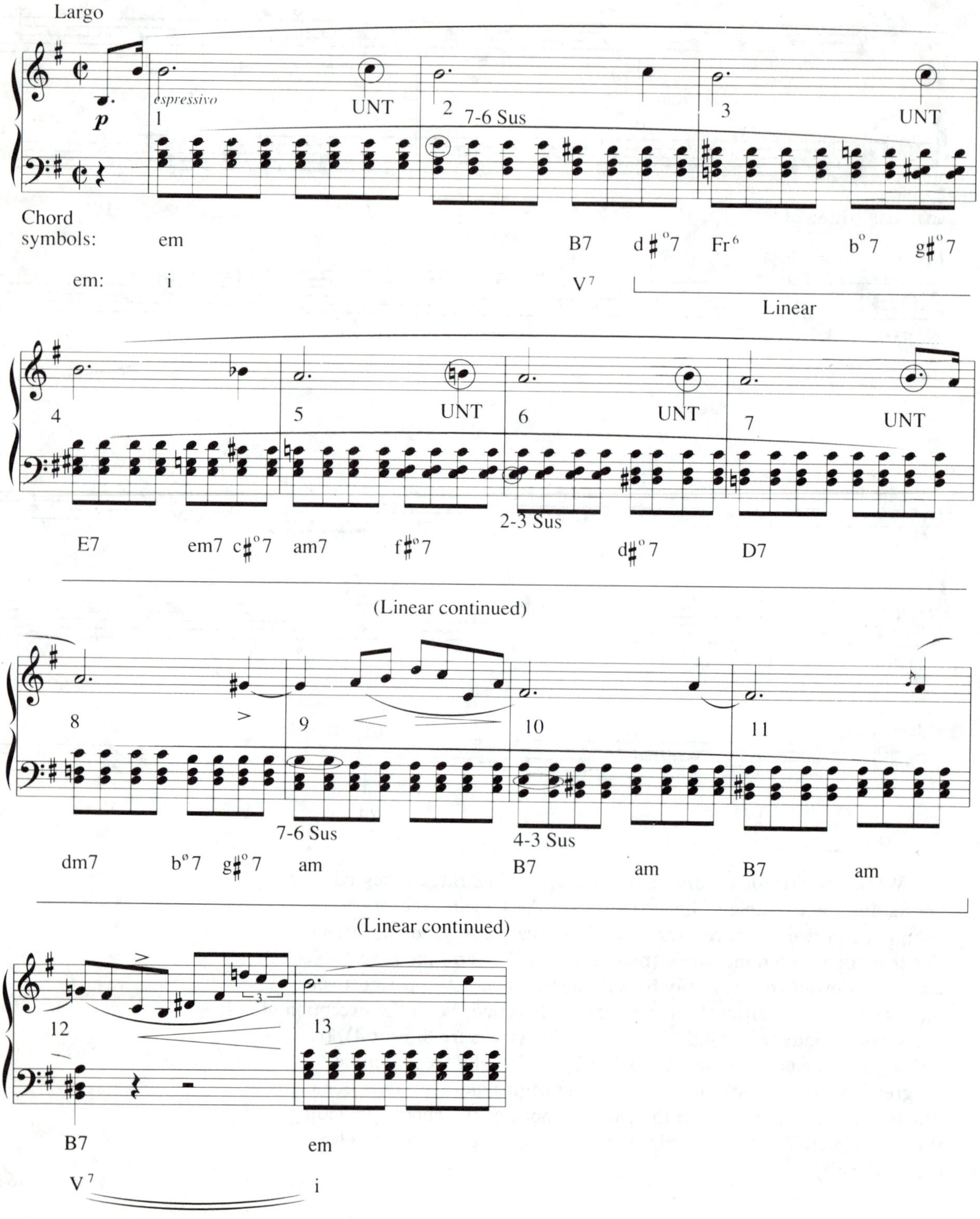

Largo

p *espressivo*

1 UNT 2 7-6 Sus 3 UNT

Chord symbols: em B7 d♯°7 Fr⁶ b°7 g♯°7

em: i V^7

Linear

4 5 UNT 6 UNT 7 UNT

2-3 Sus

E7 em7 c♯°7 am7 f♯°7 d♯°7 D7

(Linear continued)

8 9 10 11

7-6 Sus 4-3 Sus

dm7 b°7 g♯°7 am B7 am B7 am

(Linear continued)

12 13

B7 em

V^7 i

Double Slur V to I Progressions. Connect chords **V** to **I** with a double slur because these two chords are capable of establishing a tonal center.

Diminished Triads or Seventh Chords. When the root of a diminished triad or seventh chord progresses up a minor second to the root of a major or minor triad, connect the two with a dotted slur. This is done to account for leading-tone harmony, which often functions as a weaker form of dominant harmony. An example is:

Chord Symbols:	**e°7**	F	
Analysis:	**vii°7**	I	(in F Major)
or Analysis:	**vii°7/V**	V	(in B♭ Major)

Add Roman Numerals

Completing the Macro Analysis. Scan your analysis for *double slurs,* indicating possible **V** to **I** progressions. Near the beginning of the composition you should find double-slurred progressions that indicate the key of the composition.

V to I to IV. Beware that occasionally a set of circle progressions may span **V I IV,** giving the false impression that the key of **IV** has been established. Look at other double slurs in the area to confirm the key.

Indicating Modulation and Secondary Dominants

Extended Line. Where you find a strong circle progression that comes to completion in another key, start with the final chord, and place a straight line beneath it and extend the line backwards as far as the chords can be analyzed in the new tonality. Beneath the *extended line,* indicate by roman-numeral analysis the relationship of this new tonic to the original key. In the illustration below, the original key is D major and the new key (measures 5–8) is A major, so a **V** is placed below the extended line.

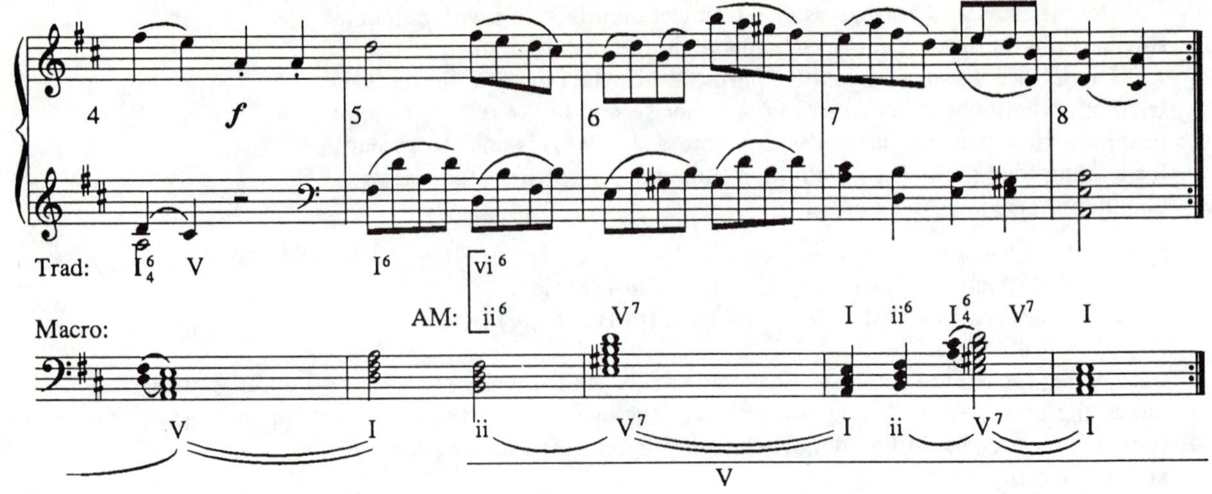

Secondary Dominants. In macro analysis, secondary dominants and modulations are both treated in the same manner—with an extended line. However, secondary dominants, easy to spot because of their short extended line, are easily contrasted with true modulations where the extended line often lasts for fifty measures or more. Since secondary dominants and modulations are but different shades of the same phenomenon (change of key), the need to devise an artificial rule-of-thumb to distinguish between them is eliminated in macro analysis.

Tonal Profile. A *tonal profile,* not essential, but a desirable option available in macro analysis, provides a summary of the ebb and flow of the composition. A tonal profile reveals at a glance the key relationships, the build up and relaxation of tension developed throughout a composition, and the relationship of larger sections, one to another. (See page 465 for an example of a tonal profile.)

An Evolving Theory

The Nature of Macro Analysis. With present ongoing research, new information about the nature of functional harmony is constantly being discovered. Each successive edition of this text will contain updated material. It is the hope of the authors that you will not become obsessed with mere analytical symbols, but will look beyond to unearth more and better ways to understand the mysteries of this golden age of music. You are invited to share your ideas with the authors who may be reached through the publisher.

Look carefully at the following example of macro analysis. It contains refinements that are more easily grasped from musical illustrations than from written descriptions.

Beethoven: Piano Sonata, op. 28 (2nd Movement)

Tonal Profile

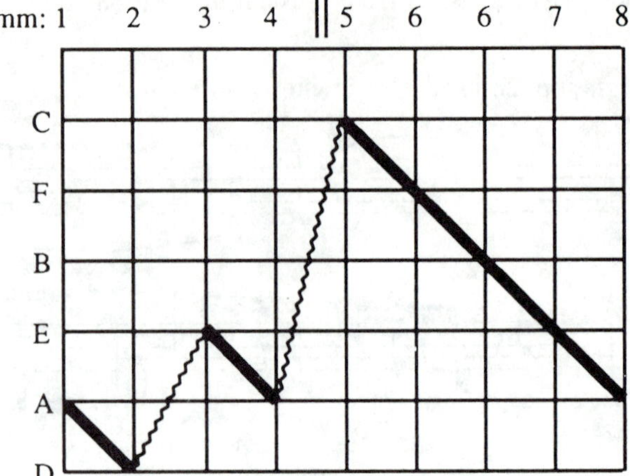

How to Read the Profile

1. The circle progressions used in this excerpt (C F B E A D) are shown at the left of the grid.
2. Think of the lines, both narrow and bold, as representing motion.
3. Forward movement is shown by lines that move **downward** (shown here in **boldface**) to reach a goal or target: A down to **D** (target), E down to **A** (target), C to F to B to E to **A** (target).
4. In each instance, after the target is reached, preparations are made for the next forward movement. The lines that move **upward** (shown here as narrow lines) represent direction away from the target. In the tonal profile above, note the movement upward between measures 2 and 3 and 4 and 5.
5. The parallel lines (||) at the top between measures 4 and 5 indicate a new phrase.
6. As shown in this tonal profile, the entire second phrase is one continuous series of circle progressions.

Deductions from Analysis of Beethoven Piano Sonata in D Major (Pastoral), op. 28 (Excerpt)

Measures	**Comments**
1–2	D minor clearly established with V-i.
3–4	Half-cadence in D minor. Here Beethoven not only employs the $vii^{\circ 7}$ of V, but also precedes it with the diatonic $ii^{\circ 7}$. A further reduction could show a basic $ii^{ø 7}$—V cadence.
5–6	A temporary visit to F major.
5–8	While the V-I in F major (measures 5 and 6) temporarily establishes that key, the remainder of the phrase (measures 5½–8) reveals the authentic cadence in F major to be only a part of a circle progression, continuing without interruption to the *target* chord (A minor) in measure 8. In general, the longer the chain of circle progressions, the greater the expectation (tension) grows to reach the target chord.

APPENDIX G

Answers to Self-Tests

Test Yourself 1 (page 25)

1. (Answers in parentheses are the alternate system of octave identification shown in figure 1.11.)

   a. e^1 (E^4) b. d^2 (D^5) c. B (B^2) d. E (E^2) e. f^1 (F^4) f. f (F^3)
   g. e (E^3) h. g^1 (G^4) i. c^3 (C^6) j. g (G^3) k. AA (A^1) l. f^1 (F^4)

2. Pairs: (a–i) (b–d) (c–h) (e–g) (f–j)

3. a. Forte should not be on the staff.
   b. 1. Improper beaming. (Should be in groups of two eighth notes or all notes beamed together.)
      2. Stem direction should be down above the third line of the staff.
   c. Improper beaming. (First eighth note should not be beamed with the others.)
   d. Half rest should not be used in this location. Should be two quarter rests.
   e. 1. Notes in first chord not in proper relationship. (d should be to the left of the stem and e to the right.)
      2. Crescendo should be below the staff.
      3. Chord on the second beat of the measure should be notated as a quarter tied to an eighth to show the third beat of the measure.
      4. Stem direction should be up on the chord on beat four.
   f. Not enough beats in this measure.
   g. The dotted half rest should not be used here. (Should be quarter rest followed by half rest to show the third beat of the measure.)

4. Notes in parentheses are enharmonic equivalents.

   a. d (e♭♭) b. g (f♯♯) c. c (b♯)
   d. g (a♭♭) e. f (e♯) f. a (b♭♭)

Test Yourself 2 (page 51)

1. a. d harmonic minor b. E major
   c. f♮ minor d. g melodic minor (ascending)
2. Names in parentheses are the minor scales.
   a. D (b) b. E♭ (c) c. D♭ (b♭) d. E (c♯)
3. a. C and F b. D and A c. B♭ and E♭ d. G and D e. G♭ and C♭
4. a. D major

b. A♭ major

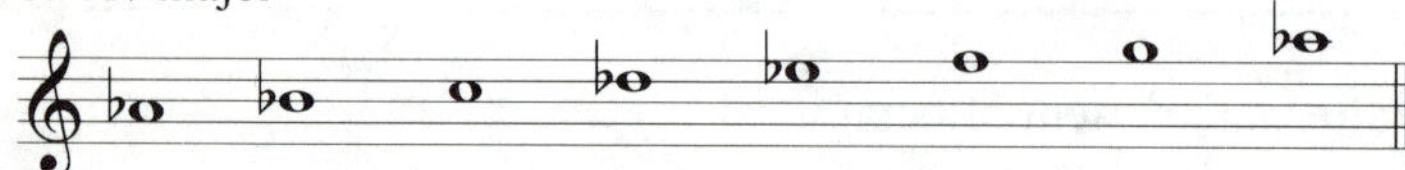

c. B ascending melodic minor

d. C♯ harmonic minor

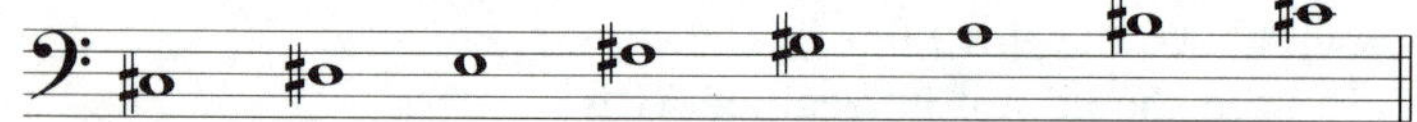

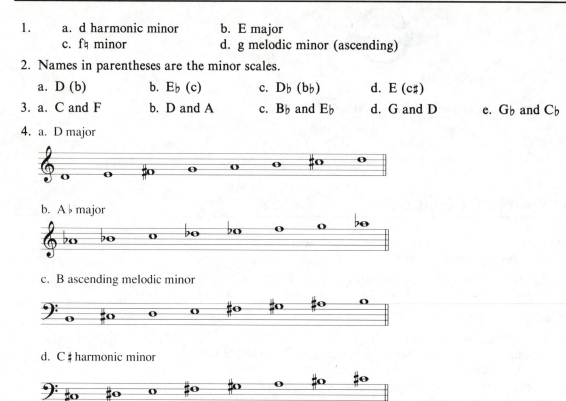

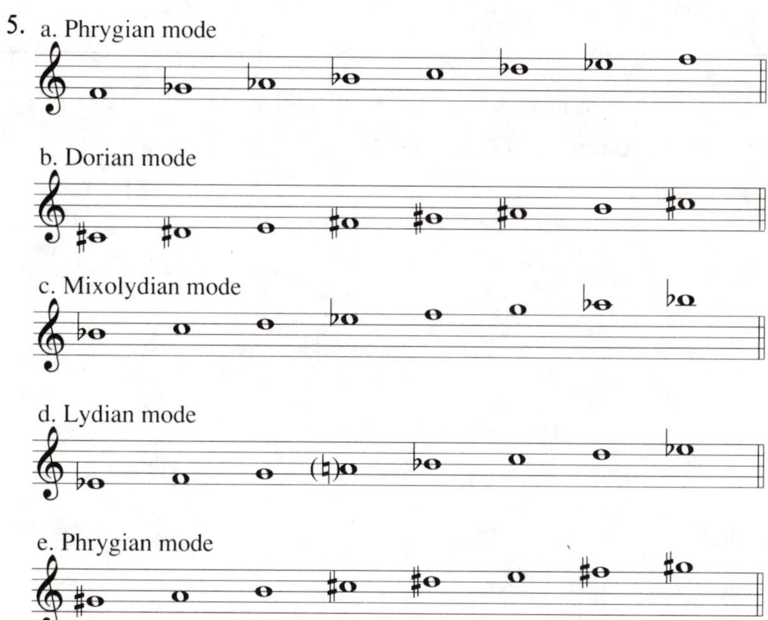

Test Yourself 3 (page 65)

1. P1, m3, M3, P5, m6, M6, P8.

2.	a. M3	b. M7	c. P4	d. m6	e. m2	f. A4
3.	a. m6	b. m2	c. P5	d. M3	e. M7	f. d5
4.	a. P1	b. M2	c. m3	d. M3	e. M6	f. m7
	g. m6	h. m10 (m3)	i. m6	j. m3	k. P4	l. m7
	m. m3	n. M2	o. m6	p. M3		

5. a. d-sharp b. c-double sharp c. a d. f e. b-flat f. d-sharp
6. a. c-sharp b. a-flat c. b-double flat d. c-sharp e. d-double sharp f. a-double flat

Test Yourself 4 (page 83)

1. a. major b. minor c. augmented d. diminished e. minor f. major
2. a. A b. Bmin c. A♭+ (or aug) d. Ddim e. Gmin f. D♭
3. a. tonic I^6
   b. subdominant IV
   c. leading tone vii^{o6}
   d. tonic I
   e. dominant V
   f. tonic I
   g. tonic I^6_4
   h. dominant V
   i. tonic I
4. a. V b. VI c. IV d. III e. I f. VII
5. a. vi b. iv c. ii d. v e. iii f. i

Test Yourself 5 (page 98)

1. Deceptive
2. Perfect Authentic
3. Plagal
4. Deceptive
5. Half
6. Half
7. Half
8. Half
9. Imperfect Authentic
10. Plagal
11. Perfect Authentic
12. Deceptive
13. Half
14. Plagal
15. Perfect Authentic
16. Deceptive
17. Plagal
18. Half
19. Half

20. Imperfect Authentic
21. Plagal
22. Perfect Authentic
23. Deceptive
24. Imperfect Authentic
25. Phrase 1 beat 15
    Phrase 2 beat 31
    Phrase 3 beat 47
    Phrase 4 beat 61

    Phrases 1 and 2 form a parallel period, while phrases 3 and 4 form a contrasting period.

Test Yourself 6 (page 117)

1. a. Plagal b. Deceptive c. Half d. Perfect Authentic
   e. Imperfect Authentic
2. a. Accented passing tone b. 4–3 Suspension c. Anticipation
   d. 4–3 Suspension e. Unaccented passing tone f. Appoggiatura
   g. 7–6 Suspension
3. The harmonic rhythm is essentially one chord per beat.
4. four
5. two
6. The first two phrases have a slow harmonic rhythm (chords extend over several measures), while the second two phrases have one chord per measure.

Test Yourself 7 (page 134)

1. 6 (first-inversion triads)
2. 3 (roots a 3rd apart)
3. 5 (repeated chord)
4. 8 (ii$^{\circ 6}$ in minor)
5. 2 (roots a 5th apart, soprano descends 2–1)
6. 9 (second-inversion triad)
7. 4 (roots a 2nd apart)
8. 7 (vii$^{\circ 6}$)
9. 1 (roots a 5th apart, keep common tone)

10. 3 (voices out of range)
11. 2 (doubled leading tone)
12. 4 (augmented 2nd)
13. 1 (parallel 5ths and 8ves)

Test Yourself 8 (page 154)

1. a. 1, 5, 7, 8, 10, 12, 14, 15, 16
   b.
   c. 2, 9
   d. 3, 4, 6, 11, 13
2. Circle progressions are more common than other progressions.
3. Circles indicate chord choices. Other answers are possible.

O Ewigkeit, du Donnerwort BWV 20 (Oh Eternity, Thou Word of Thunder)

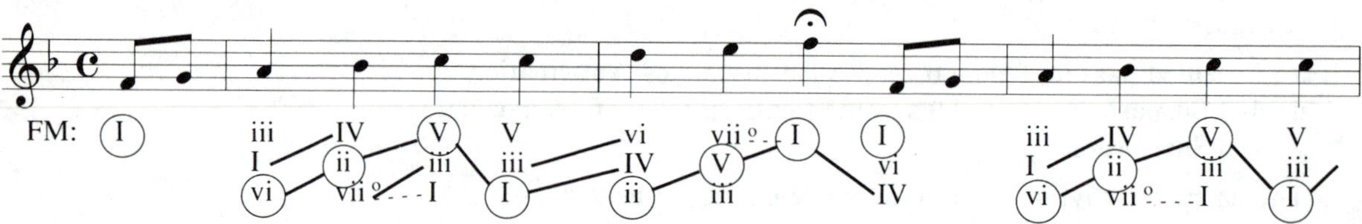

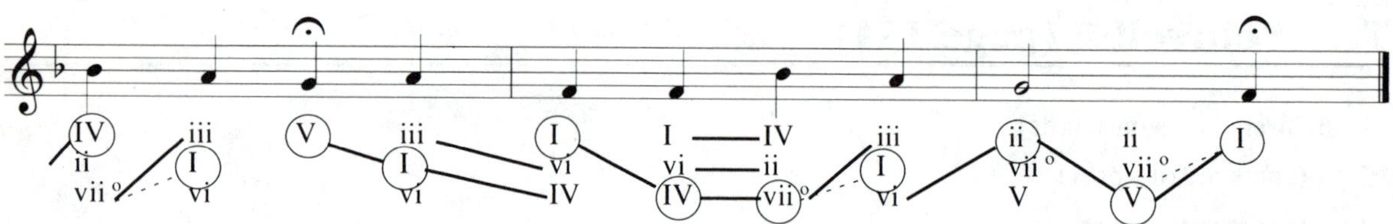

(15 circle progressions, 1 weaker circle progression)

4. Bach's setting of the chorale is on page 85 of the Workbook/Anthology.

Test Yourself 9 (page 168)

1. a. G, bass, B
   b. B, alto, D
   c. D♭, alto, F
   d. B♭, alto, D♭
   e. A, soprano, C
   f. E♭, tenor, G
2. 3, 6, 9, and 11.
3. 6
4. a. UPT
   b. 4–3 SUS
   c. UPT
   d. APP
   e. APT
   f. UPT
   g. APT
5. a. deceptive
   b. half
   c. imperfect authentic

Test Yourself 10 (page 180)

1. a. 1, 7, 8, 10, 13, 14, 20
   b. 3, 4, 17, 18
   c. 6, 12
   d. 9, 15, 16
   e. 2, 11
   f. 5, 19
2. a. Parallel 5ths (alto and tenor)
   b. 7th of the chord does not resolve downward by step.
   c. Parallel 5ths (tenor and bass)

Test Yourself 11 (page 190)

1. a. No error
   b. Parallel 5ths (soprano and tenor)
   c. A2nd (alto)
   d. No error
   e. A2nd (alto), 7th of the chord does not resolve downward by step.
   f. 7th of the chord does not resolve downward by step.

g. No error
h. 7th of the chord does not resolve downward by step.
i. No error

2.	a.	ii^7	V
	b.	IV^7	VII
	c.	VI^7	ii
	d.	iii^7	vi
	e.	$ii^{ø7}$	V
	f.	I^7	IV

Test Yourself 12 (page 208)

1.	b.	DM:	I	ii	IV	vi			
		GM:	IV	vi	I	iii			
	c.	f#m:	i	ii°	III	iv	v	VI	VII
		AM:	vi	vii°	I	ii	iii	IV	V
	d.	em:	i	III	iv	VI			
		C:	iii	V	vi	I			
	e.	fm:	i	III	iv	VI			
		D♭M:	iii	V	vi	I			
	f.	BM:	I	iii	V	vi			
		d#m:	VI	i	III	iv			
	g.	g#m:	i	ii°	iv	VI			
		BM:	vi	vii°	ii	IV			
	h.	gm:	i						
		dm:	iv						
	i.	EM:	I	ii	IV	vi			
2.		f#m:	VII	i	III	v			

a.
gm : i vi V
E♭M: vi I IV V6 I
b.
B♭M : I vi ii6
cm: ii i V6 V i
c.
A♭M : I vi V
cm: iii i ii°6 i6/4 V i
d.
cm : i i6 iv V
E♭M: VI IV vii°6 I

Test Yourself 13 (page 231)

1.

a.

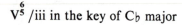

V^{6}_{5}/V in the key of A♭ major-minor

V^{6}_{5}/ii in the key of D♭ major

V^{6}_{5}/iv in the key of b♭ minor

V^{6}_{5}/vi in the key of G♭ major

V^{6}_{5}/iii in the key of C♭ major

b.

V^{6}/ii in the key of C major

V^{6}/VI in the key of f# minor

V^{6}/iii in the key of B♭ major

V^{6}/V in the key of G major-minor

V^{6}/IV in the key of A major

c.

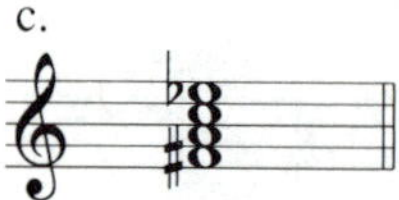

$vii^{\circ 7}$/iv in the key of d minor

$vii^{\circ 7}$/iii in the key of E♭ major

$vii^{\circ 7}$/V in the key of C major-minor

$vii^{\circ 7}$/ii in the key of F major

$vii^{\circ 7}$/VI in the key of b minor

2.
a.
b.
c.
FM: V6/ii ii
GM: vii°7/V V
cm: V4/2/VI6 VI6
d.
e.
f.
g.
E♭M: vii°7/iii iii
CM: vii°6/V V
b♭m: V6/5/VI VI
f♯m: V/VII VII
(natural)
h.
i.
j.
k.
cm: vii°7/iv iv
D♭M: vii°6/5/ii ii6
am: vii°4/2/V V6/4
AM: vii°7/vi vi

Test Yourself 14 (page 254)

1. The first section (measures 1–8) is open since it ends with a half cadence (away from the tonic chord). The second section (measures 9–18) is closed since it ends on the tonic.
2. The first section (measures 1–8) is open since it ends in the relative major (away from the *original* tonic chord). The second section (measures 9–34) is closed since it ends on the *original* tonic.
3. A *phrase* is a substantial musical thought usually ending with both a harmonic and melodic cadence. Two or more adjacent phrases may combine to form a *period.* An important characteristic of period construction is a relatively weaker cadence at the end of the first phrase (or phrases), and a strong cadence at the end of the final phrase. A *section* is a major division of a part form. Each section is a complete musical statement. By the definitions above a *phrase* can never be a *period,* since a period must consist of two or more phrases. However, a *section* may (and often does) consist of a single *period,* so a period can be a section.
4. A *rounded binary* form differs from a *binary* form in that the first section is repeated (sometimes in part) at the end of the second section. The two forms are alike in that they are divided into two major sections (often with each section repeated). The repetition just described occurs *within* the second section. It is not a separate section in itself.

Test Yourself 15 (page 267)

1. The first section (measures 1–16) is closed, since it ends on the tonic chord (C major).
2. The second section (measures 17–32) is open, since it ends away from the original tonic chord (A♭ major).
3. The B section acts as a contrasting section to the A section. It is often in a different key, and has different melodic and rhythmic material. After the B section the return to the A section is more pleasing, since it sounds "new" again.
4. In the *rounded binary form* the repetition of the first section (sometimes in part) occurs *within* the second section of the piece. It is not a separate section in itself. The rounded binary form retains its essential division into two parts.
5. The auxiliary members mentioned in the text are: introduction, transition, and coda.

Test Yourself 16 (page 278)

Test Yourself 17 (page 287)

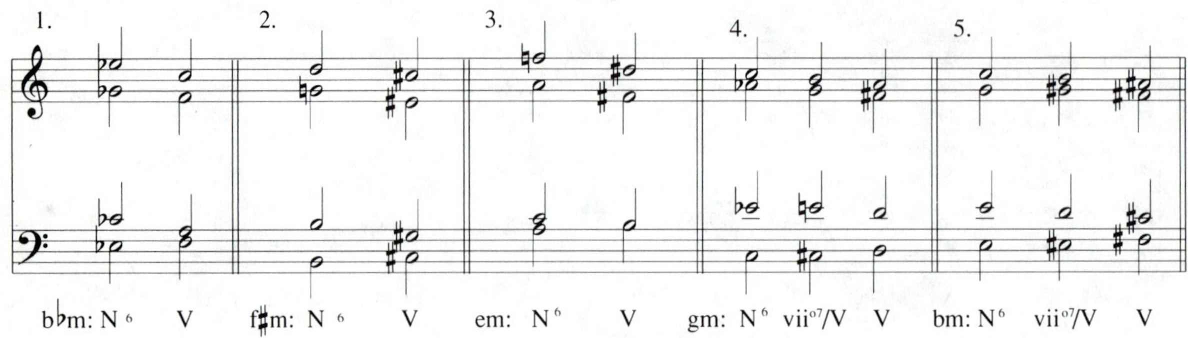

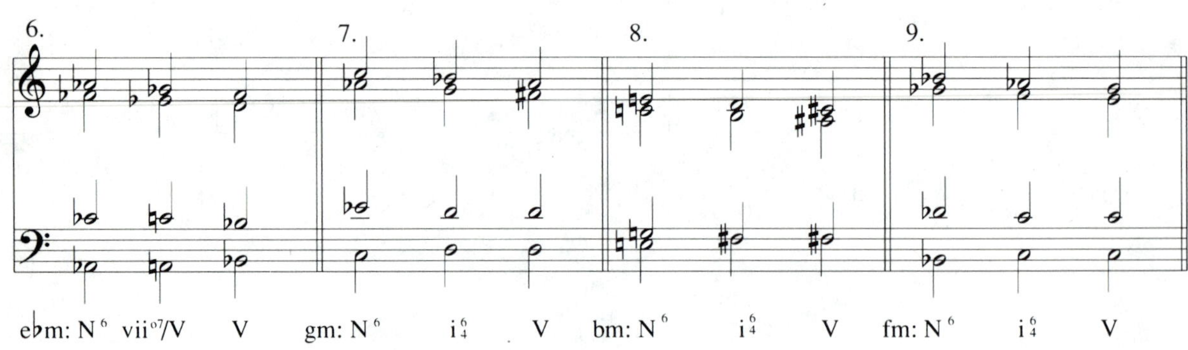

Test Yourself 18 (page 297)

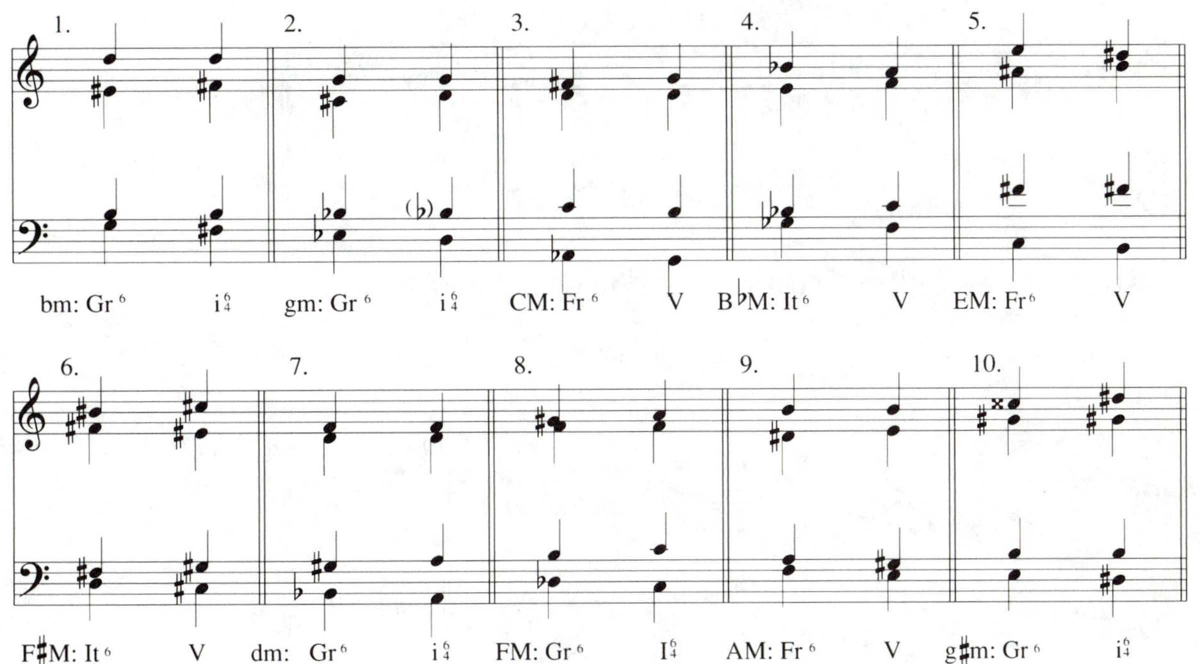

Test Yourself 19 (page 306)

Test Yourself 20 (page 314)

1. b,e
2. d
3. c
4. e
5. c
6. d
7. f
8. c
9. a
10. b,e
11. c
12. c,d
13. c,d
14. c
15. e
16. a
17. f
18. e,f
19. d

20.

B♭ Major: III ♭III ♭iii VI ♭VI ♭vi

21.

C Minor: iii ♮III ♮iii vi ♮VI ♮vi

22.

E Major: III ♮III ♮iii VI ♮VI ♮vi

23.

D♭ Major: III ♭III ♭iii VI 𝄫VI 𝄫vi

24.

B Minor: iii ♯III ♯iii vi ♯VI ♯vi

Test Yourself 21 (page 329)

1. First chord:

D♭ major:	Gr^6 (It would be spelled: B♭♭, D♭, F♭, G in this key.)
D major:	V^7 (Correctly spelled in this key.)

Second chord:

D major:	vii°^{7} (Correctly spelled in this key.)
D♭ major:	vii°^{7}/V (It would be spelled: G, B♭, D♭, F♭ in this key.)

2. C major: vii°^{7}/V (Correctly spelled in this key.)
   E♭ major: vii°^{7}/V (It would be spelled: A, C, E♭, G♭ in this key.)
3. D major: V^7 (Correctly spelled in this key.)
   D♭ major: Gr^6 (It would be spelled: B♭♭, D♭, F♭, G in this key.)
4. A♭ major: vii°^{7} (It would be spelled: G, B♭, D♭, F♭ in this key.)
   C♭ major: vii°^{7} (Correctly spelled in this key.)
5. A♭ major: Gr^6 (It would be spelled: F♭, A♭, C♭, E in this key.)
   A major: V^7 (Correctly spelled in this key).

Test Yourself 22 (page 369)

1. It is quite chromatic, (but there is some evidence of functional harmony).
2. The most common chord quality is the Mm7th chord (dominant 7th).

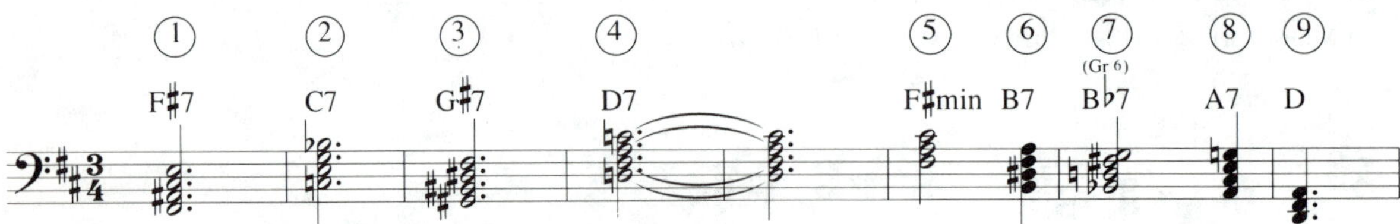

3. Chords 5–6 could be: EM: ii V^7.
   Chords 7–8 could be: DM: Gr^6 V^7.
   Chords 8–9 could be: DM: V^7 I.

   Chords 7–9 create a strong cadence in D major.

4. Chords 1–4 are tied together by several chromatic relationships, most notably the chromatic sequence in the soprano: F♯, G, G♯, A, B♭.
5. On chords 2, 4, 7, and 9 there are accented nonharmonic tones in the soprano.

a.	church modes	
b.	pentatonic scale	4 (upper part)
c.	whole-tone scale	2
d.	9th, 11th, and 13th chords	5
e.	chords of addition and omission	
f.	quartal/quintal chords	1
g.	linear cadence	
h.	third-relationship cadence	3 (enharmonic)
i.	melodic doubling at various intervals	4
j.	parallel chords (planing)	1,3

Test Yourself 23 (page 397)

a.	pandiatonicism	1
b.	polytonality	3,5
c.	dual modality	
d.	shifted tonality	
e.	free tonality	
f.	polychords	1,2,4,5
g.	quartal/quintal chords	5
h.	clusters	2
i.	changing meter	5
j.	asymmetric meter	
k.	nonaccentual rhythms	2

Test Yourself 24 (page 414)

Dallapiccola: *Goethe-Lieder* no. 2 for Mezzo-Soprano and E♭ Clarinet

	I^0	I^1	I^{11}	I^9	I^3	I^8	I^6	I^7	I^2	I^5	I^4	I^{10}	
P^0	G♯	A	G	F	B	E	D	D♯	A♯	C♯	C	F	R^0
P^{11}	G	G♯	F♯	E	A♯	D♯	C♯	D	A	C	B	F	R^{11}
P^1	A	A♯	G♯	F♯	C	F	D♯	E	B	D	C	G	R^1
P^3	B	C	A♯	G♯	D	G	F	F♯	C♯	E	D	A	R^3
P^9	F	F♯	E	D	G♯	C♯	B	C	G	A♯	A	D	R^9
P^4	C	C♯	B	A	D♯	G♯	F♯	G	D	F	E	A	R^4
P^6	D	D♯	C♯	B	F	A♯	G♯	A	E	G	F	C	R^6
P^5	C♯	D	C	A♯	E	A	G	G♯	D♯	F♯	F	B	R^5
P^{10}	F♯	G	F	D♯	A	D	C	C♯	G♯	B	A	E	R^{10}
P^7	D♯	E	D	C	F♯	B	A	A♯	F	G♯	G	C	R^7
P^8	E	F	D♯	C♯	G	C	A♯	B	F♯	A	G	D	R^8
P^2	A♯	B	A	G	C♯	F♯	E	F	C	D♯	D	G♯	R^2
	RI^0	RI^1	RI^{11}	RI^9	RI^3	RI^8	RI^6	RI^7	RI^2	RI^5	RI^4	RI^{10}	

Dallapiccola: *Goethe-Lieder,* no. 2, for Mezzo-Soprano and E♭ Clarinet

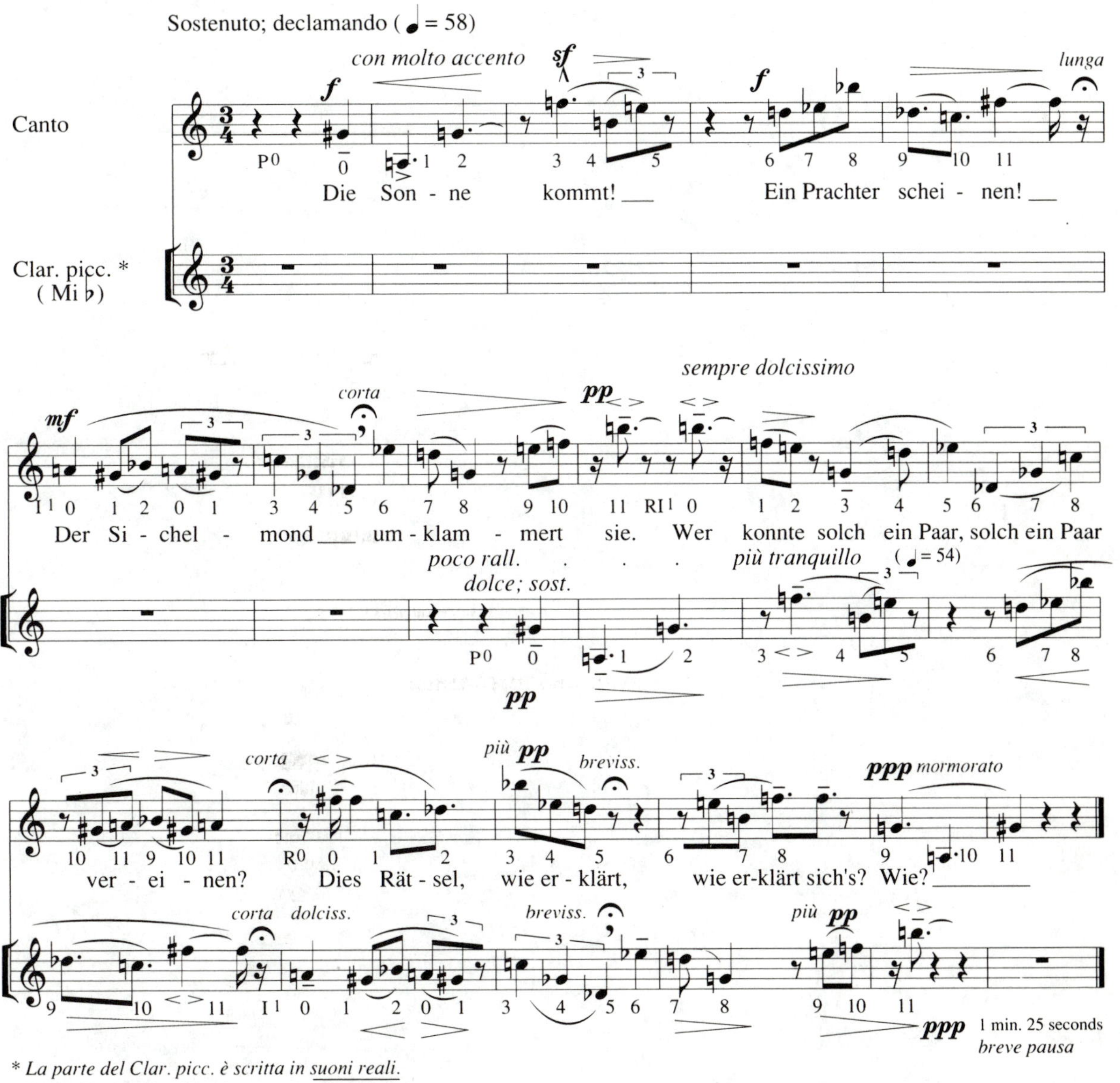

* *La parte del Clar. picc. è scritta in suoni reali.*
(The E♭Clarinet part is written at sounding pitch.)

APPENDIX H

Composers and Works

Composers	Dates	Composition	Page(s)
Babbitt, Milton	1916–	First Composition, from Three Compositions for Piano	416
Bach, J. S.	1685–1750	*Ach Gott, vom Himmel* (Oh, God, from Heaven), BWV 153	127
Bach, J. S.		*Aus meines Herzens Grunde* (From the Depths of My Heart), BWV 269	127
Bach, J. S.		*Der Tag, der ist so freudenreich* (This Day Is So Joyful), BWV 294	121,143
Bach, J. S.		*Du grosser Schmerzensmann* (Thou Great Man of Sorrow), BWV 300	195
Bach, J. S.		*Ermuntre dich, mein schwacher Geist* (Rouse Thyself, My Weak Spirit), BWV 43	120
Bach, J. S.		*Es ist Genug* (It Is Enough), BWV 60	160
Bach, J. S.		*Freu' dich sehr, o meine Seele* (Rejoice, O My Soul), BWV 25	109
Bach, J. S.		Gavotte from English Suite no. 3 in G Minor, BWV 808	243
Bach, J. S.		*Herr Jesu Christ, du höchstes Gut* (Lord Jesus Christ, Thou Highest Good), BWV 113	35
Bach, J. S.		*Jesu, meine Freude* (Jesus, My Joy), BWV 227	274
Bach, J. S.		*Keinen hat Gott verlassen* (God has Forsaken No One), BWV 369	205
Bach, J. S.		*Lass, O Herr, dein Ohr sich neigen* (Bow Thine Ear, O Lord), BWV 372	185
Bach, J. S.		*Lobt Gott, ihr Christen, allzugleich* (Praise God, Ye Christians, All Together), BWV 151	120,139
Bach, J. S.		*Nun danket all Gott* (Now Let Us All Thank God), BWV 386	122,126

Composers	Dates	Composition	Page(s)
Bach, J. S.		*O Ewigkeit, Du Donnerwort* (Oh Eternity, Thou Word of Thunder), BWV 20	186
Bach, J. S.		*O Haupt voll Blut und Wunden* (Oh Head, Bloody and Wounded), BWV 271	141
Bach, J. S.		*O Herre Gott, dein gottlichs Wort* (O God, Our Lord, Thy Holy Word), BWV 184	162
Bach, J. S.		Partita no. 1 in B-flat Major, BWV 825 (Menuett II)	239
Bach, J. S.		St. Matthew's Passion, BWV 244	283
Bach, J. S.		*Straf mich nicht in deinem Zorn* (Punish Me Not in Thy Wrath), BWV 115	139
Bach, J. S.		The Art of Fugue, *Contrapunctus VIII*, BWV 1080	59
Bach, J. S.		*Vater unser in Himmelreich* (Our Father in Heaven), BWV 416	273
Bach, J. S.		*Wahrlich, ich sage euch* (Truly I Say Unto You), BWV 86	220
Bach, J. S.		*Was Gott tut, das is wohlgetan* (What God Does Is Well Done), BWV 69a	109
Bach, J. S.		*Wer nur den lieben Gott lässt walten* (If We Will But Let God Guide Us), BWV 434	113
Bach, J. S.		*Wer weiss, wie nahe mir mein Ende* (Who Knows How Near My End May Be), BWV 166	121,126,128
Bach, J. S.		*Wir Christenleute* (We Christian People), BWV 40	175
Bartók, Béla	1881–1945	"Chromatic Invention" no. 91 from *Mikrokosmos,* vol. 3	394
Bartók, Béla		"Major and Minor" no. 59 from *Mikrokosmos,* vol. 2	375
Bartók, Béla		*Bagatelle I*	399
Beethoven, Ludwig van	1770–1827	Piano Concerto no. 2 in B-flat, op. 19 (third movement)	157
Beethoven, Ludwig van		Piano Sonata in C Minor, op. 13 (*Pathétique*) (third movement)	91
Beethoven, Ludwig van		Piano Sonata in C Minor, op. 13 (*Pathétique*) (first movement)	196
Beethoven, Ludwig van		Piano Sonata in C-sharp Minor (Moonlight), op. 27, no. 2 (first movement)	280
Beethoven, Ludwig van		Piano Sonata in F Minor, op. 2, no. 1 (first movement)	137
Beethoven, Ludwig van		Piano Sonata, op. 10, no. 1 (first movement)	172
Beethoven, Ludwig van		Piano Sonata, op. 110 (second movement)	460
Beethoven, Ludwig van		Piano Sonata, op. 28 (second movement) ("Pastoral")	465

Composers	Dates	Composition	Page(s)
Berg, Alban	1885–1935	"Marie's Lullaby" from *Wozzeck*	379
Bloch, Ernest	1880–1959	"Chanty" from Poems of the Sea	339
Brahms, Johannes	1833–1897	Intermezzo in C, op. 119, no. 3	224
Brahms, Johannes		Lullaby, op. 49, no. 4	118
Brahms, Johannes		Symphony no. 3 in F Major, op. 90 (second movement)	312
Cage, John	1912–	Aria	419
Cesti, Marc A.	1623–1669	*Bella Clori* (Beautiful Chloris)	80
Chopin, Frédéric	1810–1849	Mazurka in D Major, op. 33, no. 3	257
Chopin, Frédéric		Mazurka in F Minor, op. 68, no. 4	165
Chopin, Frédéric		Nocturne, op. 9, no. 1	329
Chopin, Frédéric		Polonaise, op. 26, no. 1	223
Chopin, Frédéric		Polonaise, op. 53	223
Chopin, Frédéric		Prelude, op. 28, no. 4	462
Chopin, Frédéric		Prelude, op. 28, no. 17	331
Chopin, Frédéric		Prelude, op. 28, no. 20	282,320,323
Chopin, Frédéric		Prelude, op. 28, no. 21	324
Chopin, Frédéric		Prelude, op. 28, no. 22	293
Dallapiccola, Luigi	1904–1975	*Goethe-Lieder* no. 2, for Mezzo-Soprano and E-flat Clarinet	414
Davidovsky, Mario	1934–	No. 3 for Cello and Electronic Sound from Synchronisms	421
Debussy, Claude	1862–1918	*Canope* (Canopic Jar) no. 10 from Preludes, Book II	371
Debussy, Claude		*Ce qu'a vu le vent de l'Ouest* (What the West Wind Saw) no. 7 from Preludes, Book I	352
Debussy, Claude		*Claire de lune* (Moonlight)	349
Debussy, Claude		*La Cathedrale Engloutie* (The Engulfed Cathedral) no. 10 from Preludes, Book I	346,356,370
Debussy, Claude		*Le Vent dans la plaine* (The Wind on the Plain) no. 3 from Preludes, Book I	348
Debussy, Claude		Menuet from *Suite Bergamasque*	350
Debussy, Claude		*Minstrels* no. 12 from Preludes, Book I	225
Debussy, Claude		Nocturnes, *"Fêtes"*	371
Debussy, Claude		*Pelléas et Mélisande*	347,370
Debussy, Claude		*Prélude à l'Après-midi d'un faune* (Prelude to "The Afternoon of a Faun")	177
Debussy, Claude		Sarabande from *Pour le Piano* (For the Piano)	353
Debussy, Claude		*Soirée dans Grenade* (Evening in Granada) from *Estampes* (Prints)	345,354
Debussy, Claude		*Voiles* (Sails) no. 2 from Preludes, Book I	43,340,341
Dodge, Charles	1942–	In Celebration	424
Duckworth, William	1943–	"Pitch City"	425
Dufay, Guillaume	1398?–1474	Mass	352
Dvorák, Antonin	1841–1904	Symphony no. 9 in E Minor, op. 95 (from the New World) (first movement)	44

Composers	Dates	Composition	Page(s)
Foster, Stephen	1826–1864	"Camptown Races"	89
Foster, Stephen		"Oh, Susanna"	41
Franck, Cesar	1822–1890	Chorale for Organ no. 2	369
Gershwin, George	1898–1937	"Nice Work if You Can Get It"	228
Gillion, Robert	1942–	Suite no. 1	381
Grieg, Edvard	1843–1907	The Last Spring, op. 34, no. 2	197
Handel, George F.	1685–1759	Chaconne in G Major (with 20/21 Variations)	192
Handel, George F.		Harpsichord Suite no. 6 in F-sharp Minor (Allegro)	185
Hatton, John L.	1809–1886	Duke Street	29
Haydn, Franz Joseph	1732–1809	Piano Sonata in C-sharp Minor, Hob. XVI:36	198
Haydn, Franz Joseph		Piano Sonata in E Minor, Hob. XVI:34 (first movement)	283
Haydn, Franz Joseph		Piano Sonata, Hob. XVI:13 (Minuet)	461
Haydn, Franz Joseph		Piano Sonata, Hob. XVI:41 (second movement)	459
Haydn, Franz Joseph		Quartet, op. 54, no. 1, Hob. III:43	330
Haydn, Franz Joseph		Sonata in A Major, Hob. XVI:5 (second movement)	241
Haydn, Franz Joseph		Symphony in B-flat Major, Hob. I:102 (fourth movement)	87
Haydn, Franz Joseph		Symphony in G (Surprise), Hob. I:94 (third movement)	27
Haydn, Franz Joseph		Keyboard Trio in G Major, Hob. XV:25 (Finale)	88
Herbert, Victor	1859–1924	Gypsy Love Song (from the opera *The Fortune Teller*)	93
Hindemith, Paul	1895–1963	Piano Sonata no. 2 (first movement)	377
Honegger, Paul	1892–1955	Symphony no. 5 *"Di tre re"* (first movement)	399
Ives, Charles	1874–1954	"Lincoln, the Great Commoner" (no. 11 of 114 songs)	398
Ives, Charles		"The Cage" (no. 64 of 114 songs)	379
Ives, Charles		Second Sonata for Violin and Piano, (third movement)	400
Johnson, Robert	1912–1938	Black Smoke Rag	178
Johnson, Robert		Sweet Home Chicago	152
Joplin, Scott	1868–1917	"Bink's Waltz"	295
Joplin, Scott		"Maple Leaf Rag"	161
Joplin, Scott		"The Augustine Club Waltz"	304
Lucerne, William	1949–	Dirge	382
Lucier, Alvin	1931–	"I am sitting in a room"	422
McCartney, Paul	1942–	"Yesterday"	265
Mercer, Johnny (and Harold Arlen)	1890–1976	"My Shining Hour"	312

Composers	Dates	Composition	Page(s)
Monteverdi, Claudio	1567–1643	*Lasciateme Morire* (Oh, Let Me Die) from *Lamento d'Arianna*	165
Morley, Thomas	1557–1602	"Nancie" (from the Fitzwilliam Virginal Book)	94
Mozart, Leopold	1719–1787	Symphony in C (Toy) (Attributed to Haydn)	88
Mozart, Wolfgang Amadeus	1756–1791	*Das Veilchen* (The Violet), K. 476	293
Mozart, Wolfgang Amadeus		*Don Giovanni,* K. 527 (Act I, Scene XIV)	173
Mozart, Wolfgang Amadeus		Fantasia in D Minor, K. 397	281
Mozart, Wolfgang Amadeus		*Phantasie,* K. 475	223
Mozart, Wolfgang Amadeus		Piano Sonata in A Major, K. 331 (third movement)	194
Mozart, Wolfgang Amadeus		Piano Sonata in A Minor, K. 310 (third movement)	33
Mozart, Wolfgang Amadeus		Piano Sonata in C Major, K. 309 (second movement)	88,92
Mozart, Wolfgang Amadeus		Piano Sonata in D Major, K. 284 (first movement)	88
Mozart, Wolfgang Amadeus		Piano Sonata in D Major, K. 284 (third movement)	175,193,197,248,463
Mozart, Wolfgang Amadeus		Piano Sonata in G Major, K. 283 (third movement)	172
Mozart, Wolfgang Amadeus		Sonata for Violin and Piano, K. 379 (second movement)	163
Oliveros, Pauline	1932–	Sonic Meditations I, "Teach Yourself to Fly"	425
Parker, Charlie	1920–1955	*Au Privave*	230
Penderecki, Krzysztof	1933–	*Threnos Den Opfern von Hiroshima* (Threnody to the Victims of Hiroshima)	427
Pisk, Paul	1893–	"Nocturnal Interlude" from New Music for the Piano	380
Poulenc, Francis	1899–1963	*"Laudamus Te"* from *Gloria*	398
Prokofieff, Sergey	1891–1953	Moonlit Meadows (from Music for Children), op. 65, no. 12	285
Prokofieff, Sergey		Piano Sonata no. 8 in B-flat Major, op. 84 (second movement)	376
Purcell, Henry	1659–1695	"Thy Hand, Belinda" from Dido and Aeneas, Z. 626	42
Purcell, Henry		Chaconne (from the opera *King Arthur,* Act V)	94
Purcell, Henry		Harpsichord Suite 8 in F Major, Z. 669	221
Ravel, Maurice	1875–1937	*L'Enfant et Les Sortilèges* (The Child and His Fantasies)	371
Ravel, Maurice		*Ma Mere l'Oye* (Mother Goose)	40
Ravel, Maurice		*Sonatine* (first movement)	295,344,349
Ravel, Maurice		*Sonatine* (second movement)	188,342,348
Ravel, Maurice		*Valses nobles et sentimentales* (Noble and Sentimental Waltzes)	303,344

Composers	Dates	Composition	Page(s)
Reich, Steve	1936–	Four Organs	429
Respighi, Ottorino	1879–1936	*Trittico Botticelliano* (Botticelli Triptych)	339
Rimsky-Korsakoff, Nicholas	1844–1908	*Plenivshis' rozoy, solovey* (The Nightingale Charmed by the Rose), op. 2, no. 2	284
Rogers, Richard	1902–1979	"Mountain Greenery"	227
Rubenstein, Anton	1829–1894	*Gelb Rollt mir zu Füssen* (Golden at my Feet)	187
Satie, Eric	1866–1925	*Gymnopedie* no. 2	351
Schmidt, Harvey	1929–	"Try to Remember" (from the musical The Fantastiks)	95,188,264
Schubert, Franz	1797–1828	*Das Fischermädchen* (The Fishermaiden) from *Schwangesang* (Swan Song), D. 957, no. 10	331
Schubert, Franz		*Das Wirtshaus* (The Inn), from *Winterreise* (Winter's Journey), op. 89, no. 21, D. 911	272
Schubert, Franz		*Der Doppelgänger* (The Double) from *Schwanengesang* (Swan Song), D. 957, no. 13	284
Schubert, Franz		*Der Müller und der Bach* (The Miller and the Brook) from *Die Schöne Müllerin* (The Beautiful Miller's Daughter), op. 25, no. 19, D. 795	280
Schubert, Franz		*Erlkönig* (Erl King), D. 328	161
Schubert, Franz		Impromptu, op. 90, no. 1, D. 899	90
Schubert, Franz		Piano Sonata in A Major, D. 959	100
Schubert, Franz		String Quartet in A Minor (first movement)	326
Schubert, Franz		Symphony in B minor, ("Unfinished"), D. 759 (first movement)	322
Schubert, Franz		Waltz, op. 9, no. 14, D. 365	330
Schubert, Franz		Waltz, op. 9, no. 22, D. 365	320
Schubert, Franz		*Wanderers' Nachtlied* (Wanderers' Night Song) II, op. 93, no. 2, D. 768	273
Schuman, William	1910–	No. 2 from Three Score Set	378
Schumann, Robert	1810–1856	*Am leuchtenden Sommermorgen* (On a Shining Summer Morning), from *Dichterliebe* (Poet's Love), op. 48, no. 12	321
Schumann, Robert		*Ich kann's nicht fassen* (I Cannot Comprehend) from *Frauenlieben und Leben* (Woman's Life and Loves), op. 42, no. 3	294
Schumann, Robert		*Im Wundershönen Monat Mai* (In the Wonderful Month of May), from *Dichterliebe* (Poet's Love), op. 48, no. 1	323
Schumann, Robert		*Kinder Sonata* no. 1	256

Composers	Dates	Composition	Page(s)
Schumann, Robert		*Kleine Studie* (Short Study) from Album for the Young, op. 68, no. 14	302
Schumann, Robert		*Papillons*, op. 2, no. 12	114
Strauss, Richard	1864–1949	*Allerseelen* (All Souls Day), op. 10, no. 8	336
Strauss, Richard		*Zeitlose* (The Saffron), op. 10, no. 7	337
Stravinsky, Igor	1882–1971	*March du Soldat* (Soldier's March) from *L'Histoire du Soldat* (The Tale of the Soldier)	16,383
Stravinsky, Igor		Sonata for Two Pianos (second movement, Var. 1)	374
Stravinsky, Igor		Triumphal March of the Devil from *L'Histoire du Soldat* (The Tale of the Soldier)	381
Tchaikovsky, Peter	1840–1893	Symphony no. 5 in E minor, op. 64 (second movement)	141
Varèse, Edgard	1885–1965	*Poème Électronique*	420
Ventadorn, Bernart de	d. 1195	*Be m'an perdut* (Indeed All My Friends)	251
Wagner, Richard	1813–1883	Overture to the opera *Rienzi*	176
Wagner, Richard		Prelude to Act I of *Tristan und Isolde*	324,334
Wagner, Richard		*Tristan und Isolde,* Act II	303
Webern, Anton	1883–1945	*Wie bin ich froh!* (How Happy I Am!), no. 1 from *Drei Lieder* (Three Songs), op. 25	403
Wolf, Hugo	1860–1903	*Das verlassene Mägdelein* (The Forsaken Maiden) from *Gedichte von Eduard Mörike*	311,338
Wolf, Hugo		*Der Knabe und das Immlein* (The Boy and the Bee) from *Gedichte von Eduard Mörike*	335
Wolf, Hugo		*Wiegenlied* (Cradlesong)	276
Xenakis, Iannis	1922–	ST/10-1, 080262	423
Ziebart, John	1952–	Overture	375
Zipoli, Domenico	1688–1726	Toccata	292

GLOSSARY

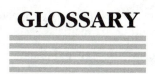

accent Emphasis on one note. Accents are of three types: dynamic, agogic, and tonic.

accidental Any of the symbols such as sharps, flats, and naturals, which are used to raise or lower the pitch of a note.

adagio A slow tempo.

additive rhythm A rhythmic system in which relatively rapid rhythmic units of equal duration are grouped together into pulses of unequal duration. An example would be 5/8 meter, consisting of two pulses with 3+2 or 2+3 eighth notes.

aggregate The total. (Example: the first six tones of a twelve-tone series form an aggregate with the second six tones.)

agogic accent An accent created when one note is longer than surrounding notes.

aleatory (also aleatoric) Interchangeable with indeterminacy. (See indeterminacy.)

allegro A fast tempo (It., lively or merry).

altered chord A chord that contains one or more factors that are not part of the prevailing diatonic system.

altered dominant A dominant triad or a 7th chord that contains a raised or lowered 5th, or in one instance, a lowered 3rd.

analog An exact representation of something in a medium different from that of the original.

andante A moderately slow tempo (It., walking).

arpeggiation Playing the notes of a chord one after another. The horizontalization of a chord.

asymmetric meter Meter in which the beats are not grouped into units divisible by two or three (examples: 7/8 and 5/4 meters). Also known as irregular or combination meter.

augmented 6th chords A type of altered chord that contains the interval of an augmented 6th. The three most common types are the Italian, French, and German 6th chords.

avant-garde	Music or composer characterized primarily by unorthodox or experimental ideas. Applies as well to other art media.
bar line	A vertical line drawn across the staff to indicate measures in a musical composition.
basso continuo	Same as figured bass. Usually performed by a cello, viola da gamba, or bassoon playing the bass line, while a harpsichord or piano plays the bass notes and adds chords as indicated by the figures (numbers).
basso ostinato	See ground.
beam	A broad, straight line connecting two or more eighth notes.
beat	The steady pulse of music. Beats form the basis of the sense of musical time.
best normal order	If a set of pitches contains two larger intervals of the same size, the best normal order is the arrangement that is most densely packed to the left of the set. (See normal order.)
bitonality	See polytonality.
blue tone	Blue tones (or "worried" notes) are tones that are between the diatonic and flatted 3rds and 7ths, which characterize the blues scale.
blues	A type of popular music coming from black vocal music, which developed in the United States in the early twentieth century, characterized by repeated chord progressions and the blues scale.
blues progression	Any of the repeated chord progressions that characterize the blues. A typical blues progression consists of twelve measures of tonic, subdominant and dominant triads with minor 7ths. (See"twelve-bar blues—standard.")
blues scale	A major scale with a flat 3rd and 7th. It must be remembered that the flat 3rd and 7th were sometimes "worried" notes; thus, their pitches did not always correspond to equal-tempered tuning.
blues scale with added flat 5th	A classic blues scale (flat 3rd and 7th) but with an additional flat 5th. This scale is a somewhat later development in blues. Flat 9ths are also included on occasion.
boogie-woogie	A modern blues style created for instrumental application. Boogie-woogie is characterized by an adaptation of the ground bass principle—a repetitious bass figure that suggests the blues chord progression.
borrowed chord	A chord borrowed from the parallel major or minor key. (Example: A, C, E♭ is a borrowed chord from [G minor] chord in G major.)
cadence—authentic	A cadence consisting of the dominant-to-tonic harmonic progression.
cadence—deceptive	A cadence made up of a harmonic progression from the dominant to a chord other than the tonic. V to VI is the one most often found.

cadence—half A cadence consisting of a harmonic progression ending on the dominant. Most half cadences conform with one of the following: IV to V, I to V, or II to V.

cadence—harmonic A formula, consisting of two chords, which brings a phrase, section, or composition to a conclusion.

cadence—linear See linear cadence.

cadence—plagal A cadence made up of a harmonic progression from subdominant to tonic. The Amen cadence (IV to I) is a typical example.

canon A melody that can be sung against itself in imitation.

chance music Interchangeable with indeterminacy. See indeterminacy.

changing meters Meter changes within a composition to show rhythmic patterns more clearly than could a single constant meter.

chorale Lutheran melodies that are the counterparts of English hymn tunes. These melodies were adapted from (1) well-known popular songs of the period, (2) Catholic hymn tunes, and (3) German hymn melodies predating the Reformation.

chord A combination of three or more pitches sounding at the same time.

chordal texture A texture in which the musical material is concentrated into chords with relatively little melodic activity.

chord cluster A chord with three or more factors, each of which is no more than a whole step from its adjacent factor. (Example: C, C-sharp, D, and E when sounded together is a chord cluster.)

chords of addition and omission Chords with added or deleted tones.

chromatic mediant chords The altered mediant and submediant triads—and 7th chords on occasion. (Example: E, G♯, and B = III in C major.) Not common in any style, but found most often in the late Romantic period.

circle of fifths A clockface arrangement of the twelve pitches in the order of the number of accidentals in the key signature.

circle progression A common chord progression that provides a structural basis for most tonal music, consisting of a series of chords with descending fifth root relationships.

clef—alto A C clef or "movable" clef. The indentation in the signature signifies that middle C is on the middle line of the staff.

clef—bass Called the F clef because dots are placed on the fourth line of the staff to indicate the F below middle C.

clef—soprano A C clef or movable clef. The indentation signifies that middle C is on the bottom line of the staff.

clef—tenor A C or movable clef. The indentation in the sign signifies that middle C is on the fourth line of the staff.

clef—treble Called the G clef because the curved line of the signature terminates on the second line of the staff to establish G above middle C.

closely related keys The keys that differ from the tonic key by no more than one accidental. In major: IV, V, ii, iii, and vi; in minor: iv, v, VI, VII, and III.

cluster See chord cluster.

combination meter Se asymmetric meter.

combinatoriality The combination of the first hexachords (first six tones) of two different set forms to produce all twelve tones. (See aggregate.)

common chord In a modulation a common chord is one that is diatonic to both keys (the original and the new).

common time Another name for a 4/4 meter signature. This meter is often indicated with a large capital C as a meter signature.

compound division The division of the beat into three equal parts.

compound meter A meter in which the beats have a compound division.

computer synthesis The synthesis of sound directly by digital computer.

consonance A combination of sounds producing a feeling of repose, or little desire for resolution. Consonances in tonal music are: P unison, P5, P8, M3, m6, m3, M6.

conventional four-chord formula In popular music, a harmonic progression pattern containing four chords. Most four-chord patterns occupy two measures. Example: I vi ii^7 V^7. Such formulas occur so often in popular songs as to be critical components of style.

cross relation A conflict, produced by a tone in one voice followed in another voice by the same tone (same letter name) altered a half step. Example: D-sharp in one voice followed immediately by D-natural in another voice.

cut time Another name for the 2/2 meter signature. This meter is indicated with a large capital C with a vertical line drawn through it. (See common time.)

degree One of the notes in a scale. Degrees are usually numbered starting with the tonic (the lowest tone of the scale).

derived set A twelve-tone set different in order from another, but retaining some particular characteristics of the original.

diatonic Any one of the common scales made of whole steps and half steps in a particular pattern.

dissonance A combination of sounds producing harsh or discordant results, or increasing the desire for resolution. Dissonances in tonal music are: M2, m2, M7, m7, P4, and all diminished and augmented intervals.

divisive rhythm A rhythmic system in which regularly recurring pulses of equal duration are divided in various ways. Most western music is characterized by divisive rhythm. (see: additive rhythm)

dodecaphonic Term used to describe twelve-tone serial writing.

dominant The fifth scale degree of a diatonic scale.

double flat A symbol, written to the left of a note head, which lowers the pitch by a whole step.

double period A succession of four phrases in which each of the first three is punctuated by a half cadence and the fourth is terminated by an authentic cadence.

double sharp A symbol, written to the left of a note, which raises the pitch by a whole step.

dual modality Simultaneous use of major and minor mode or combinations of church modes. Usually the two modes have the same tonic or final.

duodecuple scale See scale—duodecuple.

duple meter A meter consisting of two beats.

dyad Two pitches. Generally used when describing segments of a twelve-tone series. Has both melodic and harmonic connotations.

dynamic accent An accent created when one note is louder than surrounding notes. Often indicated with the accent sign.

eclecticism Derives from the word eclectic. In music it refers to the borrowing of devices or ideas from existing styles.

electronic music Music that is electronically produced and processed.

eleventh chord A superposition of five 3rds—one 3rd above the 9th of a 9th chord. (Example: G, B, D, F, A, C = V^{11} in C major.)

elision A musical situation in which the end of one pattern overlaps or coincides with the beginning of the next pattern.

embellishing tone Melodic decorations and ornaments to structural and secondary tones.

enharmonic Two tones having the same pitch but different spelling. Example: F-sharp and G-flat are enharmonic.

expanded monophonic texture A monophonic texture in which a single melody is doubled at various intervals, often in octaves.

expressionism A reaction to impressionism. Its proponents hoped to create music that would be an expression of their inner world in contrast to the impressionists, who sought to represent their impressions of the external world.

extended technique Usually refers to traditional instruments that are played in unusual ways, but may also include amplifiers and noninstruments such as sirens and auto horns.

figured bass A bass melody with numbers and musical symbols beneath it to indicate the chords to be played. Known also as basso continuo and thorough bass. A device of the seventeenth to mid-eighteenth centuries.

flag The curved shaded line extending from the end of a stem used to indicate an eighth or shorter note.

free atonality A kind of atonal writing that allows free use of the twelve tones of the chromatic scale, but does not order or prescribe the arrangement as in serial technique.

free tonality Term used to designate music that contains a definite tonal center, but which is not related to traditional major or minor keys.

French augmented 6th chord See augmented 6th chords.

fusion A form of popular music beginning in the 1970s that blended elements of jazz and rock.

German augmented 6th chord See augmented 6th chords.

grand staff A combination of the treble and bass clefs, and is commonly used to notate keyboard music.

graphic notation A score where musical textures and events are implied through the use of graphic analogs (analogies). A dark area on a score may imply loud sounds, while a white area suggests silence.

ground A short melodic figure of four to eight measures maintained in the lowest voice and repeated throughout a composition. Same as basso ostinato.

half step The smallest interval on the standard keyboard. The interval between two adjacent keys (including both black and white keys) is a half step.

harmonic progression Movement from one chord to the next; a succession of chords or a chord progression.

harmonic rhythm The frequency of harmonic changes in a composition; the rate of chord change.

harmony The study of simultaneously sounding tones or concern with the chordal structure of a musical composition.

hexachord Six pitches. In the Middle Ages and the Renaissance period, referred to six-tone segment of the total diatonic ranger, or gamut. Generally used when describing segments of the twelve-tone series. Has both melodic and harmonic connotations.

homophonic (texture) A single, clearly defined melody with chordal accompaniment. Examples: a popular song, a Mozart minuet, a Johann Strauss waltz, and nearly all music of the nineteenth century.

imitation The repetition of a melody or melodic group in close succession but in a different voice; the repetition of a melody at a different pitch level in a polyphonic texture.

imitation—real An imitation with no modifications except for the usual diatonic adjustment of half and whole steps. The exact transposition of a melody at different pitch levels.

improvise To extemporize; to play on the spur of the moment. To perform without a prepared text or composed material.

incipient three-part form See three-part form—incipient.

indeterminacy Indefinite or uncertain. Refers, in music, to some aspect of a composition that is beyond the composer's conscious control and is thus left to chance.

interval The difference in pitch between two tones.

interval class Intervals (other than the unison) may be grouped in six interval classes by the number of half steps between the two pitch classes. In this system only the numbers 1 through 6 are used.

interval—compound Any interval greater than an octave. Usually compound intervals are expressed as simple equivalents (the octave is subtracted). Example: a major tenth interval—a compound major third.

inversion (of a melody) A procedure for deriving another form of a given melody. An ascending interval in a melody becomes a descending interval (and vice versa) of the same size in the inversion of the melody.

inversion (of a twelve-tone series) The reversal of the direction (up or down) of each successive tone of the prime series, starting with the first tone.

inversion (of intervals) Occurs when the lower tone forming the interval becomes the upper tone (or vice versa). Example: major third becomes a minor sixth when inverted at the octave.

irregular meter See asymmetric meter.

Italian augmented 6th chord See augmented 6th chords.

jazz A popular music influenced by the blues, popular song, and other musical genre. Jazz is characterized by highly sophisticated improvised melodic lines over chord progressions (changes) with a steady beat and considerable syncopation.

key Music that is based on a major or minor scale is said to be in a key. Keys are identified by their tonic.

key signature An arrangement of accidentals at the beginning of a staff that indicate the pitches that will be most common in a piece of music. Key signatures are associated with particular major and minor scales.

keynote See tonic.

largetto A tempo slightly faster than largo.

largo A very slow tempo. (It., broad)

ledger line A small line written above or below the staff to extend its range.

linear cadence Melodic lines that converge or diverge at the cadence point. Oblique motion is also possible.

linear harmony Harmony that results from melodic motion without regard for traditional (functional) harmonic progression.

major scale A diatonic scale with half steps between the third and fourth and the seventh and eighth scale degrees.

measure One unit of meter, consisting of a number of accented and unaccented beats. A measure is indicated in music notation by bar lines.

melody An organized succession of pitches.

meter The system of regularly recurring pulses most often grouped by periodic accents. Example: 3/4 meter indicates that the beats are grouped by three's with the quarter note representing one beat or pulse.

meter signature A symbol placed at the beginning of a composition to indicate the meter of the piece. Meter signatures usually consist of two numbers, the lower of which indicates a note value (2, 4, 8) and the upper the number of these notes per measure.

meter—asymmetrical Those meters in which the pulse cannot be divided into equal groupings of two, three, or four in the measure. Examples: 7/4, 5/4, 11/8, etc.

meter—compound Meter in which the basic pulse may be subdivided into groups of three. Examples: 6/8, 9/8, 12/8, etc.

meter—simple Meter signatures whose upper numbers are 1, 2, 3, or 4. The basic subdivision of the pulse is in duplets.

middle C — The C nearest to the middle of the piano keyboard. This note is an important point of reference because it is on the ledger line between the treble and bass staves on the grand staff.

MIDI — Musical Instrument Digital Interface, a communications standard for connecting synthesizers to computers and other synthesizers.

mikropolyphonie — A contemporary music style featuring many-voiced, rhythmically intricate, highly chromatic counterpoint.

minimalism — The gradual process of unfolding a very limited (minimal) body of motivic material, often with a high degree of literal repetition. The material is often simple, tonal or modal, and largely diatonic.

modal mixture — A blending of the resources of the parallel major and minor scales that often results in modal ambiguity.

mode—Aeolian — A system of seven tones with the same arrangement as the natural minor key (A to A on the white keys of the piano). Not one of the original church modes; developed with the advent of polyphony.

mode—Dorian — A system of seven tones with the same arrangement as from D to D on the white keys of the piano.

mode—Ionian — A system of seven tones with the same arrangement as our major key scale (C to C on the white keys of the piano). Not one of the original church modes; developed with the advent of polyphony.

mode—Locrian — A system of seven tones with the same arrangement as from B to B on the white keys of the piano. Seldom found in music literature because of tritone relationships.

mode—Lydian — A system of seven tones with the same arrangement as from F to F on the white keys of the piano.

mode—Mixolydian — A system of seven tones with the same arrangement as from G to G on the white keys of the piano.

mode—Phrygian — A system of seven tones with the same arrangement as from E to E on the white keys of the piano.

modes—authentic — Associated with Gregorian chants. The octave ranges of the Dorian, Phyrgian, Lydian, and Mixolydian modes coincide with each modal scale, each with the final as first note.

modes—church (or medieval, or ecclesiastical) — Classified at the time of Pope Gregory I (about 600 A.D.). The church modes consist of a system of eight scales derived from the codification of liturgical chants. These scales served as the basis for musical composition until the sixteenth century.

modes—Plagal — Associated with Gregorian chants. The octave ranges of Hypodorian, Hypophrygian, Hypolydian, and Hypomixolydian modes begin a P4th below and extend to the P5th above the final.

modified twelve-bar jazz blues Variants of the standard twelve-bar blues and twelve-bar jazz blues progressions. Most variants incorporated progressions found in the popular songs of the period. In some variants the harmonic rhythm was increased to more than one chord per measure.

monophonic texture A musical texture consisting of a single melodic idea, which may be doubled in various ways. (See "expanded monophonic texture.")

musique concrète Employs "live" sounds from the environment that are recorded and processed or modified by tape techniques such as splicing and varying the speed of the tape. One of the early types of electronic music.

nationalism The use of materials that are identifiably national or regional in character, including folk music, folk stories, myths, or literature.

natural A symbol written to the left of a note head which cancels a previous sharp or flat.

natural minor scale The basic form of a minor scale with half steps between the following scale degrees: 2–3 and 5–6.

Neapolitan 6th chord A major triad based on the lowered 2nd degree of the major or minor scale. (Example: D♭, F, A♭ = N in C major.) Since the chord is most often found in first inversion, it is called the Neapolitan 6th.

neighboring tone A nonharmonic tone that moves a step away from a chord tone and returns to the same tone. (See upper neighbor, lower neighbor.)

neoclassicism A reaction to the freedom and lack of order in the form and content of compositions of the Romantic period. A return to discipline, form, and symmetry of the Classical period. Followed immediately by the Post-Romantic and Impressionistic period.

neume A symbol used in the early notation of music (circa A.D. 650 to A.D. 1350).

new-age music A form of popular music in the 1980s consisting of a blend of minimalism, jazz, and electronic music. Also called "space music."

ninth chord A superposition of four 3rds—one 3rd above the 7th of the 7th chord. (Example: G, B, D, F, A = V9 in C major.)

nonaccentual rhythms Absence of dynamic accents.

nondominant 7th chord A diatonic 7th chord that does not have dominant function. Since dominant and leading-tone 7th chords are considered to have dominant function, then all others are nondominant 7th chords.

nonfunctional harmony Harmony that is more the result of voice leading than of harmonic progression within a major or minor key. (See linear harmony.)

nonharmonic tone A tone that does not fit into the surrounding harmony. (See passing tone, neighboring tone, suspension, appoggiatura, anticipation, changing tone, escape tone, pedal tone, retardation.)

nonharmonic tone—anticipation A nonharmonic tone that anticipates a chord tone in the following chord. Anticipations are normally approached by step and the anticipated tone is repeated in the following chord.

nonharmonic tone—appoggiatura A nonharmonic tone preceded by a leap and resolved by step.

nonharmonic tone—changing tone Two successive nonharmonic tones. Leads from a chord tone by step, leaps to another nonharmonic tone, then leads to a chord tone by step.

nonharmonic tone—escape tone A nonharmonic tone that is approached by step and resolved by leap.

nonharmonic tone—neighboring tone A nonharmonic tone that is approached by step and left by step in the opposite direction.

nonharmonic tone—passing tone A nonharmonic tone that is approached by step and left by step in the same direction.

nonharmonic tone—pedal tone (pedal point) A held or repeated note, usually in the lowest-sounding voice, which alternates between consonant and dissonant relationships with the chords above it.

nonharmonic tone—retardation A nonharmonic tone similar to a suspension except that the resolution is upward instead of downward.

nonharmonic tone—suspension A nonharmonic tone that is held over from a previous chord tone and resolves downward by step. The three phases of suspension are preparation, suspension, and resolution.

nontransposing instruments Instruments in which the produced pitch is the same as the written pitch.

normal order The fundamental ordered form of a set.

notation—tablature Notation using letters, numbers, or a diagram. In the case of the vihuela, lute, and guitar, the diagrams frequently represented the strings of the instruments.

notation-mensural Measured notation. First drawn up by Franco of Cologne in the thirteenth century. Bar lines did not appear until the seventeenth century.

octatonic scale An eight-tone scale.

order number The number that represents the position of any given tone in the twelve-tone series. (Example: the 3rd tone in a given series is order number 2—remember the first tone is always 0.)

ostinato A short musical pattern that is repeated throughout a given passage. Ostinatos generally are a part of the supporting or accompanying material in a piece of music.

palindrome A literary term referring to a sentence that reads the same backward as forward. (Example: "Madam, I'm Adam.")

pandiatonicism The use of the tones of a diatonic scale in such a way that each tone is stripped of its usual function in the key.

parallel chords Chords in which all factors or voices move in parallel motion. Parallel chords are sometimes diatonic and sometimes chromatic.

parameter Independent (of each other) variables. In music the word "parameter" most often refers to such basic components as pitch, melody, rhythm, timbre, etc.

pentachord Five pitches. Generally used when describing segments of the twelve-tone series. Has both melodic and harmonic connotations.

pentatonic scale A five-tone scale. (Example: C, D, E, G, A, C.)

permutation A term used in connection with the twelve-tone series and involving a change of the order of the set.

pitch class All notes of the same name on the keyboard. A more recent term for pitch. Considered more broad because pitch class includes octave duplications while a pitch designates only a single sound.

pitch-class numbers Those numbers that represent the intervallic relationship between the first tone and any given tone of the twelve-tone series.

planing See parallel chords.

polychord Simultaneous use of two chords. Spacing is important in the use of polychords, since the chords must be spaced sufficiently apart to be heard as two distinct entities.

polyphonic texture A musical texture consisting of more than one melodic line.

polytonality Simultaneous use of two or more tonalities.

prestissimo As fast as possible. Faster than presto.

presto A very fast tempo. Faster than allegro.

prime form The form of the normal order of a set, which has the first pitch designated as "0".

prime series (in twelve-tone technique) The twelve-tone series as it is originally constructed.

primitivism A reaction to the refined and fragile music of such composers as Debussy. Its proponents sought to eliminate the subtlety and gentility of previous music and emphasize the mechanistic, violent, and more earthy aspects of music.

quadruple meter A meter consisting of four beats.

quartal chords Chords constructed through a superposition of 4ths rather than the conventional 3rds as in tertian harmony.

quintal chords Chords constructed through a superposition of 5ths rather than the conventional 3rds as in tertian harmony.

retrograde A melody, subject, motive, etc., in reverse order, or backwards. Cancrizans is another term meaning retrograde.

retrograde (of a twelve-tone series) The prime series sounded in reverse order from last to first. Symbol for the retrograde set is R^0. It is important to remember that R^0 begins on the last pitch of P^0.

retrograde inversion (of a twelve-tone series) The inversion of the prime series in reverse order from the last pitch to the first. Symbol for the retrograde inversion is RI^0. It is important to remember that the RI^0 form begins on the last tone of I^0.

rhythm The movement of music in time. A pattern of uneven duration over the steady background of the beat.

rock music The primary form of popular music in the mid-twentieth century; characterized by a heavy bass beat. Beginning as "rock 'n' roll" in the 1950s, rock came to mean any form of popular music in the 1970s. (See fusion.)

romanticism The period of musical writing from roughly 1825, or, more precisely, from 1803 to 1900. Characterized by a tendency to accentuate the impulsive, the unusual, the adventuresome, the impetuous, and the passionate attitudes toward musical composition.

round A canon at the unison. One singer begins the round and, upon reaching a certain point, is joined by a second singer who begins at the beginning. Rounds are usually in three or four parts.

scale A summary of the pitch material of a piece of music arranged in order from the lowest to the highest pitches.

scale—duodecuple The twelve tones of the octave, each with equal status. Although the older term "chromatic scale" also denotes twelve tones, its relation to key and tonal systems makes it inappropriate for present-day purposes.

sequence A melodic idea consisting of a short motive restated one or more times at different pitch levels (generally at the interval of a second or third).

serialism An extension of the twelve-tone technique, where other parameters such as rhythm, dynamics, articulations, and timbres (as well as pitch) are given a specific order.

set A collection of pitch classes, usually without regard to their order. (See normal order.)

set type Sets are classified according to the interval between the first pitch class of the set and each successive pitch class. The lowest pitch is labeled 0 and the remaining pitches are named by the interval they form with the lowest pitch.

seventh chord A triad with an added factor a 3rd above the 5th (7th above the root).

shifted tonality Sudden tonality change without preparation or modulation in the traditional sense.

simple division The division of the beat into two equal parts.

simple meter A meter that has a simple division of the beat.

solfeggio A system used to help singers to remember the pitches of the various scale degrees in a diatonic scale.

sound mass Denotes a texture of such density and complexity that the parts cannot be distinguished individually.

space music See new-age music.

spacing The interval distance between voices or factors of a chord.

staff A group of five horizontal lines on which music is notated.

standard twelve-bar blues Twelve-bar units repeated as many times as lyrics dictate. Accompanying each twelve-bar unit is a routine harmonic progression (with several variants): I, IV, I, V, IV, I, V.

step progression Selected tones from a melody that give it direction. Certain tones (usually not adjacent) proceed by stepwise motion either up or down to provide direction to the melody.

stochastic music Music written according to a system based on probability distribution.

subdivision The division of the beat in simple meter into four equal parts or in compound meter into six equal parts.

swing The rhythmic style of most jazz, in which the division of the beats is uneven and there is considerable stress on the notes between beats.

syllabic Describes a style of vocal writing in which one pitch is used for each syllable of a text. It contrasts with melismatic writing, which employs many notes per syllable.

syncopation A rhythm in which normally unaccented beats are stressed either through agogic or dynamic accent.

tactus The name given to the pulse in medieval and renaissance music. The tactus was said to be equal to the heart rate of a person breathing normally (in the range of sixty to seventy beats per minute).

temperament—equal A system of tuning in which an octave is divided into twelve equal half steps. This leaves no pure intervals except the octave, but makes possible the use of all twelve keys.

temperament—just A system of tuning in which both the fifths and thirds are pure (according to the natural overtone series).

temperament—mean-tone A system of tuning in which the pure fifths are compromised in favor of pure thirds.

temperament—Pythagorean A system of tuning in which the tones of the scale are arrived at by selecting a series of twelve pure fifths. This, of course, does not provide 2:1 octaves.

tempo The speed of the beat in music, which may be expressed in general terms or in beats per minute.

tempus imperfectum A rhythmic system of the Medieval and Renaissance periods in which rhythmic values were divided into two parts.

tempus perfectum A rhythmic system of the Medieval and Renaissance periods in which rhythmic values were divided into three parts.

ternary form See three-part form.

tessitura The average range of a particular voice or instrument in a composition. If a tessitura is "high," the notes tend to be in the higher extreme of the total range of that voice or instrument.

tetrachord Modern interpretation a four-tone scale segment. The term was adapted from Greek music where it referred to a four-tone scale segment in descending order.

texture A term which refers to the way the melodic, rhythmic, and harmonic materials are woven together in a piece of music.

theme A melodic figure or phrase that is the basis for a composition or section of a composition.

third relationship Relationship of a 3rd between roots of adjacent chords. When prominent progressions employ 3rd relationship in concentration or in succession, particularly ascending, tonal emphasis is decreased.

third-relationship cadence A cadence in which the roots of the two chords lie in 3rd relationship.

thirteenth chord	A superposition of six 3rds—one above the 11th of an 11th chord. (Example: G, B, D, F, A, C, E = V^{13} in C major.)
three-part form	A form most often found in homophonic music, but existing as well in three-part polyphony, the first and third parts of which are either the same or nearly so. Usually designated by the letters A B A, three-part form is also known as ternary form.
three-part form—incipient	Related both to two- and three-part form. Consists of three sections with the first and third similar, but with a middle section that is often shorter than the other two and that is frequently repeated along with the third section.
tie	A curved line connecting two notes, which indicates that they are to be played as a single note.
tonality	A system of tones (example: the tones of a major scale) used in such a way that one tone becomes central, and the remaining tones assume a hierarchy based on their intervallic relationship to the central tone or tonal center.
tone	A musical sound of definite pitch.
tonic	The keynote of a piece of music. The tone that is felt to be a point of rest, where the music can logically conclude.
tonic accent	An accent created when one note is higher or lower in pitch than surrounding notes.
tonicized chord	A chord that functions temporarily as a tonic (having been preceded by a secondary dominant).
total serialism	All (or at least most) of the elements or dimensions of a twelve-tone serial composition are serialized. (Example: serialization of pitch, intensity, duration, and timbre.)
transposing instruments	Instruments that produce a pitch other than that written.
transposition	The process of rewriting a piece of music or a scale so that it sounds higher or lower in pitch. This involves raising or lowering each pitch by the same interval.
triad	Strictly speaking, a triad is any three-tone chord. In tertian harmony, a triad is a chord build in superposed thirds. The four types of triads are major, minor, diminished, and augmented.
triad—augmented	A triad consisting of a major 3rd and an augmented 5th above the root.
triad—diminished	A triad consisting of a minor 3rd and a diminished 5th above the root.

triad—first inversion The position of a chord in which the 3rd factor is the lowest-sounding tone.

triad—major A triad consisting of a major 3rd and a perfect 5th above the root.

triad—minor A triad consisting of a minor 3rd and a perfect 5th above the root.

triad—root position The position of a chord in which the root is the lowest-sounding tone.

triad—second inversion The position of a chord in which the 5th factor is the lowest-sounding tone.

trichord Three pitches. Generally describes segments of twelve-tone sets. Has both melodic and harmonic connotations. The trichord is used in place of a triad by contemporary composers and theorists since the triad has key and tonal implications.

triple meter A meter consisting of three beats.

tritone The common name for the A4 or d5 interval. Usually avoided in earlier practice, it became an important structural element in much twentieth-century music.

turnaround (turnback) A term used in popular song to denote four-chord formulas that signal the repetition of a period or return to a previous period. Typical turnabout: I—vii^7—ii^7—V^7 (in popular music symbols in C major: C—B dim—Dm^7—G7).

twelve-bar blues—standard See standard twelve-bar blues.

twelve-bar jazz blues A variant of the twelve-bar blues harmony characterized by the ii^7 to V^7 progression in the ninth and tenth bars.

twelve-bar jazz blues—modified See modified twelve-bar jazz blues.

twelve-tone row Same as twelve-tone series. Series, set, and row are used synonymously. Some authors and composers of the 1960s and 1970s prefer the term *set*.

two-part (binary) form A form, often found in homophonic as well as polyphonic compositions, consisting of two organically related parts. Frequently the two parts are bound together by the same thematic material, but this is not always the case.

unison Two pitches that are the same. Several singers singing a melody together.

whole step An interval consisting of two half-steps.

whole-tone scale A six-tone scale in which each degree is a whole step from the next. (Example: C, D, E, F♯, G♯, A♯, C.)

INDEX